Edited by William R. Baker *Foreword by* Randall Balmer

EVANGELICALISM
& THE
STONE-CAMPBELL
MOVEMENT

Volume 2,
Engaging Basic Christian Doctrine

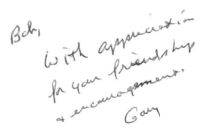

ACU
PRESS

Abilene, Texas

ACU
P R E S S ·

1648 Campus Court
Abilene, Texas 79601
World Wide Web: www.acupressbooks.com
Toll free: 1-877-816-4455

Cover photographs courtesy of Disciples of Christ Historical Society, Nashville, Tennessee.

ISBN 0-89112-512-4
Printed in the United States of America

12 11 10 09 08 07 06 / 10 9 8 7 6 5 4 3 2 1

Published in association with
Stone-Campbell International,
publisher of Stone-Campbell Journal

CONTENTS

Foreword

WILLFUL NAIVETÉ:
AMERICAN EVANGELICALISM AND THE
STONE-CAMPBELL TRADITION

Randall Balmer

The Last Will and Testament of the Springfield Presbytery changed everything. When Barton Stone and others published this document, they signaled a shift from a European orientation, suffused as it was with tradition and history, toward a kind of determined primitivism that would set the tone for evangelicalism in America ever since. Put another way, prior to the *Last Will and Testament*, American evangelicalism still looked to the East, across the Atlantic, toward Europe and Great Britain, for its cultural identity and its theological definition. After 1804, however, evangelicals shifted their gaze geographically away from the Atlantic and toward the Alleghenies. They looked for theological guidance not from the centuries immediately preceding their migration to America, but, leapfrogging history, they sought theological legitimation directly from the first century and the example of New Testament Christianity.

From Reformation to Revolution

The primitivist impulse in American Christianity goes back at least as far as the Protestant Reformation. Martin Luther, an Augustinian friar steeped in both the theodicies of Augustine and the Humanism of Erasmus, repaired to the New Testament in an effort to salve his uneasy conscience and to circumvent the centuries of theological accretions rampant within medieval Catholicism. His "rediscovery of the gospel," inspired by the study of Paul's letters to the Romans and to the Galatians, allowed him to rescue Christianity from what Luther characterized as works-righteousness, a kind of theological recidivism that had set in after Augustine. Luther's reformulation of the faith was not entirely primitivist, for he replied on both Augustine and Erasmus, but he was able to claim that his primary allegiance lay with the New Testament.

Sociological inevitabilities being what they are, Luther's followers developed their own traditions and institutions within a century of the posting of his Ninety-five Theses on the cathedral door at Wittenberg—everything from the leveling impulses of the Anabaptists and the Brownists to the doctrinal precisionism of the Reformed tradition and the calculated via media of the Church of England. By the time the Arbella weighed anchor in 1630 and tacked toward the West with its cargo of Puritans, English and European traditions had defined every group of Protestants who settled on the Atlantic seaboard.

The Puritans, for instance, still viewed themselves as part of the Church of England, albeit a people set apart from ordinary Anglicans, who had been led astray by a duplicitous Catholic monarch and the treacherous archbishop of Canterbury. John Winthrop's famous sermon aboard the Arbella, which spelled out the reasons for migration, announced that this band of Puritans, a remnant of the faithful, would construct a "city upon a hill" out of the howling wilderness of Massachusetts, a beacon to the rest of the world, England especially. To add to the pressure, Winthrop assured his auditors that the eyes of the world would be watching as the Puritans demonstrated to their confrères across the Atlantic how God intended that church and state be configured.

Winthrop and most of the first generation of Puritans were fixated with this eastward orientation across the Atlantic, but dissenters lurked even in this homogeneous community. Roger Williams, for instance, took issue with the Puritans' self-identification as Anglicans; he was banished for his heresy and founded the religiously tolerant colony of Rhode Island. But the "city upon a hill" mission imploded in 1640 when Puritans back in England took matters into their own hands by taking the king and the archbishop of Canterbury into their own hands. As news of the English Revolution filtered across the Atlantic, it became painfully clear that Puritans in England were not paying attention to the beacon so painstakingly constructed in Massachusetts, and the Puritan experiment descended into a maelstrom of reverse migration, recrimination, and spiritual declension.

By 1700, Puritanism was in disarray, but the transatlantic orientation persisted even through the dark night of declension. When the time came for renewal in a series of revivals historians refer to as the Great Awakening in the 1730s and 1740s, an Anglican priest was the major catalyst, and the preeminent theologian of the Great Awakening, Jonathan Edwards, himself influenced by European and British ideas, was careful to keep his correspondents in England and Scotland apprised of the progress of the revival. Even the infamous Anglican Apostasy at Yale in the 1720s represented a turn back across the Atlantic to England.

Further south, in the Middle Colonies, the revival there also had its roots in Europe. Since the founding of New Netherland in 1628, the ministers (or dominies) of the Dutch Reformed Church had an ambivalent relationship with their ecclesiastical superiors back in the Netherlands, but the arrival of a Dutch minister in 1720 reinfused the church with European influence, an influence that was not entirely welcome. Theodorus Jacobus Frelinghuysen had been immersed in a renewal movement called Pietism in the Old World, one that prized spiritual ardor above mere intellectual assent, and when he arrived in the New World he meant to put his Pietistic convictions into practice.

Frelinghuysen's machinations divided his congregations in New Jersey and triggered the Great Awakening in the Middle Colonies. Through his friendship with Gilbert Tennent, Frelinghuysen's Pietism spread beyond Dutch circles to the Presbyterians.

European sources made their presence felt in other colonial religious communities as well. German immigrants were also influenced by a Pietism defined by the enemies of scholasticism back in Europe. The short-lived Swedish settlements along the Delaware River sought to orient their religious life toward Uppsala, although political vicissitudes eventually prompted a redirection toward Canterbury by the time of the American Revolution. Among the English, Pietistic renewal took the form of Methodism, a movement that took its own institutional form in 1784: the Methodist Episcopal Church.

Second Great Awakening

Even during the early years of the Second Great Awakening, European influences were apparent. Among students at Yale College, Enlightenment ideas enjoyed such popularity that students referred to one another by the names of the French philosophes: Rousseau, Voltaire, et al. When Timothy Dwight, Jonathan Edwards's son-in-law, took over as president in 1796, he instituted a four-year curriculum of moral improvement to reintroduce students to orthodox Christianity, but the objects of study hailed, once again, from the eastern shores of the Atlantic, not the western. The same pattern obtained during the early years of the Great Revival in the South. As Leigh Eric Schmidt has demonstrated, the Scottish practice of sacramental seasons provided a template for the camp meetings at Gaspar River and Cane Ridge, so once again Old World forms dictated religious expressions in the New World, even so far inland as the Cumberland Valley.

Whatever one can say about the Second Great Awakening, one must say that it was a time of religious ferment and theological reconfiguration. Historians have spilled a great deal of ink portraying the social unrest of the burned-over district in upstate New York, an area opened for mass settlement by the construction of the Erie Canal. To the South, the success of the Gaspar River gathering in August 1800 caught the eye of the Presbyterian minister at Cane Ridge. Barton W. Stone organized another camp meeting for the following summer, and the spectacular scenes of the Cane Ridge revival are forever etched into America's religious consciousness.

But something else happened as well. Within a few years of Cane Ridge, which had been remarkable for its frontier ecumenicity, denominational distinctions once again reared their ugly heads. More to the point, Old Side Presbyterians in the East sought to reinforce European sensibilities—a strict Calvinist theology, an educated clergy, and decorum in worship—that Stone and the Campbells, Thomas and Alexander, considered pointless and inimical to revivals, especially on the frontier, where such niceties counted for little and arguably impeded the spread of the gospel.

In the midst of these intramural squabbles, Stone and others decided to take a stand against these denominational accretions and the European-based fustiness. *The Last Will and Testament of the Springfield Presbytery* decisively broke with tradition and officially dispensed with denominational divisiveness by positing that the New Testament alone would determine the shape and theology of the new movement. "No creed but the Bible" became the new rallying cry, and all disputed matters would thereafter be adjudged not by tradition but by Scripture alone.

Turning West

The effect of *The Last Will and Testament* on American evangelicalism was to reorient it from the East to the West, from a dependence on European forms steeped in tradition and toward the western frontier, which offered a kind of *tabula rasa*. Following the lead of the Stone-Campbell tradition, American evangelicals have reinvented themselves endlessly, most often claiming inspiration solely from the Scriptures, often explicitly disavowing any connection whatsoever with tradition.

Paradoxically, one of the ideologies that would facilitate this transformation was an interpretive device imported from Great Britain, something called Scottish Common Sense Realism. Scottish Realism would become the regnant hermeneutic of the nineteenth century. This ideology democratized biblical interpretation by asserting that the proper reading of the Bible was the plainest and most apparent one, and therefore readily accessible to the sincere and discerning reader.

The authors of the *Last Will and Testament* articulated these Common Sense principles for the Restoration movement. They directed that "the people may have free course to the Bible" and specified that candidates for ministry would "henceforth study the Holy Scriptures with fervent prayer, and obtain license from God to preach the simple Gospel, with the Holy Ghost sent down from heaven, without any mixture of philosophy, vain deceit, traditions of men, or the rudiments of the world." Common Sense Realism placed the Scriptures within reach of the masses, and nineteenth-century Americans responded by interpreting the Bible for themselves absent the filters of history and tradition.

No one in the antebellum period personified this new license better than William Miller. A farmer and a self-styled biblical interpreter from Low Hampton, New York, Miller decided that the reigning eschatology of postmillennialism, the notion that Jesus would return after believers had constructed the millennial kingdom, was mistaken. Miller elected to skip over centuries of biblical interpretation and return directly to the Scriptures. Armed with a benumbing barrage of numbers and arcane calculations, Miller announced that the second advent of Christ would take place sometime between March 1843 and March 1844. When the Lord failed to materialize as scheduled, Miller reluctantly agreed to a "tarrying time," which adjusted the date to October 22, 1844—albeit with the same result.

Miller was not the only one to strike out in a new direction. Indeed, the antebellum period was the era of religious innovation. Charles Grandison Finney's "new measures" represented a fresh approach to revivals as well as a brazen repudiation of the starchy Calvinism associated with both the theologians at Princeton Theological Seminary and the European traditions which they defended. The "new measures" proved remarkably successful, in part because the notion that individuals controlled their own spiritual destinies comported well with a people who had only recently taken their political destiny into their own hands.

Another antebellum religious innovator was confused by the proliferation of denominations and their competing claims to the truth. Joseph Smith "retired to the woods" and was instructed by an angel to hold off on joining any particular denomination and await further word from on high. The new revelation, unearthed on the side of Hill Cumorah in western New York, told of the wanderings of the people of God in the New World and minimized their connection with the Old World, another example of the reorientation from East to West. And as Joseph Smith and his followers contemplated the future, they looked not to Jerusalem, but to Jackson County, Missouri, where the heavenly city of Zion would eventually materialize.

While Smith and the Mormons adhered to a new history—or at least to a history newly discovered—other religious leaders in the postbellum period, following the lead of Stone and the Campbells, chose to ignore history. Dispensational premillennialism was another import from Great Britain, coming to the New World in the person of John Nelson Darby, but it quickly resonated with American evangelicals, who made it their own. Dispensationalism entailed a return to the Scriptures, especially the prophetic passages of Daniel and the book of Revelation. The notion of premillennialism asserted that Jesus would return at any moment, and in making such an assertion the dispensationalists willfully repudiated the eschatology of their antebellum forebears. Postmillennialism, with its corollary that believers bore responsibility for ushering in the millennial kingdom, had animated various social reform movements in antebellum America. The dispensationalists, however, chose to ignore that history in favor of a novel interpretation of biblical prophecy, one that disregarded the tradition of social reform so evident in American society only decades earlier.

Another form of primitivism emanated from Princeton Theological Seminary in the nineteenth century. The publication of *The Origin of Species* in 1859 brought Charles Darwin's ideas to America. Taken to their logical conclusion, evolutionary ideas cast doubt on the veracity of the Genesis account of creation and, by extension, the entire Bible. The second blow was the discipline of higher criticism, imported from Germany, which impugned the reliability of the Scriptures. The Princeton theologians—Charles Hodge, A. A. Hodge, and B. B. Warfield, among others— responded to these threats with what might be considered the ultimate expression of primitivism. The Bible was divinely inspired and utterly reliable, they insisted, because it was entirely without error in the original manuscripts. Yes, minor errors and inconsistencies might have crept into the extant text through the agency of copyists down through the centuries, but in its original, pristine form, the Scriptures were inerrant.

Restorationism within American nineteenth-century evangelicalism took still another form in the holiness movement, which sought to restore piety and spiritual ardor to nineteenth-century denominations that had, in the judgment of holiness people, grown complacent. The holiness movement functioned as a renewal initiative within Protestant denominations, principally Methodism. Holiness gatherings, centered in the camp meetings at such venues as Oak Bluffs, Massachusetts, and Ocean Grove, New Jersey, fairly reverberated with spiritual fervor. But their ardor alternated with denunciations of the spiritual declension they saw everywhere around them, evidenced by such middle-class emoluments as organs, robed choirs, and educated clergy. The holiness people sought desperately to restore Methodism and other denominations to the spiritual vitality that had marked their formation; they wanted these organizations to return to the piety of their origins. The primitivist efforts of the holiness people were thwarted, however, by denominational hierarchies, especially within Methodism, so reform-minded people like Daniel S. Warner, A. B. Simpson, and Phineas Bresee were forced to start anew with their own denominations.

Azusa Street

Perhaps the best example of primitivism in the history of American evangelicalism, outside of the Stone-Campbell movement, is the emergence of pentecostalism. On January 1, 1901, the first day of the new century, a young woman named Agnes Nevada Ozman began speaking in tongues after the manner of the New Testament Christians. The founder and head of Bethel Bible College in Topeka, Kansas, Charles Fox Parham, had been teaching about the day of Pentecost in Acts 2, when the Holy Spirit engulfed the early Christians "as a mighty wind," and they began speaking in tongues. Parham carried news of this phenomenon throughout Kansas, Missouri, and Texas, where it was picked up by an African-American hotel waiter, William J. Seymour, affiliated with the Evening Light Saints, who in turn brought it west to Los Angeles. His strange ideas cost him a job with the congregation that wanted to consider him as their pastor, but his preaching from a porch on Bonnie Brae Street triggered the outbreak of *glossolalia*, and when the crowds became so large they spilled into the street, the group found a new location at 312 Azusa Street. Thus began, in April 1906, the famous Azusa Street Revival, which would reshape American evangelicalism throughout the twentieth century.

"In the year 1900, Charles F. Parham, and his wife and family and a number of Bible students," Lillian Thistlewaite wrote in her account of the origins of twentieth-century pentecostalism, "gathered in the Bethel Bible School to study the Word of God, using no text book excepting, the Bible."[1] Parham, Seymour, and other pentecostals saw themselves as having recovered the first-century vision of Christianity, thereby claiming the gifts of the Holy Spirit promised in the New Testament. In particular, the gift of *glossolalia*, which had lain fallow in the centuries between the first and the twentieth, was once again available to the faithful, and anyone who resisted claiming that gift missed out on the "full gospel" of the New Testament.

One of the glorious characteristics of the early days of pentecostalism was its interracial character and its receptivity to the leadership of women, who approached parity with men. For a brief and liminal moment, pentecostalism approximated the kind of spiritual egalitarianism that Paul had talked about in Galatians 3. As the pentecostal movement matured, however, and various factions split off into their own denominations, the early promise of spiritual and earthly equality dissipated, first along racial lines and eventually in the diminished number of women in leadership positions, including the professional ministry.

The fundamentalists of the 1910s and 1920s also adhered to a kind of primitivism. In their battle against the encroachment of liberal or "modernist" ideas, they returned directly to the Scriptures to reaffirm their allegiance to such orthodox doctrines as the virgin birth of Jesus, the authenticity of miracles, and the second coming of Christ. Fundamentalists believed that their theological and ecclesiastical adversaries had erred by allowing their orthodoxy to be swept aside by the intellectual currents of contemporary culture. Salvation lay, the fundamentalists decided, in returning to the simplicity of the New Testament, absent the centuries of accumulated tradition and distractions.

Ahistoricism and the Religious Right
A final example of evangelical primitivism and ahistoricism is the Religious Right. Arising in the late 1970s in response to attempts to rescind the tax-exempt status of Bob Jones University because of its racial policies, the Religious Right emerged as a potent political force in the 1980s. Jerry Falwell, James Robison, Tim LaHaye, and others, working with Paul Weyrich and Richard Viguerie, assembled a formidable political coalition that, according to pollster Louis Harris, provided the margin of victory for Ronald Reagan in the 1980 election and helped to reelect him four years later.

In its quest for political influence, however, the Religious Right defaulted on the noble history of nineteenth-century evangelical social activism, especially in its attitudes toward women. Nineteenth-century evangelicals had set the social and political agenda for much of the century, and it was an agenda that favored the poor and the marginalized in society and sought to improve their fortunes. Abolitionism comes immediately to mind, but the temperance movement, which was in fact (contrary to contemporary perceptions) a progressive cause, also qualifies. Evangelicals sought prison reform and educational opportunities for women, for freed slaves, and for the children of the working classes. They supported women's suffrage and generally looked out for the interests of those on the margins of society.

The late twentieth-century manifestation of evangelical political activism neglected the principles of evangelicalism's nineteenth-century forebears. Despite their labored efforts to portray themselves as the new abolitionists by virtue of their opposition to abortion, leaders of the Religious Right generally have not evinced the same concern for the least among us. By cobbling together a political program that tilts heavily in the direction of white, middle-class, conservative Republicanism, the Religious Right demonstrates a disregard for its own history and tradition. Some associated with the movement, especially during the Reagan era, even sought to justify the acquisitive impulses of the so-called prosperity theology by recourse to the Scriptures, and their attitudes toward women drew more from the cult of domesticity than from the example of nineteenth-century evangelical activists.

Evangelicals and the Stone-Campbell Tradition

What, finally, is the relationship between evangelicals and the Stone-Campbell tradition? *The Last Will and Testament* decisively reoriented American evangelicalism from East to West, from a dependence on English and European theology and traditions, which had shaped American Protestantism through the Revolutionary period, to a more indigenous, primitivist definition of the faith. More often than not, evangelicals in America have followed the lead of the Restorationists in resorting directly to the Bible in matters of faith and doctrine rather than consult the precedents of history. Millerism, pentecostalism, and fundamentalism illustrate this tendency. Finally, the ahistoricism implicit in the Stone-Campbell movement has led evangelicals to ignore their own history, be it the dispensationalism of the late nineteenth century, which overturned the postmillennial optimism of the antebellum period, or the reactive, conservative agenda of the Religious Right, which ignored the heritage of nineteenth-century political activism in favor of an ethic that became virtually indistinguishable from the platform of the Republican Party.

What can evangelicals still learn from the Stone-Campbell tradition? In *The Last Will and Testament of the Springfield Presbytery*, the authors noted that "it is appointed for all delegated bodies once to die." The Restorationist movement properly takes a dim view of institutionalized religion as inimical to true piety. Campbell recognized that denominations are merely human constructions—and therefore flawed; sociologists remind us that institutions seek above all their own self-perpetuation.

At least as far back as the sixteenth century, Protestants have recognized the corruptibility of institutions, yet we repeatedly invest our faith and our energies in their construction and maintenance, despite the demonstrable perils of doing so. Pietism mobilized in conventicles among European Protestants for the purpose of reinvigorating institutions that had fallen into the torpor of scholasticism. Methodism began in a flurry of piety and spiritual ardor, and yet within decades of taking institutional form holiness people began calling for its return to the faith. Pentecostalism burst onto the scene with a religious fervor that virtually obliterated racial and gender barriers, but when it took institutional form the barriers reasserted themselves. Fundamentalists reluctantly broke with institutions corrupted by modernism—and then promptly constructed their own denominations. Even the nondenominational megachurches, which initially define themselves as transcending petty denominational intrigues, eventually become denominations themselves—Vineyard Christian Fellowship and Calvary Chapels, for instance—even if they resist the term denomination. In another example of misplaced faith in institutions, George Marsden issued an extended jeremiad about the failure of universities to remain true to their religious origins.[2]

Looking at the history of American evangelicalism, one would suppose that the routinization and institutionalization of religious impulses was a sociological inevitability, but the Restorationist movement suggests otherwise. Throughout its history, the Stone-Campbell tradition has maintained a healthy suspicion of denominational forms. Thomas Campbell back in 1804 recognized what Marsden and others fail to comprehend—that institutions, be they ecclesiastical or educational, are remarkably poor guarantors of piety. Institutions inevitably serve themselves and eventually subborn themselves to the pressures of building programs and mortgages, parking lots and pension funds. Nothing is more difficult than eliminating an institution, yet that is what makes *The Last Will and Testament* all the more remarkable—because it opens with an attestation to the health of the Springfield Presbytery, the very institution that the authors meant to kill.

Stone and his colleagues had the courage in 1804 to pronounce the Springfield Presbytery dead. Ever since, modeling themselves on the relational theology of Jesus and the primitive simplicity of the New Testament church, the Stone-Campbell tradition has generally looked askance at institutional forms, preferring to take seriously the promise of Jesus that wherever two or three are gathered, he is there. Evangelicals, by and large, have yet to appropriate that legacy of the Restorationist movement.

Postscript
A postscript. Recently I had the privilege of spending the day with Fred Shuttlesworth in Birmingham, Alabama. After several hours of reminiscing about the civil rights movement, Martin Luther King Jr., and Shuttlesworth's own brush with death on Christmas Eve, 1956, when the Ku Klux Klan detonated sixteen sticks of dynamite beneath the Bethel Baptist Church parsonage while he lay in bed, Shuttlesworth volunteered that the New Testament church was the closest that any human endeavor had ever come to fulfilling the ideals of Christianity. He added that the early Christians had been filled with the Spirit, and then they proceeded to change the world. "That's what we were trying to do in the movement," he said, referring to the civil rights struggle. I pressed him on that comment, whereupon this giant of the civil rights movement replied that he often preached from the Acts of the Apostles during the difficult days of the early 1960s, because the Acts of the Apostles provided the best model for Christian

action. He recited Acts 5:41 in particular: "And they departed from the presence of the council, rejoicing that they were worthy to suffer shame for his name."

The activists in the civil rights movement did just that. Not only did they invoke the purity of the New Testament church as their model, they did more than disregard history, which for them was a painful legacy of suffering, degradation, and injustice. They looked to the gospel not merely for the sport or the satisfaction of leapfrogging history and asserting a primitivist understanding of the faith. They appropriated the gospel of the New Testament for an even higher purpose: to change the course of history itself.

Notes

[1]Quoted in Larry Martin, ed., *The Topeka Outpouring of 1901* (Joplin, MO: Christian Life Books, 2000), p. 85.

[2]George M. Marsden, *The Soul of the American University: From Protestant Establishment to Established Nonbelief* (New York: Oxford University Press, 1996).

INTRODUCTION

William R. Baker

In October 2005, Gene Appel, a stellar preacher with pure-breed Stone-Campbell Restoration Movement genes, officially took the mantle of leadership from Bill Hybels over Willow Creek Community Church, South Barrington campus, one of the largest, most influential evangelical churches in America. For those who are still wondering if the Stone-Campbell Movement, especially those churches labeled "Independent," are evangelical, this occasion provides the irrefutable answer that it is. At least it is in the eyes of Willow Creek leaders who hired Gene, and in the eyes of Gene, who accepted.

Gene was a typical, smart-mouthed junior high kid, running through the dorms at Lincoln Christian College when I first saw him in the early 1970s. But he was Leon Appel's kid, who was vice-president at the school. Appel was being groomed to take over as president for the legendary Earl Hargrove, the most respected leader of the movement in Illinois, having previously succeeded Hargrove as minister of Lincoln Christian Church, Lincoln, Illinois. Gene Appel honed his sharp tongue, studied the Bible at LCC, and drew on his thoroughbred pedigree to emerge as a precocious, savvy leader of the Central Christian Church in Las Vegas, whose attendance exploded in the 1990s. Active in the Willow Creek Association, learning and applying its church growth and development principles in Las Vegas, Gene got on Willow Creek's radar screen as they began to plan Bill Hybel's eventual transition from direct day-to-day leadership of the church.

Blending of the Stone-Campbell Movement and Evangelicalism

When I first heard that Gene was hired at Willow Creek, my mind reeled with how to categorize what had happened. Here was one of "our" most exciting young leaders heading into the inner sanctums of evangelicalism's holiest shrine, the evangelical Mecca located in the northwest suburbs of Chicago. Why would they choose one of "ours"? Don't they know about our peculiar views of baptism and the Lord's Supper, our general heritage of suspicion among evangelicals that goes back to the beginning of our movement? After all, Alexander Campbell left the Presbyterians upon his baptism in 1816 and was (along with his Brush Run Church) expelled from the Baptists (the Mahoning Association) after a stormy ten-year relationship. Others, thinking Gene had "left us," wondered, "Why would he betray us and go there?" How could he give up on our ideas of baptism and Lord's Supper, our rich heritage and restoration plea?

Since joining Willow Creek, Appel has recruited Mike Breaux, yet another of "our" young preachers, whose time as senior minister of Southland Christian Church (Lexington, KY) from 1996 to 2003 had sparked growth from 3,500 attendance to over 8,000. My understanding is that Gene and Mike (also a LCC graduate) have been doing the bulk of the preaching at Willow Creek for quite a while. What is happening here?

Gene and Mike candidly explain their migration to Willow Creek in a 2004 *Christian Standard* interview article.[1] When questioned about his relationship with the Stone-Campbell Movement, Gene responds: "I haven't 'left' or abandoned anything. I've grown up with my Christian Church ties—they're my roots, my friends, my mentors. Now I am taking their values to a broader world." Mike adds, "I can remember sitting in Enos Dowling's Restoration history class, really resonating with 'tearing down the denominational walls'....Here at Willow I feel like I'm right in the middle of that [restoration] ideal." In the context of a Mark Taylor editorial a year earlier,[2] when the news broke of Gene's move to Willow Creek, when asked if he considered himself an evangelical, he responded, "I see myself as a Christian only." When pressed as to whether his move to Willow Creek meant he was leaving the Restoration Movement, he responded:

> I'm not sure I even understand that question. The dream of that Movement has always been to restore the kind of church we read about in Acts 2—a biblically functioning community without denominational barriers....We've always believed that the church is bigger than us. If the question means am I abandoning those ideals, then the answer is no. I've never been more passionate about giving my life for that dream.

I attended Willow Creek when Gene preached in fall, 2005. The sermon was part of a series centered on getting people to read their Bibles. Not just haranguing them to read but helping them distinguish its different genres and divisions, providing them a sharp summary of the Bible's message, aimed at simplifying things so that people who had not read the Bible much before would not be intimidated or put off by approaching it with wrong ideas. I could not help but think how much his knowledge for this sermon was drawn from his training at Lincoln Christian College. He even quoted a former professor from there who had once been his teacher. Yet, it was so "Willow Creek" too, with its polish and clarity. Challenging, biblical, and obviously memorable, the sermon displayed Gene in his very person as the perfect blend of evangelicalism and the Stone-Campbell Movement. (If this wasn't such an academic book, I would have lobbied for him to be on the cover, since he is the most recognizable face of how evangelicalism and the Stone-Campbell movement are morphing into something refreshingly new.)

Following the sermon, at the end of the service, an opportunity to participate in the Lord's Supper was provided. Those who wanted to remain to participate simply reflected, prayed, partook from several stations around the auditorium as they wished. Who says large churches can't provide the Lord's Supper regularly? I could not help but recognize yet another visible outcome of Gene's Stone-Campbell heritage emerging in this evangelical environment. In truth, the sensitive manner in which the Lord's Supper was provided at Willow Creek occurred in a more spiritually rewarding way than it is in many contemporary Christian Churches (independent) who minimize its significance even though they serve it weekly but consider themselves to be modeling seeker-sensitive churches like Willow Creek. It will be interesting to see what else unfolds in the course of Gene's ministry there.

Though surprising at first, in thinking more about it, I can begin to understand Willow Creek's predicament in contemplating Hybels' successor for the local church. Despite its enormous size and its influence on how to grow and do church in the last thirty years, Willow Creek is really just an independent, non-denominational church, governing its own affairs with its local leadership.

This in fact may be one of the keys to its growth, since study after study has shown that people today are searching for a non-churchy church without the negative ties to a denomination. They want motivational preaching centered on the Bible, near-professional quality worship, and great youth programs. In fact, more and more churches affiliated with denominations today are working hard to mask those affiliations by removing them from their sign and literature. It seems that congregations want to be viewed as an assembly of local, Bible-believing people (evangelical) first before any affiliations come into the picture. Thus, the rampant growth in "community," "cornerstone," "hope," and "faith" congregations—not just in Stone-Campbell circles—but throughout the denominations.

As a locally autonomous community of believers that is by design as generically evangelical as a church body could be, Willow Creek faced a very perplexing dilemma in replacing their founding, ideological leader. Taking it as a given that they could probably woo anyone they wanted into the most high profile church in America, would they want a great Baptist preacher who has proven himself in growing a large congregation? Or a Presbyterian, Methodist, or Lutheran? Would they want Willow Creek to become associated with one Protestant denomination, regardless of the candidate's credentials? Given the options, a successful, young preacher from "our" no-name, loose fellowship of locally autonomous churches seems the perfect solution for them. Yet, Gene's evangelical credentials had to pass muster before being invited to be hired as

Hybel's heir apparent. In this, it is invalid to assume that Gene did anything but espouse the values of the Stone-Campbell Movement before being hired or that he has done anything to suggest that he has departed from them since being hired. Willow Creek has not "converted" him nor has he "converted" them. There simply is no need given the overlap of values.

The dilemma on the side of Christian Churches (independent) is perplexing too. Is Gene still one of "us"? Do we continue to invite him to speak in our churches? Maybe we should now list Willow Creek in our Directory of the Ministry or put it atop (over Southeast Christian Church) the annual list of our mega churches (churches over 2000) in the *Christian Standard*. Should Gene speak at a main session of the NACC or be invited to be on the NACC executive committee, which would put him on track to be president of the NACC some year? That would be the normal track of one of our most successful preachers, the track he was on before he joined Willow Creek. Should we capitalize on his unique success or should we be embarrassed by it and wash our hands of him?

The answer to these questions will emerge over the next decade. However, the fact that Gene was a main session speaker at the 2004 NACC (a year after joining Willow Creek, though probably slated for this spot earlier) suggests his move to the most visible evangelical church in America will increase, not decrease, his true blue stature among the Christian Churches.

The situation with Gene Appel runs parallel to issues surrounding Max Lucado, long-time preaching minister at Oak Hills Church (formerly Oak Hills Church of Christ) in San Antonio, Texas. However, Max is far better known as one of the most highly regarded evangelical writers in America, having authored over fifty books that are devoured by Christians hungry for compelling spiritual thought.[3] Because of this, a 2004 article in *Christianity Today* dubbed him "America's Pastor," next after Billy Graham.[4] Yet, his church is notable for changing, becoming more evangelical. Among other things, "Church of Christ" has been removed from its name because it is viewed as an unnecessary "insurmountable barrier." Also, it is one of a growing number of Churches of Christ (a cappella) who have adopted contemporary Christian worship style—including instruments—in their "Contemporary Worship," while still offering a cappella style worship as a "traditional worship" alternative.[5] Despite being one of the largest and most prominent congregations among Churches of Christ (a cappella), I have heard people from that stream of the movement openly decry Lucado and Oak Hills as "not one of us" now. Yet, they still require baptism for membership, offer the Lord's Supper every Sunday, and openly embrace their Stone-Campbell heritage. Undoubtedly, Lucado, like Appel, views his migration to becoming more evangelical as a natural fulfillment of Stone-Campbell heritage, not an abandonment.

It is not my intention to get into the middle of ongoing discussions among those in Churches of Christ (a cappella), I simply want to observe that Max Lucado represents the same phenomenon as Gene Appel within Christian Churches (independent). The blending of evangelicalism and heirs of the Stone-Campbell Restoration Movement, whatever stream, is a cultural trend that has only now become obvious. However, we are only at the beginning of this train ride. What the outcome might be is anyone's guess. However, this volume is intended to aid those who want to understand both the ideas of the Stone-Campbell Restoration Movement better as well as the ideas of evangelicalism better. It is for readers themselves to determine the level of compatibility or lack of it.

The Origin and Design of This Volume

This is not a textbook in its design. Rather, the topics were developed year-to-year within a professional, academic environment. For ten years, beginning in the fall of 1996, biblical and theological scholars and teachers from two streams of the Stone-Campbell Movement met as an approved group within the annual conference of the Evangelical Theological Society. Called the Stone-Campbell Adherents Group, professors teaching at educational institutions associated with Churches of Christ (a cappella) and Christian Churches (independent) and others at ETS drawn to our presentations, met to interact with papers on topics of our own interest. With an executive committee consisting of myself, Robert Kurka (Lincoln Christian College and Seminary), Paul Pollard (Harding University), and Ed Myers (Harding University), we have been interested primarily in exploring our take on various evangelical, doctrinal discussions. With evangelicals as respondents each year, we have been able to initiate helpful dialogue and understanding about these issues. Though respondents had very little knowledge about the peculiarities of our Stone-Campbell heritage and rarely commented on these, all were delighted to become better acquainted with us and valued the high caliber of our biblical, theological, and historical reflections. They did not come away seeing us as anything but evangelical kinsmen and constantly were complementary of our rich tradition.

Presentations from the first five years (1996-2000) were published in 2002 under the title *Evangelicalism and the Stone-Campbell Movement* (InterVarsity). Still in print, this volume has sold well and appears to remain useful for classroom instruction. All considered it a high compliment to our work and to the growing awareness of our movement by evangelicals to have had a leading Christian publisher promote our work.

This present volume is the second published volume from the ETS Stone-Campbell Adherents Group meetings. It contains nineteen presentations from the past five years of meetings (2001-2005). We are excited that Abilene Christian University Press decided to include it in their growing list of scholarly titles.

The volume is organized by theological categories rather than by the chronology of the ETS programs in which they were presented. By grouping them under the categories of God, Christ, church (Lord's Supper), eschatology, and the Bible, this volume fills out the categories addressed in the first volume of conversion theology (faith, Holy Spirit, baptism) and church (general) and assumes the historical perspective on evangelicalism and the Stone-Campbell Restoration Movement provided there.

Chapters one through four, in part one, presented at the 2002 ETS Meeting in Toronto, Canada, employ the hot topic of open theism as a way of talking about views of God from the Stone-Campbell perspective. At the time, both Clark Pinnock and John Sanders (our respondent) were under scrutiny by ETS for their role in developing this intriguing line of theology. Many of us attended numerous late-night official discussions at ETS, leading up to an official vote at the 2003 annual meeting whether or not to oust these two theologians from ETS membership. Happily, at least for the sake of people developing other exploratory notions in the future, the official vote was not sufficient to approve their expulsion. Because it was a theological development of growing interest to Stone-Campbell scholars over the years, most of whom are already Arminian in general persuasion, we wanted to address it head on with one of its leading proponents. Duane Warden (Harding University) and Robert Kurka (Lincoln Christian College and Seminary) react to open theism as representatives of their respective streams of the movement, in different but helpful ways. Jack Cottrell does not reflect upon open theism as such but takes on one of the most complex but crucial elements in trying to understand God—the matter of God's relationship to time. Sanders, one of the most prolific writers on open theism (*The God Who Risks: A Theology of Providence*, InterVarsity, 1998; Christopher Hall and John Sanders, *Does God have a Future?* Baker, 2003), responds thoroughly to each presentation and thus provides readers a fair exposure to the open view of God. A postcript on Sanders: through the course of events and at the time of this publication, he was released from his contract with Huntington College as a result of his open theology and has taken up a new position at Hendrix College in Arkansas.

Chapters five through eight, in part two, originally presented at the 2003 ETS Meeting in Atlanta, deal with christology but with a unique Stone-Campbell heritage twist—a focus on the Gospel of John. Carrise Berryhill (Abilene Christian University) sets up the discussion by demonstrating historically the keen interest of the Campbells, Stone, and Scott in this Gospel. Brian Johnson (Lincoln Christian College) and Paul Pollard (Harding University) follow up by focusing on the movement's special interest in the christology of Word and of unity respectively. Gary Burge (Wheaton College), a leading scholar on the Gospel of John (*The Annointed Community: The Holy Spirit in Johannine Tradition*, Eerdmans, 1987) and an evangelical, provides a well-informed response with particular application to the Stone-Campbell Movement.

Chapters nine through twelve, in part three, originally presented at the 2005 ETS meeting in Valley Forge, Pennsylvania, contemplate the church but in its particular function of serving the Lord's Supper. Weekly observance of the ancient ceremony in the context of worship has been a bedrock conviction in the Stone-Campbell Movement from the beginning, a practice that continues in all three streams of the movement (a cappella, independent, and Disciples). Lynn McMillon (Oklahoma Christian University) shares the results of his extensive research to show that the roots of this conviction go back to Scotland a generation earlier than the Campbells, in particular to John Glas, Robert and James Haldane, and Robert Sandeman. Mark Krause (Puget Sound Christian College) follows up with fresh look at the key New Testament passages concerning the Lord's Supper, and John Mark Hicks (Lipscomb Univesity) adds an insightful look at the history and theology of the Lord's Supper. I. Howard Marshall (University of Aberdeen), well-known British evangelical New Testament scholar who has also published a monograph on the Lord's Supper (*The Last Supper and the Lord's Supper*, Eerdmans, 1980), concludes with a seasoned response.

Chapters thirteen through fifteen, in part four, originally presented at the 2004 ETS meeting in San Antonio, Texas, engage the topic of eschatology but with relevant contemporary thrust: the surging interest in the preterist position with regard to biblical prophecy of the second coming. Rick Cherok (Cincinnati Christian University) begins the discussion with an examination of historiography regarding millennial issues in the Stone-Campbell Movement, exposing the failure of early histories to recognize how eschatology motivated the early leaders. Ed Myers (Harding University) explores and critiques the roots of the groundswell toward preterism among Churches of Christ (a cappella). Grant Osborne (Trinity International University), a leading evangelical New Testament scholar in the area of eschatology (*Revelation*, ECNT, Baker, 2002) disputes the validity of strict preterism and offers a helpful panoramic evaluation of the variety of eschatological positions.

Chapters sixteen through nineteen, in part five, originally presented at the 2001 ETS meeting in Colorado Springs, Colorado, takes a look at the Old Testament in light of its marginalization within the Stone-Campbell Movement from the very beginning. Gary Hall (Lincoln Christian Seminary) documents this reality by examining the views of early leaders, from the Campbells up through David Lipscomb. Terry Briley (Lipscomb University) provides a personal reflection on the state of Old Testament studies in Churches of Christ (a cappella), while Paul Kissling (TCM International) develops a program for restoring the Old Testament in church life. Danny Carroll (Denver Seminary), highly-regarded, evangelical Old Testament scholar (*Amos—The Prophet and His Oracles*, Westminster John Knox, 2002), responds winsomely that the Old Testament has always been treated as a minority report among evangelicals.

In order to provide a helpful historical perspective in this second volume, Randall Ballmer (Barnard College, Columbia University), one of the foremost scholars of North American Christianity (*Encyclopedia of Evangelicalism*, Westminster John Knox, 2002; *Mine Eyes Have Seen the Glory*, Oxford University Press, 1989), evangelicalism in particular, has provided a foreward. By placing the Stone-Campbell Restoration Movement in its religious landscape, he offers compelling and challenging insight. This presentation was originally given at the Stone-Campbell Journal Conference in Cincinnati, Ohio, on March 26, 2003, and was previously published in *Stone-Campbell Journal* 7.2 (Fall, 2004).

Streams Converging (a Little)

The release of this volume at the 2006 North American Christian Convention, Louisville, Kentucky, is not coincidence. It is only appropriate that this volume, forged over the past five years by scholars from the independent and a cappella streams of the Stone-Campbell Movement, make its appearance at the most historic coming together of these groups in one hundred years. Marking the year when a cappella congregations were no longer counted among the Disciples of Christ by the U. S. Census (independent congregations did not begin leaving until 1913), 1906 is a year no one ever thought could be erased (or at least amended) until right now. This convention purposefully intends to replace that date with a new one, 2006, the year we "buried the hatchet." With a platform of main speakers evenly balanced from both streams of the movement, plus Restoration and Theology tracks addressing various relevant issues, past and present, this will be the new, great year for the history books.

While the 2006 NACC will be a banner year, it should be noted that many events have led up to this, beginning with the Restoration Forum, ongoing since 1983, where pioneering a cappella and independent church leaders have met for the purposes of relationship-building and discussion. In the 2006 gathering, over 3,000 were in attendance. On the more academic front, independent and a cappella scholars contributed to the completion of the respected College Press NIV New Testament Commentary series and are well on their way to completing a companion Old Testament series. A cappella and independent scholars, since 1998, have joined together as editors and contributors to publish *Stone-Campbell Journal*. The Editorial Board includes two members from a cappella churches and six from independent churches, with sixteen Consulting Editors (five from a cappella churches, eleven from independent). The board of Stone-Campbell International, the non-profit company publishing *SCJ* includes four members from independent churches, one from a cappella, and one from independent churches who now attends Willow Creek. Since 2002 scholars, ministers, and students from these two streams (plus a few Disciples) have been meeting together at the annual Stone-Campbell Journal Conference held each spring at Cincinnati Christian University.

While the converging of two streams of the Stone-Campbell Movement at a few points is thrilling, some hopeful things are occurring with regard to two other streams. First, the *Encyclopedia of the Stone-Campbell Movement* (Eerdmans) was published in 2004. This involved senior editors from independent, a cappella, and Disciples streams of the movement as well as vast participation from all three in composing the articles. This is the single most important volume ever written on the movement and in itself demonstrates a mutual spirit from all three streams forged on the commonalites of our heritage. The overwhelming success of this project bodes well for further joint projects, like a history and a primary documents critical textbook. Second, on the distant horizon, possibilities are unfolding for building relationships with a small tributary that developed from Churches of Christ (a cappella) in recent years: the International Church of Christ (formerly known as the Boston Church of Christ).

No one knows what these occurrences portend. However, this is not a movement that any longer needs to be embarrassed by its divisive past. The streams of this unity movement are at least civil towards one another now, and in many instances are doing more than that. It is also no longer a movement that need be embarrassed by its present, either. Though remaining somewhat obscure because of our non-denominational, locally-autonomous church organization, we are having an impact on the North American landscape. In particular, the independent stream, is booming. Many have heard of the 2002 report in the *New York Times* that documented their 18.6% growth in the decade of the 1990s, the largest growth in any group (of over a million) other than the Mormons.[6] Whether or not people know the heritage of these booming, suburban megachurches, their exponential growth indicates that churches of our heritage do seem to have come of age on the American Christian landscape.

This volume is intended to help us remember that we do have a great heritage to build on but one that must also be forged in light of continuing study, discussion, and dialog. This dialog should certainly take place with evangelicals as at the Evangelical Theological Society. However, it should not be limited to evangelicals. By helping to clarify our views of God, Christ, the Lord's Supper, the Second Coming, and the Bible, this volume may also contribute to meaningful discussion with all expressions of Christianity in North America and the world.

Notes

[1]Paul Boatman, "What are You Doing at Willow Creek? An Interview with Gene Appel and Mike Breaux," *Christian Standard* (June 27, 2004), pp. 4-8.

[2]Mark Taylor, "God's Call to a 'Christian Only,'" *Christian Standard* (April 6, 2003), p. 3

[3]These fifty books involve sales of over 33 million books. Popular early examples are: *God Came Near* (Sisters, Ore.: Multnomah, 1987); *He Still Moves Stones* (Waco, Tex.: Word, 1993). More recent are: *Cure for the Common Life* (Nashville, Tenn.: W Publishing Group, 2005); *Come Thirsty* (W Publishing Group, 2004).

[4]Cindy Crosby, "America's Pastor," *Christianity Today* (March, 2004), pp 58-63

[5]A sidebar with no by-line accompanies the Crosby article, entitled "An Unusual Church of Christ," *Christianity Today* (March, 2004), p. 62. This article notes the church's name change as well as the addition of instrumental "praise" music. It also briefly and sensitively explains to CT readers the special characteristics of the Stone-Campbell tradition.

[6]Laurie Goodstein, "Conservative Churches Grew Fastest in 1990s, Report Says," *New York Times* (September 18, 2002), p. 22

Part 1

Understanding God through Dialogue with Open Theism

1

OPEN THEISM AND
CHURCHES OF CHRIST (A CAPPELLA)

Duane Warden

*When in the beginning God created the human race, he left them free to make
their own decisions: if you choose, you can observe the commandments; you
can keep faith if you are so minded. He has set before you fire and water:
reach out and make the choice. Mortals are offered life or death: whichever
they prefer will be given them. (Sir 15:14-17)*

One turns to the subject of God with hesitancy. We fear we will say too much or
too little. Still, myriads of religious, ethical, philosophical, social, and psychological concerns compel us to apply our minds to know him. With Job's sense of resignation, we
echo the words of the patriarch, "Yet I am not reduced to silence by the darkness or
by the mystery which hides him."[1] Though hesitant, we risk making statements about
God. We are encouraged in that God invites us to know him. Whatever we think of
God, our conclusions soon prove to have ramifications stretching across the full range
of theological concerns. Nowhere is this more evident than when we turn to the subject of God's sovereignty and human free will. The question put simply is this: How are
we to understand God to be sovereign and humans to be free?

In recent years, a number of scholars have approached the question with fresh
vigor. They have maintained that God in his sovereignty has chosen to create a world
where humankind is able to enter into relationship with him. To that end, they have
argued, God has granted "significant freedom"[2] to the people he has created. He allows
individuals to make choices whose outcome may disappoint, please, or surprise him.
Open theists, or free will theists, maintain that God works out his purposes as a partner
with his creation, not as an all-determining sovereign. If humans are free, it means of
necessity that God is liable to surprise, that he learns from human behavior; and that
humans are a source both of joy and of grief to him. All this is true because when free
creatures make real choices the future is inherently unknowable. Omniscience, according

to one open theist, means that God "knows everything it is logically possible to know."[3]

This study will enter into conversation with those who maintain that God of necessity risks himself if he wills to have a relationship with his creation. A few pertinent reflections on God from within the Stone-Campbell tradition will also be examined. The questions to be explored are: How have those in the movement understood divine sovereignty and human freedom and what are the implications of this for the value of open theism? But let us first seek to understand the principle notions of this new model of God.[4]

An Open God

According to Richard Rice, the open view of God is built on two biblically based convictions: First, love is the essential quality of God. Further, when one understands God's sovereignty as his exhaustive control of natural and human events, his love tends to be overshadowed. Love requires God to respond sensitively to what people do. Not only does it require that God act in human lives, but that he allow them to act in his. "God's will," Rice asserts, "is not the ultimate explanation for everything that happens; human decisions and actions make an important contribution too."[5]

Second, open theists maintain that God does not stand over time. He lives within time because there is no other way to live. Hasker writes regarding God's timelessness, "Probably the most common response to this doctrine in recent philosophy of religion is to dismiss it as incoherent or unintelligible."[6] The argument is that God knows events as they take place. Rice sets forth two streams of biblical evidence to support a real-time, interactive view of the God-human relationship. The first consists of statements affirming God to be responsive to what happens in the world. What people do evokes emotions from God, in some cases causing him to change his mind and his plans. The second consists of passages that affirm human freedom.[7]

What, then, is the source of the notion that God is an immutable sovereign, untouched and unmoved by human events? Openness advocates argue that Christian theology in its formative stages found the formulations of Greek metaphysics to be useful as it made statements about God. The result was a biblical-classical synthesis that has been and continues to be accepted by theologians who have little inclination to measure it by the inter-personal model of God offered in Scripture.[8]

Greek philosophical speculation developed a god of changeless perfection. Plato argued that god was immutable because any change in perfection could only be a change for the worse. When Christian theology was in its infancy, Philo had already begun to think of the God of Israel in Greek categories. For Philo, God is transcendent and unmoved by human events. This Alexandrian wise man paved the way for the Christian thinkers who were to follow.[9]

Augustine was the most significant western theologian in formulating the biblical-classical synthesis. He believed divine foreknowledge and human freedom were compatible. God foreknows all but in a way that allows the exercise of choice.[10] Further, Augustine asserted that the fall of Adam resulted in a complete corruption of humankind that made humans incapable of good. Since faith in God is good, a special act of God on the individual is necessary if one is to believe. Augustine prayed that God might impart the will and the ability to do what he had commanded to be done. He predicated divine grace and love on an immutable, impassible God, more akin to the timeless God of Greek philosophical speculation than to the inter-personal, covenantal God of the Bible. From Augustine the biblical-classical synthesis passed with little change into the Middle Ages and the Reformation.[11]

Clark Pinnock with characteristic verve presents the view of an open God with evangelistic zeal. He maintains that Christians believe their lives de facto to be in conversation with God, their prayers to make a difference, and their choices to be free. He contrasts a model of God as an aloof monarch, removed from the world, unchangeable in every part, his power all encompassing and irresistible, with a model of God who enters into a loving, personal, responsive relationship with humanity. In this latter model people make real choices; they surprise one another and on occasion surprise God.[12]

Pinnock's attack on traditional Reformed Theology is withering. He writes, "To say that God hates sin while secretly willing it, to say that God warns us not to fall away though it is impossible, to say that God loves the world while excluding most people from an opportunity of salvation, to say that God warmly invites sinners to come knowing all the while that they cannot possibly do so—such things do not deserve to be called mysteries when that is just a euphemism for nonsense."[13]

God is immutable, Pinnock asserts, in that the Trinity is unchangeably what it is. But if immutability means that God is immobile, that he cannot change in response to the pleas and acts of his people, God is not immutable. Pinnock finds the doctrine of God's impassibility, that God is utterly unaffected by what people do, particularly revolting. In the Bible God loves, hates, and repents; he responds as we expect a personal God to respond. To say God loves means God opens himself so that he can be hurt, as does anyone who loves.[14]

With other open theism advocates, Pinnock rejects the notions that God is a timeless being, striding over the past, present, and future. All things that are logically possible are possible with God, but knowing the future choices that free creatures will make is nonsense, as a square-circle is nonsense.[15] The assertion that past, present, and future are all present in God's being is a concept beyond human experience or comprehension. That being the case, it is a claim that has no meaning.[16] If God is timeless, what of biblical assertions that God makes plans and carries them out in time? How can a timeless God act within time to mold and redeem a people?[17]

It is hardly unexpected that Calvinists have been vehement in their criticism of open theists.[18] Arminians have been more congenial, but many express concern about the denial of God's foreknowledge.[19] Neo-orthodoxy does not dominate theology as it did some years ago, but we may expect open theism to draw criticism from that quarter.[20] Neo-orthodoxy is likely to have trouble with open theism because, like process theologians, open theists reject the isolation of faith from science, a viewpoint that has given renewed interest to natural theology in recent decades.

Those who advocate the openness model are at pains to distinguish their affirmations from those of process theology. Not all will agree that they have been successful. The vocabulary and concerns of process theology crop up with fair frequency among open theists.[21] Open theism advocates maintain that their position is different from process theology in that they believe God is altogether separate from the world, that neither his existence nor his attributes are dependent on the material universe. Pinnock writes, "In the openness model, God still reserves the power to control everything, whereas in process thought God cannot override the freedom of creatures. This is a fundamental and crucial difference."[22] Detractors have not been convinced.[23]

The Stone-Campbell Tradition and the Openness Model

If it is true, as Highfield has argued, that the intellectual and spiritual leaders of the nineteenth-century Stone-Campbell tradition developed no distinctive doctrine of God, it is not true that they "embraced the traditional doctrine mediated by the Reformed Tradition."[24] Highfield cites a portion of the Westminister Confession to illustrate affirmations about God that have been embraced by the Stone-Campbell tradition; however, he cites selectively. The Confession's assertion, "God from all eternity did by the most wise and holy counsel of his will freely and unchangeably ordain whatever comes to pass,"[25] has not weathered well in the Stone-Campbell Restoration Movement. While it is true that those who identify with the Stone-Campbell Movement have produced very little theological reflection on the nature of God, they have had considerable to say about the other end of the equation, namely, human freedom.

Campbell himself discussed Arminian and Calvinistic positions on a number of topics that have implications for the doctrine of God. For example, in an engagement with an Arminian theologian, Campbell argued that when an Arminian tells an unregenerate soul that he must pray for God to give him faith, the difference between the Arminian and the Calvinist are indistinguishable. Campbell took issue with both when he declared that faith is a human choice, a choice of the individual when he hears the word of God. He insisted that it is logically contradictory to pray for faith. Prayer already implies faith.[26]

The implications of Campbell's argument are unmistakable. Belief or unbelief is the choice of the unregenerate when he hears the gospel. While his words may come more properly under the heading of soteriology or anthropology, neither can be approached in isolation from a consideration of God's sovereignty. Campbell implied that God allows people the choice of believing or not believing when he confronts them with the gospel. Campbell openly confessed that he had changed his theological viewpoints during the course of his ministry. He spoke candidly of "my former and primitive Calvinism."[27]

In a later issue of the *Millennial Harbinger* a letter directed to Campbell by one S. K. Milton rejected both the Calvinistic position that Christ died only for the elect and the Arminian viewpoint that none can obey God until the Spirit operates. With some disdain for Arminianism, Milton noted the irony of calling for people to choose obedience when "the Spirit will operate only when and where he pleases."[28] For Milton as for Campbell, faith was a choice the unregenerate made when confronted with the gospel. Since it was not his custom to let conclusions stand unchallenged when he disagreed with them, the fact that Campbell printed the piece by Milton without comment implies his agreement.

When Bruce Ware examined prevenient grace in Arminian/Wesleyan theology, he concluded that the doctrine was a linchpin that lends understanding to the way God has foreknown and chosen those who have saving faith. He maintained, further, that the Calvinistic concept of irresistible grace was woven finely into the doctrine of God's calling and election. Ware concluded, "It should be evident that Arminian and Calvinist soteriologies stand or fall on their respective doctrines of saving grace."[29] For the Calvinist, God predetermines who will believe; for the Arminian, God foreknows who will believe and extends prevenient grace to all so that those whom he foreknew will be able to believe. Both agree that as a consequence of Adam's sin, humankind is totally corrupt and cannot come to faith without direct divine intervention. Campbell rejected this. He believed that the individual had within himself the resources to believe. Call it high Pelagianism if you wish, but it is the implication of his words.[30]

The viewpoint that individuals make a free-will decision to respond to God, either to believe or to reject the gospel, has been the dominant position of past and present adherents to the Stone-Campbell Movement. At the same time, it is safe to say that nineteenth-century Restoration leaders tended to regard the Calvinist position on God's sovereignty as more consistent than the Arminian. Arminianism asserted human freedom but maintained that one must pray for God to give the faith he foreknew the individual would embrace. Campbell's position was this: If a person is free when presented with the choice of belief or unbelief, Adam's sin notwithstanding, he needs to choose faith, not to "pray through" until God gives faith.

Campbell and his colleagues might have argued that their position was a more consistent Arminianism than that of the Arminians. The same charge has been leveled at those who advocate open theism. If people are free either to believe or not believe, the conclusion that people cannot believe until the Holy Spirit has operated makes little sense.[31] It is safe to say that those of the Stone-Campbell Movement have been dissatisfied with both the Calvinist and the Arminian views of divine sovereignty. They have maintained against both that God has created human beings so that they are able to make significant, free choices.

Toward the end of the nineteenth century, T. W. Brents published *The Gospel Plan of Salvation,* a work that has proven to be widely influential among Churches of Christ (a cappella). Among other things, Brents addressed the foreknowledge of God. Some of his statements could have been written by open theists. Brents seems to understand the implications of exhaustive foreknowledge. He writes, "If God knew before He gave Adam the law in the garden that he would violate it when given, then he was not free; for he could not have falsified God's foreknowledge if he would: hence to violate the law was a necessity."[32] However, at times Brents is less than clear. He seems to use the words "foreknowledge" and "predestination" interchangeably. Further, he suggests that God could have foreknown the future but chose not to.[33] As far as I can see, that nullifies his previous argument. If the future is foreknowable, it is of necessity determined. While Brents may not be altogether coherent, he illustrates at least this much: Leaders among Churches of Christ (a cappella) have recognized the tension between assertions of significant human freedom and God's exhaustive foreknowledge.

That people make free choices has been an uncompromising staple in Stone-Campbell thinking. Because the doctrine of election is inseparable from the question of sovereignty, it is not accurate to assert that nineteenth-century Stone-Campbell leaders embraced the traditional doctrine of God mediated by Reformed theology. They certainly did not embrace it in toto. Neither is it true that their twentieth or twenty-first century descendants have done so.[34] Predestination and original sin have been decisively rejected, and with this the doctrine of God that undergirds such doctrines. When Robert Shank published his books challenging Calvinistic conceptions of perseverance, election, and the underlying concepts of sovereignty, he found a ready reception among those of the Stone-Campbell Movement.[35]

Another indication of the friendly interest those of the Stone-Campbell Movement might be expected to show open theism is the favor they have shown to "conditional prophecy."[36] Conditional prophecy implies that the events God brings to pass depend on the responses—the choices people make—after God has foretold the future. If prophecy is conditional, the future is not set. People have choices to make that God has not determined.

Many Stone-Campbell adherents have embraced God's foreknowledge, but the doctrine has stood alone as a statement of God's nature; it has not been anchored to doctrines of human sinfulness inherited from Adam and of prevenient grace. What is lacking among those of the Stone-Campbell Movement is a serious examination of the implications of their steadfast trust in human freedom for the doctrine of God's exhaustive foreknowledge. Still, that omission hardly implies an uncritical acceptance of the doctrine of God as expressed in Reformed Theology.

Observations, Questions, Reflections

Those who advocate understanding God on an openness model are persuasive. Highfield comes across as a bit condescending when he suggests that the model is for the theologically naive.[37] Though open theism is attractive, serious unresolved questions remain. But then, unresolved questions continue for every model of God. In what follows I want to set forth some of the persuasive aspects of open theism as well as some of the questions that have not been sufficiently addressed.

First, advocates of open theism have not only drawn support for their model from Scripture, they have made a good case that biblical teaching, not philosophical speculation, has driven them to ask the questions they ask and reach the conclusions they do. Sanders has devoted a significant portion of his book to the biblical evidence, as does Gregory Boyd.[38] The argument, in summary, is that when the Bible presents God in relationship with humanity, when he gives commands, offers choices, expresses surprise or repentance, the narrative should be taken at its face value.

Second, the claim that exhaustive foreknowledge and predestination come out at the same point is accurate. If we imagine a marble rolling down a maze until it drops out in a bucket at the bottom, it makes little difference to the marble whether it reached its destination because of the maze itself or because the designer of the maze determined its final destination. The marble comes out at the same place. The formal distinction between God's foreknowing all and his being the causal agent of all is of little consequence when questions of human freedom are at issue. If God foreknows all, we are driven to the conclusion that every future event has somehow been determined.[39] Reformed Theology with its emphasis on God's sovereignty is a more internally consist way of viewing God than is the Arminian/Wesleyan position, embracing foreknowledge and prevenient grace. Neither middle knowledge nor the concept of a timeless God eliminates the demand for causal relationships that result in a determinism as ironclad as any Calvinists affirm.[40] In either case, human freedom is eliminated.

Third, open theism expresses the way Christians typically understand their relationship with God more adequately than do the traditional models advanced by Arminian or Calvinist theologians. Pinnock writes of an "as if" factor.[41] We live "as if" we had real choices to make. We do not live "as if" the outcome will be the same regardless of the choices we make. Open theism is more existentially satisfying than determinism. That does not prove the model to be true. However, if people are to engage their minds as well as their hearts in their relationship to God, it is hardly satisfying to pray for God's intervention in their lives when they have decided beforehand that each detail of life has already been mapped out.

Calvinists claim that the doctrine of election provides reassurance for Christians that adds vigor to Christian living. Packer writes, "Election is a pastoral theme, spelled out for believers' encouragement, reassurance, support, and worship."[42] Strangely, the problem is that Calvinists themselves assert that nobody can be perfectly sure he is among the elect. Marshall observes,

> Whoever said, 'The Calvinist knows that he cannot fall from salvation but does not know whether he has got it,' had it summed up nicely.... The non-Calvinist knows

that he has salvation because he trusts in the promises of God but is aware that, left to himself, he could lose it. So he holds to Christ. It seems to me that the practical effect is the same."[43]

Christians who understand themselves to share a personal relationship with God bask in this relationship. They feel no compunction to fret over whether they may or may not be among the elect. They offer love freely to God who has demonstrated his love by allowing them to choose to love God or not to love him.

Fourth, scientific understanding of the material world has revealed that uncertainty and chance are built into the created order. God has created the world so that not only human beings but the cosmos itself may surprise him. The days have long past when a Spinoza could predicate a mechanical determinism on the universe. Things as diverse as eddy currents, quantum mechanics, and DNA molecules suggest that God has built randomness into creation. Pinnock writes, "Seeing the future as partly open and partly settled fits hand in glove with what we are discovering about dynamic systems in science today."[44] According to his will, God steps into the cosmos and does whatever he chooses, but he also seems to leave himself open for the possibility of surprise.

Fifth, when critics argue that open theism is idolatry, an attempt to make God in human form, the critique is a caricature, not a fair assessment of the model.[45] God invites us to understand his nature through human analogy. When Deborah pictures God rising up in Edom, shaking himself off like a mighty man, causing the heavens to thunder and the mountains to quake, it is an anthropomorphism, but the depiction offers insight into the ontological reality of God. God in his Being hears his people and responds to their pleas. Our choice is to use anthropomorphic language or not to speak of God at all. I'm not sure what all the implications of *imago Dei* are, but if humans in some sense have been created in the image of God, it cannot be a great error for these same humans to attempt to understand God based on the image they see in themselves. Since God is free, since God's freedom is of his essence, can it be far wrong to suppose that when he expressed his love by creating humans, he gave them some measure of his own freedom?

Open theism is no attempt to make God in the image of humans, but it is a willingness to understand some things about God by making reference to humans.[46] The alternative is for us to reason abstractly about God and then to pronounce him to be what we have determined him to be. It is to the point to ask, "Can we understand any aspect of God's being on a model that defies experience?" Westblade writes, "The certain future God sovereignly guarantees to his chosen saints depends upon their fulfilling moral conditions, yet at no expense to the certainty of that guaranteed future."[47] One reads the statement and wonders whether God might, after all, dig a hole so deep that he could not fill it.

To say first that the future depends on human performance of moral imperatives and second that God sovereignly guarantees the future with no regard for human performance stretches language beyond tolerable limit. Centuries of reasoning on the part of Reformed theologians fail to convince that one exercises freedom by any reasonable definition of the word when every act one takes has been sovereignly decreed to take place from eternity. The appeal to mystery cannot justify the jettisoning of experience and reason.

While open theists make a convincing case, difficult, unresolved questions remain. First, though one applauds Sanders for the space he devotes to the biblical text, open theists have given too little attention to the exegesis of texts that are difficult to fit into their model of God. Calvinists tend to spend a great deal of time with texts such as John 6:35-45, Romans 8:29-30, Romans 9-10, and Ephesians 1:3-11, but in fairness, they also attempt to deal with passages such as Hebrews 2:1-4; 3:6-4:13; 6:4-6 that call their system into question.[48] Open theists tend to respond by decrying the use of proof texts and asserting that they take seriously the narrative portions of the Bible where a loving God has a relationship with his people. Even if we concede the point, still open theists cannot dismiss passages that call the model they offer into question.

Second, open theists have difficulty fitting specifics into the discussion at a number of levels. One sympathizes with the assertion that God operates in broad, comprehensive ways as he works his will. The problem is that God's overall strategy must be realized through a working together of specific occurrences. For example, when the prophets call Nebuchadnezzar or Cyrus God's servant, the instrument of his judgment upon his people, the rulers appear to be under God's control, not in dialogue with him. Judas seems to be appointed to his deed.[49] Where does dialogue enter the picture? Is God in dialogue with some, controlling the thoughts and actions of others? If God respects human freedom, isn't it reasonable to expect him to respect the freedom of every person in every circumstance? Perhaps these questions can be answered by appealing to God's infinite flexibility and resourcefulness, but the answer has the appearance of desperation.

Third, while open theists make a good case when they claim to have been driven to their conclusions by the Bible, one is left uncomfortable with the ease with which the model accommodates itself to the individualistic obsession, not to say the hubris, of Western culture. In spite of the efforts of open theists to distinguish their conclusions from those of process theology, the two viewpoints converge at crucial points.[50] When process theologian Ian Barbour writes, "God presents new possibilities but leaves the alternatives open, eliciting the response of entities in the world.... This is a God of persuasion rather than coercion,"[51] the words are the same as open theists. Process theologians tend to hold a low estimate of Bible as divinely inspired. When reflecting on the intersection of science and theology, they also evidence pantheistic or deistic leanings. Those who hold God to be personal, both standing over creation and independent from it, find themselves uncomfortable with the company open theism keeps.

Fourth, open theists have difficulty accounting for the universality of human sin.

Did the sin of Adam taint human nature so that humans can do no good? Do people contribute to their own salvation or is it the work of God? If free will is a necessary corollary to sin and guilt, then we must allow for the possibility of human goodness. How do the sin of Adam and its consequences fit into open theism? Must we look at Eden as God's failed experiment?

Fifth, a related question arises when we ask about the consummation of the age, life in the *eschaton*. Will there be free will in heaven? If it is inherent in the nature of God that he wills to relate to humankind so that people are able to make choices, will there be choices in heaven? If so, must we allow for the possibility of sin in heaven? How can that be if this mortal will be swallowed up with immortality, and the wages of sin is death, and God will wipe away every tear? If being in relationship to his creatures is in God's nature, why will the same qualities of choice in this age change in the age to come?[52]

Conclusion

Risking a global judgment, it appears to me that the reasoning and the conclusions of open theism resonate positively with doctrinal stances evident in the Stone-Campbell Movement. Those in the Stone-Campbell Movement in some ways have been more Arminian than the Arminians. They have insisted that in order to be saved, people must hear the gospel, believe it on their own volition, and obey it. People seem to make real choices and to exercise a measure of freedom. They pray expecting God to hear and act; they expect prayer to make a difference. Jesus seemed to expect people to believe what he said, and he held them culpable when they did not believe. All of this fits admirably into open theism's model of God's being in a relationship with his people.

The sticking point for those of Stone-Campbell persuasion is in the denial of exhaustive foreknowledge by open theists. Long before open theism appeared, I viewed predestination and exhaustive foreknowledge to be the same. If both viewpoints are essentially deterministic, and if Stone-Campbell adherents reject determinism, they should reconsider holding to God's exhaustive foreknowledge.

Questions raised by open theists are at least as much about the nature of humanity as they are about the nature of God. Predicating a sovereign God who has exhaustively determined every human act offers some comfort. However, if adopting such a view of God is based more on an internally coherent theological system than on biblical teaching, it is an abdication of human responsibility. Open theism forces the question, "Can we live in a world that we ourselves, at least in part, are responsible for?" To adopt the stance of open theism implies that people live in a world where what they do makes a real difference. The implications spread across the entire span of Christian theology, from soteriology, to judgment, and beyond.

Open theism faces a philosophically well-conceived classical-biblical synthesis on the right and a philosophically well-conceived process theology on the left. Open theists respond that both philosophical systems, well conceived though they be, do not measure up to the biblical presentation of God.

Open theists must confront difficult and unresolved questions. Yet, difficulties are present with any model of God. Still, God invites us to understand him to the degree that we are able. We make statements about God with caution, and we acknowledge with Job, "These are indeed but the outskirts of his ways; and how small a whisper do we hear of him! But the thunder of his power who can understand?"[53] In the end we must accept a model of God that seems to conform best to the portrayal of him in Scripture. To that end, the viewpoints and conclusions of open theism are appealing and invite further study.

Notes

[1]Job 23:17 (REB).

[2]"Significant freedom" are the words of Clark Pinnock, et al., "Preface," *The Openness of God: A Biblical Challenge to the Traditional Understanding of God* (Downers Grove, Ill: InterVarsity, 1994), p. 7. The suggestion is that however one slices human freedom, when it is within the constraints of God's exhaustive foreknowledge, middle knowledge, or predestination, the result is no "significant freedom."

[3]William Hasker, *God, Time, and Knowledge* (Ithaca: Cornell University Press, 1989), p. 53.

[4]Pinnock, *Openness of God*, includes contributions from David Basinger, William Hasker, Clark Pinnock, Richard Rice, and John Sanders. Antecedent volumes edited by Pinnock include *Grace Unlimited* (Minneapolis: Bethany, 1975) and *The Grace of God, the Will of Man: A Case for Arminianism* (Grand Rapids: Zondervan, 1989). Not all the articles in the earlier volumes question God's exhaustive foreknowledge as strongly as the latest volume does.

[5]Richard Rice, "Biblical Support for a New Perspective," in Pinnock, *Openness*, p. 15.

[6]William Hasker, *God, Time*, p. 144.

[7]Rice, "Biblical Support for a New Perspective," p. 16.

[8]John Sanders, "Historical Considerations" in Pinnock, *Openness*, p. 60.

[9]Ibid., p. 70.

[10]Augustine, *The City of God,* trans. Marcus Dods (New York: Random House, 1950), p. 154: "We assert both that God knows all things before they come to pass, and that we do so by our free will whatever we know and feel to be done by us."

[11]John Sanders, "Historical Considerations," pp. 81-87.

[12]Clark Pinnock, "Systemic Theology," in Pinnock, *Openness*, pp. 103-104.

[13]Ibid., p. 115. In a later work, *Most Moved Mover: A Theology of God's Openness* (Grand Rapids: Baker, 2001), 16, Pinnock writes, "It astonishes me that people can defend the 'glory' of God so vehemently when that glory includes God's sovereign authorship of every rape and murder, his closing down the future to any meaningful creaturely contribution, and his holding people accountable for deeds he predestined them to do and they cannot but do."

[14]Ibid., pp. 117-119.

[15]Ron Highfield, "The Problem with the 'Problem of Evil': A Response to Gregory Boyd's Open

Theists Solution," *Restoration Quarterly* 45 (2003):175-176, misses the point of the square-circle analogy. It is not as if a square-circle is some desirable entity that God cannot bring about. The point is that reference to square-circles is, as Highfield acknowledges, gibberish. It is the same kind of gibberish one encounters in the proposal that God has determined human affairs in all their minutia and yet people act freely when they do what God has determined they will do.

[16]Existentially we operate within the realm of human meaning. The attempt to deal with meaning in God's level is hopeless.

[17]Pinnock, "Systemic Theology," p. 120.

[18]Bruce A. Ware, *God's Lesser Glory: The Diminished God of Open Theism* (Wheaton: Crossway, 2000), p. 20, states it this way: "In a word, what is lost in open theism is the Christian's confidence in God." Ware wants to reduce the choices to open theism or Calvinism. Arminian foreknowledge, he argues, implies open theism (p. 41). See also John S. Feinberg, *No One Like Him: The Doctrine of God* (Wheaton: Crossway, 2001); John M. Frame, *The Doctrine of God* (Phillipsburg, N.J.: Puritan & Reformed, 2002).

[19]See, for example, Robert E. Picirilli, "An Arminian Response to John Sander's *The God Who Risks: A Theology of Providence," JETS* 44 (2001): 467-491.

[20]One expects neo-orthodox thinkers to criticize open theism based on a negative assessment of the Reformed-Arminian discussion of God's sovereignty for Christian faith and practice. One boldly affirms the paradox that God is sovereign and people are free. End of discussion! I suspect this is the direction Ron Highfield, "Does the World Limit God? Assessing the Case for Open Theism," *Stone-Campbell Journal* 5 (2002): 86, wants to go when he writes that he would dismantle an argument by Hasker and "construct an alternative theological perspective within which human freedom and God's complete foreknowledge are reconciled." One wonders, of course, what that alternative might be.

[21]Process theology and open theists express considerable interest in the relationship of the scientific enterprise and theology. Both emphasize God's personal involvement with events of nature as well as humankind. For a summary of process theology see D. W. Diehl, "Process Theology" in *Evangelical Dictionary of Theology,* ed. Walter A. Elwell (Grand Rapids: Baker, 1984), pp. 880-885.

[22]John B. Cobb, Jr. and Clark Pinnock, eds., *Searching for an Adequate God: A Dialogue Between Process and Free Will Theists* (Grand Rapids: Eerdmans, 2000), p. xi. This volume also offers a list of concerns that are common to process theologians and open theists (pp. ix-x).

[23]See S. M. Baugh, "The Meaning of Foreknowledge" in *Still Sovereign: Contemporary Perspectives on Election, Foreknowledge, & Grace,* eds. Thomas R. Schreiner and Bruce A. Ware (Grand Rapids: Baker, 1995), p. 184-185; D. A. Tiessen, "The Openness Model of God: An Examination of Its Current and Early Expression in the Light of Hartshorne's Process Theism" (M. Div. Thesis, Providence Theological Seminary, 1998).

[24]Highfield, "Does the World Limit God?" p. 69.

[25]Westminster Confession, 3.1.

[26]Alexander Campbell, "Response to Mr. Waterman," *Millennial Harbinger* 4 (1833): 411.

[27]Ibid.

[28]S. K. Milton, "Sectarian Inconsistencies Exposed," *Millennial Harbinger* (1834): 513-514.

[29]Bruce A. Ware, "Effectual Calling and Grace," in Schreiner and Ware, *Still Sovereign*, p. 208

[30]Among the charges Baptists brought against Alexander Campbell and his associates was a "Pelagian doctrine of the sufficiency of man's natural powers to effect his own salvation," *Millennial Harbinger* (1831):78. Many would call Campbell's position on human freedom and responsibility, semi-Pelagianism. Robert Richardson, *Memoirs of Alexander Campbell,* 2 vols. (reprint ed., Indianapolis: Religious Book Service, n.d.), 2:349, cites the above indictment and Campbell's later response that he was "not guilty" of the charges. This is not the place for a discussion of the nuances on human freedom

that follow from Pelagianism vis à vis semi-Pelagianism, but we may at least observe that distinctions are finely drawn. See discussion and references in "Pelagius, Pelagianism" and "Semi-Pelagianism" in *Evangelical Dictionary of Theology*, ed. Walter A. Elwell (Grand Rapids: Baker, 1984), pp. 833-834; 1000-1001.

[31]See J. Henshall, "Calvinism and Arminianism," *Millennial Harbinger* (1846): 323-324.

[32]T. W. Brents, *The Gospel Plan of Salvation* (1874; reprint ed., Nashville: Gospel Advocate Company, 1957), p. 96.

[33]Ibid.

[34]A survey of the *Restoration Serials Index* compiled at Abilene Christian University (www.acu.edu/rsi/index.php) uncovers scores of articles on predestination, Calvinism, and irresistible grace. Simply perusing the titles of the articles makes it evident that those of the Stone-Campbell Movement, like Pelagius, have rejected the notion that children are born tainted with the sin of Adam. Heirs of the Stone-Campbell Movement have been no great friends of Reformed Theology.

[35]*Life in the Son: A Study of the Doctrine of Perseverance* (Springfield, Mo. : Westcott Publishers, 1960); *Elect in the Son: A Study of the Doctrine of Election* (Springfield, Mo.: Westcott Publishers, 1970).

[36]See F. Furman Kearley, "Biblical Prophecy and the Middle East Crisis," *Inman Bible Forum* 1 (Parkersburg, W. Va: Ohio Valley College, 1983), p. 2.

[37]Highfield, "Does the World Limit God?" p. 92.

[38]John Sanders, *The God Who Risks: A Theology of Providence* (Downers Grove: InterVarsity, 1998), 39-139; Gregory A. Boyd, *God of the Possible: A Biblical Introduction to the Open View of God* (Grand Rapids: Baker, 2000).

[39]Calvinists tend to see this clearly. Donald J. Westblade, "Divine Election in the Pauline Literature," in Schreiner and Ware, *Still Sovereign*, p. 71, summarizes Jonathan Edwards as follows: "Infallible foreknowledge of an event presupposes the necessity of that event and therefore precludes its real freedom." See Jonathan Edwards, *Freedom of the Will*, ed. Paul Ramsey (New Haven: Yale University Press, 1957), pp. 257-269.

[40]See Augustine's discussion of Cicero cited by Hasker, *God, Time*, p. 5.

[41]Pinnock, *Most Moved Mover*, p. 155.

[42]J. I. Packer, "The Love of God: Universal and Particular," in Schreiner and Ware, *Still Sovereign*, p. 281.

[43]I. Howard Marshall, *Jesus the Savior: Studies in New Testament Theology* (London: SPCK, 1990), 313.

[44]*Most Moved Mover*, p. 130. See further, Arthur Peacocke, *Theology for a Scientific Age: Being and Becoming* (Minneapolis: Fortress, 1993), p. 65.

[45]Norman Geisler, *Creating God in the Image of Man? The New "Open" View of God: Neotheism's Dangerous Drift* (Minneapolis: Bethany, 1997).

[46]Rice, "Biblical Support for a New Perspective," p. 35 asks, "To avoid turning God into an enlarged human being, must we deny not only that God shares our physical properties but our intellectual, volitional and emotional properties too?" He responds, "If human beings and God have nothing whatever in common, if we have utterly no mutual experience, then we have no way of talking and thinking about God and there is no possibility of a personal relationship with him." Sanders, *God Who Risks*, p. 35 and passim, returns often to the theme, "We cannot think and speak of God other than as a being in relation to us."

[47]"Divine Election in the Pauline Literature," p. 77.

[48]Wayne Grudem, "Perseverance of the Saints: A Case Study in the Warning Passages in Hebrews," in Schreiner and Ware, *Still Sovereign*, pp. 133-182.

[49]Sanders, *God Who Risks*, pp. 98, takes up the case of Judas. He implies that things might very

well have turned out differently with Judas than they did. He argues that Judas's misplaced zeal led to the tragic result of betrayal. But the narratives present Judas as a traitor, not merely misguided. Could God have worked out his will in this particular aspect of Jesus' death had Judas made some other choice than the one he made? It is difficult to argue that in the light of passages such as John 6:70-71.

[50]See Clark Pinnock, "Introduction," in *Searching for an Adequate God: A Dialogue Between Process and Free Will Theists* (Grand Rapids: Eerdmans, 2000), pp. ix-x, for a summary of viewpoints that free will theists share with process theologians.

[51]*Nature, Human Nature, and God, Theology and the Sciences* (Minneapolis: Fortress, 2002), p. 34.

[52]Pinnock, *Most Moved Mover*, p, 31 speculates about the status of free will in the *eschaton*. Perhaps the period of probation will come to an end, he says, and we will be able to love reliably. Perhaps the purpose of our probation on earth will end and freedom will be withdrawn. The speculations are not satisfying. If love is essential to God, and if love calls for risk on the part of God and free will on the part of humankind, one wonders why things should be different in the world to come. If they are not different, we must reckon with the possibility of sin.

[53]Job 26:14 (NRSV).

2

OPEN THEISM AND
CHRISTIAN CHURCHES (INDEPENDENT)

Robert C. Kurka

When Bethany College in West Virginia began as a Christian educational institution in the nine-teenth century, its revivalist founder wrote into its charter that it would never have a professorship of theology, and its main textbook would always be the Bible.[1]

Alexander Campbell's antipathy towards theology has long served to guide his descendents in their exegetical efforts but has also proven to be a bane. As a consequence of their reticence to construe theological models, Stone-Campbell adherents have tended to foster doctrinal suspicion among evangelicals (for example, being accused of belief in water regenerationism) and have tended to provide a breeding ground for non-orthodox movements to grow and develop (Mormonism, Christadelphianism, and the International Church of Christ).

This tendency, then, suggests a two-pronged response to open theism among those in Christian Churches (independent) of the Stone-Campbell Restoration Movement.

Stone-Campbell Historical Perspective

First, Stone-Campbell adherents should give open theism an attentive audience. As a movement that has prided itself in its confessional freedom ("No Creed but Christ") and defined itself in terms of theological suspicion, those in the Stone-Campbell Movement, both independent and a cappella, can hardly do less that give a charitable hearing to a proposal that claims to be biblically-driven and non-Calvinistic.[2] Stone-Campbell literature cautions against allowing theological models to dictate what exegetical conclusions should be reached. This preference for "letting the Scriptures speak" led to placing baptism in the realm of soteriological discussion rather than in its traditional evangelical treatment in the doctrine of the church.[3]

Given their preference for the narrative and functional (Acts) over the didactic and theological (Romans), the Stone-Campbell fathers were brief on the doctrine of God. In the nearest thing to a systematic theology Alexander Campbell did, he devoted a scant three pages to theology, proper, in contrast to the twelve pages he gives to baptism and its role in conversion.[4] In a terse statement that surely will draw a few comparisons to that of the Westminster Catechism, Campbell comments:

> But the Scriptures speak of his divinity, or Godhead, as well as of the unity, spirituality, and eternity of his being. We have not, indeed, much said upon this incomprehensive theme; for who by searching can find out God, or know the Almighty to perfection?[5]

On the other hand, Campbell denounces those who "conceive of God as a mathematical unit," a reductionism that is "not in harmony with the *sacred style of inspiration.*" Campbell then asks why "there cannot be a plurality of *personal manifestations* in the divine nature any more than in the angelic or human, especially as man was created in the image of God?"[6]

Anticipating contemporary discussions of God from *theomorphic* and *Trinitarian* perspectives, much like Vanhoozer's *First Theology,*[7] Campbell refuses to let philosophic constructs determine his model of God. One's admiration for Campbell's short but insightful comments on God are tempered, however, when one reads these words on the Trinity in *The Christian Baptist*:

> I have been asked a thousand times, "What do you think of the doctrine of the Trinity?"…Some, nay, many think that to falter here is terrible…or not to speak in the language of the schools, is the worst of all errors and heresies. I have not spent, perhaps, an hour in ten years, in thinking about the *Trinity*. It is no term of mine. It is a word which belongs not to the Bible…I teach nothing, I say nothing, I think nothing about it, save that it is an unscriptural term, and consequently, can have no scriptural ideas attached to it.[8]

While the above words were penned by the less mature Campbell prior to producing *The Christian System*, they nonetheless served the non-Trinitarian biases of fellow Restorationist, Barton Stone, as the latter campaigned against the use of "unbiblical" creeds.[9]

Following the lead of their heritage's forebears, Stone-Campbell descendents have generally shied away from the rigors of developing theological models, especially God-models, preferring the less formulaic but equally demanding tasks of New Testament (and to a smaller degree, Old Testament) exegesis. One notable exception has been the present-day Cincinnati Bible Seminary theologian, Jack Cottrell, who made Stone-Campbell history by producing a well-received three-volume Arminian-oriented work on *God, The Creator, Ruler, and Redeemer.*[10]

The absence of God-thought specifically, and systematic theology in general, have rendered contemporary Stone-Campbell adherents, as well as other restorationist/atheological movements like pentecostalism, more vulnerable to novel, theological presentations than their more confessional neighbors. Yet, while Stone-Campbell adherents historically have been reticent about developing coherent systems, they have not generally embraced construals of God's self-limitation, such as those promoted recently in the writings of Hasker, Pinnock, Sanders, and Boyd. While Stone-Campbell history would seem to yield a qualified interest in open theism, the minimalist theology found in the thinking of Campbell, Stone and most recently Cottrell, would mitigate against an acceptance of open theism.

In *The Christian System*, the more mature Campbell notes that in each of God's attributes (among them, wisdom, power, and goodness) he is "infinite, immutable, and eternal."[11] Even the "trinity-suspicious," and militantly anti-Calvinistic Stone still concedes "that God is a sovereign" although "we neither understand or believe many things which are said on that subject."[12] In a far more substantial manner, Cottrell offers up a model of God that fails to draw a ready comparison to open theism: a sovereign God who has "absolute Lordship...absolute dominion over all things."[13] While one could argue that these three voices represent a pre-openness era and therefore might be subject to change to this newer form of Arminianism, the Stone-Campbell Movement never entertained a concept of God that radically departed from that of historic Christianity. While it is somewhat surprising that Stone-Campbell thinkers could say so much about baptism, church polity, and Christian unity without saying much about God, one can only assume that the "received model" of deity was essentially consistent with a "common-sense," plain reading of the Bible.[14]

However, open theism has now arrived! Theological convictions once held implicitly must now carefully be thought out and expressed. I therefore offer a theological critique of John Sanders.[15]

John Sanders' Historical Perspective

The belief that God is the ultimate cosmic explanation for each and every thing, including all the bad things we experience, is quite widespread, at least in North America. About fifteen years after the death of my brother I attended the funeral service of a young child whose parents were close friends of mine.... Several weeks later when I was visiting these friends, they had a question for me: "Why did God kill our baby girl?"...They had always been told that questioning God is a sin. In answering their question, I sought to provide them with a different model of God—the one that is explained in this book...(that) God takes risks in bringing about this particular type of world.[16]

With these words, philosopher-theologian John Sanders launches readers into one of his more recent experiments in "neo-Arminianism," offering a project that seems to arise genuinely out of the "knottiness" of everyday human existence. One cannot help but be impressed by the pastoral context for a book on providence. Too often God's preservation and government (and concurrence) become the abstract discussion of systematic theologians rather than concrete wrestlings of shepherd-teachers who are trying to make sense as to how the Lord is really working amidst the apparent incongruities of life. Sanders deserves commendation, then, for grounding this topic in the all-too familiar world of *angst*. However, I question the actual helpfulness of his risk-taking God as well as its biblical grounding

In this volume, Sanders articulates a more sustained and comprehensive version of a theological pilgrimage that has been largely traveled along the "edge" of traditional evangelical belief. As a young Bible instructor at Oak Hills Bible College in Minnesota in 1989, Sanders served notice that classic, absolutist models of God needed to be subsumed under "personalistic lenses" in a essay titled "God as Personal,"[17] authored for Clark Pinnock's 1989 "Arminian Manifesto," *The Grace of God, The Will of Man*. In this work, Sanders indicated an early penchant for setting God's kingship against his covenant love, portraying the former as "those who prefer to speak of God in Greek philosophic terms."[18] Unfortunately, the more mature Sanders still chooses to cast the discussion in these terms of incommensurate models of God (sovereignty/love) instead of acknowledging that both attributes have strong scriptural attestation. This portrait of a loving deity was extended into Sanders's 1992 soteriological work, *No Other Name*, as the God who does not want any to perish (2 Pet 3:9), offering a salvation that includes devout believers from other religions.[19] While Jesus Christ is still the source of redemption , a Rahner-like implicit faith is presented as a solution to the dilemma of those who have not heard the explicit claims of the Gospel.[20]

In what has become a bit of a controversial chapter on "Historical Considerations," in *The Openness of God* in 1994, Sanders contended that traditional theism itself was a "novel" imposition on early Christianity's teaching about God, a mixture of Greek deterministic ideas foreign to the libertarian notions of the church fathers.[21] For Sanders, libertarianism constitutes an implicit nod towards open theism that inevitably leads to denial of exhaustive foreknowledge. Thus, he gladly includes Jacob Arminius as a co-laborer in his historical treatise. However, Sanders omits citing the one genuine example of early theologians who explicitly combined these two key themes: Leo (and Faustus) Socinus. Robert Strimple, among others, has brought this "oversight" to the forefront, noting that Socinianism provides the most demonstrable parallel to open theism in church history, even to the "most basic arguments."[22] One can understand Sanders's reticence to cite support from these sixteenth-century thinkers in his open theism cause, since their theological movement also denied the full deity of Christ, his substitutionary atonement, and justification by his imputed righteousness, earning them a heretical label.

The God Who Risks: A More Biblical Alternative to Classical Theism?

Sanders's *The God Who Risks*, written in 1998[23] is one of the most comprehensive projects to appear from the proponents of open theism. Any serious interaction with open theism must engage this book.

Sanders's Core Assumptions

The God who Risks is built upon three "core assumptions." First and most critical to Sanders's understanding of divine providence is his portrayal of God as a fundamentallyrelational being. Four control beliefs govern this relational construct: (1) God loves us and desires that we enter into a reciprocal, loving relationship with him, as well as with our fellow human beings. (2) God has sovereignly decided to make some of his actions contingent upon human requests and actions. He establishes the project and elicits our free collaboration with it. (3) Consequently, God chooses to exercise a general rather than specific form of providential control. (4) In order that a truly personal love relationship between personal humans and himself actually occurs, God has granted His creation genuine *libertarian freedom.*[24] These control beliefs will mitigate against certain characterizations of God that have long prevailed in classical models, such as God as sovereign, king, and judge.

A second core assumption concerns Sanders's understanding of God-talk, or language describing the emotions and actions of deity. In contradiction to traditional discussions of anthropopathism and anthropomorphism, he argues for a "reality-depicting language." Since God is a primarily relational being, he would hardly choose to relate to his human creatures in ways that create a distance or hinder the intimacy incumbent upon such a relationship. Classical theism, with its highly impersonal transcendent deity, could never bring itself to accept a "literalness" to God's repentance or apparent changes in action; these fluid expressions had to only be divine accommodations to our finite minds."[25] On the other hand, the personal God of Scripture does not "lisp" to us as a nursemaid to a young child (Calvin's motif) but engages us in meaningful adult discussion that presumes a common experiential context. Sanders comments, "Our knowledge of God as Creator comes from 'inside' the world. We do not reach from the inside to the outside. God reaches us as an insider."[26]

The above two core assumptions, then, provide the "systematic principles" that undergird a third: how biblical narrative should be read. The "God who risks," then, is a relational being who is involved with his image in a genuinely interactive, give-and-take manner. According to Sanders this means that he cannot possess exhaustive foreknowledge in the traditionally-understood manner. Rather, he only knows the past and the present in some comprehensive way (presentism). Except for a relatively small number of things that he has predetermined to do, God's future knowledge is largely derivative. When he determines or promises to act certain ways, these are derived from his reading of past and present events, a reality-based omniscience that would affirm that God has supernatural knowledge of all real things (the future is not an ontological reality). Subsequently, this past-and-present knowing God will make mistakes and even risk failure as he works out his plans with his creaturely co-agents. The biblical story, then, is the drama of this risk-taking God in a reality-depicting manner that is nothing short of scandalous to the adherent of classical, all-controlling notion of deity. Human beings, in their exercise of genuine libertarian freedom, can actually bring about a change in events that God could not foresee; such is the nature of loving non-coercive relationships.

While God's eschatological "promises" (a carefully nuanced term) will reach fruition, this will not occur due to a prescribed script; in fact, the *eschaton* will bring surprises because it is not set in concrete."[27] Rather, God's intended good ultimately will triumph due to his proven track record of bringing redemption out of human failure, a faithfulness more befitting a covenantal relationship than a meticulous blueprint.[28]

"The Story of Risk": An Exposition of Sanders's Version of the Biblical Narrative
Sanders skillfully employs his core convictions as he weaves his way through the biblical narrative. Instead of encountering a story of God's monumental sovereignty in redeeming a fallen universe, people enter a drama of temporary failure. Such a deity is introduced in the opening verses of Genesis where the traditional notion of *ex nihilo* creation is turned into a *relational battle* between Yahweh and his cosmic opponents. While this portrayal is not all that unusual among Old Testament scholars (as in polemic vs. Near Eastern cosmologies), Sanders's reasons for adopting such are certainly understandable, given his governing ideology. From the moment of initial creation forward, nothing is really safe for the "God who risks."

As readers move through the remainder of the creation narrative to Adam and Eve, they are ushered not into a "tent of security" but rather an open-air bazaar of free trade for God's creatures. The Fall of Genesis 3 is not something foreknown by God but a cosmic surprise: the "Implausible Happens," as Sanders puts it.[29] However, because of his great love for his creation (his chief attribute), God changes his mind over the death sentence he gave in Genesis 2:17.[30] Another occurrence of divine love rescinding judgment is found in Genesis 6-9, where God's parental pain causes him: first, to recognize he has put his creation project in jeopardy (6:1-6); second, to find in Noah someone who could rehabilitate this negative situation (6:8); and third, to decide "to try different courses of action in the future."(9:11-16).[31]

The Abrahamic narratives continue this story of God's developing learning curve. In the Isaac episode (Gen 22:1-12), Yahweh gains genuine knowledge of Abraham's deep faith.[32] Exodus tells of Moses risking divine wrath by interceding for his rebellious nation, trusting that Yahweh is enough of a fair dialogue partner that he won't exercise his anger.[33] The subsequent pages of the Old Testament are then concluded with these words: "God expected positive results, but all things have not gone as God desired. God nevertheless invested himself in the project in the hope of regaining what was lost."[34]

Sanders's study of the New Testament focuses upon the person and work of Jesus Christ. Jesus reveals the relational nature of God to us in familial language: God is a heavenly Father, not a distant Creator.[35] Jesus also is the incarnation of the risk-taking Godhead, whose success or failure to perform miracles is greatly affected by people's faith.[36] Even the events of Jesus' passion were not acted out in accordance with some pre-scripted plan. Jesus attempted to win over the overly-zealous but generally well-intentioned Judas right to the very end.[37] His pathos in Gethsemane demonstrated the contingency of the cross[38]; and the Christ's cry of dereliction showed that even within the Godhead, real questions existed about the purpose and end-result of the cross.[39] This passion section is where Sanders takes some of his biggest "risks." He concludes his overview of the New Testament by calling attention to God's "failed wish" to see the Gentile Church become God's reconciling agent to Israel,[40] yet expresses his confidence "that God will bring his project to the fruition He desires because God has proven himself faithful time and again."[41]

History, Philosophy, Theology, and Practicality

In the second half of the volume, Sanders argues that divine relationality is both a biblical and early patristic teaching subsequently subverted, first by Augustine,[42] and then substantially by Calvin. With the great reformer, the transition from the more personal God of the Bible to a Greek-like portrayal was made complete. Calvin's hermeneutic presupposes that sovereignty means domination, and so biblical texts that go against this understanding read differently. God graciously accommodates himself by "listening" to us as does a nursemaid to a young child.[43]

The theme of the loving God was recovered in part by Arminius and Wesley, particularly in regards to conditional election.[44] Sanders then moves to an analysis of the contemporary reexamination of the divine human relationship, calling attention to the distinct models of Tillich, Henry, and process theism. Tillich offered a paradigm of no relationship. Henry, on the other hand, saw a strong divine-human relationship but no reciprocity. Process theologians make all things essentially or necessarily contingent.[45] Sanders rightly notes that "the God of process thought is pervasively conditioned by the creatures."[46] Furthermore, Sanders criticizes process for its "lack of a proper Trinitarian theology" and its denial of creation *ex nihilo*, thereby creating an "ontologically needy God."[47] While Sanders is adamant about distancing his risk-taking God from the process divinity, his articulation of the former draws him nearer to process theology than he wishes to admit.

Sanders's treatment of providence provides an illustration of the controlling assumptions that govern his conclusion. A Christian doctrine of providence must affirm (1) God's loving care for the creatures wherein he seeks their greatest well-being, (2) God's involvement with us in the flow of history, and (3) God's intended goals for creation.[48]

If these are, indeed, the only criteria for assessing providence (and related categories like immutability, omnipotence, and foreknowledge), then Sanders's model wins hands down. He has established the rules of the game that allow him to disqualify a traditional Arminian understanding of foreknowledge ("simple") as useless,[49] seriously curtailing divine freedom by "making God a prisoner of his own omnipresence."[50] In this discussion of foreknowledge, at least three of the four controlling convictions of the author are in operation: the loving God, a libertarian notion of freedom, and a very general providence. Obviously, these will challenge classical postulates on God's power (it is self-restricted due to love),[51] and the divine will that ultimately "implies the failure of humans to reciprocate the divine love and the failure of God to reclaim everyone."[52] In Sanders's risk-taking model, divine failure necessarily becomes fundamental theological vocabulary, chilling though it may be.

In the final section he addresses evil and prayer. On evil, he offers what he terms a "logic-of-love defense," pointing out that this is a world of "gratuitous evil."[53] However, through Christ, God is working to overcome both moral and natural forms of evil through suffering and by the resurrection. As long as God is still working, hope for a future much different from our present earthly experience continues.[54]

Prayer ceases to be a purely God-directed activity but an actual give-and-take dialogue between God and his people. Sanders argues that if a Moses or a Hezekiah had not prayed in key Scriptural narratives, the outcome would have been different.[55] A dialogical understanding of prayer, such as Sanders offers, communicates some positive values that classical models cannot. Christians believe circumstances can be improved, and they can become genuine instruments of God to bring blessings that would not have occurred otherwise.[56] On the other hand, God may sometimes risk granting requests that are not necessarily in the prayer's best interest or even in his. But this must be so if the requests of finite, sinful people are held in highest respect.[57] Like a human parent, God is perfectly capable of granting questionable requests in an educative manner.

According to John Sanders, prayer is also an activity of the Christian community and a primary means by which God "helps to shape the future" of the body of believers.[58] Failure of community members to pray for one another directly affects the well being of the community. God's denial of blessing to a needy brothers or sisters may be due to the absence of prayer on their behalf. With his risk-taking view of prayer, Sanders takes the admonition of James very literally: "You do not have, because you do not ask God" (Jas 4:2).

Positive Assessment of Sanders's "Risky" Proposal
Several commendable points come to mind in reaction to Sanders's provocative proposals. First, his attempt to go beyond the rather aloof and not always biblically accurate portrayal of God in classical constructions is laudable. While lip service is often given to divine immanence, Sanders seriously explores God's relationality. Recent non-openness

endeavors to refocus theology proper, such as John Feinberg's *No One Like Him*,[59] have provided critical reassessment of classical attributes of God, such as divine simplicity (God's inviolable unity; he cannot be separated into parts) and impassibility (God is not affected by things that take place in this world; notably, he does not experience suffering and pain) in part because of problems brought to the forefront by advocates of open theism like Sanders. This is bringing about a general recognition that the God of the Bible is personal.

Second, Sanders's emphasis on the relational God has also forced theologians to deal with the genuine complexities that accompany the divine self-portrait in the Bible. It has been much too easy simply to dismiss difficult passages as anthropocentrisms or anthropopathisms and not truly wrestle with a deity whose character of "I AM" thwarts such formulaic reductionism. Even Calvin can be accused of limiting the variegated mystery of God when he piously notes "that in the enumeration of his perfections, he is described not as he is in himself, but in relation to us, in order that our acknowledgement of him may be more…than empty visionary speculation" (*Institutes* 1:X:2).[60] Subsequently, for Calvin, the difficult passages of Scripture that Sanders delights in, are hardly problematic: the divine being is so unlike the creation that he must necessarily utilize the limitations of human language for communicative purposes.

Third, Sanders's relational model of God's providence provides fresh impetus to prayer, especially petitionary prayer. Proponents of a more classically-understood theism find themselves "reducing" petitionary prayer to little more than a transforming exercise for the pray-er, an opportunity to gain God's perspective of reality. Since God has perfectly foreordained all things, prayer is certainly not going to alter his plan, although he commends prayer. Sanders rightly comments "proponents of the no-risk model of sovereignty cannot legitimately claim that God responds to our prayers or does something because we prayed."[61] Obviously, Sanders's model of risk-taking gives dynamic dignity to praying that classic paradigms lack. However, as developed later in this study, embracing open theism is not the only route to believing God genuinely hears people's prayers

Fourth, Sanders's relational God gives new dignity to the day-to-day decisions enacted by his creatures, both angelic and human. Instead of merely being chess pieces whose movements have been determined from the beginning, people become true participants in a divine drama. Again, Sanders's openness corrective is not the only option to the very tight and deterministic sovereignty that he posits as the foe. The choices for a more workable sovereignty/human freedom model may be greater than the very limited menu Sanders provides. A spectrum of "real choice" theologies span both Calvinist and Arminian camps. Nevertheless, John Sanders should rightfully be thanked for forcing people to deal with a complex portrait of God in Scripture, one that demands admission of difficulties rather than denial.

Negative Assessment of Sanders's "Risky" Proposal

Despite its contributions, Sanders's volume generates more problems than it resolves. First, while "risk" is the operative concept in the book, the term is not defined. Paul Helm, whose risk-free presentation of providence is in Sanders's sights, relates that risks can range from those that place both our preferences and expectations at stake to lesser varieties that merely involve our expectations.[62] Though a stronger variety of risk seems assumed, the omission of other risk nuances enables the author to cast God's intentions and activities in the most precarious and fallible ways possible, revealing Sanders's general tendency to categorize concepts in binary opposites. Either God operates in a sterile, risk-free providence or he exerts his control in a realm of unpredictable risk. Either he is a distant Sovereign or an intimate Lover. Either one is a classical theist or an openness proponent (although Arminianism represents a partial step in the right direction). For Sanders, the middle is always excluded.

Moreover, "risk" ironically seems to be the kind of anthropomorphism that Sanders wants to eschew. From the finite, human vantage point, the turns and twists of the biblical narrative with its very fallible human characters would indeed be a risky proposition. However, this is not a discussion of human abilities but abilities of the triune God who brought this world into being. "Risk" is a carefully nuanced creaturely concept not a divine one that binds creation with its own contingency. Sanders's risk-taking God falls into the common error made in discussing Heisenberg's Principle of Indeterminacy[63]: making human perception of reality an attribute of the cosmos. Sanders makes human perception of God an actual attribute of God.

Second, Sanders's hyperliteral interpretation of written language seems overly rigid for one who is bent on challenging classical paradigms. His controlling assumptions compel him to ignore the rich elasticity and resident ambiguities of human language that makes interpretation both science and art.[64] Robert Picirilli correctly observes:

> We may say two things that seem contradictory, when both are true. We may say, for example, that "God does not change" and that "God changes," without intending contradiction—or else the laws of logic about contradiction would be violated. Both sentences depend, finally, on what one means by them, on perspective and content.[65]

Sanders's insistence that statements of divine repentance (Jn 4:2) be read as wooden admissions of God's short-sightedness is as naïve an approach to biblical interpretation as any literal fundamentalist.[66]

Where does such literalism end? At divine corporeality? In critiquing openness theologian, Gregory Boyd,[67] William Lane Craig notes:

> It is striking how similar Boyd's literalistic hermeneutic is to that of Mormon theologians, who apply it to justify their belief in a God who is notoriously ignorant of future contingents but is a physical being with human form. Like Boyd, the Mormon theologian insists on taking the biblical descriptions of God at face value.[68]

Craig goes on to add that Mormon theologians have seen the similarities between their hermeneutics of theism and those of openness theologians like Boyd, Sanders, and Pinnock and have opened the lecture halls of Brigham Young University to them.[69] Sanders does not intentionally associate his work with the interpretive schemes of either biblical fundamentalists or Mormons, but his approach to reading Scripture is suspect in its proximity to such fringe interpreters.

Third, while Sanders affirms a "creator/creation" distinction,[70] his views do blur this demarcation. As one would expect from his controlling assumptions, Sanders's depiction of Yahweh and his relationship to creation is more a mastery over his opponents than a story of God's sovereignty.[71] In this, he follows a popular line in Old Testament studies that emphasizes Yahweh's subjugation over cosmic forces, an approach that is plausible given the polemic-like nature of the creation language. Yet, these presently rebellious entities were in the beginning created good and placed in a harmonious order by the one true God. The entrance of human sin brought about the disorder and conflict that is so much a part of ancient cosmologies. In fact, the Genesis account provides a corrective to this common animistic belief in capriciousness. Sanders's cosmological view, on the other hand, moves dangerously in the direction of an embodied deity, a concept that process theologians espouse.[72] Sanders's somewhat confusing statements give an impression that his view is not fully process, but then, again, not clearly evangelical: "God creates a world different from himself, yet it is no more different than he desires...despite Yahweh's almighty power in creating and his claim as king of the creation; the unfolding of the intended relationship is not guaranteed but is, given God's resourcefulness, a live option."[73]

Fourth, Sanders's controlling assumptions about God create a startling reversal in standard biblical interpretation. A cardinal principle of hermeneutics has been the interpretation of less clear texts by those that are more clear. *The God Who Risks*, on the other hand, gives interpretive precedence to the "difficult" statements and subordinates the less nuanced ones. Unambiguous declarations of God's unchangeable nature, admittedly in covenantal contexts (Ps 33:11; 89:34-37; 102:25-27; Heb 1:10, 12; 13:8; Jas 1:7), are placed under the divine repentance texts (Jon 3:10). Furthermore, in Sanders's presentation these "unexpected" descriptions of God's mind and activity become the more normative understandings of the biblical Yahweh. In short, an "unchangeable God" becomes the anomaly in the scriptural portrait.

Many of Sanders's examples of God's "limited knowledge" (the "I thought" passages, Jer 3:7, 19-20; 20:3; Ezek 12:3) are in judicial contexts in which Yahweh has acted to lessen the probability of Israel's sin."[74] While he desires that his people will respond positively to his activity, God knows all too well that they are hardened in their ways. The uncertainty in Yahweh's voice is related to the covenant he has made with the nation: He will spare judgment upon them, if they return to him. However, in what should be a positive response to his grace, God's heartfelt "hope" turns out to be but another chapter in Israel's disobedience (Jer 3:19: "I thought you would call me 'Father' and not turn away from following me"). Even Sanders's revised understanding of divine prophecy should credit God with enough historical memory to predict what his obstinate people will do. It is perplexing how Sanders can be so focused on specific words in a discourse and ignore the rhetorical context.

Fifth, due to his controlling assumptions, Sanders engages in speculative exegesis. In his examination of the Abraham-Isaac narrative (Genesis 22), Sanders departs from most standard commentators by arguing that God really did not know how his Abraham was going to respond to the test.[75] When Yahweh declares that "now I know that you fear God" (22:12), he is genuinely acknowledging that he has learned something from this episode.[76] Sanders cites Old Testament scholar Walter Brueggemann as one who agrees with his thesis of God's discovery. However, Brueggemann hardly models an orthodox view of God. Brueggemann, who delights in portraying God (or any theological theme for that matter) in dialectic, has no difficulty seeing Yahweh as both all-knowing and limited in knowledge.[77] While Sanders's citations of Brueggemann do not necessarily indict him as a theological "bedfellow," one has to ask why theologians on the edge of orthodoxy seem to be the major supporting voices of his risk-taking deity? For that matter, why is it that the Socinians, a group that was deemed heretical both by Protestants and Catholics bear the clearest resemblance to open theism's doctrine of God.

As questionable as Sander's rendering of the Abraham narrative is, his presentation of Judas's betrayal of Jesus (Jn 13:18-30) teeters on the very edges of orthodoxy. He writes these astonishing words:

> Judas may have thought that Jesus and the high priest could resolve their differences and bring about needed reforms. Jesus, no doubt, had his own agenda in mind for such a meeting. Regardless, Jesus instructs Judas to carry out this mission…it is clear that Judas is not betraying Jesus and that Jesus is not issuing any prediction of such activity.[78]

While the Gospels record Jesus' (self-imposed) ignorance of his *parousia* (Mk 13:32), they uniformly portray his mastery over the *kairos* of his death (especially John's references to "my time" (Jn 2:4; 7:6; 12:23; 17:1). Furthermore, John 6:70-71 indicates early in Jesus' ministry that one of his twelve disciples was a "devil," who in turn, would betray him. The, evangelist, then, adds a parenthetical note that Jesus "meant Judas," implying that the Lord indeed knew the identity of his betrayer.

Not only does Sanders view Jesus' knowledge of his passion to be limited, he presents a picture of Judas that exonerates the "son of perdition" as one who merely is attempting "to force Jesus to show his hand…to take on the role of political liberator and thus become a 'genuine' messiah."[79] Judas's main sin, then, is not his betrayal of Christ but rather his different conviction about what Israel's Messiah should be like.[80]

Sixth, like process theologians before him, Sanders has elevated one attribute of God, his love, to supreme status. While classical theism might be rightly accused of not

giving sufficient attention to the divine agape in its portrayal of God's ontological difference, openness proponents travel to the boundaries of immanence in offering a deity
who is sensitive, feeling, vulnerable, and respectful of others' choices. How does this
portrayal do any more justice than the classicist's in defining the biblical God's love?[81]

Sanders cites the works of Vanstone and Brummer approvingly that define love by
such characteristics as vulnerability, limitlessness, precariousness, intentionality, and reciprocity.[82] While these descriptions certainly connect with the human heart, they hardly do justice to the *agape* of the cross. These are, instead, the feelings of a finite God.
Indeed, process theologian, David Ray Griffin, has commended Sanders's colleague
Clark Pinnock for articulating an understanding of divine love "that could have been
written by a process theologian."[83]

Sanders's elevation of love to the defining attribute of God cannot successfully be
argued as Scripture's dominant divine motif. John Frame states, "It is especially difficult to
make a Scriptural case that God's love is more important than his leadership," going on to
note that the word "Lord" occurs some 7,484 times in the NIV.[84] Furthermore, "Lord" is
the translation of the divine name that God gave Moses, and in turn becomes the fundamental Christian confession, "Jesus is Lord." The Bible, then, organizes God's love (and all
other attributes) around his character as Lord, rather than the other way around.

Seventh, in spite of Sanders's protests, process theology does appear connected to
open theism. He does attempt to distance himself from process theology several times
during the course of his work, such as when he contrasts process theology's God of
"powerless love" from that of openness's "powerful love."[85] Yet, Sanders offers such a
finely nuanced understanding of God's omnipotence (one who has existential relations
with, rather than sovereignty over his creation) that one wonders whether open theism's
difference from process is more matter semantic than ontological. At the conclusion of
his discussion on "Risk and the Divine Character," Sanders attempts to vindicate his
orthodoxy by acknowledging the charge from Process theologians that openness presents "only a revision" of classical notions of God.[86] There are genuine differences
between openness and process conceptions. In the former, God is ontologically distinct
from creation, the creation was created *ex nihilo*, God's love is not a metaphysical necessity, and there is the hope of a definitive eschatological victory over evil. Yet, Sanders's four
major points of relational theism (God's love, limited sovereignty, general providence, and
libertarian freedom) compares well with crucial aspects of process theology.[87]

Eighth, Sanders needs to answer a very practical question: How does his risk-taking
God really help people? While one can sympathize with the Sanders's repudiation of
strong deterministic models, one wonders if his resulting deity, whose knowledge is
limited, whose project is vague, and whose will is sometimes thwarted, is of that much
comfort to the already questioning believer. Is a God who dialogues with the pray-er
a genuine improvement over a Father who "knows what you need before you ask him"
(Mt 6:8) and will never give his beloved children anything other than what they really

need (Lk 11:13)? More pointedly, in the tragic death of Sanders's brother, how much of an advantage is a God who could not foresee such an event as opposed to one who was caught off-guard? The God who risks seems too much like an evangelical version of Harold Kushner's hurting but impotent deity in the rabbi's popular book on grief, *When Bad Things Happen to Good People*.[88] On this basis, Sanders's God might be excused from the charge of not intervening on an evil that he knew was impending, but how does this ultimately contribute to a more pastoral theodicy? If God does not know exhaustively what lies in the future and evil takes him by surprise, then we might ask, is anyone or anything in charge of this universe?

Consider yet another practical dimension of the Christian life: prayer. Bruce Ware notes the conundrum that Sanders's brand of providence creates with this inseparable aspect of faith: "God is too wise to need or benefit from our help, but not wise enough to remove all doubt or lack of confidence in him."[89] Ware's observations suggest another major problem that open theism brings to Christian experience: divine guidance. Traditionally, believers have regarded God as the paradigm of wisdom, whose guidance is always reliable.[90] However, with Sanders's risk-taking deity—a God with a proven track record of failed plans—one's confidence in his ability to direct life has to be shaken.

Ninth, Sanders collapses the traditional distinctions between God's will and desire into one, seamless concept, thereby making his failed desire a thwarting of his will. Sanders comments, "Divine risk taking allows for some things occurring in the creation that God does not specifically intend to occur. God does not want sin and suffering for instance."[91] According to this quotation, God's intention and God's wish ("want") are virtually synonymous, an equation that is virtually unheard of in systematic theology, whether Calvinist or Arminian.[92]

God does not want any person to perish (1 Tim 2:4; 2 Pet 3:9), yet he does not always (frequently) get his wish because he "honors" the choice of his human creation, even rejection. On the other hand, does this mean that his will has been thwarted or defeated? One must question whether his will was ever to save everyone irrespective of their relationship to him (Acts 4:12). Rather, God intends all who come to his amazing grace through Jesus to be saved and that intention is never thwarted. While Calvinists and Arminians may disagree on the exact nature of what coming (and staying) in Christ involves, there is agreement that one's salvation resides solely in the event of the cross and empty tomb.

Tenth, the ninth criticism leads into this final observation of Sanders's volume: Is not the God who risks a somewhat necessary construal for one who has already adopted a more inclusive soteriological scheme? If God's intentions (purpose) and desires are one in the same—and love is his dominant attribute—then two "paradoxical" things will come true: (1) the explicit Gospel has not, nor probably will be heard, nor accepted, by every human being; (2) God has an implicit Gospel that he will reckon as belief in Christ. In other words, sincere people belonging to other world religions will be included in the "throng around the throne." (Rev 7:9) In spite of the failed risk he took to have the good news preached to every creature, his overwhelming love for all will enable him, one final time, to redeem a "lost" situation.

In a sense, God will "change his mind," again, and in an ultimate, eschatological gesture of kindness, enlarge the "Christ-circle" to include the many who did not hear. This is certainly an attractive postulate to many evangelicals, today, who well know the immensity of the evangelistic task. And yet, one has to question whether such a proposal goes beyond the legitimate "boundaries" of biblical soteriology? Sanders begins with an eschatological paradigm that demands a "risk-taking God" who is "free" to admit that his previous conditions were a bit unrealistic, as well as potentially damaging to his cardinal attribute of love.[93]

A Mediating Proposal for a Doctrine of God

Despite reservations about his thought and method, Sanders provides a challenge to rethink classical models of God. Non-openness theologians have also recognized the need to come to grips with divine immanence. Not only are simplicity, immutability, and impassability candidates for serious review, but the growing body of literature on God and time reveal an evangelical consensus that the Being we encounter in Scripture is not Aristotle's "Unmoved Mover."[94] However, the choice is not simply between classical expressions and openness, despite Sanders'sSanders's tendency to posit these starkly contrasting choices. The following proposals are offered to facilitate a successful negotiation between Augustine (or Paul Helm) and John Sanders, between a risk-free and a risk-taking God.

First, biblically based personalism offers more potential than either the classical or open theism. The God whom we meet in the initial words of Scripture is a personal being, immanent not only with his creation but within himself. Trinity is not peripheral to his being but essential to it. As Graham Cole notes, "The God of biblical testimony is proactive (Eph 1:1-22), interactive (Ex 32:1-14) and reactive—a storyline is the logical outcome of a God who, in Himself, is proactive, interactive, and reactive—as Father, Son, and Spirit."[95] Within this model, God is perfectly personal, so that if he changes his mind (Jn 3:10), he is not changing his essential nature and purpose. Unlike classical theism, which emphasizes his sovereignty (proactivity) at the expense of his relational nature (interactive and reactive), or openness, which promotes God's interactivity and reactivity at the expense of his proactivity (sovereignty), a biblical personalism maintains the necessary balance. All three of these actions are inseparable to the Three-In-One God.[96]

Second, rather than understanding Scripture's description of God strictly in terms of anthropomorphisms, better results come from starting with the divine himself and moving theopathically. Obviously, biblical statements about God's "finger" or "eye" must be understood in an anthropomorphic sense. Sanders would offer no disagree-ment with many of these. However, perhaps statements about God's anger, grief, and joy should not be understood as analogous to human experiences but rather to the divine personality merely reflected in his human creation, the imago dei. Again, Cole is helpful: "Indeed when Bible writers speak of God's grief it may not be so much a matter of God being anthropopathic (humanlike) but of our being theopathic (Godlike) as bearers of the divine image."[97] In other words, when people feel things like joy, pain, and grief, it is precisely because they are made in the image of One who is inherently a feeling being.[98]

Third, it would be helpful to revisit the implications inherent in the Bible's creator/creation distinction, especially as this impacts understanding of human freedom. A view of freedom that either denies its reality (extreme determinism) or describes it in the unrestricted manner of libertarianism is not acceptable. A finite, bounded creation necessitates a certain limitation in human choices, externally and internally. As an Arminian, ideas of libertarian free-will seem overly ambitious, both in the realm of human experience and in the teachings of Scripture. On the other hand, neither of these realities is easily reconciled with a notion that people are like the pre-set tracks of a compact disc, with thoughts and actions awaiting their appropriate "play" in the sequence of time.[99]

Cole's analogy of a jazz concert appears to offer a paradigm that more seriously takes the nuanced notions of human freedom and responsibility suggested by the Bible and life. In this model, there is both definition ("Rhapsody in Blue" will always be that piece and no other, like this created universe) and improvisation (people can play freely within the confines of the work). The jazz concert better pictures the interplay of divine sovereignty and human freedom, a recognition that both elements are present in the relationship of the Creator and his creation.

Fourth, a personal relationship with God need not be egalitarian, as Sanders seems to assume. If God is truly a king he cannot be a friend; whereas if he really is a friend, he cannot operate in a hierarchical, (or monarchial) manner to his human creation. Once again, a choice between these extremes is not mandated, either in Scripture or in everyday human experience. A student may have a close, collegial, and intimate rela-tionship with a professor, but that does not mean that the student dictates the course requirements or her own personal course grade. Furthermore, the common workplace provides scores of examples where employers and employees work together as a "team" without operating in a purely egalitarian fashion.[100]

Fifth, Arminians are not required to follow Sanders and open theism in the pursuit of a more "coherent Arminianism," as Pinnock terms their quest.[101] In fact, the open-ness brand of Arminian theology jettisons the historic distinction between divine (exhaustive) foreknowledge and election, that an individual's election to salvation is based upon God's prior knowledge of what that person would do in response to the preeminent work of the Spirit. Sanders replaces a more Calvinistic God who fore-knows and ordains with one who neither foreknows nor chooses, the precise opposite of the Reformed paradigm rather than an updated Arminianism. Furthermore, Sanders emphasizes the libertarian freedom issues far more than Arminius or his more legiti-mate followers ever would. Contemporary science provides a fitting analog that illus-trates the traditional Arminian perspective. Scientists, given the accuracy of their mod-els, can predict with great accuracy what will occur in a given situation without caus-ing such to happen. This is one of the defining marks of good science. If this is the case, cannot the omniscient Maker of the Universe predict his creatures' behavior—with 100% accuracy—also without direct causation?

Sixth, God's prior knowledge (foreknowledge) of future events need not preclude him from experiencing these events in a fresh new manner when they actually unfold in time. If people are created in the image of the triune God and both know in cog-nitive and experiential ways (in a sense, out of time and in time) does this not reflect how he knows? Biblically speaking, do we not encounter a God who knows that the prodigal will return home but the impact of that repentance action is not fully "under-stood" until it occurs and produces a "knowledge" of inexpressible joy? (Lk 15: 20). In a theopathic sense, then, I can relate the recent wedding of my eldest daughter: I knew that on December 29, 2001, Holly Kurka would become the wife of Randal Zehr, but I could hardly predict the wide range of emotions that event would bring when I finally experienced it.

Conclusion

The recent challenges to classical theistic models from open theists like John Sanders call attention to classical attributes of God (simplicity, impassibility, immutability) that present a divine being who is less than the personal deity of Scripture. Negligence to critique these insufficiencies has opened the door for open theism to go beyond the parameters of orthodoxy, despite the fact the resulting exposure of long-standing prob-lems is commendable. On the other hand, the Sanders reconstruction does not offer a paradigm that merits jettisoning past constructions. The model proposed may cause valid alterations on a handful of divine attributes, but its serious weaknesses disqualify it as the biblically-based, conceptual replacement. The ancient paradigm may not even need to be so radically overhauled but just more carefully nuanced.

Sanders's openness model deserves recognition as a legitimate proposal in contem-porary, evangelical discussions of God, even though its reality-depicting portrait of God appears less than the Scripture's unique triune being and more a courtship with process theism's world-embodying God. Yet, in spite of failed efforts that have been made to silence open theism in the Evangelical Theological Society by removing Sanders and Pinnock from its membership,[102] the evangelical community would do well to imple-ment a hallmark of the Stone-Campbell Movement: refuse to make biblical exegesis the handmaiden of pre-set theological formulas. Rather than allowing evangelical confessional models (historically, more often than not, Reformed) or even openness theism models to dictate the parameters of scriptural inquiry, let the Bible have its total say on this matter and others, no matter how uncomfortable that testimony and no matter how impossible it might be to harness its entire witness into a systematic model. To do less than this plays into the hands of heresy.

Notes

[1]Stanley Grenz and Roger Olson, *Who Needs Theology? An Invitation to the Study of God* (Downers Grove, Ill: InterVarsity, 1996), p. 50.

[2]Alexander Campbell in Robert Richardson, *Memoirs of Alexander Campbell,* 2 vols (Cincinnati: Standard Publishing, 1897), 1:372, well expressed his movement's "openness" to dialogue and more importantly unity with a veritable panoply of Christians: "We plead for the union, communion and so-operation of all such (believers); and wherever there are in any vicinity a remnant of those who keep the commandments of Jesus, whatever may have been their former designation, they ought to rally under Jesus and the apostles and bury all dissensions about such subjects as those vexing questions about trinity, atonement, depravity, election, effectual calling, etc. If it had not been for this most unreasonable war about Arian or Unitarian orthodoxy, the name Christian would not have been traduced in the land as it has been, and much might have been done to promote the union of all who love our Lord Jesus Christ sincerely." This reveals that the Restoration father would not only fellowship with Clark Pinnock and John Sanders but also a host of other "believers" that would probably be on the generous boundaries of faith in openness estimations.

[3]See, for example, Robert C. Kurka, "The Stone-Campbell Understanding of Conversion: A Misunderstood '*Sola Fide*,'" Evangelical Theological Society Annual Meeting, 2001, which argues for the traditional Restorationist association of baptism with salvation (actually with "saving faith") without succumbing to a water regenerationism.

[4]Alexander Campbell, *The Christian System* (Cincinnati: H.S. Bosworth, 1866), pp. 19-21; 55-67.

[5]Ibid., p. 20.

[6]Ibid., p. 21.

[7]Kevin J.Vanhoozer, *First Theology* (Downers Grove, Ill.: InterVarsity, 2002).

[8]Alexander Campbell, *Christian Baptist* 7 (1830) cited in B.W. Stone and John Rogers, *The Biography of Barton Warren Stone* (Cincinnati: J.A. and U.P. James, 1847), p. 325.

[9] Stone and Rogers, *Biography*, pp. 322-329.

[10]Jack Cottrell, *What the Bible Says About God the Creator* (Joplin, Mo.: College Press, 1983); *What the Bible Says About God the Ruler* (Joplin, Mo.: College Press, 1984); *What the Bible Says About God the Redeemer* (Joplin, Mo.: College Press, 1987).

[11]Campbell, *System*, p. 20.

[12]Stone and Rogers, *Biography*, p. 225.

[13]Cottrell, *God the Ruler,* p. 266.

[14]See my discussion of Campbell's Scottish Common Sense Realism (and its hermeneutical application) in "The Role of the Holy Spirit in Conversion: Why Restorationists Appear to Be Out of the Evangelical Mainstream," in *Evangelicalism and the Stone-Campbell Movement*, ed. William R. Baker (Downers Grove, Ill.: InterVarsity, 2002), pp. 138-151, esp. 144-148.

[15]Church of Christ (a cappella) scholar Ronald Highfield (Pepperdine) has contributed two recent articles critical of open theism from a Stone-Campbell perspective: "Does the World Limit God? Assessing

the Case for Open Theism," *Stone Campbell Journal* 5:1 (Spring, 2002): 69-92; and "The Function of Divine Self-Limitation in Open Theism: Great Wall or Picket Fence?" *Journal of the Evangelical Theological Society* 45 (2002) 279-299.,

[16]John Sanders, *The God Who Risks: A Theology of Providence* (Downers Grove, Ill.: InterVarsity, 1998), p. 10.

[17]John Sanders, "God as Personal," in *The Grace of God, the Will of Man,* ed. Clark Pinnock (Grand Rapids: Zondervan, 1989), pp. 165-180.

[18]Ibid., p. 173.

[19]John Sanders, *No Other Name: An Investigation into the Destiny of the Unevangelized* (Grand Rapids: Eerdmans, 1992).

[20]Karl Rahner, *Theological Investigations* 6 (Baltimore: Helicon, 1969), p. 394. According to Rahner, through the mediation of the Spirit, Christ is present and working in non-Christians and their non-Christian religions.

[21]John Sanders, "Historical Considerations," in Pinnock, *Openness of God*, pp. 73-81.

[22]Robert Strimple, "What Does God Know," in *The Coming Evangelical Crisis,* ed. John Armstrong (Chicago: Moody Press, 1996), pp. 140-141.

[23]Sanders, *Risks*.

[24]Ibid., p. 282.

[25]Ibid., p. 33.

[26]Ibid., p. 34

[27]Ibid., p. 125.

[28]Ibid., p. 12. The third "core assumption" is also noted by Robert Picirilli in "An Arminian Response to John Sanders's *The God Who Risks: A Theology of Providence,*" *Journal of the Evangelical Theological Society* 44.3 (2001): 467-491.

[29]Ibid., p. 46.

[30]Ibid., p. 48.

[31]Ibid., p. 50.

[32]Ibid., p. 52

[33]Ibid., p. 63.

[34]Ibid., p.89.

[35]Ibid.,p.91-92.

[36]Ibid., p. 97-98.

[37]Ibid., pp. 98-99.

[38]Ibid., pp. 98-101.

[39]bid., pp. 105-106.

[40]Ibid., pp. 123.

[41]Ibid., p. 129.

[42]Ibid., pp. 147-151.

[43]Ibid., p. 156.

[44]Ibid., pp. 157-158.

[45]Ibid., pp. 158-161.

[46]Ibid., p. 161.

[47]Ibid.

[48]Ibid., p. 168.

[49]Ibid., pp. 200-206.

[50]Ibid., p. 201.

[51]Ibid., pp. 224-228.

[52]Ibid., p. 230.

[53]Ibid., pp. 267-268.

[54]Ibid., p. 268.

[55]Ibid., p. 271

[56]Ibid., p. 272.

[57]Ibid., pp. 273-274.

[58]Ibid., pp. 274.

[59]John Feinberg, *No One Like Him* (Crossway, 2001).

[60]John Calvin, *Institutes of the Christian Religion,* 2 vols.; trans. Henry Beveridge (Grand Rapids: Eerdmans, 1973), 2:88.

[61]Sanders, *Risks*, p. 271.

[62]Paul Helm, *The Providence of God* (Downers Grove, Ill.: InterVarsity, 1993), p. 40.

[63]Werner Heisenberg, *Physics and Beyond: Encounters and Conversations,* trans. A.J. Pomerans (New York: Harper & Row, 1971).

[64]Kevin Vanhoozer, *Is There Meaning in this Text?* (Grand Rapids, Eerdmans, 1998), p. 339, poignantly comments: "The rules that govern literary forms are flexible....An author enjoys freedom within limits; the author is a citizen of literature. (Yet) literary genre holds communicative freedom and determinism in constructive tension." Given this linguistic fluidity, Vanhoozer challengers interpreters to "recognize and participate in various forms of communicative activity" and avoid mismatching text genres and reading genres (p. 338)—like Sanders appears to be doing. Douglas M. Jones, "Metaphor in Exile," in *Bound Only Once*, ed. Douglas Wilson (Moscow, Idaho: Canon, 2001), pp. 40-41, argues that Sanders specifically (and openness proponents, generally) have in actuality embraced an Enlighten-ment (and even Greek) prejudice against imagination and metaphor; a distaste that was engendered due to the latter's mathematical and reductionistic view of language. Jones, "Metaphor," p. 50, notes that while Sanders would like his readers to understand him as taking metaphor seriously (Sanders calls for new, "iconoclastic" metaphors such as "God as risktaker"), his dismissal of anthropomorphism as a legitimate interpretation of genuine, divine purposes, emotions, desires, love, suffering (these must be taken in a strictly univocal sense), indicate that he has already determined "such language cannot remain truly figurative." Whereas openness proponents chide classical theists for positing a God that is staid, boring and predictable, it is actually they who limit "the glory of new songs and fresh poems and creativity...the sort of metaphor an aesthetic dimension mathematically precluded by the Open-ness method. One, therefore, cannot hold to openness assumptions and grasp the depth of poetry."

[65]Picirilli, "Arminian Response," p. 483.

[66]One is somewhat ironically reminded of classical dispensationalism's dictum "to rightly divide the word of truth" (2 Tim 2:15), and literally they divide the Scriptures (into multiple dispensations). Furthermore, theologians of this stripe regularly have extolled their hermeneutical principle, "Consistent Literalism," to the point of creating a certain (unintended) theological dissonance to such key doctrines as salvation and the church. Sanders's theology of risk follows a similar plea for excessive literalism, with consequences that appear to be far more damaging to orthodox convictions.

[67]Gregory Boyd, *God of the Possible: A Biblical Introduction to the Open View of God* (Grand Rapids: Baker, 2000), has written perhaps the most "accessible" primer on open theism.

[68]W. L. Craig, "A Middle Knowledge Response," in *Divine Foreknowledge: Four Views*, ed. James Beilby and Paul Eddy (Downers Grove, Ill.: InterVarsity, 2001), p. 59.

[69]Ibid.

[70]Sanders, *Risks*, pp. 41-43.

[71]Ibid., p. 42.

[72]See for example, David Ray Griffin, "Process Theology and the Christian Good News," in *Searching*

for an Adequate God, eds. John B. Cobb, Jr. and Clark Pinnock (Grand Rapids: Eerdmans, 2000), p. 5, who offers a list of core process doctrines, including "the doctrine of internal (as well as external) relatedness… the basis for understanding causation as incarnation, for regarding the presence of God in all things and the presence of all things in God as fully natural, and for developing a fully ecological view of reality."

[73]Sanders, *Risks*, pp. 42-43.

[74]A "judicial" context is a pericope in which God (or his prophet), as "prosecutor," is raising questions in a manner of cross-examination, often of Israel (the "defendant"). These are not information-gathering requests but clearly, in the context, questions that will serve to confirm the Lord's indictment (see Gen 3:9; 11:5; 18:20-21; Deut 13:3; Pss 44:21; 139:1, 23-24). See also John Frame, *No Other God: A Response to Open Theism* (Phillipsburg, N.J.: R&R Publishing, 2001), pp. 194-198, on these and other "judicial contexts."

[75]Sanders, *Risks*, p. 53.

[76]Ibid., pp. 53-54.

[77]In fact, Walter Brueggemann, "The Costly Loss of Lament," *Journal for the Study of the Old Testament* 36 (1986): 59, himself describes Yahweh in terms of being put "at risk" in discussing the believers lament According to Brueggemann, the human supplicant, frustrated by God's apparent silence, is facilitating a new development in the divine personage. See also Walter Brueggemann, *Genesis*, Interpretation (Atlanta: John Knox, 1982), p. 187.

[78]Sanders, *Risks*, pp. 98-99.

[79]Ibid., p. 99.

[80]I could not help but think of the portrayal of Judas in Andrew Lloyd Webber's "Jesus Christ, Superstar" as I read Sanders's version: both contemporary accounts implicitly put the blame on Jesus for creating such an ambiguous messianic figure for a fairly rational and noble Judas! John Feinberg, normally a more charitable critic of openness than some of his other Reformed colleagues, in a personal discussion nonetheless termed this revisionistic rendering as "near blasphemous."

[81]In a recent essay, Geoffrey Grogan, "A Biblical Theology of the Love of God," in *Nothing Greater, Nothing Better: Theological Essays on the Love of God*, ed. Kevin Vanhoozer (Grand Rapids: Eerdmans, 2001), p. 58, argues that God's love is especially expressed when he is dissatisfied with the subjects of his love and is witnessed in his rebukes and chastenings (Prov 3:12; Heb 12:6; Rev 3:19) and that God's love for his elect nation is enforced by his punishment for her sins, a stark contrast from the scorned lover of Sanders's volume.

[82]Sanders, *Risks*, pp. 178-180.

[83]Griffin, "Process Theology," p. 19.

[84]Frame, *No Other God*, p. 54, notes that "Lord" is the translation of the covenant name God gave to Moses (Exod 3:13-15), the name that his mighty works would give testimony to (Ex 6:7; 7:5, 17; 8:22; 10:2; 14:4,18), and the fundamental early Christian confession ("Jesus is Lord"; see Rom 10:9; 1 Cor 12:3; Phil 2:11).

[85]Sanders, *Risks*, p. 190.

[86]Sanders, p. 207. Again we want to defend Pinnock, Sanders, et.al., from the reckless charges that openness is but a thinly-veiled version of process theology; there are significant differences. However, there are enough unsettling similarities to suggest that the "risk-taking God" is less a modification of classical theism and more a conservative appropriation of process. Indeed, Cobb and Pinnock, *Searching for an Adequate God*, p. xiv, in spite of their points of disagreement, find that "there are inclinations in each community that move toward the other."

[87]Clark Pinnock, *Most Moved Mover* (Grand Rapids: Baker, 2001), pp. 142-143, has noted the following convictions that openness and process theologians share: Both, make the love of God a priority, hold to libertarian human freedom, are critical of conventional theism, seek a more dynamic model of

God, contend that God has real, and merely rational, relationships with the world, believe that God is affected by what happens in the world, say that God knows what can be known (which does not amount to exhaustive foreknowledge), appreciate the value of philosophy in helping to shape theological convictions, and connect positively to Wesleyan/Arminian traditions.

[88]Harold Kushner, *When Bad Things Happen to Good People* (New York: Schocken, 1981).

[89]Bruce Ware, *God's Lesser Glory: The Diminished God of Open Theism* (Wheaton, Ill: Crossway, 2000), p. 208.

[90]Frame, *No Other God*, p. 208.

[91]Sanders, *Risks*, p. 171.

[92]See Millard J. Erickson, *Christian Theology*, 2nd edition (Grand Rapids: Baker, 1998), p. 387; and R. Picirrilli, "An Arminian Response," p. 485.

[93]In actuality, according to Sanders, *No Other Name*, p. 218-221, God has already been enlarging the "circle of faith" throughout history a significant number of persons have been saved in the past ("Old Testament believers") without explicit knowledge of Jesus Christ. Consequently, if soteriological details were unnecessary for them, why should we expect that those who live after the Christ-event will not be saved in a similar manner? The key issue, then, is not: What do you think of Christ?" but rather, "How have you responded to the generalized revelation of God that has been given to all persons via nature and the human conscience?" The intended answer is simply "faith"—a Rahner-like belief in a vague deity that enables the "believers" to participate in Christ's work, although they have no idea that such ever occurred. These "anonymous Christians" (Rahner's term) are "soteriologically-challenged" in only the sense that they do not know the fullness of God's riches that are available in Christ; otherwise, they, too, are to be found in the "great multitude" around the Lamb's eschatological throne (Rev 7:9). While Sanders's inclusivist view certainly strikes a responsive chord with any evangelical who seriously considers the enormity of evangelizing a world approaching six billion people, this latter day version of *apokatastasis* cannot be legitimately derived from the biblical data, only imposed upon it. Instead of engaging in a purely speculatives discussion concerning the "fate of those who have not heard the gospel," I would much rather be oriented towards a clear New Testament (especially Pauline) "obsession"; namely, preaching the Gospel "where Christ is (was) not known" (Rom 15:20). The Apostle's preoccupation with evangelism should rightly be our own, challenging us to set aside unprofitable (and unprovable) "faith principles" for the perspicuous *kerygma*. If God does have an alternative salvific program, he surely has not told any of us what it is.

[94]See W. L. Craig. *Time and Eternity* (Wheaton: Crossway, 2001); Feinberg, *No One Like Him*; Alan Padgett, *God, Eternity, and the Nature of Time* (New York: St. Martin's, 1992).

[95]G. A. Cole, "The Living God: Anthropomorphic or Anthropopathic?" *Reformed Theological Review* 59:1 (2000): 24-25.

[96]In many respects, the model of Cole, "The Living God," echoes the theological project undertaken by the early Greek theologians, the Cappadocians. Contemporary orthodox thinker, John Zizioulas, has argued that these church fathers inherited a Greek philosophic system, but they also rejected its monistic view of reality for one more compatible with the biblical narrative. Taking seriously the biblical doctrine of creation, the Cappadocians insisted that a real difference existed between God and the world, a distinction that enabled him genuinely to interact with his creation. This was a challenge to the traditional Greek notion ("Aristotelian") where God was simply the "unmoved mover" of the materialistic continuum. Furthermore, this distinct God had revealed himself to be triune, which of course meant that there was a real difference within God, an ontological impossibility in a classical metaphysical system. Consequently, these early Greek theologians replaced the static and monistic "being" constructions of the philosophers with both a creator/creation demarcation and an understanding of deity that affirms a oneness (Trinitarian) that defies materialistic simplicity. Rather than the abstract "uncaused cause" of Aristotle,

the Cappadocians posited the realities of hypostases, plurality, love, and communion. In contrast to the Western fathers who tended to make the Trinity subservient to God's substance, according to John Zizioulas, *Being as Communion* (Crestwood, N.Y.: St. Vladimir's, 1985), p. 41, the Greek theologians argued that "the substance never exists in a 'naked' state...without hypostasis...outside the Trinity, there is no God."

[97]Cole, "The Living God," p. 24.

[98]Dembski, *Intelligent Design* (Downers Grove, Ill.: InterVarsity, 2000), has used the related term, theomorphism, to express such ideas as God's fatherhood, rather than yielding to feminist theologians' contentions that the biblical "father" needs to be jettisoned from our "God-talk" references to language due to its patriarchal (and misogynist) associations. A theomorphic move, conversely calls us to critique our human understandings from above" by a divinely-defined model. Approaching the Scriptural text theomorphically might also lessen the "unintelligibility" of such doctrines as the Trinity, in that the Triune God defines oneness, notably in a communitarian context.

[99]Cole, "The Living God," p. 25.

[100]Note also Eph 6:5-9 where redeemed relationships do not preclude definable slave/master roles. Scripture presents a God who relates to people as colleagues but is clearly firmly in control.

[101]Pinnock, *Most Moved Mover*, p. 106.

[102]At the annual meeting of the Evangelical Theological Society in Toronto, November 20-22, 2002, members voted (by a fairly narrow margin) to bring before the examination of the society's executive committee the issue of whether or not the openness theologies of Clark Pinnock and John Sanders violate the ETS doctrinal basis ("inerrancy"). The executive committee recommended that Sanders be excluded from ETS but that Pinnock not be. A vote of the ETS membership sustained the membership of both. As quoted in "Closing the Doors on Open Theists?" *Christianity Today* (January, 2003), p. 25, Craig Blomberg, Denver Seminary (not an openness advocate), expresses the evaluation of many of the Evangelical Theological Society members at the Toronto gathering: "They [Pinnock and Sanders] are not denying that God cannot choose to know in advance what creatures can do, but that he has chosen not to know everything in advance."

3

UNDERSTANDING GOD:
GOD AND TIME

Jack Cottrell

Afterdeciding to address the issue of God and time, I soon regretted my choice, especially after seeing William Craig's comment, "Apart from the idea of God, I know of no concept so profound and so baffling as that of time. To attempt an integration of these two concepts therefore stretches our minds to the very limits of our understanding."[1]

The issue here is to explain how God relates to time. As Christian theologians we accept that God is infinite, and therefore infinite with respect to time. This is called God's *eternality*: God is eternal. The Bible[2] calls him "the eternal God."[3] Though we all agree about this, we do not agree as to what this eternality means. It has been interpreted in two distinctly different ways. In one view, "God is eternal" means that he exists everlastingly, on a time line that has no beginning and no end. On another view, "God is eternal" means that God exists outside of and apart from time as such; the categories of time do not apply to him at all. These views are at opposite ends of a spectrum; some position themselves between these extremes and attempt to combine them in various ways.

What is at stake in this matter of God and time? Obviously the very nature of God is at issue. How we understand God's eternality will affect how we interpret his omniscience, his immutability, his simplicity, and his sovereignty.[4] Also at stake is how God relates to the world. For example, our understanding of how God relates to time affects our understanding of creation, the incarnation, and God's providential intervention into the world. Specifically at stake is the status of God's foreknowledge. How does

God's relation to time affect his ability to know the future—if indeed there is a "future" from God's perspective?

I understand time to be that characteristic of existence according to which the relation between events may be described in terms of before and after, or earlier than and later than. It involves a sequence or succession of moments which may be described as past and future in relation to a present or now.

The two main views of God's relation to time in this sense are quite simple. Either this characteristic of existence applies to God, or it does not. Either God is in the flow of time, or he is outside of it. Either his being and experience pass through a succession of moments, or they do not. Simply, God is either temporal or atemporal.

Here I will briefly present these two main views, then I will look at some attempts to combine them. My own view is in this last category.

God Is Timeless

The view that God is timeless is called atemporalism and eternalism. It is associated with classical theism, an approach that is traceable to ancient Greek philosophers such as Plato and Plotinus, and to early and medieval Christian theologians such as Augustine, Boethius, Anselm, and Thomas Aquinas. Modern representatives of this view are Paul Helm and Norman Geisler.

Explanation of Divine Timelessness

In this view God is timeless in the sense that he totally transcends all categories of time and exists outside the flow of time altogether. The concepts of succession or sequence of moments, before and after, past/present/future, simply do not apply to him. In his being, God exists in an eternal, unchanging NOW of "infinitely extended, pastless, futureless duration."[5] He exists in a beginningless, endless, eternally enduring present. This applies not only to God's being, but also to his knowledge. The timeless God knows all things in a single, self-contained moment of cognition. This would mean, says Feinberg,[6] "that God always has the same thought," that "he is always thinking everything, and that there is never any variation in what he thinks." As Geisler affirms, "What he thinks, he has forever thought."[7] His knowledge is changeless, eternally all-inclusive, and non-extended. Created history is neither past nor future in God's perception; its whole scope is present before him in one eternal NOW.

This also applies to God's actions. Though his actions occur sequentially within the creation, from God's own perspective they are not sequential but simultaneous. Everything that God does is performed at exactly the same time in the one eternal NOW. This means that they are never not occurring. God never begins to do anything or never does anything for the first time, and he never ceases to do whatever he does. His "one timeless act" is forever the same; "it never begins or ends."[8]

Thus, for a timeless God there exists nothing except the single, eternal, changeless, frozen *present*. The key concept is *simultaneity*. As Boethius said, "Eternity is the complete possession of an endless life enjoyed as one simultaneous whole." An eternal being "grasps and possesses simultaneously the entire fullness of an unending life."[9]

Time itself is regarded as altogether a created phenomenon. "Time began with the space/time universe," says Geisler.[10] Since time is an essential part of the creation, "then it cannot be an attribute of the uncreated."[11] Since (according to modern science) space and time necessarily co-exist, time could not have existed before space itself. Thus "time began with the universe."[12]

The Basis of the Divine Timelessness View

Upon what is the concept of divine timelessness based? Geisler and House say it is clearly taught in the Bible.[13] Craig agrees that "certain New Testament passages also seem to affirm a beginning of time."[14] Thus, God is described as being "in the beginning" (Gen 1:1) and thus "beyond time."[15] He is described as existing "before the world was" (Jn 17:5), and "before the foundation of the world" (Eph 1:4; see Ps 90:2). He is "the High and Lofty One who inhabits eternity" (Isa 57:15, NKJV). God's grace "was given to us in Christ Jesus before time began" (2 Tim 1:9, NKJV; see 1 Cor 2:7). God promised us eternal life "before the beginning of time" (Tit 1:2, NIV), literally, "before eternal times." Jude 25 attributes glory to God "before all ages, now and forevermore" (NIV). Through his Son God "made the world" (Heb 1:2), or literally "framed the ages."[16] He is the timeless "I AM" (Ex 3:14; see Jn 8:58). There are of course many texts that depict God in temporal terms, but atemporalists say they are all anthropomorphic.[17]

Besides being based on these specific biblical texts, divine timelessness is also said to be logically inferred from other attributes of God.[18] For example, the attribute of simplicity—that God cannot be divided into parts—must imply timelessness because a temporal God's existence would be separated into an endless succession of moments.[19] Also it is said that immutability implies timelessness, since a God proceeding through an endless succession of moments would be constantly changing.[20] Likewise, according to Anselm, God's perfection (God defined as "the greatest conceivable being") implies timelessness, since timelessness is greater than temporality.[21] Such conclusions as this last one, says Helm, are grounded ultimately upon our intuition.[22]

Problems with Divine Timelessness

Critics of the atemporal view of God see a number of problems with it. One is that the supposed biblical basis is inconclusive, since the passages usually cited in its support can be understand in terms of temporal eternity (everlastingness, discussed later). This leads Paul Helm, an eternalist, to say that even though the teaching of Scripture is consistent with God's timeless eternity, this teaching is nonetheless "somewhat underdetermined" in that "the language of Scripture about God and time is not sufficiently precise so as to provide a definitive resolution of the issue one way or the other. So it would be unwise for the eternalist to claim that divine timeless eternity is entailed by the language of Scripture."[23] Nicholas Wolterstorff, a temporalist, likewise asserts, "The scriptural passages traditionally cited as supporting divine timelessness provide no such support whatsoever."[24] His attempt to demonstrate this, though, is very weak.

In reference to the texts cited above which allegedly establish God's timelessness, the basic alternative interpretation is that they are referring to God's priority to this world's time, not to time itself. God is the Creator of this universe and its history; thus he obviously existed "in eternity" before all the past aeons of this creation. But these texts in themselves do not explain the nature of the "eternity" in which the Creator existed "prior to" the beginning of this universe. More will be said about this below.

The second problem with the timelessness view is that its other basic foundation is also shaky. Not only is its alleged biblical basis questionable; so also is the atemporalist version of the other divine attributes from which it is logically derived. This is true especially of the two principal attributes, simplicity and immutability. As they are taught in classical theism, both of these attributes are victims of philosophical extremism.

Regarding the doctrine of simplicity, I have earlier warned against carrying this to an extreme,[25] as does John Frame in his recent work.[26] Frame argues that simplicity does not rule out complexity.[27] Feinberg questions the whole concept of simplicity, saying that the Bible does not explicitly teach it[28] and concluding that it is not a divine attribute[29] and should be abandoned altogether.[30] At the very least, as Morris has shown,[31] one can hold to spatial simplicity without holding to temporal simplicity.

Regarding the doctrine of immutability, I argued in 1987[32] that the classical view is an unwarranted extreme and must be modified. I pointed to an "emerging consensus" that God is unchanging in his essence and character, but changes in his states of consciousness and in his activities.[33] Such a view of immutability, itself established by Scripture, in no way entails absolute divine timelessness. Feinberg agrees that "immutability needs a more nuanced definition," one that is "consistent with God being in time."[34] Morris argues that, contrary to the classical theistic view, not all changes must be either for the better or for the worse. Some changes are value-neutral.[35] Temporal changes may well be in this category. Frame says he sees no reason to say that immutability entails atemporality.[36]

The third problem with divine timelessness is that it seems to present a view of God that is just the opposite of the biblical picture. This is the sense in which Stephen Davis[37] declares that "a timeless being cannot be the Christian God" because "a timeless being cannot be the personal, caring, involved God we read about in the Bible."[38] From beginning to end the Bible portrays a God who personally interacts with his creatures in ways that presuppose and exhibit temporality. He acts upon the world at certain specific points in its history, and he reacts and responds to events that happen in the world. Especially in his mental life is God's relation to the world described in personal terms:

he remembers, deliberates, anticipates, decides, intends, is grieved, becomes angry, and rejoices.[39] Likewise his actions and reactions are personal and presuppose temporal sequence: he plans for and sends a Redeemer, he forgives sins in response to repentance, he answers prayers, he issues warnings, and he punishes the wicked.

All such activities naturally involve temporal sequence, not just for the creatures who observe them but for the divine subject himself.[40] As Feinberg says, these are "things that an atemporal being cannot do, and Scripture does portray God as doing those things."[41] As Reichenbach puts it, "Remembering and forgiving are acts which are meaningless without the rememberer or forgiver experiencing a before and after."[42] Attempts to explain the whole phenomenon of divine response in atemporal terms are especially strained.[43]

Divine actions that are most difficult to explain on the atemporal model are major events such as the creation, the incarnation, and the cross. If what appear to us to be distinct, separated-by-time divine acts are actually for God one eternal, non-extended, simultaneous act, then God is never not creating, never not incarnate, and never not dying on the cross. The doctrine of creation *ex nihilo* becomes meaningless.[44] If God was truly incarnate in Jesus Christ, how could the time-sequenced actions of Jesus— God the Son—not also be time-sequenced actions for his divine nature?[45]

The point is that this is the consistent biblical picture of God and his personal, time-oriented activities in relation to the world. Atemporalists say this is all anthropomorphic. But as Reichenbach says, if this is so, "there is little left in revelation to inform us about the character of God himself since most properties which Scripture ascribes to God are time-related."[46] He concludes, "Timelessness is inconsistent with the scriptural God."[47]

The fourth problem with the view of timelessness is that the very concept of simultaneity, which stands at its heart, seems incoherent[48] and even bizarre. The idea of a timeless being is "probably incoherent," says Davis, especially in requiring "that for God all times are simultaneously present."[49] The following illustration shows the outrageousness of such a notion. In response to the above objections related to creation and the incarnation, Paul Helm (an atemporalist) declares that the universe may well indeed be eternal and without a "first moment of creation."[50] "There was no time when the Creator was not, any more than there was a time when the creation was not."[51] Likewise for the incarnation, there is no time in the existence of God the Son "when he was not incarnate," says Helm.[52] "There was no time when the eternal God was not Jesus of Nazareth."[53] No wonder Feinberg says, "It is hard to make sense of the notion of atemporal eternity."[54]

God Is Temporal

The other main view of God and time is that God is temporal. This means that God is in some sense "in time," that in his very nature—and not just in his relation to the world—he experiences the flow of time in terms of past, present, and future. Craig says,

"God is temporal if and only if He exists in time, that is to say, if and only if His life has phases which are related to each other as earlier and later. In that case, God, as a personal being, has experientially a past, a present, and a future."[55]

The Biblical Data

How does this relate to the Bible's clear teaching that God is eternal, or infinite in relation to time? It means that God is everlasting. He has a past, but that past has no beginning. He has a future, but that future has no end. Thus instead of timelessness a temporalist speaks of everlastingness. God's time is quantitatively infinite. He experiences the succession of moments on an infinite time line. Another term applied to this concept is sempiternity: "The fundamental idea of sempiternity is existence at all times. God never had a beginning, nor will he die, but his existence extends backwards and forwards through every moment of time."[56] It is the concept of infinite, everlasting duration.

Temporalists point out that this is the most natural way to understand the many Bible texts that describe God as eternal. It should be noted that the relevant Greek and Hebrew terms (aion and olam) in themselves conclusively support neither the temporal nor the atemporal view.[57] However, these terms most certainly can refer to "endless duration through time," as Frame says.[58] Frame also agrees that the passages that speak of God as having no beginning and no end most likely "say only that God is everlasting—persisting through time, rather than transcending it."[59]

The fact is that the biblical teaching about God's eternity almost always refers to his originless, unending duration. He is pictured as existing from eternity past. He is the one who is "enthroned from of old" (Ps 55:19): "Your throne is established from of old; You are from everlasting" (Ps 93:2). "Are You not from everlasting, O Lord?" (Hab 1:12). He is "the Ancient of Days" (Dan 7:9,13,22).

God's existence is also projected into eternity future. He is the one who "lives forever" (Isa 57:15; Dan 12:7), "abides forever" (Ps 9:7; 102:12), and is "on high forever" (Ps 92:8). God's own oath is "as I live forever" (Deut 32:40). But he is not God just "forever"; he is "our God forever and ever" (Ps 48:14). "The LORD is King forever and ever" (Ps 10:16); "Your throne, O God, is forever and ever" (Ps 45:6). He is worshiped as "Him who lives forever and ever" (Rev 4:9-10; 10:6; 15:7). He is "the everlasting King" (Jer 10:10). His righteousness is everlasting (Ps 119:142), as is his lovingkindness (Ps 118:1-4; 136:1-26).

Many texts combine God's everlasting past and his everlasting future. He is "from everlasting to everlasting" (Ps 41:13; see Ps 106:48). "Before the mountains were born or You gave birth to the earth and the world, even from everlasting to everlasting, You are God" (Ps 90:2). "Of old You founded the earth, and the heavens are the work of Your hands. Even they will perish, but You endure....But You are the same, and Your years will not come to an end" (Ps 102:25-27; Heb 1:10-12). God's glory is "before all time and now and forever" (Jude 25). God is the one "who is and who was and who is to come" (Rev 1:4,8; see 4:8). God declares, "I am the first and the last" (Isa 44:6; 48:12); "I am the Alpha and the Omega, the beginning and the end" (Rev 21:6; see 1:8). As the infinite Creator his essence is incorruptible (Rom 1:23) and immortal (1 Tim 6:16). No wonder he is "the Everlasting God" (Gen 21:33; Isa 40:28). "The number of His years is unsearchable" (Job 36:26).

The concept of eternal duration specifically affirmed in all these texts is the key to our understanding of Ps 90:4, "For a thousand years in Your sight are like yesterday when it passes by"; and 2 Pet 3:8, "With the Lord one day is like a thousand years, and a thousand years like one day." There is no hint of timelessness here; time passes for God, even as it does for us. But for one who is everlasting, one finite period of time (a thousand years) is no more significant than any other finite period (a day). Even a thousand years is quite short when compared with eternity.

This abundance of texts affirming God's everlastingness, combined with the consistent biblical picture of God as personally acting in and interacting with our history, seems to support the view that God is temporal.

Time as an Attribute of God

To say that God is temporal means that in some sense he exists "in time." Does this mean that God is subject to time, that time is somehow a higher or more fundamental force to which God must bow? No, it means simply that time, in the sense of a succession of moments and the experience of past/present/future, is a part of God's own essence or being. As Pinnock says, "Time, in a certain sense, must be a property of God" or an attribute of God.[60] He adds, "Time is the concomitant of God and of personal life. It exists because of God's nature." Also, "I suggest God knows the passage of time as a dimension of his own endless existence."[61]

This means that in its most general sense, time is not a created reality, and is not exclusively associated with our space/time universe.[62] Stephen Davis has adopted this view, that "time was not created; it necessarily exists (like numbers); it depends for its existence on nothing else."[63] Most temporalists would agree with the first part of this affirmation, but not necessarily the second part. They would say rather that time depends for its existence on God, in the sense that it is a part of his nature. Davis goes on to present this as a possibility: "Time, perhaps, is an eternal aspect of God's nature rather than a reality independent of God." This is a much better way of thinking. But still, as Davis notes, "the point is that God, on this view, is a temporal being."[64]

When viewed thus, time is an attribute of God in the same way that logic is. Frame affirms, "God acts and thinks in accordance with the laws of logic. This does not mean that he is bound by these laws, as though they were something 'above' him that had authority over him. The laws of logic and rationality are simply the attributes of his own nature."[65] The temporalist thinks of time in a parallel way. It is not "above" or "over" God, but is an attribute of his own nature.

Thus, God's thoughts and actions are not locked into one single, unchanging, ever-frozen now, but are experienced by God in an ever-flowing now. His past is past, and his future is future. This is contrary to Frame's judgment, that "God does not sense one moment of his own transcendent consciousness flowing into another."[66]

Advocates of Divine Temporality

Representatives of this view are spread across the whole spectrum of theology. From earlier times William of Ockham[67] and the Socinians[68] rejected God's timelessness. In more recent times divine temporality has been included in process thought, and in less-than-evangelical theologians such as Oscar Cullmann.[69] Nicholas Wolterstorff defends this view in *God and Time* as "unqualified divine temporality."[70] Frame says, "At present one may speak of a consensus among theistic philosophers that God is in time."[71] The Christian philosopher Stephen Davis is clearly among them.[72]

Geisler criticizes that "extreme Arminians teach that God is temporal."[73] By "extreme Arminians" he means Neotheists, his name for openness theologians. It is true that temporality is a major characteristic of openness theology.[74] But it is not limited to "extreme Arminians," or even to Arminians as such. The Reformed theologian J. O. Buswell, Jr., was a temporalist,[75] as is John S. Feinberg.

God Is Metatemporal

Combination Views

Some have attempted to combine temporality and atemporality, and to say that God partakes of both in certain ways. Frame, for example, develops the view that God is (most likely) atemporal in his transcendence and temporal in his immanence,[76] concluding, "He really exists in time, but he also transcends time in such a way as to exist outside it."[77] Another example is Craig, who says that God was timeless before the moment of *ex nihilo* creation, and temporal afterwards.[78] Prior to creation the categories of time (such as past/present/future) did not apply to God, but the act of creation brought time into existence and brought God into a temporal relation with the world.[79]

Alan Padgett also attempts to present a hybrid view, one he calls "relative timelessness." He offers this as an alternative to both the atemporal view and everlastingness.[80] He says God himself exists as pure duration that is relatively timeless in the sense that his duration is infinite but immeasurable, contrary to the measured time of creatures, of which he is the source and Lord.[81] Padgett believes his view "has the coherence of the everlasting view but respects the intuition of the traditional notion of timeless eternity, by pointing to several ways in which God 'transcends' time."[82]

Two Kinds of Time

My own understanding includes the essence of temporality but attempts to combine it with atemporality in some ways.[83] My view is closer to Padgett than to either

Frame or Craig, since I believe that God was temporal in his essence prior to creation, and that he is temporal in his essence even in his transcendence. His very essence is temporal; time is an attribute of his being, as described above. Thus I refer to God as *tempontological*.

Not only does God's *being* exist along a time line; so also do his consciousness and his actions. God's consciousness passes through the succession of moments, both in his non-relational life and in his relation to his creatures. His consciousness dwells in the ever-flowing now; he looks back on the past and looks ahead to the future. Likewise, his actions are always oriented to specific points along the time line, according to the location of the now. God and his creatures share the same now; when God acts in the now of this world he is acting in his own present. Even for God, some of his actions are now past, and some are yet to come.

God's time line is infinite in the sense that it is eternally everlasting. This is the point of the many Scripture references cited in the discussion of the temporal view. Thus, I accept almost everything with regard to the temporal view as described above.

This is not the whole story, however. God is temporal, but he is not merely temporal. He is *metatemporal*. He both exists in time and transcends time. The latter is true in reference to his creation. When God created our world ex nihilo, he brought into existence this whole universe of both space and time. God did not create time as such, but he created our time. God's own time is infinite; created time is finite. God does not transcend his own time, but he transcends created time.

The difference between uncreated and created time is not just quantitative but also qualitative. God's time is infinite in the sense that it has no beginning and no end; ours is finite in that it had a beginning. But God's time is infinite in a qualitative sense also. The divine dimension, even in its aspect of time, qualitatively transcends every created dimension. Just as God is outside of our space, so is he outside of our time; yet he interacts with us in reference to both. Our time is not his time, yet it is not unlike his time. God is qualitatively different from man, yet we are made in his image. In a similar way, God's infinite time and our finite time are qualitatively different; yet our time is made "in the image of" God's time.

Thus, I agree with Craig and others who insist that "time" had its beginning when God created the world *ex nihilo*, but I believe this applies only to finite, created time and not to God's metatime. Thus Craig's argument—that since God existed "before" the moment of creation and thus "before" the beginning of time, he "must therefore be atemporal"[84]—appears to be a *non sequitur* from my perspective.

In what sense does God transcend created time? Not in the sense that he is outside of time altogether, and therefore in a dimension of timelessness. I reject the concept of timelessness, and especially its concomitant of ontological simultaneity. Nevertheless God transcends our created time in the sense that his consciousness (his knowledge) is not limited to its now. Though the created now corresponds to the divine now, so that

God's history coincides with our world's history, it is nevertheless true that God is still outside of created time just as he is outside of created space, and he is not bound by the flow of created time. From the perspective of the infinite divine dimension, God sees the entire scope of created time from its beginning into its unending future. As Nash well observes, "A defender of the view of God as everlasting may insist, quite consistently, that God is still Lord over time and can still behold all time simultaneously."[85] Herein lies the basis for God's comprehensive foreknowledge, which should be regarded as a non-negotiable biblical doctrine. God knows each person's past and future, as certainly as he knows their present.

Arguments Against Divine Temporality
Though God is metatemporal, existing in his own transcendent, infinite dimension of time, he still exists in time along a quantitatively everlasting time line. Several arguments have been raised against such a view; these will now be considered.

First, it is argued that divine temporality cannot be true because it is inconsistent with other divine attributes, especially simplicity and immutability. Temporality does contradict these attributes as they are understood by classical or Thomistic theists. However, I agree with those who say that the classical understanding of divine simplicity and divine immutability is incorrect, and that these attributes need to be redefined along less absolute lines.[86]

Second, do not both science and Scripture say that time had a beginning? But surely God's existence did not begin when time began. Therefore God's existence must be apart from time, or atemporal. In response one may note again the distinction explained above between created time and uncreated metatime. This space/time universe had a beginning. This is the point of all the Scripture references that refer to "the beginning" (such as Gen 1:1; Jn 1:1) or that refer to God's existing "before the ages," or before the earliest aeons of this created universe. All of the texts cited by Geisler and House[87] can easily and fairly be understood in this way. Thus, when Heb 1:2 says that through his Son God "framed the ages," it is indeed declaring that God created the "unfolding temporal periods" of this universe.[88] But this is referring only to the temporal periods of this universe, not to the divine temporal dimension. Or, to say that "before the world was" in John 17:5 means "before time began"[89] is true, but only in reference to this world's time. The same applies to Ephesians 1:4, 2 Timothy 1:9, and Jude 25.

A third argument is closely connected to the preceding, namely, the contention that time is inseparable from space and (some say) even from matter. Thus, if God is temporal, he must also be spatial and even material.[90] This is clearly a false assumption, as can be shown by a moment's reflection upon the life of created beings who are pure spirit. Angels are temporal beings, yet they are distinct from our visible universe with its space and matter. Likewise our own disembodied spirits during the intermediate state will be separated from this space/time universe, but will be quite temporal. Purely mental activity need not be connected with either space or matter. The transition from one mental state to another, an activity surely true of God, involves the succession of moments. As Craig says, "The events which serve to generate time need not be physical events; a sequence of mental events would suffice."[91] Hence this argument is completely without merit.[92]

A fourth argument is that temporal existence is a less-than-perfect existence, and since God is perfect, he cannot be temporal. In what sense is such existence less than perfect? The contention is that if one exists along a time line, then his life exists only in the moment of the now; therefore all the goodness of past moments is forever lost to his experience, and all future goodness can only be anticipated. But it would surely be more desirable and therefore greater to be timeless, so that all the goodness of the divine life can be experienced at the same time and without beginning or end. Therefore, since God is the greatest conceivable being, he must be timeless. Craig calls this the argument from "the incompleteness of temporal life."[93] Helm calls it the argument from divine fullness, and presents it as his basic rationale for timelessness.[94] He points out that it was a major argument of the earliest Christian defenders of divine timelessness: Augustine, Boethius, and Anselm.[95]

Three main responses defeat this argument. First, how do we know that simultaneous experience is a greater or fuller life than sequential experience? Helm basically appeals to intuition.[96] Wolterstorff well asks, "What epistemological status does this 'intuition' have?"[97] Surely this is a judgment call, one with which not everyone need agree. Second, Craig responds that "considerations of divine omniscience mitigate the argument's force."[98] He explains, "When we recall that God is perfectly omniscient and so forgets absolutely nothing of the past and knows everything about the future, then time's tooth is considerably dulled for Him."[99] Third, some of God's experiences are far from pleasant, e.g., the grief he felt upon viewing the pre-flood world (Gen 6:6), and the infinite suffering of God the Son on Calvary. One could well argue that a temporal experience of such events is better than a timeless one.

The fifth argument against divine temporality is the one I consider to be the most difficult to answer. It is the philosophical argument that an actual infinite is logically impossible. Ironically this is an aspect of the *kalam*[100] (or *kalaam*) cosmological argument for the existence of God; it is used to prove that the *universe* cannot have existed from eternity past and therefore must have had a beginning. When applied directly to God, it is said to likewise prove that God himself cannot have existed temporally from eternity past; therefore he must be timeless.

The argument basically states that a series increasing toward infinity can exist, since it is just getting started; but an actually infinite series cannot exist because it can never be completed. This means that an actual infinite can never come to exist since this could happen only through successive addition to any series of units. However, to any series of units it is always possible to keep adding "just one more," thus never completing an actually infinite series.[101] This is said to rule out the existence of a temporally infinite God because, if an infinite series of moments were to exist prior to now, this series could be formed only by adding one moment after another. But if the series (the life of God as divided into temporal units) were infinite, this present moment would never have arrived. But this moment has arrived. Therefore the past cannot have been temporally infinite, not even for God.[102]

In other words, if God has existed for eternity past, then an infinite number of moments must have elapsed prior to the present moment. But the key problem is that "it is impossible for an infinite number of events to have elapsed."[103]

How may we respond? Feinberg, a temporalist, leaves the argument hanging by saying it raises problems for both temporalists and atemporalists.[104] In my judgment, however, three observations may be offered. First, the argument is nonsense because in effect it makes an actually infinite series of time-units no different from a series of no units at all: infinity becomes equated with nothing. This can be seen as follows. The key idea is that an actually infinite series of moments prior to the present would never arrive at the present. Let us think of a moment, then, that occurred ten years before the present. Would the actually-infinite series ever have reached that moment? The argument says no. Let us retreat further into the past, then, to ten thousand years ago. Would the actually-infinite series ever have reached that moment? The argument says no. Let us retreat further, to ten billion years ago. Would the actually-infinite series ever have reached that moment? The argument says no. How far back, then, would we have to go, before we finally "meet up with" the advancing actual infinite? The argument implies that it would never happen—even if we kept going back *infinitely* (in the sense of a potential infinite). But surely this is absurd—as absurd as any of the problems faced by the manager of Hilbert's Hotel.[105]

A second observation is that the argument from no actual infinite quite possibly does not apply to time at all. This conclusion is based on Craig's reference to the French philosopher Henri Bergson's distinction between "real duration" and mathematical time. Craig says,

> Bergson held that the analysis of time on the model of a geometrical line composed of points (in this case instants) is a mere conceptual construct that we impose on time, whereas time itself is not composed of instants but is an uncomposed flowing or duration. The "mathematization" of time is a convenient fiction for scientific purposes, but the metaphysician should not take literally the concept of time as a point-set of instants....I think that Bergson is, in fact, correct.[106]

In other words, time is unique. We cannot apply to time the properties of numbers, which this argument attempts to do. But if Bergson is indeed correct, does this not make the "no actual infinite" argument inapplicable to God's temporal eternity?

A final observation is that even if this argument were applicable to time itself, what is true of finite, created time is not necessarily true of infinite, uncreated time.

My suggestion has been that God is not just temporal, but metatemporal. Though his existence involves the experience of the passing of time, it is still qualitatively different from our space/time continuum. This may well be the point of 2 Peter 3:8, "With the Lord one day is like a thousand years, and a thousand years like one day." Thinking of his everlasting past in terms of "moments" or "units in a series" may be presumptuous. As Morris says, "Thus, it is not the case that, on the temporalist view, God is the sort of being to whom this sort of argument clearly applies."[107]

The sixth argument against a temporal God is the puzzle of divine inactivity: if God had existed for eternity prior to the creation of the universe, why did he wait so long—infinitely long—to do it? What was he doing before this? As Craig puts the question, "Why would God delay for infinite time the creation of the universe?"[108] Why did he not create the world sooner? Why endure "an infinite period of creative idleness"?[109] Craig's own view is that before creation God was timeless and thus "changelessly alone."[110] Padgett's answer is very similar: before creation God's time was nonfinite and immeasurable, therefore no actual amount of time passed. We may "consider all of the infinite past before the first change [creation] as a single 'moment' of eternity."[111]

In my judgment, it is an unwarranted assumption to think that God was doing nothing prior to the creation of this universe. For one thing, some kind of communion existed among the three persons of the Trinity. For another thing, why should we assume that our universe is the first one God ever made, or that the creation of our world is the first and only thing he ever did? Helm declares that, as far as we know, "there is only one universe."[112] As far as we *know*, yes; but we cannot rule out a countless number of prior universes. Morris remarks:

> But the worrisomeness of the alleged delay is surely dealt with to some extent by the possibility that God has always, or very frequently (to put it mildly) been creating and bringing into existence good things prior to the creation of our universe. Nothing in the Bible or in the fundamentals of Christian faith requires us to hold that the bringing about of our universe is the only creative endeavor in which God has ever engaged. Thus, we need not live with the specter of an infinite delay in God's creative impulses, if we endorse the temporal interpretation of divine eternity. [113]

My judgment is that none of these arguments is strong enough or conclusive enough to force us to look for some non-literal interpretation of the Bible's abundant affirmations of God's temporal everlastingless.

Foreknowledge and the Metatemporal God

A final question is this: how does the question of foreknowledge fit into this portrait of a metatemporal God? Most of the issues regarding foreknowledge cannot be discussed here: How is it possible? Does it preclude free will? How does it facilitate providence? All I am seeking to do is to explain how I believe foreknowledge relates to God and time.

God the Creator (written in 1983) explains what I considered then to be a reasonable, logical order of God's pre-creation counsels:

> 1) Decision to create a universe. 2) Decision to create a universe with free-will creatures. 3) Knowledge of all possible futures of all possible universes with free-will creatures. 4) Decision to create this particular universe. 5) Foreknowledge of the real future of this particular universe. 6) Decision to include redemption in the plan. 7) Creation. [114]

Being uncertain then about how exactly God relates to time, I was careful in that volume to suggest that the sequence of these counsels was logical, not chronological.[115] In light of this current study, I now suggest a modified list of counsels, and I now consider the nature of the sequence to be chronological as well as logical.

My present judgment is that the sequence begins with God's knowledge of all possible futures of all possible universes. This includes a knowledge of all possible acts by all possible free-will beings, as well as a knowledge of all God's own possible responses to such acts. This may include knowledge of how he will actually decide to respond to any such acts, if they ever become realities. Sanders calls this the "knowledge of all possibilities view."[116] Ware refers to the last part of this knowledge as a divine "contingency plan" and disparages it,[117] but I have no problem with God's having a "contingency plan."

All of this knowledge of possibilities is simply an aspect of God's omniscience, which includes a knowledge of all reality as well as all possible reality. He has had this knowledge of all possibilities for eternity.

The next relevant item in the sequence is God's decision to create this particular universe. But if this decision is part of a chronological sequence, does this mean that there was a time in God's eternity past before this decision was made? Yes, it does. This raises a question to which I have given much consideration: Can God think a new thought? I have concluded that he can. But since he has eternally known all possibilities, the only kind of thoughts that can be new for God are his own personal decisions to do something new. His decision to create this particular world was such a new thought, made at some point along his eternal time line. (The question of "When?" is irrelevant, as is the question of "Why now and not sooner?" See 2 Pet 3:8.)

This amounts to a rejection of classical immutability, since the content of God's consciousness is viewed as capable of change. This is consistent, however, with my previously published ideas about such a change in God's consciousness.[118] It also means that at no point is God's knowledge absolutely all-inclusive, since he at no point knows all of his own future decisions, including the realities that will actually spring from them. This in effect places a limit on God's foreknowledge, since I cannot affirm that "God has complete and infallible knowledge of the future," as Hunt words the "traditional doctrine."[119] I must disagree with Hunt when he says, "Then since God foreknows *everything*, his own future actions are among the things he foreknows."[120]

On the other hand, this helps to solve the problem of the divine *freedom*. Feinberg says the traditional doctrine of foreknowledge raises "a dilemma about *divine* freedom. Of all the beings in the universe, one would think that God would be free, but if God knows all things, including whatever he will do in the future, then there seems to be no way for him to avoid doing those things. And if this is so, how can he be free?"[121] Rice agrees that "the concept of absolute foreknowledge renders meaningless any notion of divine freedom," if he indeed foreknows "everything he is ever going to decide."[122]

I reject the common fallacy that God's foreknowledge of a future act, whether it be divine or human, rules out the free-will character of that act. But even if that were true, since God does not know all his future decisions and acts, he is indisputably free. His own future is open.

This brings us back to the question of God's new thought in the form of his decision to create this particular universe. A key element of it is his decision to create free-will beings, including both angels and the human race. Since God has determined to create free-will beings who themselves will make decisions that determine their own futures, God's decision to create does not include a divine predetermination of every detail of this universe. If free will means anything, then in its details God must leave the future open to wherever his free-will creatures will take it, within the limits of his own creation purposes, permissive will, and providential intervention.

In this sense I am fully comfortable with the concept of divine risk. In God the Creator I said, "God's purpose to bestow love on and receive glory from free moral creatures involved a risk, but it was a risk he was willing to take."[123] But this should not be surprising, since (as Ware notes) all nondeterminist models of creation involve some degree of divine risk.[124] Sanders correctly states the other side of the coin, that only absolute determinism avoids risk altogether.[125]

Thus I fully agree with Sanders that a God with simple foreknowledge is no less a risk taker than a God with present knowledge only.[126] I even agree with Sanders that God's risk includes the fact that he does not know in advance how things will turn out (a notion of risk that the Arminian Picirilli rejects[127]). But I do disagree as to the extent of this risk. To me the risk exists only prior to and in connection with the initial decision to create this particular (free-will) universe; once the decision has been made, the risk is off-set by what happens next.

The next event in the temporal sequence of God's experience is that the entire future history of the planned cosmos is completely unfolded to God's consciousness, with the result that from this event forward he has a total foreknowledge of the realities and actualities (and not just a knowledge of possibilities) that will come to pass in the new universe. Craig acknowledges that such an approach to foreknowledge is possible, but labels it "exceedingly strange" and "peculiar," and declares that it "diminishes the role of God's wisdom in creation."[128] Sanders acknowledges that this view exists, but his equation of this view with "simple foreknowledge (Arminianism)" is a mistake,[129] as Picirilli rightly points out.[130] As Picirilli notes, for most Arminians God's foreknowledge is immediate, intuitive, and eternal,[131] and not derivative as I have described it here.

As I now understand God's foreknowledge of this creation, it is not eternal. I no longer can say, as I did in 1983,[132] that God's "knowledge is eternally the same"; nor can I say that he "at all times" has a complete knowledge of time's eternal scope.[133] I cannot agree with those who say that "God has always been as certain about the future as he is about the past" (as Boyd[134] describes non-openness views). But neither do I agree with openness theology's main tenet, that God never has true foreknowledge of contingent events. Though his foreknowledge is not eternal, it is nevertheless absolute and complete with regard to our universe prior to the act of creation. Thus I would modify Hunt's summary[135] of the doctrine of divine foreknowledge—"God has complete and infallible knowledge of the future"—to read as follows: "Once God has made his decision to create this universe, he has complete and infallible knowledge of its future."

I have modified my understanding of foreknowledge in another way. I formerly described it as instantaneous, or as registering in God's mind in a single, simultaneous act. In *God the Creator* I said that God's "consciousness embraces the whole of time in a single act of knowing,"[136] and in God the Redeemer I said that "once God in his pre-creation counsels had determined to create this particular world, he immediately foreknew its entire history in one act of cognition."[137] I now think of God's foreknowledge as registering in his mind progressively or incrementally, with the future of the intended universe unfolding in his consciousness in accord with its sure historical sequence. This is how Sanders describes what is to him a view that others (not himself) might hold, a view he calls "incremental simple foreknowledge."[138] However, whereas in his description of the view the unfolding of the future is only logical and atemporal, I regard it as happening in a temporal sequence in God's experience.

How fast does the future universe's history unfold? How long does it take? This is completely unknown, and in view of 2 Peter 3:8 it is irrelevant. Though time passes, from God's perspective it makes no difference if it is equivalent to our ten seconds or our ten billion years. It could happen almost instantly, to be sure, in view of the infinite power of God's mind. This leads me to picture what is happening in God's mind in this preview of our history as something equivalent to science's portrayal of the "big bang." Just as the universe (supposedly) began at a single point of space and almost instantaneously exploded to form the massive universe we now observe, so did God's *foreknowledge* of the entire history of the universe begin at a single point of time and then expand in a kind of noetic "big bang." This noetic "big bang" or explosion of foreknowledge was an event in the life of God, an event that occupied "X" amount of time. Before this event, God had no knowledge of this actual world; after this event he knows its entire history. Since the knowledge occurs prior to the actual creation of the world, it is true foreknowledge.

What God foreknows is not the unfolding history of a self-contained universe, with God himself being just an observer of what created causal forces (such as free will) will bring about. Rather, this is the time when God makes his decisions and his plans regarding his own intervention into the unfolding historical process, or else regarding his deliberate permission to allow the created causal forces to proceed unhindered. The history that unfolds in God's mind is not just the world's history; it is his own history too.

In this event of the noetic "big bang," God is determining when and how he will intervene in human history. In so doing he is in a sense thinking more new thoughts: he is making new decisions concerning his own actions. In another sense they are not really new, since from all eternity he has had a complete knowledge of all possible worlds and all possible contingencies, and has eternally known his own potential responses to whatever contingencies will ever arise. So during the "big bang" process God does not have to ponder or weigh possible courses of action. He simply has to convert them in his mind from possible future acts to certain future acts.

How is it *possible* for God, given his temporality, to know the entire future of a world not yet created? I really do not know. We should remember that God's time is not just quantitatively but also qualitatively different from created time. His time is infinite, and he transcends the time line of creation in ways we as finite creatures cannot understand. Even if he transcends our created time in no other way, he at least transcends it with respect to his knowledge.[139]

It is legitimate to leave this in the realm of mystery. Hunt admits to being agnostic on this question of how foreknowledge is possible,[140] as was William of Ockham.[141] Other views have their own versions of mystery. In Molinism (the "middle knowledge" view), how God can know the counter-factuals of freedom is no less mysterious than how God can know future contingencies.[142] Crabtree, a determinist, says that "an appeal to divine 'mystery' is a common but suspicious move."[143] But his fellow determinists do not hesitate to make such an appeal. In defending timelessness Paul Helm declares that

> [I]t is surely not a reasonable requirement for a satisfactory articulation of a doctrine such as timeless eternality that one must be able accurately to describe what it is like to be timeless. Part of what it means to say that God is incomprehensible is to say that though we believe that God is timeless we do not and cannot have a straightforward understanding of what his timeless life is.[144]

Robert Strimple says that the question of how God's timeless decree and knowledge relate to our free and responsible choices is "an ultimate *mystery*." Contrary to openness theology, "it is not God's knowledge but our finite human understanding that is limited. The ultimate mystery exists for our limited minds."[145]

What follows the "big bang" explosion of foreknowledge is the actual creation of this universe. God implements his decision to create, and thus initiates his own pre-planned involvement in its history. As the history of this universe passes, God not only stands above the created time line but also exists along with it and acts within it. All that he foreknew and foreplanned now unfolds in reality, and God experiences the actualities of the world as they happen.

Because of foreknowledge, none of these actualities is totally new to God; no event or no human choice takes him by surprise. All the so-called "surprises" occurred during the foreknowledge event as the preview of history was unfolding within God's mind. But even then nothing was a total surprise, because of God's eternal knowledge of all possible futures.

Does such foreknowledge mean that God's participation in the actual course of history is not genuine but is instead impersonal and robotic, as openness theologians claim?[146] Hardly. Even on the human level, the anticipation of future events of which we are fairly certain in no way negates the pleasure (or pain) of the actual experience itself. Thus also with God, the foreknown confrontation with the "unexpected," the foreknown feelings of regret and frustration, and the foreknown testing of individuals like Abraham in Genesis 22:12[147] are all experienced in reality with genuine interpersonal interaction. God is not simply re-living the "big bang" explosion of foreknowledge; he is living it for the first time with all the attendant feelings.

Conclusion

The metatemporal view of God lies between the classical view of God and open theism. By including temporality within the nature of God it is more like open theism than the classical view, but it nonetheless preserves the crucial element of the classical view which openness rejects: a comprehensive pre-creation foreknowledge of our world. At the same time it posits a genuine openness for God in his temporality: his own future remains open, since he is free to think new thoughts and make new decisions about possible new universes in his infinite future.

Notes

[1] William Lane Craig, *Time and Eternity: Exploring God's Relationship to Time* (Wheaton: Crossway, 2001), p. 11. Reading this made me want to throw in the towel before embarrassing myself, especially after I saw that Craig, "The Middle-Knowledge View," in *Divine Foreknowledge: Four Views*, ed. James K. Beilby and Paul R. Eddy (Downers Grove: InterVarsity, 2001), p. 57, has discerned "philosophical naïveté" in Gregory Boyd's position also represented in the same volume as "The Open-Theism View." I confess up front to a large measure of philosophical naivete.

[2] Unless noted otherwise Scripture references are taken from the New American Standard Bible (1995 ed.).

[3] Gen 21:33 [NIV]; Deut 33:27; Rom 16:26; see Isa 40:28; Rom 1:20; 1 Tim 1:17.

[4] See Norman Geisler and H. Wayne House, *The Battle for God: Responding to the Challenge of Neotheism* (Grand Rapids: Kregel, 2001), chs. 2, 4, 5, 8.

[5]Eleonore Stump and Norman Kretzmann, "Eternity," in *The Concept of God*, ed. Thomas V. Morris (Oxford: Oxford University Press, 1987), p. 225.

[6]John S. Feinberg, *No One Like Him: The Doctrine of God* (Wheaton: Crossway, 2001), p. 429.

[7]Norman Geisler, "God Knows All Things," in *Predestination and Free Will: Four Views of Divine Sovereignty and Human Freedom*, ed. David Basinger and Randall Basinger (Downers Grove: Inter-Varsity, 1986), p. 73.

[8]Feinberg, *No One Like Him*, p. 402.

[9]Cited in William Hasker, *God, Time, and Knowledge* (Ithaca, N.Y.: Cornell University, 1989), pp. 6-7.

[10]Norman Geisler, *Chosen But Free: A Balanced View of Divine Election* (Minneapolis: Bethany, 1999), p. 110.

[11]Ibid., pp. 111-112.

[12]Geisler and House, *Battle for God*, pp. 70, 73.

[13]Ibid., pp. 66-70.

[14]William Lane Craig, *Time and Eternity*, p. 19.

[15]Geisler and House, *Battle for God*, p. 66.

[16]Ibid., p. 67.

[17]Geisler, "God Knows All Things," p. 73; Geisler and House, *Battle for God*, p. 71.

[18]See Feinberg, *No One Like Him*, pp. 384-387.

[19]Geisler, "God Knows All Things," p. 67; see Feinberg, *No One Like Him*, p. 326-327; and Thomas V. Morris, *Our Idea of God: An Introduction to Philosophical Theology* (Downers Grove, Ill.: InterVarsity, 1991), pp. 121-124.

[20]Geisler and House, *The Battle for God*, pp. 73, 80-81; see Feinberg, *No One Like Him*, pp. 387-388; Morris, *Our Idea of God*, pp. 127-128.

[21]See Feinberg, *No One Like Him*, pp. 384-385; Morris, *Our Idea of God*, pp. 129-130.

[22]Paul Helm, "Divine Timeless Eternity," in *God and Time: Four Views*, ed. Gregory E. Ganssle (Downers Grove, Ill.: InterVarsity, 2001), p. 29-31.

[23]Ibid., p. 31.

[24]Nicholas Wolterstorff, "Unqualified Divine Temporality," in Ganssle, *God and Time*, p. 190.

[25]Jack Cottrell, *What the Bible Says About God the Creator* (Joplin, Mo.: College Press, 1983), pp. 37-40.

[26]John M. Frame, *The Doctrine of God* (Phillipsburg, N.J.: Presbyterian & Reformed, 2002), pp. 225-230.

[27]Ibid., pp. 705.

[28]Feinberg, *No One Like Him*, p. 329.

[29]Ibid., pp. 335, 337.

[30]Ibid., p. 433.

[31]Thomas V. Morris, *Our Idea of God*, pp. 113-118, 121-124.

[32]Jack Cottrell, *What the Bible Says About God the Redeemer* (Joplin, Mo.: College Press, 1987), ch. 8.

[33]Ibid., pp. 476.

[34]Feinberg, *No One Like Him*, pp. 404, 431-432.

[35]Morris, *Our Idea of God*, pp. 127-128.

[36]Frame, *The Doctrine of God*, p. 551.

[37]Stephen T. Davis, *Logic and the Nature of God* (Grand Rapids: Eerdmans, 1983), p.11.

[38]Ibid., p.14.

[39]See Hasker, *God, Time, and Knowledge*, p. 150.

[40]See Davis, *Logic and the Nature of God*, p. 14.

[41]Feinberg, *No One Like Him*, p. 399.

[42]Bruce Reichenbach, "God Limits His Power," in Basinger and Basinger, *Predestination and Free Will*, p. 113.

[43]Feinberg, *No One Like Him*, p. 396-398. Craig, *Time and Eternity*, p. 84, takes the view that an atemporal God could have the capacity for all such personal activities and relationships, but once he actually engages in them, he becomes temporal.

[44]Craig, *Time and Eternity*, pp. 210-215; Craig, "Timelessness and Omnitemporality," in Ganssle, *God and Time*, p. 65. See Davis, *Logic and the Nature of God*, pp. 11-13.

[45]See Wolterstorff, "Unqualified Divine Temporality," pp. 209-210.

[46]Reichenbach, "God Limits His Power," p. 113.

[47]Ibid., p. 114.

[48]Alvin Plantinga, "On Ockham's Way Out," in *The Concept of God*, ed. Thomas V. Morris (Oxford: Oxford University Press, 1987), p. 176.

[49]Davis, *Logic and the Nature of God*, pp. 14-15.

[50]Paul Helm, "Divine Timeless Eternity," p. 49.

[51]Ibid., p. 52.

[52]Ibid., p. 54.

[53]Ibid.

[54]Feinberg, No One Like Him, p. 428.

[55]Craig, Time and Eternity, 15. Since my own view includes much of what is said below, for the most part I am presenting divine temporality as a valid concept.

[56]Feinberg, *No One Like Him*, p. 255.

[57]Ibid., p. 263.

[58]Frame, *The Doctrine of God*, p. 545.

[59]Ibid., p. 554.

[60]Clark H. Pinnock, *Most Moved Mover: A Theology of God's Openness* (Grand Rapids: Baker, 2001), p. 97.

[61]Ibid., pp. 98, 99.

[62]This is contrary to the view I took in Cottrell, *God the Creator*, pp. 250, 264, though I was somewhat ambivalent about it then (pp. 251, 263).

[63]Davis, *Logic and the Nature of God*, p. 23.

[64]Ibid.

[65]Frame, *The Doctrine of God*, p. 511.

[66]Ibid., 556, n37.

[67]Hasker, *God, Time, and Knowledge*, p. 12.

[68]Frame, *The Doctrine of God*, p. 546.

[69]Oscar Cullmann, *Christ and Time* (London: SCM, 1951), p. 63.

[70]Wolterstorff, "Unqualified Divine Temporality," 187-213.

[71]Frame, *The Doctrine of God*, p. 548.

[72]See Davis, *Logic and the Nature of God*, p. 23.

[73]Geisler, *Chosen But Free*, p. 111.

[74]See John Sanders, *The God Who Risks: A Theology of Providence* (Downers Grove, Ill.: InterVarsity, 1998), p. 319, n78; and Pinnock, *Most Moved Mover*, pp. 32-33, 96-97.

[75]James Oliver Buswell, Jr., *A Systematic Theology of the Christian Religion* (Grand Rapids: Zondervan, 1962), 1:42, 47.

[76]Frame, *The Doctrine of God*, 549.

[77]Ibid., p. 559.

[78]Craig, *Time and Eternity*, pp. 233, 235.

[79]Ibid., pp. 235-236, 241. Pinnock, *Most Moved Mover*, 98, leaves a door open to Craig's view: "The really important thing to say is that at least from the moment of creation, God enters into temporal rela-

tions with his creatures. One might speculate that God is timeless without creation and temporal subsequent to creation."

[80]Alan G. Padgett, "Eternity as Relative Timelessness," in Ganssle, *God and Time*, p. 92.

[81]Ibid., pp. 106-108.

[82]Ibid., p. 108.

[83]See Cottrell, *God the Redeemer*, p. 485.

[84]Craig, *Time and Eternity*, p. 20.

[85]Ronald H. Nash, *The Concept of God* (Grand Rapids: Zondervan, 1983), p. 81.

[86]I believe this is true, totally apart from any connection with the question of God and time.

[87]Geisler and House, *Battle for God*, pp. 66-70.

[88]Ibid., p. 67.

[89]Ibid., p. 69.

[90]Geisler, *Chosen But Free*, p. 112; Geisler and House, *Battle for God*, p. 73.

[91]Craig, *Time and Eternity*, p. 66.

[92]See Feinberg, *No One Like Him*, p. 416.

[93]Craig, *Time and Eternity*, p. 67.

[94]Paul Helm, "Divine Timeless Eternity," pp. 29-35.

[95]Ibid., pp. 33-34.

[96]Ibid, pp. 29-31.

[97]Wolterstorff, "Unqualified Divine Temporality, p. 70.

[98]Craig, "Timelessness and Omnitemporality," p. 64.

[99]Craig, *Time and Eternity*, p. 72.

[100]*Kalam* is an Arabic term (literally, "speech") that designates a certain approach to God in medieval Islamic theology and philosophy. It is associated with a particular form of the cosmological argument for God's existence. See William L. Craig, *The Kalam Cosmological Argument* (New York: Barnes & Noble, 1979).

[101]See Craig, *Time and Eternity*, pp. 226-229.

[102]Geisler, *Chosen But Free*, p. b111.

[103]Paul Helm, *Eternal God* (Oxford: Clarendon, 1988), p. 38.

[104]Feinberg, *No One Like Him*, pp. 389-391.

[105]The problem of Hilbert's Hotel is discussed by Craig, *Time and Eternity*, pp. 221-226.

[106]Craig, "Timelessness and Omnitemporality," p. 118.

[107]Morris, *Our Idea of God*, p.126.

[108]Craig, *Time and Eternity*, p. 25.

[109]Ibid., pp. 229-230.

[110]Ibid., p. 236.

[111]Alan G. Padgett, "Eternity as Relative Timelessness," pp. 108-109.

[112]Paul Helm, "The Philosophical Issue of Divine Foreknowledge," in *The Grace of God, the Bondage of the Will,* vol. 2, ed. Thomas R. Schreiner and Bruce A. Ware (Grand Rapids: Baker, 1995), 489.

[113]Morris, *Our Idea of God,* .p. 124.

[114]Cottrell, *God the Creator,* p. 182.

[115]Ibid., pp. 180, 181, 183.

[116]Sanders, *The God Who Risks*, p. 196.

[117]Bruce A. Ware, "Defining Evangelicalism's Boundaries Theologically: Is Open Theism Evangelical?" *Journal of the Evangelical Theological Society* 45 (June 2002):204.

[118]Cottrell, *God the Redeemer*, p. 486.

[119]David Hunt, "The Simple-Foreknowledge View," in Beilby and Paul Eddy, *Divine Foreknowledge*, p. 65.

[120]Ibid., p. 93.

[121]Feinberg, *No One Like Him*, p. 391.

[122]Richard Rice, "Divine Foreknowledge and Free-Will Theism," in *The Grace of God, the Will of Man*, ed. Clark H. Pinnock (Grand Rapids: Zondervan, 1989), p. 126.

[123]Cottrell, *God the Creator*, p. 181.

[124]Bruce A. Ware, *God's Lesser Glory: The Diminished God of Open Theism* (Wheaton: Crossway, 2000), p. 48.

[125]Sanders, *The God Who Risks*, pp. 171, 195.

[126]Ibid., p. 203.

[127]Robert E. Picirilli, "An Arminian Response to John Sanders's *The God Who Risks: A Theology of Providence*," *Journal of the Evangelical Theological Society* 44 (September 2001):490.

[128]William Lane Craig, *The Only Wise God* (Grand Rapids: Baker, 1987), pp. 134-135.

[129]John Sanders, "Be Wary of Ware: A Reply to Bruce Ware," *Journal of the Evangelical Theological Society* 45 (June 2002): 225-226. See Sanders, *The God Who Risks*, p.196.

[130]Picirilli, "Arminian Response," p. 471.

[131]Ibid.

[132]Cottrell, *God the Creator*, p. 285.

[133]Cottrell, *God the Redeemer*, p. 485.

[134]Gregory A. Boyd, "The Open-Theism View," in Beilby and Eddy, *Divine Foreknowledge: Four Views*, p. 13.

[135]Hunt, "The Simple Foreknowledge View," p. 65.

[136]Cottrell, *God the Creator*, p. 255.

[137]Cottrell, *God the Redeemer*, p. 493.

[138]Sanders, *The God Who Risks*, pp. 201-202.

[139]Davis, *Logic and the Nature of God*, p. 24, says, "He can still have complete knowledge of all past, present and future events. (If he 'transcends time', it is only in the sense that he has this power-a power no other being has.)"

[140]Hunt, "The Simple-Foreknowledge View," p. 67.

[141]See Hasker, *God, Time, and Knowledge*, p. 15.

[142]J. A. Crabtree, "Does Middle Knowledge Solve the Problem of Divine Sovereignty?" in Shreiner and Ware, *The Grace of God, the Bondage of the Will*, 2:438. Craig, "The Middle-Knowledge View," pp. 133-134, suggests that seeing God's foreknowledge as conceptual (innate) rather than perceptual (derivative) explains how such knowledge is possible. However, his presentation of this idea is an assertion rather than an explanation, and is quite unsatisfying.

[143]Crabtree, "Does Middle Knowledge Solve the Problem of Divine Sovereignty?" p. 438.

[144]Helm, "Divine Timeless Eternity," p. 38.

[145]Robert B. Strimple, "What Does God Know?" in *The Coming Evangelical Crisis*, ed. John H. Armstrong (Chicago: Moody, 1996), p. 147.

[146]Rice, "Divine Foreknowledge and Free-Will Theism," pp. 133-134, 137.

[147]Boyd, "The Open-Theism View," pp. 23-33

4

RESPONSE

John Sanders

One question that immediately came to my mind as I have prepared my remarks is this. Why have Stone-Campbell adherents embraced exhaustive definite foreknowledge? What purpose does the doctrine serve in Stone-Campbell thought? That is, doctrines are supposed to accomplish tasks-to be useful. Of what use is foreknowledge? T. W. Brents, a restorationist, wrote *The Gospel Plan of Salvation* (Cincinnati: Chase & Hall, 1874), which was widely read in the nineteenth century by members of the Stone-Campbell Restoration Movement. Brents's book was the closest thing to a systematic theology used by Stone-Campbell students for many decades. This volume includes an entire chapter called "The Foreknowledge of God" (pp. 92-108) where he rejects exhaustive definite foreknowledge as unbiblical. He cites many of the same biblical passages used by proponents of open theism and raises many of the same arguments.

Response to Duane Warden

Warden's presentation of open theism for the most part is accurate. This I truly appreciate, as well as its irenic tone that demonstrates interest in dialogue.

Let me respond, though, to Warden's very legitimate questions. First, he asks whether open theists dismiss passages that call our model into question. Proponents of open theism have discussed texts such as Romans 8:29-30, 9-11; Ephesians 1:4 and others presented as supporting "determinism."[1] Generally, though, open theists don't see the need to rehearse all the explanations already developed by Arminian scholars over the years when we agree with them, such as on John 6 or other passages.

Second, regarding the passages about Cyrus and Judas, open theists are not in agreement. Boyd tends to agree with the explanations given by L. D. McCabe, a nineteenth-century Methodist who wrote two lengthy volumes in favor of open theism. In this view, God occasionally overrides human freedom in order to carry out his plans. Though I think this is possible, I try to explain the texts without appealing for God to override human freedom. I believe Cyrus was a title rather than a person in this biblical text and that the prediction about Judas was conditional—he did not have to do it. It was an implicit warning just as Jonah's prediction about Nineveh. Though stated unconditionally, both were implicitly conditional.

Third, are open theists overly individualistic? Perhaps we reflect our evangelical heritage in our efforts to apply our model to issues that focus on individual piety. Quite correctly, open theists need to apply our model in wider social arenas such as social ethics and ecology.

Fourth, Warden wonders if open theists have difficulty accounting for the universality of human sin. Open theist accounts of sin can range from Augustinian to Wesleyan to Eastern Orthodox views. Open theism does not require a particular understanding of this issue. After all, there are many Reformed theologians who affirm both divine temporality and the dynamic omniscience view.

Finally, Warden wonders if there will be sin in heaven if humans continue to have libertarian freedom. I have addressed this question at length elsewhere.[2] Here, let me simply say that this is an issue for all proponents of libertarian freedom, including Arminians and Eastern Orthodox, not just open theists. My short answer is that in heaven we may voluntarily ask God to confirm our characters in such a way that we forever freely choose the good.

In his conclusion Warden notes that any model of God will have difficulties. I agree. Sometimes theological positions are decided by which problems one chooses to live with.

Response to Robert Kurka

Kurka's presentation helps me appreciate the opportunity to clarify and correct my views on various topics. The opportunity provided to correct misstatements made about open theism in his presentation is greatly appreciated, though I may not have time or space to address them all.

First, he claims that I present the debate in terms of a polarity between sovereignty and love. No, the question is: Which view of sovereignty is to be affirmed since more than one view exists (as so with regard to such issues as baptism, the millennium, and election)? I affirm that God sovereignly decided not to tightly control everything we do. This is called general sovereignty and it is incompatible with what is called specific sovereignty (God tightly controls everything we do). If Kurka believes that the Calvinist view (specific sovereignty) is the only legitimate view of sovereignty, then I simply disagree. Later on he calls my view "limited sovereignty." Since general sovereignty has been a standard Arminian view affirmed by people such as Jack Cottrell (a well-published, Stone-Campbell theologian), Kurka must conclude that Cottrell and many other Arminians affirm limited sovereignty.

On a couple of occasions he states my position as "limited foreknowledge." Open theists do not believe God's foreknowledge is "limited" in any respect. The debate centers on the nature of the future: Does "the future" actually already exist in some way? Open theists affirm a widely accepted position known as the dynamic theory of time. According to this view, the future does not now exist—it is not a reality—so there is literally no "thing" (fact of the matter) to be known. God would be limited if facts were available to be known, and he was prevented from knowing them. This also gets into complex philosophical questions regarding the nature of truth and whether statements about future contingent events are true now.

Third, he accuses me of historical selectivity, stating "Socianism provides the most demonstrable parallel to open theism in church history even to the most basic arguments" (p. 44). Kurka correctly notes that Socinians denied the deity of Jesus, the atonement, the Trinity and the like. Open theists, however, do not reject these doctrines. So, should we not be labeled Socinians? After all, the very same accusation that Kurka makes was made against Arminius himself. A letter written in Arminius's day says that with incredible zeal "some persons accuse this man of schism and others of heresy; some charge him with the crime of Pelagianism and others brand him with the black mark of Socinianism."[3] Also, the dynamic omniscience view has been affirmed by a number of orthodox Christians throughout history. Calcidius, a late fourth-century Christian writer propounded it, and the nineteenth-century witnessed an explosion in the number of proponents including T. W. Brents (the leader in the Stone-Campbell Movement mentioned earlier), many Methodists, and Isaac Dorner. The actual historical forerunner for open theism is L. D. McCabe who wrote two lengthy volumes defending it.[4]

Fourth, he claims I was "stacking the deck" in my three criteria for a doctrine of providence. This is curious since these criteria are widely accepted by Arminians. After all, Arminians believe God is involved with people in the flow of history. Kurka is simply mistaken to think that these three criteria rule out the traditional Arminian understanding of foreknowledge. My arguments against the simple foreknowledge view are independent of these criteria.

Fifth, Kurka writes: "Risk is a creaturely concept not a divine one" (p. 48). If this means that it is impossible for God to take risks, then Kurka is quite out of the Arminian mainstream. Freewill theists from C. S. Lewis to Phillip Yancey state that God took a risk in creating beings with libertarian freedom. The freewill defense to the problem of evil is predicated upon divine risk taking. That is, God could not create us with free will and also guarantee that we would never commit a moral evil. In the same vein, Arminianism has maintained that God wants to save every single individual but, unfortunately, God takes the risk that some will refuse divine grace. Both of these situations entail that God takes risks in some areas. Though the term "risk" may not have been used much in theology, the concept of divine risk taking is certainly there.

Next, he accuses me of a "hyperliteralism." However, I specifically said that biblical language about God is comprised of conceptual metaphors.[5] He says we must think theomorphically rather than strictly anthropomorphically. I made this very point only six pages later in the same book, quoting Abraham Joshua Heschel: "God's concern for justice and love is not an anthropomorphism; rather, our concern for justice and love is a theomorphism."[6] In my view, biblical statements like "God does not change" and "God changes" are metaphors and can both be true depending on what is meant by "change" in the various texts. He accuses me of taking the divine change of mind texts in a "wooden" manner reminiscent of fundamentalists and Mormons. Did Kurka read my discussion of the metaphorical nature of all Scripture? In particular, on page seventy-two where, after criticizing those who see contradictions between God not changing and God changing, I say, "A better approach for handling the divine repentance texts is to acknowledge that they are metaphorical in nature. Metaphors do not provide us with an exact correspondence to reality but they do provide a way of understanding reality." So, he is quite incorrect that my views "logically lead" to fundamentalism or Mormonism.

Kurka thinks that I have broken an axiom of biblical interpretation by subordinating clear teaching on divine immutability to unclear teachings of divine mutability. However, I don't believe either the immutability or mutability texts have to be subordinated to the other for I see no tension between them.[7] My position is that the divine nature does not change but God can change in certain respects. Kurka himself says, "God is perfectly personal, so that if he changes his mind (Jon 3:10), he is not changing his essential nature and purpose." Amen! This is precisely my view.

Kurka says I engage in some very speculative exegesis. His example is Genesis 22:12 where God says "now I know that you fear me." What is my speculative exegesis? That God learned something about Abraham. Well, how can it be speculative when that is what the text says? We may have good reasons to claim that the text does not mean what it says but Kurka does not provide any such reasons. Would not most people in the Stone-Campbell movement accept the biblical texts as reality depicting unless we have good reason not to do so? In line with this he says the feelings I attribute to God resemble a "finite God." The biblical writers portray God as having feelings such as joy, anger, and even inner turmoil over what to do with his people (Hos 11:8). I wonder if Kurka would say the feelings that the biblical writers attribute to God resemble a finite God? I find it highly ironic that someone in the Stone-Campbell tradition hurls insults at me for taking the biblical portrayal of God seriously.

Kurka says my understanding of omnipotence could easily be seen in a description of process theology's aims. Really? How could a process theologian agree that God sovereignly decided to make some of his decisions contingent? The God of process theology cannot do that because all of God's actions are contingent—God cannot act unilaterally in process thought. For process theology it was not God's sovereign decision that humans be given libertarian rather than compatibilistic freedom. In process theology God cannot determine anything in the creation. This pattern in Kurka's paper, of using loaded language and attempting to tar us with guilt by associating us with process theologians and Socinians, is quite disappointing.

At the end of his paper Kurka gives his own proposal, but I find no fundamental difference between his proposal and mine. He says my portrait is of an emotionally unpredictable God. If he thinks I believe God is overwhelmed by emotions as we are apt to be, then he is mistaken. Elsewhere, I have discussed God's love, wisdom and faithfulness at length.[8] I simply do not recognize my view in Kurka's accusations.

Also, Kurka describes how God uses his knowledge to make decisions. He uses an illustration of a scientist making predictions based on knowledge of the past and then he claims that this is the "traditional Arminian perspective." It is not. Arminians affirm a view known as simple foreknowledge whereby God just "previsions" everything that will ever happen. Proponents of simple foreknowledge do not believe God prognosticates based on his exhaustive knowledge of past and present-that is the God of open theism. Again, I am left wondering where is the difference between us since each of the five points in his proposal are affirmed in my work.

I thank Kurka for stating some of the positive elements that the discussion of open theism has raised. Also, I agree with him that openness is not the "only option" to Calvinism. In my book I said that open theism is just one form of what may be called freewill theism or relational theology, a major position throughout church history.[9] Though I believe that openness is the best form of relational theism, I view other relational theists as allies and dialogue partners.

Response to Jack Cottrell

I enjoyed working through this thought-provoking paper. Over the years I have learned much from Cottrell's work. So I am delighted to be able to respond to this paper.

Cottrell defines time as the "relation between events may be described in terms of before and after, or earlier than and later than. It involves a sequence or succession of moments which may be described as past and future in relation to a present or now." This is a psychological rather than a metric definition of time. That is, it addresses the experience of consciousness that personal beings experience. God can experience sequence without any sort of creation. Measurable (metric) time requires a creation with distance between objects. Cottrell is correct that psychological time, as an attribute of God, does not make God subject to time anymore than God's eternal knowledge of mathematical truths makes God subject to math.

Also, his exposition and critique of divine timelessness is correct. Divine timelessness is incompatible with core doctrines of Arminian theology: conditional election, resistible grace and that our prayers can affect God. A timeless being could not respond to creatures, so election would have to be irresistible, and a timeless being could not be affected by our prayers. These considerations led the influential Methodist theologian, John Miley, to reject timelessness, concluding that exhaustive definite foreknowledge would also need to be rejected if it was shown to be incompatible with God interacting with us.[10]

Cottrell says God transcends created time both quantitatively and qualitatively. He transcends it quantitatively in the sense that God had no beginning and will have no end. I agree with this. But in what way does God qualitatively transcend metric time? What is meant by God "outside of our time?" He writes: "Though the created now corresponds to the divine now, so that God's history coincides with our world's history, it is nevertheless true that God is still outside of created time" (p. 71). How can God's time correspond to our time if God qualitatively transcends our time? If God is not in the flow of created time in what possible sense could his history coincide with created history? He says, "Our time is not his time, yet it is not unlike his time" (p. 70). In what ways it is similar and in what ways it is different?

Next, Cottrell claims that divine metatemporality allows God to prevision all of the future. "Herein lies the basis for God's comprehensive foreknowledge" (p. 71). But how does it accomplish this?

In his section, "Foreknowledge and the Metatemporal God," Cottrell says that God can think new thoughts. In the scholarly realm, this is a major break with traditional conceptions of omniscience, but a break in the right direction. However, does God's ability to think new thoughts come to an end according to Cottrell after God decides to create? Once God makes the decision to create this type of world, then God acquires the knowledge of all that creatures will do in the future and all the actions that God will do in the future. Hence, it seems God's ability to think new thoughts is limited to the time prior to creation. Now that God knows all that will obtain in the future, it would seem impossible for God to ever again think a new thought.

Yet, Cottrell indicates that God can continue to formulate new decisions. He writes: "It also means that at no point is God's knowledge absolutely all-inclusive, since he at no point knows all of his own future decisions, including the realities that will actually spring therefrom. This in effect places a limit on God's foreknowledge, since I cannot affirm that 'God has complete and infallible knowledge of the future'" (p. 75). For Cottrell, God does not know all of his own future actions. This view is very similar to the dynamic omniscience view affirmed by open theists.

Naturally, I resonate with Cottrell's affirmation of divine risk-taking. He affirms that a God with simple foreknowledge is no less a risk taker than the God of open theism. However, Cottrell says he disagrees with me concerning "the extent of this risk" because the risk is only prior to creation but not after God acquires exhaustive definite foreknowledge. Yet, I fail to see how this helps. Cottrell says that he affirms what I call "incremental simple foreknowledge" (ISF). The way ISF works is that God gains his knowledge of what both God and creatures will do in the future incrementally. The reason this is necessary is that Cottrell seems to acknowledge that it is logically impossible for God to make an event not occur that God knows with certainty will occur. For example, once God knows for certain (previsions) Israel's idolatry with the golden calf, God cannot bring it about that they do not commit this act of idolatry. Hence, God works his way through our future, seeing what we will do and then deciding what action he will take. Then he looks a bit further ahead to see what we will do and decides what action he will take. Elsewhere, I have explained at length that for ISF, divine providence works out in precisely the same way that a God with dynamic omniscience (open theism) works it out.[11]

The only difference is that the God of openness is working it out in time as we go along whereas Cottrell's metatemporal God worked it out prior to the final act of creation. For instance, say that God would like for Billy Bob to give assistance to Sue. For open theists, God seeks to get Billy Bob motivated to do so but God does not know whether his efforts have been successful until after the time of Sue's need. For Cottrell's metatemporal God, God runs the tape of the future prior to creation and sees Sue in need so he decides to encourage Billy Bob to help. Then God runs the tape forward to see whether his efforts were successful. If Billy Bob did not help Sue at the necessary time, then once God knows that Sue did not receive the help he wanted her to have, God cannot "go back" and find someone else to meet that need. Once God knows what will actually happen (not what might happen), that Sue does not, in fact, get the help she needed God cannot change this since that would render his foreknowledge incorrect. God knows prior to creation that Sue will not get the help she needed but God cannot do anything about it. So, I fail to see what difference this makes to the extent of risk God takes.

Cottrell says, "Contrary to openness theology, it is not God's knowledge but our finite human understanding that is limited" (p. 78). I agree. However, simply to say our understanding is limited does not settle the question as to which view, if any, most approximates reality. Also, for open theists it is not correct to say we believe God's foreknowledge is limited. We deny that the future exists which means there are no "facts of the matter" for God to know. God's knowledge would only be limited if there were knowable facts of which God was ignorant. But that is not our position. It is no limitation to say that God does not know what is not real.

I do not know whether Cottrell affirms the dynamic (A-theory) or the stasis (B-theory) of time. He seems to go back and forth between these. At times he speaks of God's history unfolding with ours and that the future is contingent. If so, then it would seem that the "future" is unreal-it does not exist (the dynamic view). At other times, God is able to see the future, which sounds as though it exists (the stasis view). If

Cottrell affirms the stasis theory of time then why speak of God experiencing time at all? If he affirms the dynamic theory of time in which the future is not real, then what reality is it that the metatemporal perspective provides access to?

Finally, though Cottrell acknowledges that his paper does not address how this view "facilitates providence," that is a question I am most interested for him to discuss. If doctrines are supposed to accomplish tasks, what does metatemporality accomplish for divine providence? What does incremental simple foreknowledge accomplish for divine providence? What good does it do God to have them? What can God accomplish with them that he could not accomplish without them? I do not see any advantages for God to have these as opposed to having dynamic omniscience and temporality.[12]

In conclusion, I deeply appreciate the fact that Cottrell is willing to wrestle with these thorny problems. Many Arminians simply dismiss these issues, but, as Miley in the nineteenth century, Cottrell realizes how serious they are for the core doctrines of Arminian theology. He now acknowledges that some of God's knowledge changes in that God comes to know at a later time something he did not know at an earlier time. This means that, for Cottrell, exhaustive definite foreknowledge is not essential to the divine nature. Also, he freely acknowledges that God takes risks, and I argue that the degree of these risks is exactly the same in his view as they are in open theism. Cottrell and I agree that both before God makes his decision about what sort of world to create, and immediately after he makes that decision, God does not know in full detail what the future will be. Where we differ is in how quickly God acquires the knowledge of what will happen. I hold that God acquires the knowledge as time goes on, whereas for Cottrell God "learns" this somewhat faster. But this makes no difference whatsoever to God's providential control, or to the degree of risk taken by God. Viewed in this light, how important can the difference between the two of us be?

Notes

[1]John Sanders, *The God Who Risks: A Theology of Providence* (Downers Grove, Ill.: InterVarsity, 1998, pp. 81-87, 120-124 and Gregory Boyd, *God of the Possible* (Grand Rapids: Baker, 2000), pp. 21-51.

[2]See John Sanders, "The Assurance of Things to Come" in *Looking to the Future*, ed. David Baker (Baker, 2001), pp. 281-294.

[3]John Andrews, "Address to the Reader," *The Works of James Arminius*, trans. James Nichols (Grand Rapids: Baker, 1991), 2:686.

[4]On Calcidius see J. Den Boeft, *Calcidius on Fate: His Doctrine and Sources,* Philosophia Antiqua (Leiden: E, J. Brill, 1970), p. 52. For a summary of McCabe's arguments see William McGuire King, "God's Nescience of Future Contingents: A Nineteenth-Century Theory," *Process Studies* 9 (Fall, 1979): 105-115 and David Alstad Tiessen, "The Openness Model of God: An Evangelical Paradigm in Light of Its Nineteenth-Century Wesleyan Precedent" *Didaskalia* (Spring, 2000): 77-101.

[5]See John Sanders, *The God Who Risks*, p. 15. Brents takes an extremely literalistic approach to the texts, as in Gen. 18:20-1 ("I will go down to see whether...").

[6]Sanders, *God Who Risks*, p. 21.

[7]See Christopher Hall and John Sanders, *Does God have a Future?* (Grand Rapids: Baker, 2003), pp. 124-129.

[8]Sanders, *God who Risks*, pp, 173-194.

[9]Ibid., pp. 161-164

[10]John Miley, *Systematic Theology* (New York: Eaton and Mains, 1892): 1:192, 214-215.

[11]See my fuller account in John Sanders, "Why Simple Foreknowledge Offers No More Providential Control than Open Theism," *Faith and Philosophy* 14 (1997): 26-40; and Sanders, *God Who Risks*, pp. 200-206.

[12]John Sanders, "Open Theism: A Radical Revision or Miniscule Modification of Arminianism?" *Wesleyan Theological Journal* 38.2 (Fall 2003): 69-102.

Part 2

Understanding Christology through the Gospel of John

5

BELIEF, UNION AND MISSION: THE USE OF JOHN'S GOSPEL BY EARLY RESTORATION MOVEMENT LEADERS

Carisse Mickey Berryhill

John's Gospel is the fifth most-frequently-cited biblical book in Dave McWhirter's *Millennial Harbinger Index*.[1] It is the second most-frequently-cited biblical book in Raymond Person and Eugene Boring's index to Alexander Campbell's 1839 *Christian System*, where it trails only Acts and precedes Hebrews, 1 Corinthians, and Romans in frequency.[2]

John's language about belief, salvation, and unity became very important to Alexander and Thomas Campbell, Barton Stone, and Walter Scott because they faced twin problems in their ministry context. In the first place, the can-do optimism of the opening American frontier clashed with the passive submission of would-be believers under Calvinistic soteriology. In the second place, American democratic ideas clashed with clerical authority and denominational turf wars. If Tony Dunnavant and Hiram Lester are right, the evangelistic impulse is the driving force: mission is the motive in which the interlocking American themes of freedom, restoration, and unity function.[3] The land is too big, there are too many people to reach, there is too much to do to build a new and beautiful world, therefore Eurocentric factions must not obstruct faith. After a few comments about the genres of early Stone-Campbell Restoration Movement studies of the Gospel of John, this study will focus on three specific chapters that received great attention from Stone, the Campbells, and Scott. I assume that the frequency and force of their citations reflect their chief concerns as they contextualized their message. How often we, too, find that a passage we had scarcely heeded before comes alive, cutting through to the marrow of some new ministry situation we face.

This examination must read the material situationally, recognizing the theological and polemical situation the founders faced: their struggle against Calvinism; against accusations of universalism and Arianism; their eschatological progressivism reflecting their sense of America's manifest destiny as the new world; and their local life situations, such as their own spiritual struggles, the baptism of a newborn child, personal alliances and disappointments, and their developing responsibilities and leadership roles.

The available materials about John's Gospel are in a variety of formats and genres. In the way of textual studies, we have Alexander Campbell's 1826 translation of the New Testament.[4] In systematics, we have his *Christian System* and Walter Scott's *Gospel Restored.*[5] Polemical items include Thomas Campbell's 1809 *Declaration and Address,* Barton W. Stone's 1804 *Compendious View of the Gospel* (published with the *Last Will and Testament of the Springfield Presbytery*), Stone's *Address to the Christian Churches* and a number of published debates by Alexander Campbell.[6] Nine extant Alexander Campbell manuscripts preserve notes of dozens of early sermons by Thomas Campbell as well as his own.[7] Periodicals to consider include Stone's *Christian Messenger,* Alexander Campbell's *Christian Baptist* and *Millennial Harbinger,* and Walter Scott's *Evangelist* and *Christian.*

I have collected references to the Gospel of John from these sources between 1800 and 1852, using print indexes and online search functions for texts available electronically. I have paid special attention to the unpublished Alexander Campbell manuscripts because of their valuable but hard-to-access information about the topics preached by Thomas and Alexander between 1800 and 1815. In the more than 300 citations to John in my sample, the most frequent citations are to chapters 3 (18.6%), 1 (16%), 17 (14.2%), 6 (9.4%), 20 (8.5%), and 5 (8.2%). (See Appendix, page 293, for entire compilation). This study will examine chapters 20, 17, and 3 in some detail; but first, a word about 1, 6, and 5.

Chapters One, Six, and Five in John

With its emphasis on the Word incarnate, the prominence of John 1 in the early Stone-Campbell Movement is not surprising. References to John 1 are fairly evenly dispersed throughout the sample, whether early or late, regardless of which speaker we examine. This is a natural result of the importance of the chapter to Christian faith in general; but it also reflects the simmering discussion of trinitarian ideas among the reformers and with their opponents who accused them of Unitarianism or Arianism. Stone's 1821 *Address,*[8] for example, contains at least seven references to John 1 as Stone defends his ideas about the nature of the Son. Thomas Campbell preached three times in 1802 on 1:11-12.[9] Campbell's 1839 *Christian System* has twenty references to John 1.[10] Scott's 1852 *To Themelion* refers twice to how the prophets and the Baptist pointed to Jesus.[11]

John 6, with its Bread of Life discourse and subsequent discussions on Jesus' origin and mission, is prominent throughout the founding period. One of the three earliest sermons listed as preached by Thomas Campbell, in 1800 while still in Ireland, was on

John 6:27, "Do not work for the food that perishes."[12] Of particular interest to Stone in 1827 was the question of whether Jesus' statements about believers being drawn to him, and given to him, supported the doctrine of predestination.[13] Scott took up the same topic in 1829.[14] Alexander Campbell attended as well to the latter part of the chapter in his 1839 *Christian System*.[15]

References to John 5 are clustered around the use of 5:39, "Ye search the Scriptures, for in them ye think ye have eternal life," as a motto, "Search the Scriptures." This motto use appears at the head of Stone's 1804 "Compendious view of the Gospel"[16] and six times in Alexander Campbell's 1811 first year of preaching.[17] However, in 1830, Alexander Campbell announced that the grammar of the sentence did not support treating "search" as an imperative, and the motto disappears.[18] Its extinction indicates the exegetical rigor of Campbell's hermeneutic.

Chapters Twenty, Seventeen, and Three in John

John 20 appears very early in our sample, when in 1804 Barton Stone argues from 20:30-31 ("These are written that ye may believe") that the Word has "sufficient evidence in itself" to produce faith.[19] This view of the capacity of the gospel to produce faith was the Reformers' exit from the widely-held Calvinistic view that sinners were incapable of belief unless they were elected to experience new birth from the Holy Spirit. Instead, they understood the gospel itself as having power "sufficient" to produce faith. They are relying here on Scottish common-sense realism's doctrine of the power of testimony to compel faith. For example, Stone says, "The word has sufficient evidence in itself to produce faith."[20] According to Scottish philosophy, one must deliberately ignore testimony to avoid its power to compel belief. So Stone says of John 12:39-40 that those who do not believe have blinded their eyes.[21]

Stone wrote a four-part series of essays on John 20:30-31 in 1827 and published them in the *Christian Messenger* in his series, the "Christian Expositor."[22] In the first article he maintained that the written word is "the cause and foundation of our faith."[23] In the second, he asserted that the object of our faith is that Jesus is the Christ, the son of God.[24] His third essay proves "that the Scriptures afford sufficient evidence of this fact to produce faith."[25] The final essay in the series asserts that "eternal life is the fruit of this faith."[26]

Alexander Campbell in 1824 produced a series of nine, closely-reasoned articles on the work of the Holy Spirit in conversion, the main point of which is that through the word, the Spirit provides sufficient evidence for belief. In the course of this series, he quotes John 20:30-31 to the same effect as we have seen in Stone.[27] Alexander Campbell had preached from John 20:17 in 1809,[28] but the above 1824 use is the first instance of his employing 20:30-31 in the same way Stone had applied it previously. Scott makes virtually the same use of the passage as early as 1823 and as late as 1852.[29]

Thus, using John 20:30-31 to teach that persons come to belief through the preaching of the word instead of at the mourner's bench is a consistent thread in our sample. No longer should Christian preachers urge persons to pray in agony for the gift of the power to believe. The preacher, rather, should explain the gospel clearly and remove irrational barriers to understanding it. The preacher's work, therefore, is expository before it is motivational.

John 17 appears earliest in our sample in a list of sermons by Thomas Campbell, preaching from 17:3 ("This is eternal life, that they may know you.") in 1802, then again in 1805 and 1806.[30] Alexander Campbell repeated this same text in a sermon in 1809.[31] Meanwhile, Stone uses 17:17, "Sanctify them through thy truth; thy word is truth," and 17:20, "Those who will believe in me through their word," in his 1804 *Address to the Christian Churches* to argue that the word is the cause of belief.[32] In 1809, Thomas Campbell urged the readers of the *Declaration and Address* to heed the "last and ardent prayers" of the Savior for the unity of the church.[33] In 1824, Thomas quoted 17:17-20 in an article in the *Christian Baptist* in support of the statement that "both the beginning and progress of Messiah's kingdom are ascribed to the word."[34] The "unity prayer" theme and the "believe through their word theme" are united when Alexander Campbell discussed 17:20 in 1825 in the third "Restoration of the Ancient Order of Things." He said, "The word of the Apostles, the unity of those who believe it, and the conviction of the world are here inseparably associated."[35] In 1839 Thomas Campbell's two-part essay on "Christian Union"[36] includes this striking sequence:

> Indeed, Is not this the very thing that is wanting in order to restore the churches to the enjoyment of the Apostles' doctrine, and fellowship; in holy unity, unanimity, and cooperation? which never can be till they all speak the same thing, and so be perfectly joined together in the same mind and in the same judgment. And this never can be, till they all speak the dictations of the Holy Spirit, as delivered by the holy Apostles and Prophets. And, upon the whole, would not such an exhibition of Christianity answer all the purposes for which it was divinely intended; namely, the holiness and happiness of the believing and obedient subjects; and through them, the conversion of the world? See John xvii. 20, 23.[37]

In 1844 Walter Scott published an essay on "Union" in his *Protestant Unionist* with "That they all may be one" as the head-note on the first page. The essay contemplates whether Jesus' prayer for unity failed to be answered, in view of the imperfection of the unity of the visible church. Scott says the prayer has been answered in the unity of Christian character, which, he hopes, "will lead at last to unity or communion, and God's people will thus become one finally, both in character and incorporation." In the mean time, he says, "we must love one another."[38]

Thus, John 17 was used to address both prongs of the ministry dilemma faced by the Reformers. They found in it both the power of the word to bring sinners to belief and a grand vision of the unity of believers.

John 3 is the most frequently cited chapter of John's Gospel among the early

Stone-Campbell Movement leaders. We know that Thomas preached a sermon on 3:16 in 1804 in Ireland,[39] while in the same year in the United States, Stone cited the chapter at least eight times (3:3, 16, 17, 18, 27, 34, 35, 36) in his "Compendious View of the Gospel," addressing such points as man's need for regeneration, God's love, the role of Christ as the savior of the world, and the dependence of faith on the word.[40] Stone also refers three times in his 1821 *Address to the Christian Churches* to this chapter, citing 3:5 on regeneration as the work of God, 3:16 and 18 on Christ as the only-begotten Son, and 3:36 on spiritual life as the fruit of faith.[41]

Alexander Campbell's Use of John 3: A Case Study

John Mark Hicks has pointed out in his "Campbell and the Design of Baptism" that Alexander Campbell's views on baptism were not static between 1809 and 1828. He says Campbell "moved from Presbyterian (1809) to Baptist (1812), then to modified Baptist (1823), and finally to his mature view of the ancient gospel (1828)."[42] These adjustments can be illustrated by observing his use of material from John 3.

On November 4, 1810, Alexander Campbell preached a sermon on John 3:3 which he wrote out in detail in the Manuscript E.[43] The text is quoted as, "Except a man be born again he cannot see the Kingdom of God." His view of conversion is still thoroughly Presbyterian. He begins with the importance of the subject, "upon the true and correct knowledge of which much of our peace and happiness depend, and without the experimental knowledge of which we cannot be saved." His first point, defining new birth, says, "Thus when the grace of God changes the sinner's hear." Obedience occurs after regeneration: "As when a living child is born it will certainly move and act; so when the sinner is born again he will repent, believe, love, obey, and worship." He defines regeneration as "changes wrought by the power of the Holy spirit, upon the understanding, will, and affection of a sinner which is the commencement of a new kind of life: and which gives a new Direction to the judgment, Desires, pursuits, and conduct." And what of baptism? He remarks, "Some say that baptism is here represented and/or the emblem of the new birth. Baptism is the outward sign of regeneration, but not Regenerations itself." He concludes by urging unregenerate persons to pray with the Psalmist for a clean heart, and encouraging believers to be "renewed more and more."

Two years later, on October 12, 1812, after the birth of his first child and his own immersion, Campbell preached a sermon on John 3:18-21 regarding the mission of Jesus to give light to the world.[44] After discussing why Jesus came (to save the world) and how Jesus accomplishes this errand (to give light to those in darkness), he considers the question "How does it then come to pass that so many of the sons of men are still condemned, shut up in darkness, hear not his voice, and are lost…and perish eternally?" He answers that it is because they "shut their eyes" against the light, "rejected his testimony and so became more miserable than if the light had never shone." But "those who received his testimony are and were saved." He ends the sermon by an "address to all who hear": "God now speaketh to all men by his son." To those who are "complaining" for want of light, and to those who do not desire it "above all things," he says "love addresses" them: "walk while you have the light." He does not mention baptism in the sermon; but clearly his view of regeneration has changed.

The next appearance of John 3 in Campbell is in the MacCalla debate, after a complete re-study of the design of baptism, including discussions with Scott and Thomas Campbell over a tract by Henry Errett, a Scotch Baptist in New York.[45] For the first time, the story of Nicodemus is included in passages about baptism. "He placeth baptism on the right hand of faith," Campbell asserts, continuing, "Again, he tells Nicodemus, that 'except a man be born of water and of the spirit, he cannot enter into the kingdom of God.'"[46] As Hicks has pointed out, Campbell's idea of baptism in the MacCalla debate distinguishes between the "real" remission of sins at the point of belief, and the "formal" or "personal" remission when the believer receives through baptism as God's assuring pledge.[47]

In January 7, 1828, Campbell mentions John 3:5 in his *Christian Baptist* series on the ancient gospel, as he is discussing immersion as the "bath of regeneration."[48] Seeing in baptism the antitype of the laver in the Tabernacle, he takes what Hicks calls his "mature" position, that baptism is the objective ground of assurance for the believer.[49] Campbell encourages his readers to meditate on John 3:5 in conjunction with Ephesians 5:26, Titus 1:5, and Hebrews 10:23.[50]

Conclusion

So we see that the great Restoration themes of the Word, belief, and the unity of believers are mirrored by the use of John's Gospel in the preaching and writing of early Stone-Campbell Restoration Movement leaders to empower their hearers to believe the Word that provides the basis for faith and for the union of believers.

We have heard as early as 1804 from Barton Stone a characteristically Scottish Common-Sense reading of John 20:30-31 that the word of the Gospel is sufficient to produce belief. Clearly this emphasis arises from the ministry need to rescue himself and others from the soteriological impasse which Calvinism presented on the frontier. From the Campbells, beginning as early as the *Declaration and Address* (1809), we consistently hear from them, as well as from Stone and Scott, the use of John 17 to emphasize Christian unity, not as an end in itself, but for its apologetic and evangelistic power. What is unmistakably clear is that their emphasis on John 17 and John 20 is related to their evangelistic vision in their historical and theological setting.

If we consider our own setting, and ponder how this Gospel will speak to our time, we might do well to observe the powerful motive for unity to be gained from a desire for ministry together. In an ever more pluralistic global society, our task is to bear witness to the uniqueness and Lordship of Jesus Christ, to serve the poor, and to form authentic Christian community. More than ever we need one another to accomplish our task.

Notes

[1]David I. McWhirter, *An Index to the Millennial Harbinger* (Joplin, Mo.: College Press, 1981).

[2]Raymond Person, Jr., and M. Eugene Boring, "Appendix I: Christian System Scripture Index," in Eugene Boring, "Forming a Tradition: Alexander Campbell and Scripture," *Disciples Theological Digest* 2 (1988): 55-59.

[3]Anthony Dunnavant proposes a model in which mission is the substrate for the other three RM themes. See his "Evangelization and Eschatology: Lost Link in the Disciples Tradition," *Lexington Theological Quarterly* 28.1 (Spring 1993): 43-54; and see Mark Toulouse on Dunnavant in *Joined in Discipleship*, rev. ed. (St. Louis: Chalice, 1997): 10-11, 15, n. 13. Lester has connected the American Restoration Movement with ecumenical-evangelical revivalism in Ireland. See Hiram Lester, "The Form and Function of the Declaration and Address" in *The Quest for Unity, Peace, and Purity in Thomas Campbell's Declaration and Address*, ed. Thomas Olbricht and Hans Rollmann (Lanham, Md.: Scarecrow, 2000): 173-192.

[4]*The Sacred Writings of the Apostles and Evangelists of Jesus Christ, Commonly Styled the New Testament....* (Buffaloe, Va.: A. Campbell, 1826).

[5]*The Christian System, in Reference to the Union of Christians, and a Restoration of Primitive Christianity, as Plead in the Current Reformation*, 2nd ed. (Pittsburg, Penn.: Forrester & Campbell, 1839); Walter Scott, *The Gospel Restored, a discourse...the Evangelist for the current year* (Cincinnati, Oh.: O. H. Donogh, 1836).

[6]For the *Declaration and Address*, see the critical text in Olbricht and Rollman (2000); Stone's *Compendious View of the Gospel* was published with *An Apology for Renouncing the Jurisdiction of the Synod of Kentucky* (Lexington, Ky.: Joseph Charles, 1804); *Address to the Christian Churches in Kentucky Tennessee, and Ohio on Several Important Doctrines of Religion*, 2nd ed. (Lexington, Ky.: author, 1821).

[7]The manuscripts and their microfilm versions are described in the introduction to Carisse Mickey Berryhill, "Descriptive Guide to Eight Early Alexander Campbell Manuscripts" (Unpublished Guided Research paper; Harding University Graduate School, 2000) available at http://www.mun.ca/ rels/rest-mov/texts/acampbell/acm/ACM01.HTM.

[8]Barton W. Stone, *Address to Christian Churches,* 2nd ed. (Lexington, Ky.: author, 1821).

[9]Alexander Campbell, Untitled list of sermons preached by Thomas Campbell, Ms. L, p. 371.

[10]Person and Boring, "Appendix I," p. 56.

[11]Walter Scott. *TO THEMELION: The Union of Christians on Christian Principles* (Bethany, Cincinnati, Lexington: C. A. Morgan, 1852): 9, 20.

[12]Alexander Campbell, Ms. L, p. 371.

[13]Barton W Stone, "Christian Expositor Series: John 6:37-40," *Christian Messenger* 1 (1826-27): 253-256.

[14]Walter Scott, "Election – No. IV," *Christian Baptist* 7 (October 1829): 596.

[15]Campbell, *Christian System,* pp. 43, 128, 273.

[16]Barton Stone, "Compendious View of the Gospel," 61.

[17]Alexander Campbell's Ms. B, p. 167, lists sermons on this passage delivered on September 23, 1811, and October 7, 1811; Ms. D, p. 99, adds January 20 and February 19, 1811; Ms. D, p. 73, has a sermon on this text dated 1811; and Ms. L, p. 377, adds February 19, 1811.

[18]Alexander Campbell, "Samuel Roger's and Dr. Wilson's Mount Pleasant (Missouri) Circular: Examined as Coming from the Vantage Ground; and Andrew Fuller's Regenerated Unbeliever: with Strictures on Text-Preaching," *Millennial Harbinger* (1830): 21.

[19]Stone, "Compendious View," p. 206.

[20]Ibid.

[21]Stone, "Compendious View," p. 217.

[22]Barton W. Stone, "Christian Expositor: John 20:30-31," *Christian Messenger* 1 (1826-27): 125-132, 151-155, 174-177, 199-204.

[23]Barton W. Stone, "Christian Expositor: John 20:30-31," *Christian Messenger* 1 (1826-27): 126.

[24]Ibid., pp. 126, 152.

[25]Ibid., pp. 126, 177.

[26]Ibid., pp. 126, 199.

[27]See, for example, Alexander Campbell, "Essays on the Work of the Holy Spirit in the Salvation of Men, No. 4," *Christian Baptist* 2.4 (November 1, 1824): 103.

[28]The sermon is recorded in Alexander Campbell's Ms. E, p.18.

[29]Walter Scott, "On Teaching Christianity—No. I" *Christian Baptist* 1.2 (September 1, 1823): 11; "On Teaching Christianity—No. II" *Christian Baptist* 1 no. 4 (November 1, 1823): 24; *TO THEME-LION; the Union of Christians on Christian Principles* (Bethany, Cincinnati, Lexington: C. A. Morgan & Co., 1852): 19, 25.

[30]This list of his father's sermons was written by Alexander in Ms. L, p. 371.

[31]Ms. E, p. 17.

[32]Stone, *Address*, pp. 61, 82.

[33]Thomas Campbell, *Declaration and Address*, p. 13.

[34]Thomas Campbell, "To the Editor of the Christian Baptist," *Christian Baptist* 1. 2 (June 7, 1824): 65.

[35]Alexander Campbell, "Restoration of the Ancient Order of Things." *Christian Baptist* 2. 9 (April 4, 1825): 139.

[36]Thomas Campbell, "Christian Union," *Millennial Harbinger* (1839): 134-144; 155-164.

[37]Ibid., p. 144.

[38]Walter Scott, "Union," *Protestant Unionist* 1 (1844): 1.

[39]Alexander Campbell, Ms. L, 371.

[40]Barton W. Stone, *Compendious View*, pp. 192, 193, 194, 195, 196, 198, 206, 214.

[41]Barton W. Stone, *Address to the Christian Churches,* pp. 82, 19, 87.

[42]John Mark Hicks, "Campbell and the Design of Baptism," (November 21, 2000) is published in two parts on his website http://johnmarkhicks.faithsite.com/content.asp?ListSG=419. The quotation appears at the end of Part 2 at http://johnmarkhicks.faithsite.com/content.asp?CID=10074 (accessed April 2, 2006).

[43]Alexander Campbell, Ms. E, 35-39. For manuscript locations and films, see note 7, above.

[44]Ms. 322, 5. For manuscript locations and films, see note 7, above.

[45]Hicks, "Campbell and the Design of Baptism, Part 1." Http://johnmarkhicks.faithsite.com /content.asp?CID=10075.

[46]Alexander Campbell, *A Debate on Christian Baptism* (Buffaloe, VA: author, 1824): 100, 114.

[47]Hicks, "Campbell and the Design of Baptism, Part 1." Http://johnmarkhicks.faithsite.com /content.asp?CID=10075.

[48]Alexander Campbell, "Ancient Gospel. No. 1: Baptism," *Christian Baptist* 5.6 (January 7, 1828):402.

[49]Hicks, "Campbell and the Design of Baptism, Part 1." Http://johnmarkhicks.faithsite.com /content.asp?CID=10075.

[50]Alexander Campbell, *Christian Baptist* 5.6 (January 7, 1828): 402.

6

WORD CHRISTOLOGY IN THE GOSPEL OF JOHN

Brian D. Johnson

"In the beginning was the Word."[1]

T he first phrase of the Gospel of John opens a panoramic view of time, suggesting that the concerns of the Gospel's author are much wider than the earthly life span of Jesus. This study will suggest that when the author of the Gospel of John presents Jesus as the Divine, pre-existent Word, he is presenting a view of reality and particularly of Jesus' relationship to reality that is consistent with the person of God. This makes it possible for the person of God to be revealed to those who will trust fully in this Jesus. Jesus is the "truth" in the sense that he presents for those who will believe in him a way of knowing reality.

In the earliest history of the Stone-Campbell Movement, Christology was an important concern, however Word Christology was not the normal way of approaching this subject. Instead, the thinkers in the early Stone-Campbell movement seemed to focus upon the Word as the written Word while Christology is expressed in the statement "Jesus is the Christ, the son of God."[2] The idea of the Word was limited to the written Word of God through which one could come to know the truth.

Part one of this study will briefly survey Stone-Campbell treatments of Word Christology, but it will turn quickly to recent discussions of the nature of knowledge to which Word Christology can make a positive contribution. For the Gospel of John, Word Christology expresses a much wider concern than simply seeing the Word as written Scripture. Because Jesus is the Word, he provides the fullest expression of God made known to humans. It is Jesus as the Word, who reveals God, and who makes it possible to know God. This will be demonstrated in the final section of this study.

However, before that, this study will interact with two recent contributions from evangelical scholars, both of whom focus on the significance of Word Christology to show how Word Christology can be profitable in discussion of communication and epistemology. Further, it will be shown that Word Christology in the Gospel of John provides a useful framework for contemporary discussion of correct of language and communication. This discussion has broad implications for the Stone-Campbell Restoration Movement as well as for scholarship in general.

Word Christology in the Stone-Campbell Movement

The prologue of the Gospel of John has not played as large a role as has other parts in the formation of doctrine in the Stone-Campbell Restoration Movement. The prayer of Jesus in John 17 and the Nicodemus Discourse in John 3:3-5 from have been much more central in the movement.[3] The "Word of God" was central, but it was the *written* Word of God in Scripture that was emphasized. If the purpose of the movement could be characterized as "Unity in Truth," the written Word of God was the medium of that truth. Furthermore, the means by which this truth was accessible was through a "common sense," unbiased reading of Scripture.[4] In Thomas Campbell's *Declaration and Address*, for example, the phrases "Divine word," "the Word of God," and simply "the word" are used several times, but in every case they refer to the written word of the Bible. For example early in the Declaration and Address the statement is made: "Taking the *Divine* word alone for our rule; the Holy Spirit for our teacher and guide, to lead us into all truth; and Christ alone, as exhibited in the word, for our salvation."[5]

This Word of God is equated with the authority of Jesus, but a Word Christology *per se* is not developed. Later in the *Declaration and Address*, Thomas Campbell says: "With you all we desire to unite in the bonds of an entire Christian unity—Christ alone being the *head*, the center, his word the *rule*."[6]

In a later period, when B. W. Johnson wrote *The People's New Testament*, he comments on the concept of the Word in John 1.

> God exhibits his creative power through the Word, and manifests his will through the Word. There are mysteries belonging to the divine nature and to the relation between the Son and the Father that we have to wait for eternity to solve. They are too deep for human solution, but this is clear: that God creates and speaks to man through the Word. As we clothe *our* thoughts in words, God reveals his will by the Word, and when that Word is clothed in flesh, as the Teacher of men, we recognize it as Jesus Christ.[7]

Johnson does recognize the communicative nature of Jesus as the Word but fails to deal with how this takes place: "They are too deep for human solution." Later in this chapter Johnson comments on John 1:18: "But he was manifested as the Word, and at last the 'only begotten Son hath declared him.'" While this is correct, Johnson is not interested in developing an advanced theory of how this "manifestation" took place, or of the implications and significance of this for how people come to know God. Thus, Word Christology was not highly developed in the early history of the Stone-Campbell Movement, nor did it play a central role in the formation of doctrine.

More recently, however, a discussion within the Stone-Campbell Movement makes the development of Word Christology crucial. Since the inception of the *Stone-Campbell Journal,* one of its hallmarks has been discussion of epistemology and more particularly the impact postmodernism is having upon the traditional formulations of the movement.[8] The inaugural issue of the *SCJ* features an article by John Castelein, "Can the Restoration Movement Plea Survive If Belief in Objective Truth Is Abandonded?"[9] This article was, in part, an invitation to establish a dialogue. The second issue of the *SCJ* included an article by Thomas Scott Caulley: "'Truth on the Slant': Towards a Restoration Biblical Studies for the Next Generation."[10] Caulley suggests a "hermeneutic of grace" as the way forward for Stone-Campbell biblical studies to which he ties to the idea of *agape.*[11] This is similar to the approach taken by Kevin Vanhoozer, one of the two authors to be featured in Part two of this study.

In the third issue of *SCJ,* Philip D. Kenneson, one of the scholars who received attention in Castelein's article accepted his invitation to dialogue and wrote, "Can the Christian Faith Survive if Belief in Objective Truth Is Abandoned? A Reply to John Castelein."[12] In answering "yes" to the question, Kenneson explains that "objective truth" is a recent philosophical concept: "If a plausible argument can be made that the church had no such concept for the first eighteen centuries of its existence, then what grounds would Christians…have for believing that the contemporary church could not exist without it?"[13] Kenneson argues that the concept of objective truth carries with it a context of cultural change, particularly regarding the nature of truth. Is labeling "truth" objective, a way of "suggesting that there are different kinds of truth?"[14] He further discusses metaphors regarding truth and knowledge and the way they can be helpful or harmful. Finally, he suggests that a concept of intersubjectivity might be helpful as a concept in understanding the way we come to truth.

Thus, the Stone-Campbell Movement currently is engaged in questions about the nature of truth and knowledge. From the beginning, though, it has been influenced by the philosophical questions current in its surrounding culture, Common-Sense Realism, Modernism, or a Poststructuralist/Deconstructionist philosophy. This is positive in that the movement does not remain stagnant in past notions. Negatively, the movement appears too easily affected by cultural whims in approaches to knowledge. Is it possible to present a consistent view of knowledge that is not is not subject to ever-shifting philosophical perspectives? This study suggests that Word Christology in the Gospel of John can make a fruitful contribution to this discussion as well as provide a foundation on which to build a stable epistemology.

Two Recent Contributions to Word Christology[15]

Kevin Vanhoozer and Robert Gundry are evangelical authors who have made significant contributions to understanding Word Christology in John's Gospel. Vanhoozer, a theologian and philosopher, employs Jesus as the Word to provide a real alternative to postmodern pessimism about the possibility of communication.[16] Gundry, a New Testament scholar, uses Word Christology to provide a cultural critique of North American Evangelical Christianity, suggesting that now is the time for the church in North America and particularly its academics ("cultural elites") to begin to take the message of the Gospel of John seriously.[17] Along the way, however, he makes some meaningful observations about John's presentation about the use of language.

Despite being the later publication, Gundry's contribution precedes Vanhoozer's logically. His biblical understanding of Word Christology is foundational for Vanhoozer, not surprisingly, since Vanhoozer was once Gundry's student.[18] In his dedication, Vanhoozer refers to Gundry as "scholar, teacher, mentor, friend." So in regarding Vanhoozer as Gundry's Telemachus, his use of Word Christology is influenced by Gundry. Thus, Gundry will be summarized first.

Robert Gundry

Gundry argues that the message of the Gospel of John is especially pertinent for North American Evangelicals and particularly for that group he calls North American Evangelicalism's "elites". He presents this argument in three parts. First, in his chapter entitled, "Jesus the Word," Gundry traces the use of "word" throughout the Gospel. In the second chapter Gundry attempts to show that John was a sectarian. The third chapter is a cultural critique, both apt and timely.[19]

Gundry begins his argument in his first chapter by noting that several scholars have suggested the prologue of the Gospel of John is a later addition, and even if not, the introduction of the word (logos) does not seem to carry over to the rest of the Gospel. As Gundry notes, "logos never recurs as a title."[20] So it might be asked if there is a Word Christology in the Gospel of John, or if it would be more proper to speak of the Word Christology of the prologue of the Gospel of John. Gundry, however, surveys the language of the Gospel "to show that a Christology of the Word dominates the whole of John's Gospel more than has been recognized before."[21] Gundry's claim is: first, that Word Christology "*dominates,*" and second, that it appears in the whole of John's Gospel.

Gundry argues that John's Gospel emphasizes the words of Jesus. When compared with the Synoptic accounts of the same events, the long discourses expand Jesus' teaching.[22] Gundry also examines the vocabulary of the words *rhēmata* and *logos* in both the singular and the plural forms as they refer to the "words" or "word" Jesus speaks, noting that these terms are also used to refer to Jesus speaking the word or words of God.[23] Additionally, Gundry notes the use of *to speak* (*laleo*) in John's Gospel in reference to Jesus' speech.[24] Gundry states:

John has gone far out of his way to multiply references to Jesus' words qua words…and to concentrate them primarily into the singular of logos and thus line them up with Jesus the logos. The words that Jesus speaks, he speaks as the Word; and since he speaks as the Word, the plurality of his words constitutes the singularity of his word, a reminder of who he is. And since as the Word he was with God in the beginning, and was God, his word is at one and the same time God's word. Thus the rest of the Fourth Gospel dovetails with the Prologue.[25]

Gundry also shows that the word *commandment* (*entolē*) in John's Gospel always refers to Jesus' commandments rather than the Old Testament commandments.[26] This underlines the special, authoritative, quality of Jesus' words.

Gundry then carefully examines individual pericopae to demonstrate that Jesus is presented as the one doing the majority of the speaking in the Gospel of John. This speech is Divine in origin, and this speech points to Jesus' identity. Gundry's treatment of John 8:31-32 is a prime example of his thorough argument. Here, Jesus says to those Jews who have believed in him, "If you abide in my word (logos), you are truly my disciples, and you will know the truth, and the truth will set you free."[27] Gundry notes that the Gospel elsewhere speaks of abiding in Jesus (15:4-7), and further in just a few verses later in 8.36 Jesus says "If therefore the Son sets you free" (8:36)" Gundry writes, "Jesus the Son of God the Father (v. 38) is the truth revealed in Jesus' word, i.e. Jesus as the Word."[28]

Gundry's overall conclusions are convincing:

> Throughout the Gospel of John, then, Jesus the Word gives voice to the words that God his Father gave him to speak….The words that the Father has given him to speak deal almost entirely with Jesus himself….The proclaimer and the proclaimed have also become one and the same. In John, Jesus is what is spoken even as he does the speaking.[29]

The identification between the Son and Father throughout John's Gospel adds weight to the evidence that Jesus is both one revealing and the one revealed. This crucial revelatory role receives further significance when paired with the fact that truth is also presented in John's Gospel as residing solely in Jesus. Gundry is correct, then, that Word Christology permeates John's Gospel. Word Christology also incarnates the author's view of truth and the means by people can know God.

Kevin Vanhoozer

Vanhoozer's *Is there a Meaning in this Text?* has a broader concern than Gundry. However, a significant element of Vanhoozer's argument is built upon the concept of Word Christology. Central to Vanhoozer's purpose is attempting to deal honestly with postmodern claims regarding language. In his introduction he writes, "It would be no exaggeration to say that language has become the preeminent problem of twentieth-century philosophy."[30] The strength of Vanhoozer's approach is that he first attempts to understand poststructuralist and deconstructionists sympathetically, on their own terms. He strengthens his promotion of a sympathetic hermeneutic by applying this hermeneutic himself.[31]

In the second half of his volume, "Redoing Interpretation," Vanhoozer builds on this positive contribution. He suggests that it is possible to present a philosophically sound position where the author is given authority in issues of meaning. He then proposes the use of speech acts as a useful way to understand the connection of utterances to reality. Finally, he proposes an "ethical" view of reading, which takes the role of the reader seriously, yet holds the reader to a standard of interpretive rigor. Vanhoozer's hermeneutic of love rather than suspicion invests the reader with the responsibility to treat the interpretive process seriously.

This approach is thoroughly theistic, not only in the sense of being acceptable to a traditional theist but also in the sense that Vanhoozer grounds this approach in the person and nature of the Trinity. This is how Word Christology becomes an important element of Vanhoozer's suggestions. My purpose is not to deal with Vanhoozer's important book full but only those places where Word Christology impacts his presentation.

Vanhoozer's survey of deconstructionist interpretation regarding Derrida notes his criticism of logocentrism, which Vanhoozer defines as "the belief that there is some stable point outside language—reason, revelation, Platonic Ideas—from which one can ensure that one's words, as well as the whole system of distinctions that order our experience, correspond to the world."[32] Observe that revelation, which would seem to require language, is placed "outside language." We must be very careful here not to confuse the idea of language as necessary for communication with one, particular language-system. According to Vanhoozer, Derrida understands logocentricism as an error extending back to the time of Plato. Vanhoozer shows that Plato thought "that there is a realm of truths…to which reason has direct access without having to go through language."[33] Plato, therefore, seems to present language as a kind of "second best," but is it even possible to interact with reality in any meaningful way that does not include language? What kind of alternative to language are we to imagine existing? For Derrida and other deconstructionists the idea of the universality of language is significant and influences their understanding of the necessity of language in mediating reason and really anything else. Vanhoozer suggests that "Derrida locates the origin of logocentrism in Plato's preference for speech as the paradigm for the way language and thought are related to the world."[34]

Vanhoozer goes on to quote Richard Rorty: "Can the ubiquity of language ever really be taken seriously," and then suggests, "Rorty here agrees with Derrida: *we can never break out of or rise above language to make sure that our words correspond to the world.*"[35] Here deconstructionists have a valid point. Though the implications they draw are questionable from a theistic standpoint, the universal nature of language does seem to fit reality. Word Christology corrects the deconstructionist's skepticism regarding the ability of people to "rise above language" to assess the world they in which they live.

Vanhoozer in summarizing this section writes, "What I wish to highlight in this account of deconstruction is the connection between the undoing of the author and the undoing of the metaphysical dimension of theology and philosophy. In both cases, what is undone is the claim that language corresponds to some non-linguistic presence."[36] For the deconstructionist the universality of language points to the arbitrary "grasp of reality."[37] If all people have is language, and if language is no more grounded in the transcendent than other cultural institutions, then language is an arbitrary way to connect with reality. Vanhoozer shows how this arbitrariness leads to an interpretive agnosticism: "The claim to see texts are they are is illusory. Every reader sees what one can see from one's own position in society, space, and time."[38] The Gospel of John, however, provides, a transcendent view.

At the very end of the first section of his book, Vanhoozer points out this connection:

> The ethics of deconstruction follows, I believe, from its tacit theology: to be exact, from its understanding of transcendence and immanence. On the one hand, the otherness of the text transcends all attempts to know it; on the other hand, all attempts at knowledge are immanent, 'from below,' driven by local interests and entangled in political struggles.[39]

In this Vanhoozer summarizes the implications for theology of the position he has been examining, but he also points to the solution he will propose in the second half of his book. Transcendence provides the view from outside, and God becoming immanent makes this outsider view available to humans. In other words, central to this program is the doctrine of the pre-existent Word becoming flesh.

Vanhoozer begins his constructive approach to interpretation in the second half of his volume by confronting the deconstructionist view that language is an arbitrary system of signs: "Sentences are not simply products of a language system, however, mere blips of an impersonal code, but rather meaningful personal actions."[40] Vanhoozer depends on speech-act theory, but he becomes vague regarding the nature of language, saying merely that language "is a gift of God."[41] This is true, but isn't language a constituent part of reality because it is a part of God's very nature? Vanhoozer introduces his dependence on Word Christology at this point: "God's Word was made flesh. *God's Word is thus something that God says, something that God does, and something that God is.*"[42] This last point is crucial for raising language above the immanent to the transcendent.

For Vanhoozer Scripture is a Divine speech act.[43] He argues that the Holy Spirit continues mediated its meaning. In sum, Vanhoozer's Trinitarian hermeneutic is that God the Father is revealed by Jesus, the Word Incarnate, and this revelation is mediated through the Holy Spirit.[44] This is a powerful paradigm, providing a way for the Theist to defend meaning. Vanhoozer summarizes his conclusions: "*In sum, the Word of God for today (significance) is a function of the Word of God in the text (meaning), which in turn is a witness to the living and eternal Word of God in the Trinity (referent).*"[45]

Word Christology as a Means of Communication

If Gundry is correct that Word Christology pervades the entirety of the Gospel of John, and if Vanhoozer's conclusions that Word Christology provides a way to overcome the difficulties presented in the deconstructionist's view of language, then the Gospel of John's Word Christology is crucial today for presenting a positive way of coming to knowledge and taking part in meaningful communication.

In discussing Vanhoozer's book above, it has been observed that one characteristic of deconstructionism is the concept of the inescapable nature of language. According to the deconstructionist, there is no place outside of language from which to "objectively" judge the fit of language to reality. Deconstructionists have an important point here, but a point with much different implications for the Christian Theist. In this section, I will argue that John's Word Christology provides a meaningful way to discuss not only the universal nature of language, but the necessity of meaningful communication.[46]

The Debate about Language and Reality

The Gospel's use of "truth" has long been debated.[47] The heavy use of juridical language in John's Gospel (*judge*, *krino*, and its cognates; *witness*, *martur*, and its cognates) concerns the way one comes to know the "truth."[48] Passages like John 16:29-31 connect sight to belief and belief to knowledge. Passages like John 5:31-40 express the role of testimony in coming to knowledge about Jesus. Finally, the Thomas account in John 20:24-29, and continuing into the thesis statement of the Gospel (20:30-31), concerns not only how the apostles will come to true belief but also how those who will believe without sight. Passages like these demonstrate the Gospel of John develops a nuanced theory of knowledge.

Deconstructionists recognize the universal nature of language but conclude from this that truth is thereby inaccessible. For example, Kenneson, paraphrasing Rorty, writes, "To say that truth is not out there is simply to say that where there are not sentences there is not truth, that sentences are elements of human languages, and that human languages are human creations."[49] The assumptions in this statement are questionable, specifically the assumption that sentences are more fundamental than human constructions. How would the statement change if language were viewed as constituent of reality?

Word Christology provides a way to talk about language as an absolute rather than as a strictly human production. First, God, by his very nature, is communicative. Second, differing from Vanhoozer,[50] we should recognize a distinction between language as a creative act of God and language as a part of God's very nature.

When I speak of language, I am not speaking of an individual system. Rather, language is a conscious act that combines syntax and content to create meaning. Second, consciousness is constituent of God. God is communicative by his very nature. If communication is a part of God's nature then it is not created by God. The corollary (and perhaps the proof of this) is that the Word (in its Christological sense) is not created. It is the preexistent Word. God did not create language, it is integral to his very nature, and therefore is an integral part of reality.

Within a Theistic worldview, then, God is constituent of reality. For the Theist, if there is no God, there is no reality. Therefore, language as we have defined is constituent of reality. For the Theist no possible reality exists without language. Derrida seems to recognize this: "Language has started without us, in us and before us. This is what theology calls God."[51] While this is certainly a very narrow view of God, Derrida has made a correct observation about the role of language in the shape of reality. Inasmuch as language is God's nature, it is reflected in the nature of things. Compare to this as well Rorty's notion of the "ubiquity of language." If reality, because it is God's creation is necessarily comprised of language, this ubiquity should not surprise us, but instead should be expected.

A theist using the conclusions of Rorty or Derrida is put in an awkward position. Kenneson paraphrases a statement of Rorty's in an attempt to bring his claim into a theistic world view (Kenneson's additions are in brackets):

> Truth cannot be out there—cannot exist independently of the human mind-because sentences cannot so exist, or be out there. The world [and God are] out there, but descriptions of the world [and God are] not. Only descriptions of the world [and God] can be true or false.[52]

Can Rorty's argument and point be applied to a theistic worldview? A statement from Rorty following the one above is telling:

> The suggestion that truth, as well as the world, is out there is a legacy of an age in which the world was seen as the creation of a being who had a language of his own. If we cease to attempt to make sense of the idea of such a nonhuman language, we shall not be tempted to confuse the platitude that the world may cause us to be justified in believing a sentence true with the claim that the world splits itself up, on its own initiative, into sentence-shaped chunks called "facts." But if one clings to the notion of self-subsistent facts, it is easy to start capitalizing the word "truth" and treating it as something identical either with God or with the world as God's project. The one will say, for example, that Truth is great, and will prevail.[53]

I might add that Jesus is "the Truth," or that "the Truth will set you free," or that "my words are Truth." Rorty understands the implications of the ubiquitous nature of language for those who continue to accept the foundation of God's creation of the world. The idea of an absolute contains a necessary, non-human, Divine language as well as a view of the world and reality as God's intended project. A theist might come to the same conclusion as Rorty, but he *cannot* do so from the same starting point or with the same arguments. Rorty understands that if one believes in God ("a being who had a language of his own") then the idea of Truth (with a capital "T") necessarily follows.

It is inappropriate, I would argue, to link the Christian understanding of reality and the nature of knowledge to a postmodern philosophy that at its foundation makes atheistic assumptions. There is Truth "out there" because God is transcendent, and this Truth is communicated through Jesus, the Word.

If it is true that sentences exist only within the finite human mind, then what Rorty is saying is true, but if language exists in the created, human mind and in the very nature of God, and is woven into the warp and woof of reality, then it is not. Truth can correspond to reality and can be expressed (in the mind of God) in a way that can be understood. Human finiteness makes accessing this truth necessarily contingent. But this is where the incarnation is essential to theism and the Christian attempt to make sense of reality. This is a view from "outside" that has been brought "inside."

John's Word Christology

Let us briefly examine Word Christology as it is developed in the Gospel of John to see if it provides any help in this dilemma of language's universal yet seemingly inaccessible nature. The idea of Jesus as the Word is developed in the John's prologue. The eternal nature of the Word being with God and being equivalent to God supports the idea that communication is not a creation of God but is part of his nature, and therefore is eternal (Jn 1:1-2). If Jesus, the Word, preexists then communication preexists as well. This is true not only in the sense that Jesus is the Word or message of God but also in the sense that as a person of the Divine being, he participates in communication within the Divine being.[54]

In John 1:14 the eternal, preexistent, Divine Word is said to have become flesh and to have lived among us; the Word is not only the content of truth but also the means of communicating truth to the human objects of this communication. John 1:18 begins with the assertion that "no one has ever seen God" but then describes the way this one previously introduced as the Word functions on our behalf. The last part of the verse can be translated, "The unique God, the one who is in the Father's side, made him known."

The unusual verb *made him known* (*exegeomai*) used in John 1:18 to describe this activity is the key to understanding Word Christology in the rest of John's Gospel. Jesus is the communication of God, first, because he has access to God. He is able to describe God because he participates in the most intimate way with God. However, by taking on the form by which he can communicate to humankind, he makes God known. The incarnation is the way in which the Divine Word has become human in order to communicate the full reality of God's nature in a way that is comprehensible to us.

Although the Gospel of John leaves the Word theme behind in the prologue, as Gundry has observed, he continues to show the way that Jesus communicates God's truth to us, so that he becomes "*The proclaimer and the proclaimed.*"[55] In John 5:37, within a context dealing with the validity of the testimony regarding Jesus, Jesus accuses those persecuting him by saying they have never heard the Father's voice nor seen him.

He states this in direct contrast to himself, who in fact has not only seen the Father and heard him but even now is speaking on his behalf in order to reveal him. Jesus goes on to say in John 5:38, "And you do not have his *word* remaining in you" (italics mine). The reason for this is that they do not believe the one sent by the Father.

Jesus as the one who "exegetes" the Father can also be seen in a later, where we find Jesus addressing those who will not believe despite what they have seen (Jn 12:37). This group's lack of access to the "truth" is not what prevents them from believing in Jesus. Rather, it their character (Jn 12.42b–43). In John 12:44, Jesus cries out to them beginning with the paradox, "The one believing in me, does not believe in me," but he goes on to say, "rather in the one sending me." He further states, "The one looking at me, looks at the one sending me." Jesus reveals the one who sent him. To look at Jesus is to see the nature and character of the Father. This again shows that Jesus is not only the complete revelation of God but God revealed in a way that can be comprehended.

In John 8:19-20, Jesus had already suggested that knowledge of him is equivalent to knowledge of the Father. In John 14:8-10, he responds to Philip's request to "show us the Father" by answering "After all this time, and you have not known me Philip?" and then further "anyone who has seen me has seen the Father."

The importance of Jesus as the Word is he has the proper access to God. He has seen God, he knows God, and he is able to communicate the truth of God. This fits with the well-known use of testimony in the Gospel of John. One criterion for reliable testimony is appropriate access to what is being witnessed to. A reliable witness not only had access to the even but also can understand the event well enough to explain it. Jesus fits both of these criteria in relation to God. He is "showing" God to humanity.

So, the Gospel of John, by presenting Jesus as the Word, suggests that Jesus is the complete revelation and the perfect means (or medium) by which people can know God. It also suggests that Jesus makes it possible to acquire this knowledge.

Consider further Jesus' statements in John 8. Jesus says to those disputing with him that knowledge of God is only possible through knowledge of Jesus himself. (Jn 8:19) To those who have believed in him he asserts that in order to know the truth, they must remain in his word. (Jn 8:31) Later in this same context he says that they are unable to hear his word because of their status in regard to him (Jn 8:43).

So, not only is Jesus the only one with access to first-hand knowledge about God, and not only is he the only one able to speak the truth about God, but he is also the only one through whom we can have access to this knowledge ourselves. We might say a belief in Jesus makes us able to receive the Word. According to the Gospel of John belief is the proper perspective from which to understand reality. Those who fail to recognize Jesus and fail to trust him, find their view of truth and their grip on reality called into question.

Conclusion

This view of the centrality and inescapability of language makes it necessary for the Christian to see the role of Jesus as the Word to be one of self-disclosure. He is the one who exegetes God for us. Jesus makes the unknowable, knowable; the invisible, seen; but also the unspeakable, speakable. To someone who would make a claim such as, "There is no place to stand and judge this statement as true per se,"[56] I would say that this statement is absolutely not true for a theist who believes in transcendence as the Gospel of John does. Not only has Jesus been with the Father from the beginning, but also has revealed the Father.

Remember where we started? "In the beginning was the Word." God by nature, necessity, and definition has this "view from nowhere," and through Jesus as the Word he has given us access to this knowledge.

Notes

[1]NIV. Scripture quotations throughout are my own translations unless otherwise noted.

[2]M. Eugene Boring, *Disciples and the Bible: A History of Disciples Biblical Interpretation in North America* (St. Louis, Mo.: Chalice, 1997), p. 34.

[3]See for example the Scripture index of Boring, *Disciples*, p. 501. John 3:3-5 and John 17 are the only two passages from the Gospel of John singled out for individual treatment with six references for the former passage and two for the latter.

[4]Boring, *Disciples*, pp. 19-26. See also David L. Little, "Inductive Hermeneutics and the Early Restoration Movement," *Stone-Campbell Journal* 3.1 (Spring 2000): 5-18.

[5]Thomas Campbell, *Declaration and Address*, 2nd ed. (Cincinnati: H. S Bosworth, 1861), p. 27, line 15. Italics mine. <<http://www.mun.ca/rels/restmov/texts/tcampbell/da/DA-2ND.HTM>>

[6]Campbell, *Declaration and Address*, p. 40, line 18. Italics original.

[7]B. W. Johnson, *The People's New Testament* (St. Louis: Christian Publishing, 1886). <<http://www.mun.ca/rels/restmov/texts/bjohnson/ntc3/NTC301.HTM>>

[8]See William R. Baker, "Editor's Preface," *Stone-Campbell Journal* 3.1 (Spring 2000): 1-2.

[9]John Castelein, "Can the Restoration Movement Plea Survive If Belief in Objective Truth Is Abandoned?" *Stone-Campbell Journal* 1.1 (Spring 1998): 27-44.

[10]Thomas Scott Caulley: "'Truth on the Slant': Towards a Restoration Biblical Studies for the Next Generation (1998 Dean E. Walker Lecture)," *SCJ* 1.2 (Fall 1998): 167-185.

[11]Ibid., p. 184.

[12]Philip D. Kenneson, "Can the Christian Faith Survive if Belief in Objective Truth Is Abandoned? A Reply to John Castelein," *Stone-Campbell Journal* 2.1 (Spring 1999): 43-56.

[13]Kenneson, "Christian Faith," p. 45.

[14]Ibid., p. 46.

[15]Probably the most thoroughly argued issue involved in Word Christology among biblical scholars involves the Gospel of John introducing the concept of "the Word." Against which background should his use of this word be understood? My concern is how this thought is developed in the Gospel of John, whatever the initial source may be. It should be noted that Gundry, *Jesus the Word*, p. xvi., also bypasses this discussion.

[16]Kevin Vanhoozer, *Is There a Meaning in this Text?: The Bible, the Reader and the Morality of Literary Knowledge* (Grand Rapids: Zondervan, 1998).

[17]Robert H. Gundry, *Jesus the Word according to John the Sectarian: A Paleofundamentalist Manifesto for Contemporary Evangelicalism, Especially Its Elites, in North America* (Grand Rapids: Eerdmans, 2001).

[18]Gundry, *Jesus the Word*, p. v, dedicates his book to Vanhoozer, a former student, "with large appreciation for the dedication to me of his important book," since Vanhoozer, *Meaning*, p. 5, previously cited him.

[19]Unfortunately, because of the way he has packaged this argument, I am afraid that Gundry's significant observations will be ignored. See Brian Johnson, review of Gundry, *Jesus the Word*, *SCJ* 6.2 (Fall, 2003): 308-310.

[20]Gundry, *Jesus the Word*, p. 1.

[21]Ibid., p. 3.

[22]See also Gary Burge, *The Anointed Community: The Holy Spirit in the Johannine Tradition* (Grand Rapids: Eerdmans, 1987), pp. 74-78.

[23]Gundry, *Jesus the Word*, p. 6.

[24]Ibid., p.11.

[25]Ibid., p.7.

[26]Ibid., p.8.

[27]This is Gundry's translation.

[28]Gundry, *Jesus the Word*, p.30.

[29]Ibid., p 49, italics original

[30]Vanhoozer, *Meaning in This Text*, 17.

[31]On this point and the inconsistency of the deconstructionist's position, see D. A. Carson, *The Gagging of God* (Grand Rapids: Zondervan, 1996), pp. 102-105.

[32]Vanhoozer, *Meaning in This Text*, p.53.

[33]Ibid.

[34]Ibid.

[35]Ibid., p. 55.

[36]Ibid., p. 60.

[37]Ibid., p. 62.

[38]Ibid., p. 151.

[39]Ibid., p. 186.

[40]Ibid., p. 204.

[41]Ibid., p. 205.

[42]Ibid., p. 205.

[43]Ibid., p. 263-265.

[44]Ibid., p. 265.

[45]Ibid., p. 423.

[46]See also James K. A. Smith, *Speech and Theology: Language and the Logic of Incarnation, Radical Orthodoxy* (London: Routledge, 2002), and Mark Jordan, "Words and Word: Incarnation and Signification in Augustine's De doctrina christiana," *Augustinian Studies* 11 (1980): 177-196.

[47]Andrew Lincoln, *Truth on Trial: The Lawsuit Motif in the Fourth Gospel* (Peabody, Mass.: Hendrickson, 2000).

[48]Jn 5:36-40, 7:24, 8:15-16.

[49]Philip D. Kenneson, "There's No Such Thing as Objective Truth, and It's a Good Thing, Too," in *Christian Apologetics in the Postmodern World*, ed.Timothy R. Phillips and Dennis L. Okholm (Downers Grove, Ill.: InterVarsity, 1995), pp. 155-70.

[50]Vanhoozer, *Meaning in This Text,*" is ambiguous on this point. This ambiguity reveals a crucial issue for the validity of his proposal. Early in his book, he states, "In the beginning, God created language; it is his good gift, designed to be enjoyed by this creatures"(p. 31). He returns to this theme later, again calling language a "gift of God" (p. 205). However, in his conclusion dealing with God's Trinitarian nature he writes, "From a Christian perspective, God is first and foremost a communicative agent, one who relates to mankind through words and the Word. Indeed, God's very being is a self-communicative act" (p. 456).

[51]Jacques Derrida, "How to Avoid Speaking: Denials," in *Derrida and Negative Theology*, ed. Harold Coward and Toby Foshay (Albany, N.Y. : State University of New York Press, 1992), p. 99.

[52]Kenneson, "No Such Thing," p. 159, quoting Richard Rorty, *Contingency, Irony, and Solidarity* (Cambridge: Cambridge University Press, 1989), pp. 4-5.

[53]Rorty, *Contingency*, 5.

[54]It could be pointed out that the imagery of "light" here also deals with the issue of knowledge, or things being revealed, as well as the testimony of John as the means of belief, but as this paper is focusing upon the theme of Word, these will not be taken up here.

[55]Gundry, *Jesus the Word*, p. 49.

[56]Kenneson "No Such Thing," p. 167.

7

Unity Christology in John's Gospel

Paul Pollard

Hardly any theme permeates the Gospel of John like that of unity. It is embedded in the very fabric of this gospel, and the case can be argued that "John's Gospel is conceived and developed from the standpoint of Jesus' oneness with the Father.... It is the determining factor in the interpretation of Jesus' words and works, his life and his death."[1] Played out against the unity theme is the theme of disunity, perhaps for the purpose of highlighting the former.

The unity of Jesus with the Father is one of the most profound aspects and is a central theological feature of the Fourth Gospel. The christological character of the oneness motif in the Gospel of John is unique in the New Testament, and this makes it a vital study in its own right. This brief survey will only tap the surface of this broad but crucial theme.

The Unity Theme in John's Prologue: John 1:1-18

John states in the prologue[2] the unity of the Word (*logos*) with God in that the Word is with God and is, in fact, God also (1:1). This unity has existed from before the world was created (1:2). The Gospel does not describe the nature of this unity, only stating its barest essentials. It will remain for him to clarify this relationship as his gospel unfolds.

The unity theme controls the flow of the prologue as indeed it does the entire gospel. John 1:3 sets forth the essential unity of the Word with creation in the sense that all created things came about through him. Pantheism is not in mind but only that all things exist through him. Suggestive of the Genesis creation narratives (Genesis 1-3), light comes into the world *in him* (*en auto*) and brings light to all men (1:4). Light is synonymous with life in the Fourth Gospel and people have life to the degree that they are united to Jesus the life-giving source. To accept Jesus is to accept the light and to reject him is to reject both light and life. In 8:12 he declares himself to be "the light of the world."[3] In regard to discipleship, to walk in darkness indicates that unity with Jesus has been rejected and the way of unbelief has been chosen instead. Light is consistent with doing God's will and being united in his purposes and darkness signifies sin and rejection of light.[4] Both light and darkness have important ethical implications in John's gospel.

John[5] continues with the interjection of John the Baptist and his testimony about Jesus. The Baptist's words indicate a basic unity with the message and work of Jesus but we must wonder if the function of John the Baptist's commendation of Jesus was to deflect a too high view of the Baptist held by some of his own followers. In other words, John the Baptist's words promote his personal unity with the person and work of Jesus and send a message to his followers. However, it was due to a discordant note, a too high view of John that caused it to be inserted as an anti-Baptist polemic in the first place. The Gospel of John wants to convey early on that Jesus as the Logos has no legitimate rivals. Note 1:15 where this is reinforced by John the Baptist's testimony.

Over against the discordant theme of rejection that appears again in 1:10-11, the unity of Jesus with those who believe in him surfaces. The verb *pisteuō*[6] (*believe*) dominates the discussion about relationship with Jesus as the gospel unfolds and is the key to unity with him. As an *inclusio*, belief in Jesus brackets the beginning of the gospel and the end in the great purpose statement of 20:30-31. The classic statement of union with Christ through faith is found in John 3:16. Ernst Käsemann is certainly correct that if the unity of the Son with the Father is the central theme of the Johannine proclamation, then that unity is of necessity also the proper object of faith.[7]

The apex of the unity theme in the prologue emerges in 1:14 with the joining of the *Logos* with flesh in what appears to be an anti-docetic statement. Käsemann is incorrect in his view that the Fourth Gospel represents "naïve docetism" and that John if not a Gnostic was very sympathetic to the Gnostic outlook.[8] The Gospel says that Jesus really did come in the flesh. This will, however, be the great mystery in the ensuing ages as both friend and foe try to sort out the nature of this unity. From Nicea and countless other councils to today, the christological debate surrounding the unity of the human and divine continues unabated. In some way, only known to the mind of God, this unity maintains itself in perfect balance. It is, however, this very unity that causes the greatest disturbance of harmony in the Fourth Gospel, with some denying it and others embracing it. Here again, the crux of the issue in this gospel, at least as far as plot and characterization is concerned, is whether or not Jesus will be accepted as being sent from the

Father and one with him despite his fleshly, earthly appearance and lineage.

A negative note enters near the end of the prologue with reference to the Law. The unity of humanity with the Logos causes an overflowing of his grace upon us in "wave after wave" (1:16). In contrast stands the Law. Just as the Gospel's author previously dispensed with John the Baptist as a discordant rival, it now does the same with the Law. Both grace and truth come from Jesus Christ, now mentioned in this gospel for the first time by this appellation and now identified as being the Logos (1:17). The unity theme is now almost complete in the prologue. It remains only for 1:18 to emphasize a dominating theme that plays out in many ways in the rest of the gospel, namely, that Jesus and his Father are united in being and purpose. The Son is so entwined with the Father's heart that it is the Son and the Son only who truly makes God known. Not John the Baptist, not the Law, nor anything else can do what Jesus can do because of his essential unity with the Father. He surpasses everyone else who might otherwise have been sent. Christ is the only "exegete" of the one whom no one else has ever seen.[9] The superiority of Jesus over other "rivals" is thus demonstrated in the prologue by means of the underlying unity motif that serves as the basic substructure of the gospel.

Unity Christology In the Period of Acceptance: John 1:19-4:54

The unity theme in John's Gospel takes many forms and at times is only implicitly stated. As already observed in the prologue, the unity theme is frequently played off against discordant themes, either consciously or unconsciously to highlight the unity aspect, and this is true in the rest of John 1. For example, in the prologue the statement that "grace and truth came through Jesus," is set against the Law of Moses. The implication being that the Law is inferior to Christ and "grace upon grace" comes to believers who are united with Christ (and not the Law). On the other hand, in 1:45 when Philip evangelizes Nathanael, the Gospel makes clear that in some ways Moses and the prophets are united in their affirmation of Jesus' person and work. The unity of Jesus with the Old Covenant and its teachings are made evident in Nathanael's statement that Jesus is a true Israelite with no guile (1:47), probably referring back to Jacob (Israel) and Jesus as a type of true Israel. In fact, Nathanael calls him "the King of Israel." The unity/disunity theme is nicely capsulated in the Nathanael narrative with the movement from disunity/unbelief (1:46) to unity/belief.

Jesus is not only united with the Father in several ways in the Fourth Gospel, but he is also united with the Holy Spirit, making unity with the Godhead complete. The first example of this is found in a baptismal context (1:19-28). Although not specifically stating that Jesus was baptized, the implication in 1:29-34 is that John baptized Jesus and this coheres with the witness of the Synoptics (Mt 3:13; Mk 1:9-11; Lk 3:21-22). Jesus is baptized, demonstrating not only his unity with God's purposes but also symbolically his connection with those who will be his disciples. Specifically, in 3:22 and 4:1 disciples are united with him in baptism (compare Paul's unity language in Rom 6:5), a baptism that probably looked a lot like John's (see Mt 3:11, *en hudati eis metanoian, in water for repentance*). The testimony of John is that at Jesus' baptism, the Spirit descended from heaven like a dove and remained on him. The image is of the Spirit and Jesus now united just as he is with the Father.

John emphasizes the unity theme in 1:51, thus rounding out the ideas first laid down in the prologue. The co-joining of heaven and earth is found in the person and work of Jesus. The contrast between heaven and earth and the sorting of all the characters in John into two camps—"those from above" and "those from below"—is a well-known feature in John (see for example, 3:6, 31). The unity of heaven and earth is the focus here. Instead of the angels going up and down the ladder as in the Jacob story from Genesis 28:12, the angels are going up and down on the Son of Man. Not only is the title Son of Man important for connecting Jesus to the humankind he came to save, but the angels going up and down on the Son of Man symbolizes the unity and communication from heaven to earth in the person of Jesus. Thus, John closes his opening salvo in showing the supremacy of Jesus over all rivals by underscoring the unity of Jesus with God. It is this unity that highlights his argument throughout the Fourth Gospel and is foundational for his further arguments.

In 3:26–30 John the Baptist again states his inferior status to Jesus and the author follows up on this in 3:31–36 by using the famous above and below language (*ek tēs gēs, from the earth* and *ek tou ouranou, from heaven*) found in the Fourth Gospel. Jesus comes from above and testifies to all that he has seen and heard (but no one accepts this testimony). Along with the theme of rejection, which clearly connects with the prologue, is the idea that God has sent Jesus who has the Spirit without measure. The unity between them is expressed in the love of the Father to him and the placing of all things in his hands. Uniformity of purpose and plan exists between not only the Father and Son but also the Spirit.

By the end of the first main section of John, ending in chapter 4, little controversy has emerged. This will soon change starting in John 5 with the healing of the man at the pool. After this most of the direct expressions of Jesus' oneness with the Father occur in the context of controversy with the authorities.

Unity Christology in the Period of Controversy: John 5–10

The first statement of oneness in the period of controversy (John 5–10) also involves the issue of Jesus' unity with the work of his Father. After the man is healed at the pool on the Sabbath, the Jews began to persecute Jesus. His response was to emphasize how his Father's work and his work were in unison, "My Father works until now and I work" (5:17). Jesus' argument is that he is in union with God when it comes to showing mercy and good works on the Sabbath and his people should be also.

In 5:19–23 Jesus makes several crucial statements that emphasize how closely joined he and the Father are in terms of his doing what he sees the Father doing. He is, in

other words, a carbon copy of the Father as he also states in 5:26 and 5:30. Just as the
Father gives life, so does he. If anyone does not honor the Son they do not honor the
Father (4:23). He cannot do anything on his own and from the Father he receives the
authority to make judgment. Even this authority to judge is carried out only by listening to what the Father says. He does not do his own will but that of the Father
(5:30). There can be no mistake that with these words Jesus intends to convey the total
coherence between himself and the Father. He concludes the defense of his healing on
the Sabbath by pointing to the unity of the testimony about him by John the Baptist,
by the works that he did, by the Father himself and last of all by Moses. As he will often
do, Jesus points to his unity with the Father by emphasizing that the Father "sent him."
This is not only a statement of oneness with the plan and purpose of God but of his
preexistence also argued for in the prologue.

Several texts link the closeness of Jesus and the Father with the "sending" motif. In
John 6 the discussion centers on the bread of heaven (6:32-40) and Jesus as that true
bread which came down. Here the essence of the matter is that Jesus has come down
from heaven not to do his will but the will of the Father who sends him (6:38). His will
and that of the Father are perfect mirror reflections of each other. The symbiotic relationship extends even to the matter of people coming to Jesus. No person can come to
Jesus unless the Father draws that person to Jesus, indicating the complete unity between
Father and Son in every detail (6:44, 65). Not even his teaching is his but comes from
God who sent him (7:16). In 7:28-29, while teaching in the temple in Jerusalem, Jesus
again states that he has not come on his own and that he has been sent. Jesus is vitally
connected to the Father because "I know him," "I am from him" and "he sent me." These
are crucial links in the oneness theme in John—knowing the Father because he was with
him before he came to earth and was sent by him (7:33). As usual, after statements about
his close links with the Father division and animosity follow (7:40-44).

It is interesting that some of the language in John 6 relative to Jesus' midrashic explanation of the true bread connects with later unity language in John 15.[10] In particular 6:56
highlights Jesus' saying that all who eat his flesh and drink his blood "abide in me and I in
them." The unity expressed by the "abide" language here is full orbed in 15:1-10. Just as
the vine and branches represent full and total unity, so in John 6 the partaking of the flesh
and blood of Jesus accomplishes the same purpose. The unity in John 6 is so perfect that
those who partake of Jesus' flesh and blood will "live," just as the Son "lives" because the
"living Father" has sent him (6:56-57). The circle is complete.

One of the chief characteristics of the oneness texts is the recurring statement that
Jesus "knows" the Father and accurately represents his will on earth. Often this is tied in
with preexistence. A good example is in 8:54-58 where the controversy concerns who
really knows God—Jesus or the religious authorities. They claim God but do not really
know him. To the contrary Jesus knows him intimately because he was with God from
the beginning and, to the Jews amazement, states that he lived before the time of Abraham

who wrote about him. The result of this unity talk about knowing God intimately and existing even before Abraham is to provoke murderous intent on the Jews part (7:59).

This knowing of the Father stressed so often (10:15; 14:7; 16:3; 17:3) is possibly a response to an early strain of gnostic "knowing," though the evidence for any system-atized form of Gnosticism does not occur until the second century. In John the Son knows the Father not just in intellectual terms but intimately since the Son stands in close personal relationship to the Father. This is seen in 10:15 where the shepherd knows his sheep intimately and they know him. In the same way the Father knows him and he knows the Father. The unity not only exists between the Father and Son but is also extended to the sheep. There is to be one flock and one shepherd (10:16), although there are other sheep that do not belong to the fold. The ultimate goal is the unity of all those who hear the voice of the "Good Shepherd" who lays down his life for the flock. This unity talk has the expected response of opposition and division with many thinking he was a great healer and some thinking he had a demon (10:19-21).

In John 10 conversation earlier begun about the Good Shepherd now spills over to the festival of dedication in Jerusalem. In 10:30 the statement of Jesus, "The Father and I are one," lead them to try to stone him. Unity begets disunity almost every time. In the ensuing debate Jesus makes one of his most pointed statements about his oneness with the Father when he says, "The Father is in me and I am in the Father" (10:38). This total unity of purpose, will, mission and person expressed in such statements is more than the Jews can tolerate and they again try to arrest him (10:39). As the period of controversy ends in John 12 and a new section (the Farewell Address) begins in John 13-17, Jesus makes his final public discourse in the Fourth Gospel at the close of John 12 by speaking of his oneness with the Father and with those who believe in him. The unity of the Son with the Father is such that those who believe in the Son actually believe in the one who sent him (10:44) and in the same way those who have seen the Son also have seen the Father. All of his teachings derive from God as a by-product of their perfect unity (10:50). The incredible unity that exists between Son, Father and believer is the most positive feature of this section of controversy in John.

Unity Themes in the Farewell Address[11]: John 13-17

Craig Koester says that in the farewell prayer Jesus deals with the issue of unity against the backdrop of conflict.[12] Both Koester and J. Louis Martyn argue that the problem in John has to do with the conflict of the Johannine community with the synagogue.[13] As the issues heated up between those who maintained that Jesus was the Messiah and those who denied it, a separation took place. Koester argues that the synagogue attempt-ed to discredit Christian claims about Jesus, saying that his miraculous signs were the work of a charlatan and the result of demonic forces (7:12; 10:19-21). In particular, the opponents take Jesus' claims of unity with God as a blasphemous attack on the oneness of God (5:18; 10:33; 19:7).[14]

Other unity concerns in the farewell prayer may relate to the growth of the community through evangelistic efforts. John, however, does not state why the expansion of the community raised questions about their ability to maintain its cohesiveness. It is possible that ethnic issues played a role in John's concern about unity, although he does not specify what these might be. He does quote Jesus' statement in 10:16 that he had other sheep "not of this fold," although he does not state if they are Samaritans, Greeks or some other group. The work among the Samaritans had been fairly successful (4:38), and how a group of Samaritan Christians and Jewish Christians would have gotten along, given the past background of hatred between the two groups, is not clear.[15] Such a co-mingling could have produced tensions in the Johannine community. We know from reading the Johannine letters that friction—if not outright heresy—existed in the community, and John may have been aware of that even as he penned the Gospel.[16]

Another possible factor affecting Johannine unity was geographical dispersion. Jesus speaks in 11:52 of the children of God "who are scattered abroad." As Koester remarks, it is very likely that not just one Johannine community existed but that a number of communities could have been located in several places. This in fact is what the Fourth Gospel itself reflects. The Gospel says there were groups of believers at Bethany in Transjordan (1:28; 10:40-42), Sychar in Samaria (4:5, 39), Bethany near Jerusalem (11:1-2), and perhaps in Cana and Capernaum in Galilee (2:1, 12; 4:46, 53). Not only were there significant numbers of Jews and Samaritans in their respective areas, a large number of Greeks and Romans lived in Caesarea, Sebaste, and the cities of the Decapolis (located on both sides of the Jordan).[17] The fact that John translates such common terms as "Messiah" and "rabbi" suggests further that some of the first readers did not reside only in Palestine.[18]

The last address of Jesus to his disciples before going to the cross takes place away from the public, beginning with a convoluted series of thoughts in 13:1-4. The events in the upper room from 13:1 to 13:30 with the foot washing and Judas' departure to betray Jesus are "preliminaries" to the actual "Farewell Discourse" that begins in 13:31. Jesus emphasizes that his leaving will only enhance his unity with the Father and with his disciples. By returning to the Father it is easy to seen how that dimension of oneness will be made more complete. Then the Father and Son can merge into ontological sameness as they were from the beginning before the Word became flesh. But believers also will experience that oneness, perhaps to a lesser degree than the Father and Son will, but nevertheless it will be a mutual interpenetration. As Jesus says it, "I am in my Father, and you in me, and I in you" (14:20). Furthermore, the unity envisioned by Jesus involves keeping his commands. The statement that if they keep the Son's commands then both the Father and the Son will come and make their home with them underscores that unity (14:23). The Father and the Son will move in with those who keep the relationship through obedience.

The underlying unstated implication of Jesus' statements to the disciples about his one-ness with the Father is that if the Son is that closely joined to the Father, then he has the ability to take care of the disciples after his death and they should not worry. They are in capable, totally reliable hands, as he will explain in the rest of the Farewell Address.

In 14:28 Jesus states that he goes to the Father "because the Father is greater than I." When this is seen over against the statements that he and the Father are one, the idea that the Father is greater seems strange indeed (17:11). It is clear, however, that a sub-ordinationist christology exists in John. This does not have to be taken in the direction of the ancient Arian heresy that Jesus was not fully God and was only a lower type of divinity. Rather this subordinationist language reflects the functional aspect of the Trinity. Jesus in his pre-existent state was equal with God but after his incarnation the relationship changed into that of the interaction seen in earthly fathers and sons. The statements of Jesus that he and the Father are one do not in any way contradict his asser-tion that the Father is greater than he is, because in terms of normal father/son dynamics that is truly the case. This is why Jesus says in 14:31, "I do as the Father has commanded me."[19] As the Son he is to be obedient to the Father although he is in essence equal with the Father.

The basic thrust of John 15 is the unity of the disciples with Jesus. He is the vine and they are the branches; they are to abide in him even as he abides in them. The oneness motif dominates this chapter and is predicated on the unity Jesus has with the Father. Just as the Father and Son are bound by love for each other, so are the disciples bound to Jesus. Just as the Son maintains the closest of connections with the Father by being obedient to him, so are the disciples to maintain their bonds with Jesus by obeying his commandments (15:9-10). The Father, Son and now the disciples are joined in a total mutuality with love and obedience the foundation.

This mutuality between Father, Son and disciples extends also to hatred (15:18-25). The world hates the disciples and also hated Jesus before them. By extension, those who hate Jesus also hate his Father (15:23). The world hated the works of Jesus that his Father sent him to do. For this reason they hated both the Father and the Son (15:24). The mis-sion and purposes of the Father are so totally reflected in the Son's actions that the two cannot be separated. With this kind of unity, what the world does to one they also do to the other. This unity extends also to the coming Advocate who testifies with one voice with God about Jesus (15:26).

John 17 records a prayer of Jesus. Often called the "High Priestly Prayer,"[20] it is prayed to God but with the disciples as listeners. The most common way of displaying the prayer's structure is that Jesus prayed first for himself (17:1-5), for his disciples (17:6-19) and for future disciples (17:20-26).[21] However, among the several difficulties that exist with this structure, one of the weightiest is that in 17:1-5 the primary focus is not on Jesus praying for himself but rather on his prayer for the community's salvation that is made possible by his own glo-rification. In addition, 17:20-26 is best divided into two sections: 17:20-23, focusing on the unity of the disciples, and 17:24-26, where Jesus prays that believers will be perfected in the glory of Jesus. These last two verses pick up several motifs found in the first (17:1-5) such as glory, knowing God, and the Son's pre-existence and rounds out the section.[22]

In the first part (17:1-5) unity motifs emerge which reflect the reciprocity between the Father and the Son seen throughout the Fourth Gospel: (A) the Father is called on to glorify the Son so that the Son might in turn glorify the Father; (B) his authority derived from the Father and was not his; (C) eternal life consists in knowing the Father and the Son he sent to do his will; (D) Jesus carried out the mission given to him by the Father and mutuality of purpose and will connects them; and (E) the Son preexisted with the Father. No unity of the Son with his followers he is about to leave would be possible without the *quid pro quo* that existed between the Father and Son. The Father gave them to the Son and the mutuality between them concerning the disciples is that "All mine are yours, and yours are mine" (17:10).

Since the *hour*[23] has come Jesus prays for the disciples based on the exchange of glory between the Father and the Son (17:1). The word *glory* is also like *hour* a technical term in the Fourth Gospel and at times the noun *doxa* means *divine nature*[24] or *honor*.[25] The verb *doxazō* frequently means *honor*[26] but in 17:1 the meaning seems to change in connection with the technical term hour and has to do with the crucifixion that is the means by which the Father is to be further glorified. For John, the crucifixion is *glory*[27] and this *glory* is the means by which the disciples gain eternal life (17:2). Raymond Brown says that *glory* has two aspects, being a *visible* manifestation of majesty through *acts of power*.[28] By dying on the cross the unity of Jesus and the Father is made visible in the giving of eternal life to believers. This glory consists in the accomplishing on earth of God's revelatory work through Jesus.[29]

With the total integration of mind, thought, will, and purpose between the Father and Son, it is no wonder that Jesus prays that the disciples "may be one as we are one" (17:11), a concept that foreshadows the prayer for unity in 17:20-23.[30] This is also his prayer for future disciples—which would be the community at the time the Gospel was written, as well as all future believers (17:21). This unity is achieved by those who come to faith based on the reception of the words or teaching of the disciples.

The oneness in 17:20-23 is couched in specific terms, leaving no mistake as to the intentionality of this unity. Twice, in almost the same words, probably for emphasis, he states that the oneness of the future followers is to be modeled after that of the Father in the Son, the Son in the Father and the disciples in both (17:21, 23). This unity is based on unity with God and reflected in Jesus' unity with the Father. But what does this mean for believers? Are they united in exactly the same way, or only in a similar way? According to the wording, it seems most likely that an unexplained inhabitation of the Father and Son takes place in the faithful.[31] The reason needed for this total unity is so that the *world*[32] can know the total unity that existed between the Father and Son. The purpose of this unity is, therefore, both redemptive and missiological.[33] This is demonstrated in the sending and loving of the Son by the Father and his loving the future disciples in the same intimate way. The chapter closes on the note of unity and the sharing of that love between Father, Son and disciples (17:26). Interestingly, nothing is said here about love for the world, but only love for each other.

The closeness of mission between the Father and Son naturally spills over to the disciples because just as the Father sent the Son so now they in turn are sent into the world (17:18). The world in John is frequently a place of rejection, evil, and ultimately death. Just as the Son is unified with the Father in terms of mission, so are the disciples. They will need the prayers and strength of Jesus who sends them, just as the Son needed the strong arm of the Father who sent him on his mission to the world. With few exceptions (3:16) the world is viewed as a hostile place and the arena of darkness and death. The hostility of John to the world is another well-known feature of his gospel.

All in all, the Gospel of John is a network of light and shadow, rejection and betrayal with the tone for unity and disunity set by the prologue and carried throughout John's story of Jesus.

Unity Themes in the Death of Jesus: John 18-21

The cross is the symbol most associated with the unity of believers in John. Both 10:15-16 and 11:51-52 connect the death of Jesus with the oneness of believers. Furthermore, the sign above the cross, written in Hebrew, Latin and Greek, shows that the crucifixion goes far beyond the boundaries of language and ethnicity.[34] As Koester states, the primary meaning of the cross is christological, "and Christians are brought into relationship with each other through their common bond to Jesus."[35] Above all else, the crucifixion shows the utter faith of Jesus in the Father and his dependence on him. Through his death emerges a perfect meld of the will of God and the carrying out of that will by his Son.

With regard to Peter, John 21 is important in not only showing the continued unity of Jesus with his disciples (21:1-3) but also of Peter with Jesus after his denial. His threefold discordant denial is counterbalanced by his threefold reinstatement and unification with the risen Lord in 21:15-19. In this sense John 21 serves a vital function in John's telling of his story of Jesus, not only with its continued story of Peter but also regarding the appearances of Jesus in Galilee. For these reasons (and others), it should not be rejected as inauthentic.

Survey of Viewpoints on Unity[36]

The oneness of those who believe in Jesus is taken in different directions depending on the scholar. Typical is the Roman Catholic presumption that it refers to visible church unity, meaning the unity found in the Roman Catholic Church when submission is made to Christ based on official teachings of the *magisterium*. In this view the prayer of Jesus was absolute and efficacious. Regarding this unity, if some leave the church, the church does not lose its unity because the prayer of Jesus was efficacious; likewise when new believers are added to it, they do not add anything to the unity of the church as such.[37]

George R. Beasley-Murray says that believers should understand that the prayer of Jesus has already been answered since God has made the church one in Christ. This divine unity was manifested in the earliest church in the tearing down of racial, economic, gender and cultural barriers and the creation of one body in Christ. The problem, he says, is that we live in a fallen world in which the original unity of the church is marred. His position on unity is that, although the ecumenical efforts of the World Council of Churches are often flawed, Christians should pray for all unity efforts.[38]

Other scholars maintain that the unity is spiritual, meaning that uniting churches together does not form the unity envisioned but is strictly internal among all true believers. Charles Talbert maintains that the unity is spiritual but not in the same sense as some hold. For him the unity is spiritual in that it has a spiritual root (based on fellowship with the Father and Son) and is visible in that the world can see it.[39] According to David Rensberger,

> The Johannine community confronted the world not merely with a doctrine or a creed but, as all sectarian groups do, with an alternative society, a counterculture, in which its message of the messiahship of Jesus was realized. It sought to draw people out of the world and into the messianic community, and it did this not only by its words but also by being that community.[40]

Raymond Brown also sees the unity advocated in John as a unity involving the notion of community, a view strengthened by the evidence from the Dead Sea Scrolls. In the scrolls the word yahad describes a communion of men living the same way of life and united by their common interpretation of the Law. These are bound by love and united in their opposition to a hostile world. Brown sees much in common with the Johannine picture of Christian unity and the Qumran conception.[41]

For both Rudolph Schnackenburg[42] and Moody Smith[43] the unity in John 17 is unity based on brotherly love. According to Smith, this love is not simply a feeling or disposition, but is a self-giving love on behalf of those who follow Christ—even to the point of death. When the world sees this type of love and the unity with God that it represents, this is the aim of Jesus. Schnackenburg thinks that the Johannine idea of unity is congruous with contemporary ecumenical efforts, since it "presents reunion not as something that has to be sought superficially within the institutional framework" but as a goal to be sought in the context of a faith community.[44] In a different approach, Rudolf Bultmann argues it is not love but rather the word or proclamation that unites the believers. As he says, "It is not personal sympathies, or common aims that constitute that unity, but the word that is alive in them all and that gives the community its foundation."[45]

D. A. Carson says that John 17:20-23 has to do with the unity of all true believers and that the unity is partly a function of being disciples of Jesus Christ.[46] Carson holds that organizational unity is not in view although it is not ruled out. As he says it, "organizational oneness is not fundamental or essential" and the outward manifestation of this spiritual unity is "not a neat organizational flow chart" but witness to the world.[47] Carson is careful to define what he means by true Christianity upon which this unity is based. Not everyone, he says, who claims to be a Christian is a Christian. For example, some call themselves Christian by believing in a supreme being vaguely connected to the Christian faith and others think of a Christian as some type of moralist. Still others want the term applied to anyone who has been baptized by whatever mode and who call themselves "born again" or other such terms. He rightly asks how Christian unity can be defined in an unambiguous way when the term Christian is infused with any meaning people want to give it.[48]

For Carson, if the term Christian is to have anything like its New Testament meaning a person claiming that name cannot legitimately hold to a belief structure that the New Testament disallows, or adopt practices that it explicitly forbids. "More positive, he must at least hold to what the New Testament itself insists is a minimum confession or an essential practice. If he does not, he prostitutes the term *Christian*."[49]

Carson rejects certain aspects of the ecumenical movement, saying that efforts to join all branches of "churchianity" of Christendom into one organization results only in trying to unite wheat and tares. Although he doubts that every single church has true believers in them, for the sake of argument if we assume they do, "the systematic denial of biblically required truth or the wholesale disregard for biblically mandated conduct in certain groups does not inspire confidence."[50] In other words, John 17 does not seem to advocate unity composed of both Christian members and members of the "world." An ecumenism that unites all without discrimination is in Carson's view misguided about what New Testament Christianity is all about.

On a more positive note, Carson concludes, "the things which tie together true believers are far more significant than the things which divide them."[51] In a cautionary note he adds that the divisive things are not necessarily unimportant but that these at times may be based on some major inconsistency or misapprehension of the truth. But, the things binding us together are of more vital importance. Carson's plea for unity is that

> Regardless of denominational affiliation, there ought to be among Christ's people a sincere kinship, a mutual love, a common commitment, and a deep desire to learn from one another and to come, if at all possible, to a shared understanding of the truth on any point. Such unity ought to be so transparent and compelling that others are attracted to it.[52]

Wayne Grudem, like Beasley-Murray and others, makes the strong point that the unity Jesus prayed for came about in the first-century church. Paul and many others evidence this in the calls for continued unity. As Grudem says, "Paul can command the church to live in unity because there already is an actual spiritual unity in Christ which exists among genuine believers."[53] Furthermore, since the leaders are jealous to protect the unity of the church, they give strong warnings against those who cause divisions (Rom 16:17-18; Gal 5:20-21; Jude 19).[54]

The bottom line on church unity for Grudem is that such unity does not require one worldwide church government over all Christians. In fact, he says, the unity of believers is often demonstrated very effectively through voluntary cooperation and affiliation among Christian groups. In Grudem's view,

> The existence of different denominations, mission boards, Christian educational institutions, college ministries, and so forth is not necessarily a mark of disunity of the church (though in some cases it may be), for there may be a great deal of cooperation and frequent demonstrations of unity among such diverse bodies as these.[55]

Grudem also discusses several levels and degrees of separation in Christianity. One is the formation of separate organizations (which he does not see as a major problem for unity). Two others, however, are more severe and problematical. The first is when "no cooperation" takes place. A church or Christian organization refuses to cooperate in joint activities with other churches including non-participation in evangelistic campaigns, joint worship services or mutual recognition of ordination. The second severe type of separation Grudem calls "no personal fellowship." This involves the strict avoidance of all personal fellowship with members of another church, and prohibits any joint prayer or Bible study (and sometimes even social interaction) with members of other church groups.[56]

Grudem, however, does not hold to unity at all costs and allows that good reasons exist at times for separation and disunity. While some separate for wrong reasons such as personal ambition, pride or differences on what he calls "minor doctrines or practices" (things that do not affect any other doctrine or Christian living in a significant way), there may be legitimate reasons to separate. These are: (1) Doctrinal reasons. This would be required only when the doctrinal error is so serious that the parent church has become a false church and no longer part of the body of Christ. For example, both Luther and Calvin eventually said that the Roman Catholic Church was not a true church. If reformation is not possible the only alternative may be to leave. (2) Matters of conscience. A person is not able to teach what they believe the Bible to teach (caution: some may have a distorted view of the Scripture or other problems). Or a person does not feel it right to stay in a church where the teachings are contrary to the word of God. To stay might appear to be an endorsement of the false teaching. (3) Practical considerations. Staying might cause more harm than good, or reasonable changes do not seem to be happening to make the church more scriptural. (4) No cooperation and no fellowship. At times it may be necessary not to cooperate in certain activities, but only when the other group is an unbelieving one and when the unbelieving one controls the activity. No fellowship could apply to cases of individuals under church discipline, but not in cases of differences with entire churches.[57]

Millard Erickson also makes a contribution to the contemporary discussion of unity by setting out four models of unity summarized below:

(1) Spiritual unity. Purity of doctrine and lifestyle are criteria for membership for those who see church unity primarily as spiritual. This view of church unity emphasizes that all Christians are one by virtue of their commitment and service to the Lord. They are all members in the invisible church headed by Christ. They do not have hostility toward others in different churches and love them although they have no contact on interaction with them. The existence of different denominations, even in the same area, does not pose a challenge to this unity.

(2) Mutual recognition and fellowship. Unity takes place on the practical plane instead of merely being an ideological acceptance of other Christians. Believers transfer their membership from one congregation to another, recognize the ordination of other groups, fellowship with other denominations and cooperate on special programs. This unity is not expressed by formation of an official organization.

(3) Conciliar unity. Churches band together in a council or association of churches and is basically a cooperative fellowship of denominations with each retaining its own unique identity, doctrines and traditions. The emphasis is on fellowship and action with the unity both visible and spiritual.

(4) Organic unity. With this view of church unity one organization is formed and the separate identities surrendered. When denominations unite in this way there is often a merging of local congregations as well. A prime example of this was the single denomination formed in 1925 called the United Church of Canada consisting of Methodists, Presbyterians and Congregationalists.

Organic unity has several dimensions. (A.) The usual sense is the merging of differing denominations. (B.) Another sense involves the combining of fellowships that have basically the same confessional standard. For example, several Lutheran groups in the United States have merged in recent years. (C.) At times it refers to conservative Christians remaining in their denomination that may over time have become predominantly liberal and establishing another wing. An example is the formation of Evangelical Lutherans in Mission (ELIM) by members of the Lutheran Church-Missouri Synod. (D.) Organic unity may relate to the local congregation and the decision to stay within it or leave. If a group leaves it is then a matter of a church split or schism. More people face the issue of organic unity at this level than any of the other types.[58]

Erickson also observes that when it comes to the topic of ecumenism, evangelicals have several issues. This is due to a large extent to the view that fellowship is impossible without agreement on certain basic truths. One of these is belief in an objective God whom humans relate to in faith and the acceptance of God's revelation, given at least partially in propositional form. Faith is a matter of personal trust in God and acceptance of his truths. Because of this, emotional experiences and cooperative experiences are insufficient platforms for union. As Erickson says, there must be agreement relative to most items of belief. Because of their concern for truth, evangelicals have been cautious about the degree of their involvement in ecumenism.[59]

Evangelical concerns about ecumenism can be grouped into four categories.[60] (1) *The theological issue.* Evangelicals will not unite with any group which fails to uphold basic doctrines such as: the supreme authority of the Bible as the source of faith and practice; the deity of Jesus Christ, including his miracles, atoning death, and bodily resurrection; salvation as a supernatural work of regeneration and justification by grace through faith; and the second coming of Christ. Since it is most often the case that the ecumenical movement settles for the lowest common denominator, the evangelical suspects that some members of the fellowship may not be genuine Christians. (2) *The ecclesiological issue.* Evangelicals will not join forces with groups that do not share their doctrine of the church. (3) *The methodological issue.* Since a major reason for church unity is mission to the unbelieving world, just how effective is the ecumenical movement in evangelizing the world? (4) *The teleological issue.* This issue is: what is the ultimate goal of the ecumenical movement? Is it the organic merger of all denominations? To some evangelicals this sounds like the agenda of the World Council and other groups. If this is so, then evangelicals have many problems including what the standards for church membership would be and what happens to the dissenters and nonconformists. Where could they go? Such a monolithic structure would also preclude a healthy system of checks and balances necessary in the church.

Instead of taking up these theories one by one and offering a critique, let us point out the clearest features in John's statements about unity from John 17:20-23. After that views on unity from the Stone-Campbell Movement will be examined.

What is the nature of the unity proposed in John 17:20-23? While a definitive answer may not be possible, several clear statements about unity emerge from the text:

(1) Unity with each other begins with belief in Christ caused by acceptance of his word.

(2) Unity among believers is modeled by the unity that exists with the Father and Son. This unity is reflected throughout the Fourth Gospel and this Christology based on oneness is found nowhere else in the New Testament.

(3) Unity is not something initiated by the believer but by God. Although the believer participates, the starting point is the Father.

(4) Unity with the Father and Son involves an indwelling of the believer that is not described in depth.

(5) Unity is not described in terms of an institution, organization or social grouping although some type of community can be assumed based on the relationship of disciples with Christ described in the gospels.

(6) Unity exists in diversity since the Father and Son although united display individual characteristics and have different functions.

(7) Unity is visible and not just a spiritual union since the world must be able to recognize it in order to believe.

(8) Unity is for the purpose of teaching the world that Jesus was sent and loved by God—the same message Jesus had while on earth.

(9) Unity is not simply human fellowship and friendly intermixing.

(10) Unity is not a loose union or confederation based on mutual interests.

(11) Unity involves two levels: unity with each other and unity with Jesus and the Father. Neither level is possible without the other.

(12) Unity is based on the love of the Father and Son for each other and for believers.

(13) Unity is already present among believers and does not only lie in the future because Jesus has already given his glory to them.

Unity Views in the Stone-Campbell Movement

The quest for Christian unity is certainly not new or unique to the Stone-Campbell Movement. On January 1, 1832 the followers of Barton W. Stone and Alexander Campbell joined together in Lexington, Kentucky. Although the two groups declared their unity, significant issues had not been resolved. Stone and Campbell differed on several major points including the name of the movement, the purpose and place of baptism, the work of the Holy Spirit in conversion, the frequency of the Lord's supper, church government, the meaning of the atonement, the doctrine of the trinity and other matters. Sharp tensions over these issues existed for years before and after the union.[61]

Alexander Campbell and Unity

From 1823 to 1830 Campbell edited *The Christian Baptist* and in it promoted his major message: the restoration of primitive Christianity which in turn would bring the unity of Christians which in turn would usher in the long-awaited millennial age. As Hughes and Roberts noted, Campbell apparently failed to understand, perhaps at least through 1830, "that the restoration and unity motifs, as he defined them, not only failed to complement but stood in substantial opposition to each other."[62] Whether or not he understood, Campbell believed that his movement was the first in Christian history to attempt to unite the Christian world on the basis of the Bible alone and that, at least in the early years of the movement, the essential practices of the ancient Christian faith had been fully restored.[63]

Despite his combative manner and so-called sectarian spirit, Campbell can still be called an ecumenist, but not in the usual sense. He sought to unite all Christian people, but he did not seek to unite all Christian denominations. Instead, he felt that every Christian denomination was corrupt, unfruitful and had no right to exist. His goal was to destroy denominationalism and unite the true Christian believers scattered among the sects on the basis of the primitive church and its teachings.[64] There was but one church and that was the primitive church that had been restored. He called on all authentic Christians to leave their denominations and join with others of similar belief. At the center of the program was Campbell's interpretation of the Bible and his conviction that everyone could understand it alike.[65]

One of the key factors in Alexander Campbell's ambitious program was the influence of his father Thomas Campbell. In 1809 Thomas decided to leave the Presbyterian Church and gave his reasons in the *Declaration and Address*. In it he remarked that it is not incredible to think that "the Church of Christ, in this highly favored country, should resume that original unity, peace, and purity which belong to its constitution, and constitute its glory." To attain this unity Campbell said it was necessary to conform to "the model and adopt the practice of the primitive Church, expressly exhibited in the New Testament."[66] Regarding the prayer of Jesus in John 17, Thomas pleaded that Christians not ignore the divisions and corruptions of the church saying, "His dying commands, his last and ardent prayer for the visible unity of his professing people, will not suffer you to be indifferent in this matter."

Within the *Declaration and Address* lie several major features of Alexander's later work of reformation: (1) the corrupt nature of denominationalism, (2) the need to unite all Christians, (3) the call to restore the primitive church, (4) and the foundational role of the New Testament. In addition, Thomas spelled out more completely his theology in thirteen propositions. The other twelve basically amplify the first proposition:

> That the Church of Christ upon earth is essentially, intentionally, and constitutionally one; consisting of all those in every place that profess their faith in Christ and obedience to him in all things according to the Scriptures, and that manifest the same by their tempers and conduct, and none else; as none else can be truly and properly called Christians.[67]

Thomas stresses that nothing is required for the unification of Christians but what is expressly taught in the word of God and nothing else should be admitted as "Divine obligation except what is expressly enjoined by the authority of the Lord Jesus Christ and his apostles upon the New Testament church; either in express terms or by approved precedent."[68] What Thomas lays down in theory his son Alexander will put into practice with a millennial twist first in *The Christian Baptist* and later in *The Millennial Harbinger*.

Although scholars debate the views of the early, radical Campbell and the later more mellow Campbell, as late as 1851 Campbell was hammering some of the same themes laid down by his father in the *Declaration and Address*. In a sermon delivered on October 22, 1851 before the American Christian Missionary Society, Campbell used John 17 as his text. In it he argued that the Lord had made the conversion of the world depend on the union of Christians and their union with the Lord. For this reason, he said, sectarian missionary efforts could not convert the world. For the double object of uniting Christian ranks and converting Jews, Mohammedans, and pagans to the Christian faith, he argued that Christians must renounce metaphysical and speculative Christianity and "the palpable Christians facts, precepts and promises, disentangled from Grecian, Roman, German or Protestant theories and speculations must be professed. The facts to be believed, the precepts to be obeyed, the promises to be embraced, must be clearly propounded and sustained."[69]

Barton W. Stone and Unity

Stone, like Campbell, was interested in unity and the joining of their forces in 1832 cemented their relationship, though not without serious reservations on the part of both. What was Stone's view of Christian unity?[70] In 1831 he wrote about the flawed view of uniting on the Bible alone that was being preached mightily by the Restoration preachers.[71] Stone commented: "I have long thought, and seriously thought, whether a formal union on the Bible, without possessing the spirit of that book, would be a blessing or a curse to society…whether it would not rather be a stumbling block, a delusive snare to the world."[72]

In an 1833 article Stone discussed four different kinds of unity—book union, head union, water union, and fire union.[73] Book union he defined as a "union founded on a book, containing certain articles of faith, called a creed, confession of faith or a discipline." These books have been the cause of disunion, Stone argued.

Head union is "union founded on opinion." He notes that many denounce creeds and confessions and extol the Bible. That is good, he says. They leave creeds and adopt the Bible alone as their rule of faith. However, a problem soon develops. They find out that many different opinions exist about the Bible and each one believes their interpretation and opinions to be correct and "absolutely essential to salvation." If everyone, however, accepts the opinion of A then they attain union, Stone states. Or if A accepts the opinion of B then they have union. Then Stone asks: how does this union differ from the union formed on human creeds? "This plan of uniting on opinions, whether contained in a book, or in the head is not a straw, and can never affect Christian union, or the union of primitive Christianity."

Water union is union founded on immersion in water. "But fact proves that this union is easily dissolved, and that immersion will not keep those who are immersed, united." Fire union is:

> The unity of the spirit-union founded on the Spirit of Truth. Fire affects a perfect union—so does the spirit of burning, the spirit of Jesus; and no union but this will stand, no other union is worth the name. This spirit is obtained through faith, not in a human form or set of opinions, whether written or not written, but in the Lord Jesus Christ, the Savior of sinners; and by a cheerful obedience to all his known commands. For this spirit is promised to those that obey him—to them that repent and are baptized, to them

that believe in his name. This spirit leads us to love God and his children—to love and pray for all mankind. This is the very union for which Jesus prayed, and by which the world will believe that he is the Christ of God.[74]

Stone preached much about being filled with the Spirit, saying it was not possible to love God or the brethren without it. Ultimately, for Stone, unity depended on the Spirit: "The want of this Spirit, the Spirit of Jesus, is the grand cause of division among Christians; consequently, this Spirit restored will be the grand cause of union."[75]

Reflections on Unity

The contemporary Stone-Campbell Movement is made up of three main segments: the Disciples of Christ, the Christian Church (independent) and the Churches of Christ (a cappella). This diversity precludes giving a view of unity in minute detail that applies to all three. In general, it is recognized that the Disciples are the most unity conscious and participate enthusiastically in the ecumenical movement. Likewise, the Christian Church (independent) and the Churches of Christ (a cappella) are much less inclined to ecumenism. Over the past years unity meetings have been held between these two streams of the movement but have only led to a few visible results so far. Nevertheless, they have certainly created better understanding and increased fellowship activities. Hopefully these meetings will continue in the future.

In some ways, the model of unity that best fits the early Stone-Campbell Movement is the Roman Catholic view that unity exists in the one church and in no other. While Vatican II led to the view of Christians in other churches, any uniting of forces will be done basically on their own terms. Alexander Campbell argued there was only one church and from his reading of the Scripture that is a logical conclusion.[76] Like those in the Roman Catholic Church, he believed there was one true church and that it was not represented by the various denominations but by the one visible church to which all true Christians in the denominations were called to join. Like the Catholics, Campbell argues that Jesus' plea for unity in John 17 had been achieved in the primitive church and (for Campbell) in the restored church of the Stone-Campbell Movement.[77] Others such as Beasley-Murray would also agree that Jesus' prayer had been answered but only in the first-century church. However, due to sin that early unity was lost. Campbell would partly agree but also argue that the church can be restored today just as in the first century.

The Stone-Campbell Movement never embraced the idea that unity was only spiritual and internal with no visible reference. They displayed this visible testimony in 1832 with the joining of the two branches in Lexington. When the Christians in the sects[78] came out from them, they joined the visible, restored primitive church on earth. There was no such thought of joining in a loose union with other churches; for the early leaders this was not the unity spoken of in the New Testament. Rather, a community was to be formed displaying love, united in brotherhood and standing on the teachings of the New Testament. This view differs from some evangelicals who see the unity of the church more in terms of true believers in all the denominations sharing a common, but invisible bond without requiring a visible organization.[79]

The emphasis on Scripture in the early Stone-Campbell Movement resonates with the contemporary evangelical unity stance in upholding the authority of the Word. While evangelicals would not appreciate certain interpretative moves by Campbell and other restorationists,[80] both would agree on the central importance of the Bible for any kind of unity. When asked about a possible union with the Baptists, Campbell replied that he had "no valid objection to union with our Baptist brethren, if they do not require anything from us for which there cannot be produced a clear Scripture warrant."[81] It is the exalted role of Scripture that undergirds both the unity plea in the Stone-Campbell Movement and contemporary evangelical thought.

In the early Stone-Campbell Movement it was foundational that Christians existed in the denominations. If there were no other Christians except those of the Stone-Campbell Movement, then there would be no sense in the call for Christians to come out from denominationalism and become part of the true church. Both Stone and Campbell had no problem in speaking in other churches and fellowshipping those of different convictions. As time went on, however, the movement split into two well-known divisions. The Disciples on the left wing became noted for their ecumenism and doctrinal tolerance. On the right wing the early spirit encapsulated in the slogan, "Christians only but not the only Christians" gave way to a hardened position consisting of no (or little) cooperation with other churches and a strongly held conviction that members of every denomination were lost. The only authentic Christians were in the one, true church, which they were.[82] Eventually, they too split.

Conclusion

Coming from Churches of Christ (a cappella) stream of the Stone-Campbell Movement, which for all practical purposes has given up on unity and stresses restoration instead, speaking about unity is difficult Those who write about unity or engage in unity conferences are, in fact, held as suspect by certain right-wing elements of Churches of Christ (a cappella). To talk of unity is further complicated when a people who take the "Bible only" have fragmented into so many different Churches of Christ "fellowships," most of which do not associate, fellowship or cooperate with the other. It is somewhat embarrassing to propose a unity program when we have done so poorly among even ourselves what the Lord prayed for us to do. Perhaps this can be said of every religious group in America today with the myriads of divisions within denominations. It would be a great step forward if each denomination could only mend the rifts within their own ranks.

However problematic the achieving of unity is today, the early Stone-Campbell Movement leaders believed that Christians from all denominations could be called out and unified by agreement on the essentials of the Christian faith while allowing absolute freedom on non-essentials. The obvious problem surfaces. How does one distinguish between essentials and non-essentials? Another variation on the unity plea was that virtually all doctrines and practices that are important had been detailed in the New Testament in such an obvious and clear manner that all honest people could not help but see them alike. This too proved problematical. So where do we go? Some in the movement today defend uniformity based on the idea that we can all see the Bible basically alike (if we are really honest) and others seek greater cooperation and interaction with other Protestant groups.[83]

At best, Churches of Christ (a cappella) seem to fit into the first model of unity set forth by Millard Erickson—that of spiritual unity. Some churches, however, mostly in urban areas, have moved beyond this to mutual recognition and fellowship. I do not see, however, any kind of visible organic unity in the near future for this right wing of the Stone-Campbell Movement. Some hold to the view of Stone and Campbell that authentic Christians can be found in the denominations and on that basis a kind of unity with other groups does exist. As Carson well said, "the things which tie together true believers are far more significant than the things which divide them."[84] This is well worth considering for members of my fellowship not only in terms of other Christian groups but also regarding each other.[85] Maybe the plea of Jesus for unity in John 17 has not fallen on totally deaf ears after all!

Notes

[1]Mark L. Appold, *The Oneness Motif in the Fourth Gospel* (Tübingen: J. C. B. Mohr [Paul Siebeck], 1976), p. 261.

[2]Study on the prologue has been intense. It could be a pre-Johannine piece of material he utilized and perhaps redacted but the issue is not settled. Debate continues not only about the structure but also about the meaning of logos and other terms. Much of the symbolism of the prologue surfaces later in the gospel and it definitely shapes the agenda.

[3]All the translations are my own from the Greek.

[4]Craig R. Koester, *Symbolism in the Fourth Gospel* (Minneapolis: Fortress, 1995), pp. 144-145.

[5]The authorship of this gospel receives considerable debate. Options range from another John (John the Elder) to the Johannine community that perhaps used material gathered by "John." The Beloved Disciple is thought by many to be John the Apostle and is so assumed in this paper. To argue for a single author, however, does not rule out the possibility of redaction especially in John 21.

[6]It is well known that the noun *pistis (faith)* does not occur in the Fourth Gospel.

[7]Ernst Käsemann, *The Testament of Jesus* (Philadelphia: Fortress, 1968), pp. 24-25.

[8]Ibid, pp. 65-66.

[9]Ibid., p. 23.

[10]For a discussion of the midrashic elements in John 6, see Peter Borgen, "Observations on the Midrashic Character of John 6," *Zeitschrift für die neutestamentliche Wissenschaft* 54 (1963): 232-40.

[11]While it is standard treatment by most commentators to call chapters 13-17 the "farewell discourses" there is some question as to whether John 13-17 constitutes the farewell section or whether it is

only John 13-16 and the John 17 prayer is a distinct genre on its own. In biblical examples of the farewell one often finds a blessing rather than a prayer (See Gen 49:1-27; Deut 31:30-32:47; 33). However, Jesus' farewell speech ends with a prayer (Lk 22:14-38) and Paul's farewell to the Ephesian elders in Acts 20 ends with a prayer (20:36) although it is not recorded. See also Jub 22:28-30. Overall, it is best to take 13-17 as a unit. See Rudolf Schnackenburg, *The Gospel According to St John*, Herder's Theological Commentary on the New Testament (New York: Crossroad, 1982), 3:167.

[12]Ibid., p. 223.

[13]See. J. Louis Martyn, *History and Theology in the Fourth Gospel* (Nashville: Abingdon, 1979). The synagogue crisis postulated by Martyn is not accepted by all scholars. See Charles H. Talbert, *Reading John* (New York: Crossroad, 1992), p. 62.

[14]Koester, *Symbolism*, p. 224.

[15]Ibid., pp. 225-226.

[16]George R. Beasley-Murray, *John*, Word Biblical Commentary (Nashville: Thomas Nelson, 1999), p. 307.

[17]Koester, *Symbolism*, p. 227.

[18]Ibid.

[19]The last words of John 14:31, "Rise, let us depart" raise many issues about the literary unity of the farewell discourse in John 13-17 which are beyond the limits of this paper to discuss. See Thomas L. Brodie, *The Gospel According to John: A Literary and Theological Commentary* (New York: Oxford University Press, 1993), p. 437.

[20]Raymond E. Brown, *The Gospel According to John XII-XXI*, Anchor Bible (New York: Doubleday, 1978), p. 747, says if Jesus is praying as a High Priest it is not because he is like one about to offer a sacrifice but because of its likeness to the intersession Jesus exercises in Romans 8:34 and like that of the heavenly High Priest in Hebrews who has been exalted to the right hand of God.

[21]For an excellent discussion on the literary structure and style of these verses see Appold, *Oneness Motif*, pp. 157-63.

[22]John W. Pryor, *John: Evangelist of the Covenant People* (Downers Grove, Ill.: InterVarsity, 1992).

[23]*Hour* is a technical term in John referring not to a sixty-minute chronological unit of time but to the events of the cross, including the farewell to the disciples and the actual crucifixion. See 2:4; 4:21, 23; 5:25, 28; 7:30; 8:20; 12:23, 27; 17:1. *Hour* (*hōra*) and *glory* are often found in the same context or same verse (especially note the verb form with *hora* in Jn 12:23, 28 and in 17:1 (17: 5 *doxa*).

[24]Jn 1:14; 2:11; 5:41; 12:41.

[25]Jn 5:44; 7:18; 8:50, 54; 9:24; 11:4; 40; 12:43; 17:1, 5, 22, 24. Transcendent circumstances are involved in these usages. See Walter Bauer, *A Greek-English Lexicon of the New Testament and Other Early Christian Literature*, 3rd ed.; rev. ed. Frederick William Danker (Chicago: University of Chicago Press, 2000), p. 257.

[26]Jn 8:54;11:4; 12:28; 13:31; 14:13; 15:8; 16:14; 17:4, 10.

[27]See Jn 7:39; 12:16, 23; 21:19. These verses may also have a connection to *splendid greatness* or *glorify*. See Bauer/Danker, *Greek-English Lexicon*, p. 258.

[28]Brown, *John*, p. 751.

[29]D. Moody Smith, *John*, Abingdon New Testament Commentaries (Nashville: Abingdon, 1999), p. 317.

[30]A very tight grammatical parallelism exists in 17: 20-23. Notice the three *hina* clauses and the *kathos* clause in both parts. See Brown, *John*, p. 769.

[31]Rogerio Matzerath, *The Prayer of Christ for Unity: St. John 17:20-23* (Dissertation, Pontificiae Universitatis Gregorianae, 1950), pp. 144-145.

[32]John uses the word *kosmos* (*world*) thirteen times in John 17. At times it means the material world (Jn 17:5, 11, 12, 18, 24), humanity in general (17:6, 13), or the world which is hostile to God (17:9, 11b,

14, 25). See Bauer/Danker, *Greek-English Lexicon*, pp. 561-562.

[33]R. Alan Culpepper, *The Gospel and Letters of John* (Nashville: Abingdon, 1998), p. 220.

[34]Koester, *Symbolism*, p. 237.

[35]Ibid.

[36]This survey is not meant to be exhaustive, but rather a selection of thoughts on unity from a variety of perspectives. Many others could have, and perhaps should have, been included.

[37]Matzerath, *Prayer*, p. 169.

[38]Beasley-Murray, *John*, pp. 306-307.

[39]Talbert, *John*, p. 228.

[40]David Rensberger, *Johannine Faith and Liberating Community* (Philadelphia: Westminster, 1988), p.150.

[41]Brown, *John*, pp. 776-777.

[42]Schnackenburg, *John*, p. 191.

[43]Smith, *John*, pp. 316-317.

[44]Schnackenburg, *John*, p. 194.

[45]Rudolf Bultmann, *The Gospel of John*, trans. G. R. Beasley-Murray (Philadelphia: Westminster, 1971), p. 513.

[46]D. A. Carson, *The Farewell Discourse and Final Prayer of Jesus: An Exposition of John 14-17* (Grand Rapids: Baker, 1980), pp. 201-204.

[47]Ibid., p. 201.

[48]Ibid., p. 202.

[49]Ibid.

[50]Ibid., p. 203.

[51]Ibid., p. 204.

[52]Ibid.

[53]Wayne Grudem, *Systematic Theology: An Introduction to Biblical Doctrine* (Grand Rapids: Zondervan, 1994), p. 876.

[54]Besides texts such as Eph 4:3-6, 16 and Phil 2:2, various biblical images stress unity such as the household (unity of many races in one church), bride of Christ (one bride and one body), body of Christ (many members but one body, 1 Cor 12:12-26).

[55]Grudem, *Systematic Theology*, p. 877.

[56]Ibid., p. 879.

[57]Ibid., pp. 880-883.

[58]Millard J. Erickson, *Christian Theology* (Grand Rapids: Baker, 1986), pp. 1135-1137.

[59]Ibid., p. 1142.

[60]Ibid., p. 1143. These categories used by Erickson derive from an adaptation made from William R. Estep, *Baptists and Christian Unity* (Nashville: Broadman, 1966), p. 170.

[61]C. Leonard Allen, *Distant Voices: Discovering a Forgotten Past for a Changing Church* (Abilene, Tex.: ACU Press, 1993), p. 41.

[62]Richard T. Hughes and R. L. Roberts, *The Churches of Christ* (Westport, Conn.: Greenwood, 2001), p. 16. William J. Richardson, "Ecumenical Perspectives in the Thought of Alexander Campbell," *Restoration Quarterly* 40 (1998): 166, argues that as early as his Christian Baptist days Campbell felt the tensions, for even as he stressed the need for scriptural baptism he refused to regard pedobaptists as aliens to the kingdom.

[63]Ibid., p. 17.

[64]Ibid., pp. 18-19.

[65]Richard T. Hughes, *Reviving the Ancient Faith: The Story of Churches of Christ in America* (Grand

Rapids: Eerdmans, 1996), p. 26, discusses the influence of Bacon, Locke and others on Campbell's view of scripture.

[66]Thomas Campbell, *Declaration and Address* (reprint edition; St. Louis: Bethany, 1955), p. 34.

[67]Ibid., p. 44.

[68]Ibid., p. 45.

[69]Alexander Campbell, "Sermon," *Millennial Harbinger* (March 1852): 125. Both Campbell and his leading co-worker Robert Richardson believed that Jesus' prayer for unity in John 17 was answered by the establishment of the primitive church and by the existence of true Christians in every age of the church. See Robert Richardson, "Christian Unity—No. II," *Millennial Harbinger* (March 1859): 128-29.

[70]Stone and Campbell both stressed the unity message of John 17 in sermons and articles. See Barton W. Stone, *Christian Messenger* 11 (March 1841): 232-238, for a sermon preached on John 17:20-22. Charles A. Young, *Historical Documents Advocating Christian Union* (Chicago: Christian Century, 1904), p. 5, says that John 17 was the favorite text of the leaders in the early days of the restoration.

[71]Robert Richardson was certainly a well-known exception. He says there was no New Testament in the time of the apostles and there was no such thing among the early Christians as a formal union upon the "Bible alone." Rather it was a union based on the Gospel alone. See Robert Richardson, "Reformation—No. IV," *Millennial Harbinger* (September 1847): 508.

[72]Barton W. Stone, *Christian Messenger* (August 1831): 185.

[73]Barton W. Stone, *Christian Messenger* 7 (October 1833): 314-16.

[74]Barton W. Stone, *Christian Messenger* 7 (October 1833): 316.

[75]Barton W. Stone, *Christian Messenger* 11 (June 1841): 334.

[76]What is said of Campbell here also applies to Stone.

[77]Robert Richardson, "Christian Unity—No," *Millennial Harbinger* (February 1859): 65, says that the prayer was answered because true believers have existed in every age of the church.

[78]Used in the Stone-Campbell Movement as shorthand for denomination.

[79]Carson, *Farewell*, p. 201.

[80]Some in the movement have problems with Campbell's hermeneutics. See Russ Dudrey, "Restorationist Hermeneutics among the Churches of Christ: Why Are We at an Impasse?" *Restoration Quarterly* 30 (1988): 37-42.

[81]Robert Richardson, "Union of Christians," *Millennial Harbinger* (March 1860): 97.

[82]The development of this process has been researched, among others, by Douglas A. Foster, *Will the Cycle Be Broken?: Churches of Christ Face the 21st Century* (Abilene, Tex.: ACU Press, 1994), p. 99.

[83]Tom Steed, "Alexander and Thomas Campbell's View of the Nature of Reality and Church: A Phenomenological, Rhetorical, and Metaphoric Analysis of the Restoration Movement" (Dissertation: Southern Illinois University, 2000), p. 147.

[84]Carson, *Farewell*, p. 204.

[85]The key is what Carson means by "true believer." Carson, *Farewell*, p. 203, says that a "true believer" is guided by the New Testament and is one who avoids practices that the New Testament explicitly forbids. I would add that the "true believer" is also one who only practices what the New Testaments approves.

8

RESPONSE

Gary M. Burge

I am delighted to be a part of this conversation about the Stone-Campbell Restoration Movement and the Gospel of John. I come to the topic, however, as an outsider with no experience whatsoever in this history and no academic background regarding the Stone-Campbell Movement. But as a New Testament scholar I am acquainted with the Fourth Gospel and have made its words a particular area of interest.

Berryhill, Pollard and Johnson outline persuasive cases for the centrality of John's Gospel among the earliest writers in the Stone-Campbell Movement. Given its emphasis on unity in the earliest decades, I was not surprised to see statistics that demonstrated frequent use of the Fourth Gospel. Heavy use of John 3 was probably characteristic of many frontier evangelists, even as it is today among modern preachers. But the frequent interest in John 17 is likely unique, however, since in it Jesus sounds themes that were so central to any restorationist type of movement.

Preliminary Thoughts: Alexander Campbell

Preparation for this response took me on a detour into the life of Alexander Campbell and his father Thomas. And here it seems there is a remarkable irony. The Campbells had left their Irish Presbyterian roots in the first decade of the nineteenth century. Thomas left for America in 1807 and his son Alexander, after merely a year of theological education at Glasgow, departed in 1809. Within three years Alexander was ordained into "the Christian Association of Washington" (Pennsylvania) and from there began an itinerant preaching ministry in Kentucky, Ohio, Indiana, West Virginia, and Tennessee. His followers simply called themselves "disciples of Christ." Having broken from an established European denomination, he entered the American religious fray and quickly felt compelled to renounce the myriad of ecclesiastical choices that appeared everywhere. A quick look at any restored early nineteenth-century American town (such as Galena, Illinois) depicts what Campbell must have seen. The leading members of society had built their homes, modeled from European-East Coast symbols of wealth and prestige, along rivers and ridges where property was costly. And nearby they built churches—Methodist, Presbyterian, Lutheran, Episcopal and Catholic—whose architecture and placement reflected the social status of their parishioners. The churches were rivals whose position socially seemed as important as their positions biblically. And those who did not share the expected affluence or values or cultural heritage were often disregarded, left to the mills, mines and factories where they labored.

Alexander Campbell's call for a community of Christians who might recreate the simplicity and purity of a biblical world must have sounded as prophetic to some as it sounded naïve to others. Either way, it was a remarkable vision, one that might unite true believers into a community of the faithful that looked strictly to the Bible (and not old world ecclesiastical models) for life and faith. But there is its irony: The Campbellites had to provoke some disunity, some social dislocation away from established churches, in order to form this fresh community. Their vision of unity was not a recommitment to tolerance, not a new atmosphere where Christians could hold forth shoulder-to-shoulder, *regardless* of where they worshipped. Unity would come when men and women joined Campbell's new budding movement. Rival Presbyterian and Episcopalian clerics likely did not see this as a call to Christian unity and harmony but as a call to sectarianism that in the end would fracture the church even further. And Mormons as well as Brethren in the era likely wondered why this restoration should be followed and not their version it.

Campbell and the Johannine Community

Brian Johnson deftly contrasts this social context with the portrait of John given by Robert Gundry's *Jesus the Word According to John the Sectarian*. Alexander Campbell must have read John's Gospel and felt that themes there resonated with his own experience on the frontier. In other words, Campbell intuited that John's social location was akin to his own, that the words of Jesus here treasured and recorded by John were words that needed to be heard likewise in the world of the nineteenth century. And this instinct, this intuition that Campbell felt does not surprise me or most Johannine scholars.

In the last 30 years, Johannine scholarship has suggested that if we read between the lines in this gospel it might be possible to gain a glimpse of the community of Christians who used and valued it. This is not to deny that the words of the gospel record the say-ings of Jesus or the context of Jesus (although severe critics are willing to make this step). It is simply an observation from history and sociology: people produce and preserve sto-ries that give meaning *to them*; seeing these stories as social constructs permits us to unravel what must have been going on in John's world. (A quick glance at American movie history demonstrates the point: westerns in the 1950s and 1960s, spy thrillers dur-ing the Cold War, and space/technology parables such as *The Matrix* and *Star Wars* dur-ing the 1980s and 1990s each tell the historian about the movie's audience.)

A tentative consensus among scholars believes that John's community was a circle that knew conflict. It had labored in the midst of severe synagogue struggle (John 9), had converted many from the ranks of John the Baptist, but still needed to define the Baptist's secondary position to Jesus (1:6-8; 1:19-42; 3:22-36; 10:40-41). It knew that the world was hostile (as we see in John's use of the Greek *kosmos*, see 15:18-27) and that only a remarkable experience—a conversion experience involving the Spirit of God (3:3)—could extricate a person from this darkness. John's world was strictly dual-istic: the above and the below, light and darkness, truth and falsehood. And every person was required to make a choice. It is interesting that the "drama" of Jesus' life in John's Gospel generally sets up a crisis. When Jesus speaks or acts, the audience consistently divides over the meaning of what he has done. At Tabernacles in John 7, the crowd wrestles with the dilemma of Jesus' true identity (7:25-27, 40-43). Jesus is either demon possessed or he is the Christ. He deserves either belief and discipleship or he deserves to be arrested. There is no middle ground.

Unity in a Community under Seige

In a community that lives under siege, whose place in history seems tenuous—in a community that has no recognized place in the religious landscape—*unity is an asset that cannot be compromised*. The fledgling movement of Jesus' followers would fragment and disappear if they did not share a common vision and belief and practice. And John knew this better than others. Johnson rightly underscores the "word" in this gospel. Jesus is not merely the Messiah, he is the Word incarnate; Jesus is not merely a teacher, he is the Wisdom of God now spoken in human language. And therefore true defer-ence to him, true obedience and devotion are demanded. This is a word-centered unity. Unity—and here is where Paul Pollard's contribution is helpful—is a theme that per-meates the gospel and is not simply anchored in John 17. However, this unity is one that is centered on Jesus, who he is, and what he says and deviation from these words will not do.

If there were an added feature of this study of the unity motif in John that needs exploration it would be a further examination of the letters of John. Almost every Johannine scholar sees these three letters—and particularly First John—as living with-in the theological world of the Fourth Gospel. For some scholars First John was penned at the same time the gospel was edited and the prologue was attached (compare the language of Jn 1:1-18 with 1 Jn 1). For others, First John comes immediately after the writing up of the gospel. But here is the point that bears on our subject: the letters of John betray yet a second social development that likely springs from the first (and this too has some relevance for restorationist movements).

Christian communities that underscore internal cohesion and unity, that build firm parameters on their margins, that use dualistic language and are quick to chastise those who are "in the darkness"—these communities may find that the passions that fueled their conflict with the world my erupt within their own ranks. It is curious that the language once used for the world in John's Gospel is used in First John for people who were within the ranks of John's church and now have departed. In his first letter John must again talk about unity but in this case fragmentation has begun inside the church doors. For instance, 1 John 2:18-19 suggests that the church receiving this letter has even split: some members have left the congregation in an uproar. John even uses the term "antichrist" to describe their behavior. But the trouble didn't stop there. These disgruntled former members still held a pull on the church. They were playing heavy-handed politics. They were cajoling John's faithful members to come away and join the revolt (2:26). John spares no words when criticizing these people. He calls them "children of the devil" (3:10).

Not only was this community's commitment to unity (and separation) a part of what made its later conflicts so severe, but its confident understanding of spiritual experience likewise contributed. In a word, it was John's teaching about the Spirit that may have helped form the nature of the later struggles in the church. The Gospel of John was an empowering gospel that shaped this Christian community so that it would expect dynamic spiritual experiences. Jesus and the Father were dwelling inside these spiritually reborn believers (Jn 14:23)! No other gospel speaks like this. The Holy Spirit promised to provide them with incredible powers: power to recall Jesus' very words (14:26), power to work miracles greater than those of Jesus (14:12), power to have prayer answered (14:13-14), and power to confront a hostile world (16:7). They even had the power to forgive sin (20:23). Above all, the Spirit gave them the power of prophecy, to continue speaking with Jesus' voice, revealing new things not recorded in Scripture (16:13).

John's gospel suggests that John's community was a pneumatic community. Today we might call it a charismatic community. This is not to say that the Johannine literature provides a detailed working out of the spiritual gifts as, say, Paul does in 1 Corinthians 12-14. It does not evidence that the Johannine Christians spoke in tongues (though it is not implausible). Rather, the Johannine literature evidences a community that was alert to the centrality of the Spirit and ready to experience the Spirit in its fullness. In short, Johannine theology laid the context in which a pneumatic/charismatic Christianity would flourish.

But we can only speculate that something serious happened at a later stage of the church's life. The once-unified congregation began to tear apart from within. Threats that were once external now were found within the ranks of the fellowship itself. For John, it must have been a crisis beyond belief. In 1 John 2:18 he even says that it is "the last hour" for the community.

Who were these dissenters? These were a select group of Johannine Christians who knew the Fourth Gospel well, claimed to be inspired by the Spirit, but challenged John's understanding of Jesus Christ's personhood and work. Apparently they were succeeding. The community was splitting, harsh words were being exchanged, and the vocabulary once reserved in the Fourth Gospel for those in "the world" now was being aimed at fellow Christians within the church.

Our evidence for this division is found in John's response to the crisis: the First Epistle of John. In its pages we have evidence of severe social conflict: the painful departure of the group (1 Jn 2:19-26) and warnings about "deceivers" and "liars" who twist the truth of Christ (1 Jn 2:22; 2 Jn 7). There were also severe theological debates (1 John 5:5-8) which were being fought among teachers claiming to be filled with the inspiration of the Holy Spirit (1 Jn 2:20-21; 4:1-6). The letter's repeated emphasis on love hints at the severity and desperation of the situation.

Therefore we can say that in some respect John's letters are a response written in debate with those who may be interpreting the Fourth Gospel. For some the epistles serve as a sort of commentary on the gospel. Still others would describe them as an "epilogue" to the gospel designed to circulate with it so that erroneous interpretations would not be reached.

Conclusion

If the Stone-Campbell Restoration Movement can find instructive teaching within the Johannine literature, it would be interesting to compare its history with the history of the Johannine church. To what extent does zeal for a "return" to an idealized restored past lead to sectarian instincts? To what extent does this zeal lead to good and healthy cohesion-and when does it lead intolerance? And to what extent does that zeal lead to the risk of internal fractures that can put the entire community at risk? These are the sorts of questions John would have us explore as we look at our own churches within our present history.

Part 3

UNDERSTANDING THE CHURCH
THROUGH THE LORD'S SUPPER

9

The Centrality of the Lord's Supper for 18th and 19th Century Scottish Restorationists

Lynn A. McMillon

Nearly eighty years before Thomas and Alexander Campbell and Barton Stone began their religious journeys, John Glas (1695-1773) began a similar journey in Scotland. Trained at the University of Edinburgh as a minister in the Church of Scotland, Glas assumed his first congregation at Tealing in 1719. His ministry began with an attempt to revive faithfulness in his small rural church by urging renewed loyalty to the national covenants of his church only to discover that he could produce no scriptural authority for even having covenants. The local synod struggled with Glas for the next eleven years over the issue and finally deposed him in 1730. The path of religious independency was thus set for Glas, a route he never planned but one that defined his search for a form of Christianity that was not fettered by human regulations.

John Glas and Restoration

Glas was on a clear path of upholding the New Testament as the pattern and guide for contemporary Christians to follow. That principle was clearly stated by Glas when he wrote that "the writings of the Old and the New, contain a complete revelation of the will of God to me, cannot be denied, without the highest reflection on the truth of that revelation, that plainly sets itself out as a declaration of the whole counsel of God, to which nothing can be added."[1]

Glas states his guiding principles in language that prefigures the Campbells and Barton Stone:

> Let people be consistent with their profession of making the Scriptures the rule of their faith and practice. Let them not pick and choose, but take the whole of it for their law and guide: for otherwise this conclusion must follow, that with them then the Scriptures, and the whole of it, is not a perfect rule for Christians to walk by; and that in some things, they must set aside its precepts and examples, and fashion a system according to their own notions.[2]

This would be the interpretive principle for Glas, his followers and later church members until the end of the Glasite movement in 1999.

The churches of Glas' Scottish "restitution" movement were largely known as Glasite though they referred to themselves as churches of Christ. As Independent congregational churches in England and Wales joined the movement, they became known as Sandemanian largely because of Robert Sandeman's correspondence and theological leadership among them. Sandeman was Glas' son-in-law and principal leader among the churches outside Scotland. After the death of his wife, Sandeman traveled to New England in 1764 and established a number of congregations there until his death in 1773. Several of those congregations survived until the late 1800s and some had connections with the Stone-Campbell Restoration Movement.

The Haldanes, Glas and Sandeman

Another significant Scottish connection to the American restoration movement came through the Haldane brothers of Scotland, Robert (1764-1842) and James (1768-1851), and their preacher training seminary operated by Greville Ewing from 1799-1808.

The writings of John Glas and his son-in-law Robert Sandeman (1718-1771) became the dominant theological articulation for the Glasite-Sandemanian movement for the two hundred and seventy-five years of its history. Those writings were in Ewing's school library and were often discussed by the students.[3] Ewing reported that though Robert Haldane originally disliked Glas and Sandeman, he had a change of thinking: "An extraordinary revolution in his sentiments, took place as late as the time when he began to study the works of Glas and Sandeman."[4] Ewing encouraged Robert Haldane's change of mind as seen in a statement by Ewing regarding Robert Haldane:

> The fact was that before he [Robert Haldane] had read Glas and Sandeman, he had a great dislike to them. . . . When the first class after mine, met at Edinburgh, Mr. Haldane not only kept those books out of the library, but laid the students under an express prohibition from reading them. From that moment, they seemed like forbidden fruit, to be 'good for food, and pleasant to the eyes, and to be desired to make one wise.' They had never been read by the students before with half so great and general avidity. At last Mr. Haldane was induced to read them himself, and became as much enamoured, as before he had been jealous of them.[5]

When Alexander Campbell met Greville Ewing on November 3, 1808, following the shipwreck, he "was most hospitably received."[6] On two occasions Ewing helped

Campbell secure lodging for his family. For the next nine months Campbell fell heavily under the influence of Ewing and his associates, a fact attested by Campbell's chief biographer, Robert Richardson, who wrote: "Alexander was frequently at Mr. Ewings to dinner or to tea, where he formed many agreeable intimacies with the guests at his hospitable board, and acquired, during this intercourse, an intimate knowledge of Mr. Ewing's previous religious history, and that of his coadjutors, the Haldanes and others."[7]

Campbell listed his friends in Glasgow as Ewing, Gilbert Wardlaw, seventeen other Independent ministers, and fourteen students he knew at the university and at Ewing's seminary. That Campbell inundated himself with their discussions on religious Independency appears from his own comment: "We did not attend any place of worship regularly but I was never out of the congregation at assembly on the Lord's Day." In the same entry Campbell wrote that he "attended Ewing's frequently," referring to his worship services.[8] Campbell, therefore, met, studied, and contemplated for some nine months in Glasgow the respective beliefs of Glas, Sandeman, Ewing, Wardlaw, the Haldanes, and likely others. Though the fully developed thought that Campbell attained in later years does not precisely parallel any one of the men mentioned, the overall similarity and affinity with the thought and spirit of all of them is unmistakable. He did not inherit the theological system of any one or two men, but he did fall heir to the heritage of Independency, including the restitution or restoration principle.[9]

The Haldane Influence Moves to America

During the early years of the Stone-Campbell Restoration movement, 1809-1820, various groups and individuals of similar beliefs converged. Among these were isolated individuals and congregations of Haldaneans, Sandemanians, and Scotch Baptists in America. One important example of the connection between the Scottish and American restoration was that of George Forrester and John Tassey who emigrated from Scotland to Pittsburgh, approximately 1816-1818. Forrester, a member of the Haldanean connection, was baptized after the practice of the Haldanes, and Tassey was a product of Robert Haldane's seminary.[10] Upon their arrival in Pittsburgh they established a church and an academy for secular education. In May, 1819, Walter Scott arrived in Pittsburgh seeking employment, himself newly emigrated from Scotland, and was employed by Forrester as a teacher. Scott studied the Scriptures with Forrester, and within a few weeks was baptized by him.[11]

When Forrester died unexpectedly, Walter Scott was suddenly faced with the responsibility of maintaining the congregation started by Forrester. Soon he was preaching for the church and studying the books left in Forrester's library, which he later describes:

> He [George Forrester] left behind him also an excellent library containing many volumes on Holy Scripture, as Benson on the Epistles, McKnight's Harmony of the Gospels, Catchbull's Notes, Haldane's Works, Campbell on the Four Gospels, Lock's

Reasonableness of Christianity, McKnight on the Epistles, Carson's Works with those of Wardlaw, Glas, Sandeman, Letters published Eld. Errett, New York.[12]

Theological similarities between the thought of the Haldanes and Glas are readily observed. Haldane emphasized the absolute authority of Scripture in all religious matters and stressed that the New Testament contained the pattern for all Christian service.[13] He also taught that the apostolic church provided a model for Christians in all ages to recover and practice, thus teaching the idea of "restitution" or "restoration."[14] The system of church government taught by the Haldanes was one of local congregational autonomy that set leaders over each congregation.[15] Elders were to serve as congregational leaders, and there was to be no distinction of ruling or teaching elders, a distinction made in the Church of Scotland.

James Haldane believed that each congregation should have deacons[16] and that a civil magistrate possessed no authority over God's church other than to uphold the faith as a Christian.[17] Haldane affirmed the weekly observance of the Lord's Supper.[18] In regard to baptism, he stated that there was no particular mode to be observed, though he used Glas's term "washing" in reference to baptism.[19] Three years later, however, both Haldanes accepted immersion as the scriptural mode of baptism and were so baptized. James Haldane saw the necessity for church discipline but encouraged its reasonable exercise rather than the strict form practiced by Glas and Sandeman.

In many ways the Haldanes were theological descendents of Glas and Sandeman, but the brothers exhibited a dynamic evangelistic zeal that did not exist with Glas or Sandeman. While the Haldanes might be characterized as zealous evangelists and Glas and Sandeman as pastors who tended their own flocks, their basic doctrinal beliefs, nevertheless, bore remarkable similarities.

Campbell's 1847 Tour of Great Britain[20]

In 1847 Alexander Campbell returned to Great Britain for a visit. Lasting from April to October, 1847, the tour was made to strengthen ties with Christian groups in the British Isles. He visited Scotch Baptists, Sandemanians, Congregationalists, and several Independent churches. Campbell stopped first in London where he met and preached for both General and Particular Baptist congregations which received him cordially. He then met with Scotch Baptists who were also receptive to him. Scotch Baptists had emphasized the importance of adult baptism for remission of sins and thus had split from the Edinburgh Glasites.

From England, Campbell traveled to Edinburgh where he tried to meet James Haldane and the brethren in the church with him. On the occasion Campbell reminisced that the evangelical cause and the beginning of a "new class of congregations over a considerable portion of Scotland and Ireland" had begun from the efforts of "Greville Ewing, William Ballantine, Alexander Carson, Ralph Wardlaw and Mr. Innes."[21]

Perhaps the most significant event on Campbell's tour was the cooperative meeting held at Chester County on October 1–3, 1847, because this meeting reflected the fellowship enjoyed by a wide group of churches in England, Scotland, Ireland, and Wales.[22]

The majority of the congregations from England came from the northwestern counties where the early churches of Christ after the thought of Robert Sandeman had been established eighty years earlier. From Criccieth, Wales, William Jones, a relative of John Richard Jones of that city who had led the restoration in Wales following Sandeman's trip there, attended the Chester meeting. The Welsh church was clearly of Sandemanian origin though it later openly identified with Campbell and the American Restoration Movement. The churches represented from Scotland were all from the area in central Scotland where John Glas began his work. Therefore, many, if not most, of the congregations represented at Chester were originally associated with John Glas and Robert Sandeman, Scotch Baptists, and churches after the tradition of the Haldanes.[23]

On Sunday, October 3, Campbell preached at the Chester church to 700 people; that afternoon the Lord's Supper was observed by 150 persons. Afterwards, Campbell journeyed to Liverpool, where he preached that evening and on Tuesday, October 5, Campbell boarded a steamship for his return to America.[24]

Glas, Sandeman and the Lord's Supper

Having established the primary path by which the teachings of John Glas and Robert Sandeman entered the thinking of Alexander Campbell and other early American restoration leaders, attention is now focused on the specific teachings of Glas and Sandeman regarding the Lord's Supper, their central theological tenet.

Issues regarding the Lord's Supper first arose in the summer of 1730 soon after Glas had moved his family to Dundee. Family and friends urged him to take a holiday, and during his absence the question arose as to whether the Lord's Supper could be observed without the presence of an "ordained minister." Opinions in the church quickly split into two camps with one contending that the men who had formerly served as elders in the Church of Scotland could administer the communion while the other group insisted they could not since they were "ruling elders" and not "teaching elders," a distinction made by the Church of Scotland.

James Don and George Miller were chosen to go to Dunkeld where Glas was resting and seek an answer to the problem. Glas returned to Dundee and met with the members who were assembled and waiting for him. The matter was considered in light of Acts 20:17–18, 1 Timothy 3, and Titus 1. The men decided that since "apt to teach" was a qualification for elders, anyone who lacked such ability was not truly an elder; thus, the twofold distinction of elders, held by the Church of Scotland, was dropped by the Dundee congregation.

Their study also revealed that the Scriptures contained no requirements for an educated or ordained ministry, only requirements of character and ability. So, after several days of fasting, the Dundee church selected Glas and James Cargill, a handloom weaver, to serve as elders. Thus, the principle of searching the Scriptures for answers to questions was set on a permanent course for these followers.

The New Covenant Signified in the Lord's Supper

The doctrine of the Lord's Supper was central to the theological system of the Glasites, as they were called in Scotland and Sandemanian as they were known in England and New England. So central to the theology of the Glasites did the Lord's Supper become that in 1743 Glas wrote a 250 page treatise covering a wide range of aspects of the Lord's Supper. The Lord's Supper was the theological hub that connected several significant doctrines held by Glasites and Sandemanians. The first of those was the belief that an important distinction existed between the Old and New Testaments and that the New Testament, not the Old, was the pattern for the church. This belief was a major departure from the Church of Scotland that had built its justification for a national church on the theocracy of the Old Testament.[25]

Glas and Sandeman explained that the covenant in Christ's blood is declared in his supper and is the new covenant in contrast to the previous covenant with Israel which was only temporary.[26] The new covenant of grace can give eternal life not because humanity can have perfect obedience, but because of God's gracious gift. Therefore, eternal life comes from ending the curse of the old covenant and recognizing the hope brought by the new covenant. The new covenant signifies salvation through the death of Jesus which puts to death the curse of the law.[27]

The first covenant was written on tablets of stone and the second or new covenant is written on the hearts of people. Glas explained this concept as the work of regeneration and new birth without which a person cannot enter the kingdom of God.[28] It is an act of God's grace that came by the blood of Jesus and is signified in the Lord's Supper.

Glas reasoned that the new covenant was to be distinguished from the old covenant by three divine promises. The first promise was that God would make a new covenant (Jer 31:31). The second promise was that all would know the Lord from the least to the greatest (Jer 31:34). On this point Glas wrote: "As the people of the new covenant are distinguished from all others by their knowledge of the Lord....This is the new spiritual brotherhood, different from, and far excelling the old fleshly brotherhood of the first covenant."[29] The third promise Glas identified was also from Jeremiah 31:34: "For I will be merciful to their unrighteousness. And their sins and their iniquities will I remember no more."[30] From these promises, Glas concluded that the new covenant is grounded in the blood of Christ: "We are made to know and obey Jesus Christ because the remission of our sins is in him through his blood."[31] Thus, it is the blood of Christ that Christians are to remember and honor with their worship and their lives.

The Nature of the Church and the Lord's Supper

The nature of the church is also integrally interwoven with Glas's understanding of the Lord's Supper. Christ's church communes in the sacrifice of Jesus and his blood as one unified body. Glas saw in the description of the church an emphasis on the union of the church. Christ is the head of this unified body called the church. This new body, the church, is distinguished from the "body of Moses" in the Old Testament. This new church, which is the body of Christ, is the only true church, whereas the church of the Old Testament was just a figure of the true church to come.[32]

> A church of the New Testament, that comes together in one place to eat the Lord's supper, as the church in Corinth, is not the true church, the body of Christ itself, but the sign of it; even as the bread and cup are signs of his broken body and shed blood; and it is called the church, and the body of Christ, in the same sense wherein the bread that we break is called his broken body, and the cup his blood: so that, as there is but one Christ that was sacrificed for us, though his broken body and shed blood be represented to us in many different places in the Lord's supper by the bread and wine, which is called his body and blood; even so there is but one church, the body of Christ, though it be represented and shewed forth in every church that, according to his institution, comes together any where to eat his supper.[33]

Glas reasoned that every gathering of Christians for the purpose of observing the Lord's Supper is a church. He further stated that there was not any larger group of Christians than what might assemble in one place to observe the Lord's Supper. That group, Glas reasoned, is a sign of the body of Christ and must not be divided just as Christ was not divided. On this point Glas observed that baptism must precede one's partaking of the Lord's Supper.[34]

Perhaps the most significant point for Glas was that in order for the church to commune with Christ and the sacrifice of his blood, they must all partake together in harmony else the body of Christ is divided.[35] From this belief followed the conclusion that the Lord's Supper could not be observed by an individual person or administered to an individual person.

> And this is a remarkable difference betwixt baptism and the Lord's supper: for though we be all baptized into the same body of Christ, the true church, which is represented in the Lord's supper…but the nature of the lord's supper will not admit of a believer's receiving it alone…and therefore there is no instance of it in the New Testament.[36]

The Eldership and the Lord's Supper

The eldership of a local church was interwoven with the meaning of the Lord's Supper. First, a church did not exist as a true church unless it had a plurality of elders. Second, the elders had responsibility to maintain the unity of the church by exercising discipline as a means of preventing disharmony among members and sin which disrupted the church. As the physical body of Christ was unified so the church, the body of

Christ, must be unified in order to observe the Lord's Supper and the Lord's Supper was the primary reason for assembling on the Lord's Day.[37]

Of the Sandemanians in New England in 1766, Ezra Stiles, President of Yale, reported "That upon any difference they practiced Christ's rule immediately till it was bro't before the Church and settled and made up in the week; for there could be no communion (which they celebrate every Lord's Day) if a single member had aught against a brother [sic]."[38] Sandeman agreed with his father-in-law John Glas, that the church, a local congregation, had to have elders to be scripturally organized and they were to be present in the Sunday worship to oversee the observance of the Lord's Supper, which the deacons typically administered to the congregation.[39]

Church Discipline and the Lord's Supper

Because the visible church represents the true church and the body of Christ, then the unity of the visible church must be maintained and always preserved. That means that when members forsake the assembly or have sins of a public nature or are not in harmony with one another, that the church, the body of Christ is not one and thus cannot observe the Lord's Supper.[40] Sin among the members disrupts the bond of peace which Glas interprets to be the new covenant in the blood of Jesus.

The church must be visibly one as it was in Acts 11:21-26 and Acts 20:7 when it assembled on the first day of the week for the purpose of breaking bread. Faithful continuance in assembling to break bread demonstrates the perseverance of the church in its faith and hope in the gospel. On this point Glas stated:

> A church that comes together in one place to eat the Lord's Supper, being thus united as a body, must take care to be without schism or division among themselves in assembling to that ordinance; that so they may perceive the union and communion of the body of Christ, the true church.[41]

Self-examination, Glas reasoned, is essential for each person and for the church to avoid division. Each person must know whether their life is in harmony with the principles of the gospel and they must be aware of their union with the body of Christ.[42]

Discipline was to be exercised within the church to maintain the unity of the church. Citing Matthew 18:17, Acts 15:4, 22; 16:26 and 1 Corinthians 5:9-11, Glas emphasized that the whole church was to act together in matters of discipline and the elders were to be the leaders in all disciplinary situations. The elders, too, were first to be in harmony among themselves on matters of discipline and only then could they lead the whole church to act. Glas interpreted Jesus' statement to the disciples, "Whatsoever ye shall bind on earth, shall be bound in heaven; and whatsoever ye shall loose on earth, shall be loosed in heaven," as a reference to the discipline process led by the church elders.[43] The elders were to follow only the word of God, the "keys of the kingdom," in a matter of discipline and that was also their authority to do so. The whole demeanor of discipline was to be in love including all admonitions and words spoken to the person.[44] Finally, "When a whole church trespasses, the Lord himself chastens them, as he did Corinth; and if they repent not, he removes their candlestick, as he threatens the Ephesians."[45]

Music and the Lord's Supper

Discussion among the members apparently occurred regarding what music was appropriate prior to observing the Lord's Supper. This is suggested by a letter from an unnamed brother to Robert Sandeman dated November 17, 1760, in which he asked Sandeman what hymns they sang at the Lord's Supper,[46] and though Sandeman's reply is not known one might assume that the hymn "Thy Worthiness is all our Song" was the likely and preferred hymn for that purpose. The hymn, written by Glas, was later glued into the front cover of *The Book of Psalms in Metre* which was used for singing in worship. In a letter from elder Gerard Sandeman dated September 2, 1984, he stated that the Lord's Supper was "concluded by singing—'Thy worthiness is all our song.'"[47] That was the same practice on a Sunday in January, 1985, when I visited the Barony Street congregation in Edinburgh. The three stanzas of the hymn read:

1. Thy worthiness is all our song;
   O Lamb of God! For thou wast slain;
   And by thy blood bought'st us to God
   Out of each nation, tribe, and tongue;
   And we shall reign upon the earth.

2. Salvation to our God, who shines,
   In face of Jesus, on the throne,
   The only just and merciful:
   Salvation to the worthy lamb,
   With loud voice, all the Church ascribes;
   Amen! Say angels round the throne.

3. To Him who loved us, and wash'd
   Us from our sins in his own blood,
   And who hath made us kings and priests
   To his own Father and his God,—
   The glory and dominion be
   To Him eternally. *Amen!*[48]

Worship Service Order, the *Agape* Feast and the Lord's Supper

The order of Sunday services was apparently arranged so as to avoid having non-members be present to partake of the Lord's Supper. The Barony Street congregation in Edinburgh was the last extant congregation of this fellowship, and they began their worship each Sunday at 11:15 am, when I visited in 1985. The service consisted of a little over an hour of prayers, scripture readings and the singing of Psalms. That service was followed by the agape or love feast that was a simple fellowship lunch upstairs in the feast room. Following a prayer the group had soup followed by beef, carrots and potatoes. The meal was concluded with a song and the kiss of charity that passed around the table.[49] This noon meal was a standard practice of churches in Scotland, England and New England and earned the Scottish churches the name "Kale Churches" because of the traditional cabbage soup that was served. The *agape* or love feast was a fellowship meal that was typically open only to members and had no connection with the Lord's Supper.

Following the love feast, the congregation enjoyed a rest for half an hour and then the afternoon service at 2:15. This service included prayers, scripture readings, singing of Psalms, a collection and the weekly Lord's Supper.[50] Some references suggest that the doors of the meeting house were opened to the public for only the service portion that did not include the Lord's Supper. The account by Ezra Stiles indicates that the doors were shut prior to the Lord's Supper. In New England the Lord's Supper came in the final hour of a six hour service or at about 4 in the afternoon. Stiles reports that "The Assembly dismissed; and Chh [sic] stay & Doors shut"[51]

Further Spiritual Meanings of the Lord's Supper

Glas saw meaning in each of the several names used for the "ordinance" as he designated it. He stated that it was called a supper because Jesus ate it in the evening of the Passover and so it should be distinguished from a regular meal. Furthermore, the Lord's Supper was to be observed in the evening and not morning or mid-day. Breaking of bread was another term Glas identified though he recognized that term also to be used of a common meal which he took to be the love feast or *agape* feast.[52] The expression breaking of bread, in his understanding, came from the action of breaking the bread that Paul refers to in 1 Corinthians 10:16 and without which the observance was not complete.

The Lord's Supper is also called the communion, upon which Glas observed:

> Therefore the communion, or joint partaking, of the bread and of the wine by Christ's disciples as one body, must be most carefully observed, as that which is of very great significance…and without which it is no more entire than it would be without the bread or the cup.[53]

Though the Scripture makes no use of this name [eucharist], Glas stated, "Yet that from which it is taken is very express in the institution of this ordinance."[54] He goes on to explain the meaning of this term as "blessing" or "thanksgiving" and that "The Lord himself blessed or gave thanks at the institution of his supper."[55] Sacrament is the final term addressed by Glas—a term that does not appear in scripture but is used in the Latin Bible for mystery. As such the term might well express the hidden meanings of Christ's sacrifice that are not fully understood.[56]

Remembrance of Jesus, his life, his teachings and all that he came to accomplish are essential aspects of observing the Lord's Supper according to Glas. Because the Lord's Supper is the most solemn outward act of worship, a serious remembrance of Jesus as the fulfillment of all that God has done is proper observance.[57] Jesus' statement "this is my body and my blood" reminds us that Jesus came to this earth to be with us in flesh and blood and that to remember him is to remember his earthly life. It is to recall that the word became flesh as John states and that He was born into this world of a virgin because God was sending his son into this world for our sakes. The whole reason for the four gospels, according to Glas, was to keep Jesus' life in remembrance. [58]

Christians are to remember Jesus' poverty, pain and suffering of both body and mind as a proper remembrance. "The remembrance of him in the holiness of his life, when he dwelt among us, serves to posses us with a true notion of a holy life...and to keep us from being misled by false examples."[59] He was the essence of truth and sincerity and his character was meek and patient with the injuries he received, returning good for evil and forgiving his enemies. These are things that must be remembered about Jesus as he lived a life of obedience to the father here on earth, because they inspire the same attitude and behavior in his disciples today.[60]

Remembrance of Jesus' infinite love is recognition of God's greatest gift, the gospel. "Now in the human nature of the Son of God, thus furnished with the grace of the Holy Ghost, we find the nearest imitation of the divine love; and his obedience to the death is the most perfect conformity to that love."[61] Christians further remember him as the seed of Abraham who came as a blessing for all nations and the fulfillment of the Law of Moses, "Thus all that he did and suffered, in the days of his flesh, was in love to his people of all nations, without difference."[62] So, as Paul expressed his imitation of the love of Christ, so we also are to do the same with our lives, showing love to those around us. Glas states that when we remember the love of Jesus in giving his life by giving his body and his blood, and by praying for those who persecuted him that they might have eternal life; we can then look on ourselves as no more deserving of his dying love than were they.[63]

Jesus' love to his disciples is the pattern of love required of his disciples one to another. He was humble in his love to his disciples and so they are to be humble in love to each other. Thus, Glas concludes that as Jesus washed the feet of his disciples as an expression of humble love so are we to do the same even as the ministering widow or deaconess did in 1 Timothy 5:10. Likewise, the "kiss of charity" was an expression of brotherly love one to another that Glas believed should be practiced among Christians.[64] So in remembering Jesus' "broken body and shed blood" Glas says there are three aspects of that loving gift that cannot be forgotten. First, Jesus lived his love for humankind rather than just speaking of it. Second, his love was based on self-denial of his own comfort and life, and third, his love was from a pure heart.[65]

The whole concept of remembrance, Glas observed, suggests that Jesus has ascended to heaven and is no longer present on earth in bodily form, thus calling his disciples to remember him, and that he was born into the world and has left the world to return to the Father.[66] To remember him is to remember that he left to become our intercessor. Jesus' return to heaven is also a great reminder of our utter dependence on him for forgiveness and that we have no merit in ourselves. As the supper is observed, therefore, it must be eaten in total confidence in his sacrifice and intercessions.[67]

The very fact that Christians rest from their work each week and remember him is a sign of the truth of God's promise, Glas believed. "This remembrance of Him is to be continued during His absence, and till He comes again."[68] This, then, is the primary reason for assembling on the first day of the week, to remember Jesus until he comes again.

Greville Ewing first introduced into the Glasgow tabernacle weekly Lord's Supper and congregational government composed of elders and deacons.[69] "The keeping of the Lord's day is a solemn profession of the faith, love, and hope that is in Christ, as well as the eating of the Lord's supper" Glas reasoned.[70] This remembrance and anticipation of his return encourages faithfulness in God's people, Glas explained.[71]

> At the very heart of the Lord's Supper and the Christian faith is the death of Jesus Christ as the one and only true sacrifice, a theme emphasized many times in Glas' theology. He explained "In the institution of sacrifices, God appointed emblems of the defilement of the conscience by sin; whereby sinners are separated from God...."[72]
> Furthermore, "In the emblematical purification and atonement, God shewed the method of the true sacrifice; for we see the defilement by the dead transferred on the heifer, whereby they are cleansed from that uncleanness (Num. xix.7, 9)."[73]

From the Old Testament examples of sacrifice, Glas explained that the laying on of hands on the head of the sacrifice signified the transfer of guilt. Glas also explained that the daily sacrifices intimated that God's judgment against sin was not truly executed in them nor was justice satisfied by those animal sacrifices.[74] Drawing together several ideas, Glas explains:

> The Lord's supper plainly declares the sacrifice of Christ already offered as the end of all the offerings for sin, as he says, in the institution of it, *This is my blood for the new testament, which is shed for many for the remission of sins*: for thus he evidently sets forth himself in his death as the sacrifice for sins, the blood of the new testament, or covenant; that is, the covenant wherein God says, *Their sins and their iniquities will I remember no more.*[75]

Since the Lord's Supper shows the death of Jesus as the true and actual sacrifice, there is then no repetition of his sacrifice in the supper.[76] That is, Christ is not repeatedly sacrificed each time the Lord's Supper is observed. In the supper we declare Jesus to be both the sacrifice and the altar. "The body and blood of the Lord, itself, is the only sacrifice whereof we eat and drink, and wherein we have communion with God in the supper."[77] The supper also demonstrates that Jesus' death was the true sacrifice of the

Passover lamb. His disciples, therefore, are to purge from themselves malice and evil and from the church they are to purge those who are found living in wickedness.[78]

Conclusion

The ideal of restoring the faith and practice of the New Testament was the goal of the eighteenth-century Scottish leaders, Glas, Sandeman, the Haldanes, and the later nineteenth-century American restorationists. But though there were direct connections and influences between the two movements, there was a definite difference in theological emphasis. Glas and Sandeman both developed a theological system that upheld the sacrifice of Jesus as the central and foundational principle of the Christian faith. From that emphasis the doctrine of the Lord's Supper became the practical as well as theological hub of their thought. In that supper they saw all of God's love and grace to humankind exhibited. They saw the all sufficient sacrifice of Jesus in its meaning as well. This differs from Stone-Campbell restorationists in the next century, who gave much of their attention to the meaning of baptism due to the close relation to the Baptists.

Notes

[1]John Glas, "The Right of the Christian People, and the Power of their Pastors, in the Ordination of Ministers of the Gospel Asserted," in *The Works of Mr. John Glas,* 5 vols. (Perth: R. Morison and Son, 1782), 2:232-33; John Glas, "A Treatise on the Lord's Supper", *Works*, 5:13; and John Glas, "A Second Letter to Mr. Aytone, Containing Remarks Upon His Review", *Works*, 1:377.

[2]John Glas, *Remarks on the Subject of Modern Religious Divisions* (Edinburgh: n.p., 1801), p. 35-36.

[3]Harry Escott, *A History of Scottish Congregationalism* (Glasgow: The Congregational Union of Scotland, 1960), p. 78.

[4]Greville Ewing, *Facts and Documents Respecting the Connections Which Have Subsisted Between Robert Haldane, Esq. and Greville Ewing* (Glasgow: James Hedderwick and Co., 1809) p. 133.

[5]Ibid., p. 82.

[6]Alexander Campbell, "Journal of a Voyage from Ireland Towards America, 1808" (Nashville: Disciples of Christ Historical Society).

[7]Robert Richardson, *Memoirs of Alexander Campbell,* 2 vols. (Nashville: Gospel Advocate, 1956): 1.149.

[8]Campbell, "Journal of a Voyage."

[9]Thomas W. Grafton, *Alexander Campbell: Leader of the Great Reformation of the Nineteenth Century* (St. Louis: Christian Publishing Co., 1897), p. 43.

[10]Winfred Ernest Garrison, *Religion Follows the Frontier* (New York: Harper and Brothers, 1931), p. 109.

[11]William Baxter, *Life of Elder Walter Scott* (Cincinnati: Bosworth, Chase and Hall, Pubs., 1874), pp. 38, 45.

[12]Walter Scott, *The Messiahship, or Great Demonstration, Written for the Union of Christians on Christian Principles* (reprint ed., Kansas City: Old Paths Book Club, n.d.) p. 7.

[13]James Alexander Haldane, *A View of the Social Worship and Ordinances by the First Christians* (Edinburgh: J. Ritchie, 1805), pp. 17-18.

[14]Ibid., p. 39. See also, pp. 93, 169.

[15]Ibid., pp. 143, 220. See also, p. 225.

[16]Ibid., p. 145. See also, pp. 252, 284.

[17]Ibid., pp. 102, 132. See also p. 432.

[18]Ibid., pp. 89, 295. See also, pp. 293, 297, 301.

[19]Ibid., pp. 327, 339.

[20]Thomas Chalmers, *Alexander Campbell's Tour in Scotland* (reprint ed., Nashville: Gospel Advocate, n.d.).

[21]Alexander Campbell, "Letters from Europe, No. XXV," *Millennial Harbinger* (April, 1848): 220.

[22]Alexander Campbell, "Letters from Europe, No. XXXII," *Millennial Harbinger* (October, 1848): 565-66.

[23]E. Roberts-Thomson, *Baptists and Disciples of Christ* (London: Carey Kingsgate Press Ltd., n.d.), p. 38.

[24]Campbell, "Letters, No. XXXII," p. 574.

[25]John T. Hornsby, "John Glas: A Study of the Origins, Development and Influence of the Glasite Movement" (Ph.D. dissertation, University of Edinburgh, 1936), gives a fairly thorough discussion of Glas' theological thinking.

[26]John Glas, *A Treatise on the Lord's Supper* (London: Sampson, Low, Marston, Searle and Rivington, 1883), p. 130. This same treatise first appeared in John Glas, *The Works of John Glas*, 4 vols.(Edinburgh: Alexander Donaldson, 1761), 4:1-191. Citations for this chapter are made from the later 1883 copy due to the fragility of the 1761 volume in the author's library.

[27]Glas, Treatise, p. 135; and Robert Sandeman, Letter No. 3 to Jean Smellom, Perth, 10th March 1736, from Robert Sandeman," in *Letters in Correspondence By Robert Sandeman, John Glas, and their Contemporaries* (Dundee: Hill and Alexander, 1851), p. 14.

[28]Ibid., p. 144.

[29]Ibid., pp.149-150. The version quoted here and elsewhere in this chapter by Glas is uncertain. It is possibly his own translation.

[30]Ibid., p. 151.

[31]Ibid., p. 156.

[32]Ibid., p. 163.

[33]Ibid., p. 165.

[34]Ibid., p. 169.

[35]Ibid., p.171.

[36]Ibid., p. 172.

[37]Robert Sandeman, *Letters on Theron and Aspasio,* 2 vols.; 4th ed. (London: J. Chater, 1768), 2:197-199.

[38]Ezra Stiles, "Memoirs concerning Mr. Robert Sandeman, 1764" (Yale University, Beinecke Manuscript Library, Stiles Manuscripts), p. 29.

[39]Ibid. See also Letters in Correspondence, "Robert Sandeman to Samuel Newham, Edinburgh, December 31, 1759," pp. 41-42.

[40]Glas, *Treatise*, p. 180.

[41]Ibid., p. 185.

[42]Ibid., p. 190.

[43]Ibid., p. 203.

[44]Ibid., p. 210.

[45]Ibid., p. 215. See also *Supplementary Volume of Letters and Other Documents, by John Glas, Robert Sandeman, and their contemporaries* (Perth: Morison and Duncan, 1865), p. iii.

46 *Supplementary Volume*, "Mr. J. Densham to Mr. Sandeman, London, 17th Nov., 1760," p. 100.

47 Personal letter from Gerard Sandeman of Edinburgh, Scotland to Lynn McMillon (September 2, 1984).

48 The hymn is pasted to the inside cover of *The Book of Psalms in Metre* (Edinburgh: George Waterston and Sons, 1902).

49 Lynn McMillon, "Research Trip to Edinburgh and London, January 4-13, 1985" unpublished personal notebook, p. 9.

50 Ibid., pp. 12-13. The author was permitted to be present but was not allowed to partake of the Lord's Supper. In Letters in Correspondence, "Memoranda of John Glas and Robert Sandeman," 119, the frequency of the Lord's Supper is discussed and concluded from Acts 20:7 to be a weekly and not monthly observance.

51 Stiles, "Memoirs," p. 31-34.

52 Glas, *Treatise*, p. 24-25.

53 Ibid., p. 28.

54 Ibid., p. 29.

55 Ibid., p. 30.

56 Ibid., pp. 32-34.

57 Ibid. 41.

58 Ibid., pp. 45-46.

59 Ibid., p. 47.

60 Ibid., pp. 49-50.

61 Ibid., p. 51.

62 Ibid., p. 53.

63 Ibid., p. 56.

64 Ibid., pp. 63-64.

65 Ibid., pp. 65-66.

66 Ibid., p. 67.

67 Ibid., p. 72.

68 Ibid. Song XVII in *Christian Songs*, 14th ed. (Perth: Morison and Duncan, 1872), p. 33, is a specific song about and for the Lord's Supper.

69 Alexander Haldane, *Memoirs of the Lives of Robert Haldane of Airthrey, and of His Brother, James Alexander Haldane* (New York: Robert Carter and Brothers, 1853), p. 322.

70 Glas, *Treatise*, p. 77.

71 Ibid., p. 78.

72 Ibid., p. 80.

73 Ibid., p. 81.

74 Ibid., p. 83.

75 Ibid., p. 85.

76 Ibid., p. 87.

77 Ibid., p. 104.

78 Ibid., p. 119

10

THE LORD'S SUPPER IN THE NEW TESTAMENT

Mark S. Krause

The Eucharist is Jesus.
Gospel of Phillip, 3rd Century

T ackling the subject of the Lord's Supper is a project both daunting and timely. It is daunting because of the enormous literature that exists concerning this topic. It touches Jesus studies, Gospels studies, Pauline studies, study of Christian origins, and several other areas of biblical and church historical studies. Furthermore, every Bible dictionary/encyclopedia, Christian theological handbook, or systematic theology will include an article on the subject written by one of the best contributors. This study is more complex than the simple comment from the *Gospel of Phillip*.

The task is timely because the Lord's Supper has received renewed interest in the twenty-first century. For example, John Paul II proclaimed October 2004 – October 2005 as the "Year of the Eucharist," with special events aimed at renewal of this practice in the Roman Catholic Church. At the same time the United Methodist Church is actively endorsing weekly communion among its congregations as a way of promoting a "richer sacramental life."[1] Another ongoing trend showing intense interest in the Lord's Supper is found in the postmodern "emerging church" with its neo-primitivism that seeks to rediscover the mystery of worship and liturgy.[2]

Preliminary Matters

Limits on the Study
This study will first be limited by confining itself to the New Testament, with no attempt to explore the Lord's Supper in its history and development. Four primary

texts will be examined (Mt 26, Mk 14, Lk 22, and 1 Cor 10-11), along with a few other passages with eucharistic overtones.

Even within the New Testament, though, there are a number of historical questions related to this study that have had no satisfying answers. Perhaps the most perplexing have to do with trying to understand how the Last Supper of Jesus and his disciples (as portrayed in the Synoptic Gospels) became the Lord's Supper of the early church (as evidenced in 1 Corinthians). This includes the following specific questions: (1) How did it shift from a meal originally on Thursday to an event on Sunday? (2) How did it shift from a fellowship meal to a symbolic ritual celebrated in the context of worship? (3) How did it shift from an annual Passover meal to a more frequent (perhaps weekly) celebration? The tie between the Last Supper and the Lord's Supper is undeniable (particularly in 1 Corinthians), but this does little to resolve the tension created by these substantial changes between the two events.

Therefore, a second limiting factor in this study will be to concentrate more on the theological significance of the Lord's Supper and less on historical investigation of its origins and development. A previous generation was often preoccupied by trying to determine exactly what Jesus said and did at the Last Supper and how this became the Lord's Supper of the early church.[3] While some important findings emerged as a result of these studies, their tendency for fragmentation and speculative reconstruction some-times overlooked the theological intent of the New Testament author-theologians.

Historical Aspects

Some important historical aspects related to these texts cannot be ignored. As Leonard Goppelt has noted, the Synoptic Gospels record the Last Supper as part of their narrative, thus fulfilling their particular audiences' need for "catechism about Jesus' ministry." Goppelt also sees the account in 1 Corinthians as likely a decade or more earlier arising from Paul's need for corrective instruction concerning the "liturgy of celebration at the Lord's Supper."[4] Therefore, even though these four accounts have obvious similarities (and differences) between, the *Sitz im Leben* of each author is substantially different, and each will yield a distinctive theological perspective. As John Reumann has observed, it is an error to see the New Testament presenting the Lord's Supper in "simple purity," while the post-New Testament era begins a fall into confusion and "decadence."[5] Even in the New Testament era there appears to have been a "good deal of variety in the way in which Christians observed their common meal."[6]

Terminology

A necessary consideration for this study is choice of terminology. Marshall finds four distinct terms used by the New Testament authors for this congregational event: Holy Communion, Lord's Supper, Breaking of Bread, and Eucharist.[7] Stein adds a fifth to this list, the Table of the Lord.[8] Each of these presupposes a certain theological emphasis and will at times be useful for this study, employing them as their theological entail-ments demand. The usual default designation will be the Lord's Supper.

Theological Themes
Previous studies have offered lists of major theological themes subsumed under the cat-egory of the Lord's Supper. For example, an important document in this regard is "Baptism, Eucharist, and Ministry" (BEM), an ecumenical effort of the World Council of Churches that was finalized at Lima, Peru in 1982.[9] BEM distinguished five "mean-ings" for the Lord's Supper: 1) Thanksgiving to the Father (Eucharist), 2) Memorial of Christ (*Anamnesis*), 3) Invocation of the Spirit (= presence of Christ), 4) Communion of the Faithful, and 5) Meal of the Kingdom. These are helpful for BEM's ecumenical purposes, but they incorporate a mixture of understandings of the Lord's Supper from the New Testament and the influence of later church practice.

Eduard Schweizer finds three theological motifs concerning the Lord's Supper in the New Testament: 1) Proclamation of the death of Jesus (1 Cor 11:26), 2) new con-firmation of God's covenant with the church (1 Cor 10:18-22), and 3) anticipation of the messianic banquet of the future (Mk 14:25).[10] These, too, are helpful categories, and come closer to what I have found, although my divisions are different.

My own analysis observes three primary areas for fruitful theological investigation concerning the Lord's Supper in the New Testament: as a Typological Meal, a Covenantal Meal, and as an Eschatological Meal. Despite overlap between the categories, each adds a distinct, theological perspective for understanding the Lord's Supper that will raise appreciation for this most fundamental of all Christian practices.

The Lord's Supper as a Typological Meal

Which is the medicine of immortality, the antidote against dying
Ignatius of Antioch, c. AD 110

Though typology is a neglected area of biblical interpretation today, it is a common feature of many New Testament writers.[11] Most readers are familiar with New Testament "fulfillments," but these are usually thought of in terms of predictive prophecy. In the predictive prophecy scheme, a God-spokesman in the Old Testament utters a prediction that comes true in the New Testament. The related scheme of typol-ogy also speaks in terms of "fulfillment," but with important differences. Typology is a way of understanding a person, event, or institution in the Old Testament as a prefig-uring or foreshadowing of a person, event, or institution in the New Testament.[12] The theological underpinning of typology is that the same God is operating in both the Old Testament and the New Testament, so related patterns may be detected running throughout the Bible.

Typology in 1 Corinthians 10

Richard M. Davidson has identified six New Testament passages in which the author has used typology as a hermeneutical tool to present his case.[13] Central to this identification is the presence of some form of the *typos* (type) word group employed to relate Old Testament scriptures or events to a New Testament issue. Two of these six are in 1 Corinthians 10.

This chapter displays the most extended use of typology of any New Testament passage. Within the context of Paul's corrective instruction of theologically dangerous actions in the Corinthian church, the Apostle employs a carefully drawn typological analogy from the history of the Exodus. His argument is initially summarized in 10:5, where the cumulative message is:

> These ancients had a lot of similarities to the contemporary people of God (the church, YOU!). They even had a type of baptism, a type of Lord's Supper, and a type of the presence of Christ in their midst, but these things did not make them immune from displeasing God.

This study does not intend to unravel all the features of Paul's argument in 1 Corinthians 10. However, since this typological line of reasoning is necessarily theological, it may provide help to appreciate Paul's understanding of the nature of the Lord's Supper. Three things may be noted. First, Paul refers to the Exodus ancestors as eating *to auto...brōma* (*the same food*, 10:3) and drinking *to auto...poma* (*the same drink*, 10:4).[14] What does Paul mean by "the same food," and "the same drink?" The repeated *to auto* (*the same*) should not be seen as saying that the wilderness Israelites celebrated the Lord's Supper like the Corinthians. The "sameness" refers to the historical fact that all the Israelites ate the same fare: manna and water. No "bread of breads" and "drink of drinks" was reserved for leadership or priesthood. Only one item appeared on the daily menu for all of them, and one choice for beverage. What this reveals is the unity that Paul finds in the act of eating and drinking the Lord's Supper as the gathered people of God. As he goes on to say, "We all eat from one loaf, showing that we are one body" (1 Cor 10:17, NTL). As Israel was united (at least in meal choices) so is the church united by participation in the Lord's Supper.

Second, Paul refers to the wilderness cuisine as *pneumatikon brōma* (*spiritual bread*) and *pneumatikon...poma* (*spiritual drink*). What is his intended meaning in referring to the manna and water as *pneumatikos*?[15] The English translations are nearly unanimous in rendering this as "spiritual," normally an acceptable equivalent.[16] This word appears frequently in 1 Corinthians (15x),[17] occasionally in other Pauline literature (9x),[18] and rarely in the rest of the New Testament (2x).[19] The word is used as an antonym for that which is material (*sarkinos*)[20] or physical/natural (*psychikos*).[21] Nowhere else, however, does Paul use *pneumatikos* in the context of physical nourishment.

The basic meaning of the *pneu** root is "blowing" with its connotations of invisible yet discernible air movement.[22] It is tempting to see *pneumatikos* as having the meaning "supernatural" or "miraculous" here.[23] However, this makes it difficult to understand the typological analogy that Paul is drawing for the Corinthians. The Corinthians had not been taught that staging the Lord's Supper was a continuing miraculous event. They did not consider the loaf and cup to be supernatural food. In fact, the abuses that Paul seeks to remedy with regard to the Lord's Supper indicate the opposite; that they treated the Lord's Supper far too casually for his tastes. Yet, it cannot be ignored that Paul presents the manna/water of the Exodus as prototypical of the loaf/cup of the Lord's Supper. How?

Perhaps the key to understanding this is found in the third theological point to be drawn from this text, that the Israelites also had a *pneumatikes petra* (spiritual rock) accompanying them in the wilderness. Whatever the source of Paul's picture of the shifting boulder, even more startling is his assertion that *hē petra…en ho christos* (the rock was the Messiah). Typologically this point is straightforward. As the Israelites had the *typos* of the presence of God (Christ) with them, so the Corinthians have the *antitypos* (antitype) of the presence of Christ (God) among them, especially during the Lord's Supper. Furthermore, Christ is the source of nourishment; physical for Israel, spiritual for Corinth. He is not the spiritual food and drink; he is the giver of these things.[24] It would follow that the Lord's Supper is Christ's meal, the *trapezēs kyriou* (table of the Lord, 10:21). As at the Last Supper, he is the host. Now, however, he must needs be the pneumatikos host, for he is not physically present.

Typology in John 6
Connecting the Lord's Supper and the Exodus also occurs in the Bread of Life Discourse in John 6. The Fourth Gospel does not include accounts of either the baptism of Jesus or the institution of the Lord's Supper. Both baptism and the Lord's Supper find their way into John's narrative indirectly, however, and in ways that reveal the theological priorities of the author. With Jesus' baptism, the act is not recounted, but the accompanying descent of the Holy Spirit is described from the lips of the Baptist himself (Jn 1:31-33). John's extended chronicle of the Last Supper (John 13-17) does not include anything like the "institution" of the Lord's Supper as found in the Synoptic Gospels and 1 Corinthians 11, but some of Jesus' words in the Bread of Life Discourse are bizarre and incomprehensible if they do not have reference to the Lord's Supper. This reaches a high point in 6:53-56. In this section, Jesus refers to his flesh as *alēthēs…brōmis* (*true food*, 6:55) and his blood as *alēthēs…posis* (*true drink*, 6:55). Jesus promises that the one who eats and drinks his flesh and blood will have *zōēn aiōnion* (*eternal life*, 6:54) and will *en emoi menei* (remain in me, 6:56).

While the connection between the Lord's Supper and the manna of Exodus is somewhat parallel to Paul's typological argument in 1 Corinthians 10, the context and the lesson are different. Here the manna discussion arises because of the feeding miracle of

Jesus. Expectations arising from this miracle lead the crowd to draw a comparison to the manna of the wilderness (6:31). Rather than assert the *pneumatikos* (spiritual) nature of this provision of God, Jesus points out that eating manna did nothing to prevent the natural death of the ancestors (6:49). What Jesus offers, then, is like the manna in that it is "from heaven" but unlike the manna in that it is "living bread."

As Dunn has noted, "eating" Jesus' flesh in John 6 is a metaphor for believing in him.[25] Although this text has been used extensively to support a sacramental, even magical view of the Lord's Supper, this is not John's point. The major theological issue of the Fourth Gospel is faith versus unfaith as in John 1:12; 12:39; 20:31. For the Johannine audience, participation in the Lord's Supper was an act of faith, an act of fellowship with the one in whom they had placed their faith. Understanding the Lord's Supper as action is theologically important. Guzie claims the shift from the Eucharist as an action to the significance of the elements themselves (as found in some Christian traditions today) is first written about by Radbert of Corbie, approximately AD 830, seven centuries after the New Testament period. Guzie comments, "None of the earliest christian writers described the eucharistic elements as objects [sic]."[26] John, therefore, is not teaching Ignatius's lesson of the Eucharist as the "Medicine of Immortality,"[27] unless Ignatius is content with the metaphor of eating/drinking Jesus = believing in Jesus.

The Lord's Supper as a Covenantal Meal

> *In tender memory of his grave*
> *The mystic bread we take*
> William Cullen Bryant, 1864

In all four accounts of Jesus' institution of the Lord's Supper at the Last Supper, the authors have him referring to the cup as *diathēkē* (covenant) and relate this to his blood. Some authors have drawn a distinction between the Mark/Matthew version[28] of this (blood of the covenant) and the Luke/1 Corinthians version[29] (new covenant in my blood). For example, Dunn sees the Mark/Matthew version as placing an accent upon the blood, thus pointing to a soteriological emphasis. The Luke/1 Corinthians wording (in Dunn's analysis) places an emphasis upon the covenant, thus giving eschatological prominence.[30] This distinction should not be drawn too tightly, however, for surely both soteriological and eschatological significance accrue to the Lord's Supper.

Remembering the Covenant

A covenant has no continuing value unless it is remembered by the parties involved. If a meal of remembrance is thought of as a covenant meal, several theological concepts emerge. With regard to the Lord's Supper, the connection to the Passover meal of the Jews becomes vital.

Exodus taught that the annual Passover celebration was to be a "day of remembrance"

(Ex 12:14, NRSV). This was highlighted by symbolic actions surrounding a meal, particularly the ritual slaying and eating of a Passover lamb.[31] It was a time of high fellowship, of celebrating the past deliverance of Israel in anticipation of the future deliverance of Israel. The Last Supper (from which the Lord's Supper is derived) was some kind of a celebratory Passover meal.[32] Should we, then, understand the Lord's Supper as a Christian Passover?[33] While the Passover origins of the Last Supper are undeniable, the two have important differences: 1) No lamb or meat is eaten at the Lord's Supper; 2) the Lord's Supper is not a sacrificial meal; 3) the Lord's Supper is celebrated more than annually, perhaps weekly; 4) the Lord's Supper has no specified presider;[34] and 5) the idea of drinking blood, even symbolically, would have been abhorrent to Jews and has no counterpart in the Passover celebration.[35]

Blood Covenant

What covenant, then, is being remembered with the celebration of the Lord's Supper? The traditional words of Jesus indicate this is a "blood covenant," a concept with rich Old Testament antecedents. Blood was associated with the covenant of Abraham,[36] with the covenantal act of circumcision,[37] and with the Sinai covenant of Moses.38 Blood offerings were a part of the sacrificial system of the Tabernacle/Temple, particularly for the Day of Atonement.[39] The covenant remembered in the Lord's Supper is all of these in some ways, and none of these in other ways.

Hebrews expresses a Jewish belief of the day when it says, "Without the shedding of blood there is no forgiveness of sins" (Heb 9:22b, NRSV). Pauline theology in particular emphasizes the shedding of the blood of Jesus as symbolic of his atoning, sacrificial death for human sins. Romans 3:35 states, "God put [Jesus] forward as a sacrifice of atonement by his blood." In 1 Corinthians 1:16, Paul reminds the Corinthians, "The cup of blessing that we bless, is it not a sharing in the blood of Christ?" The human sacrifice of God's Son as a propitiation for sin finds Old Testament background in the Jewish sacrificial system but no complete parallel. It is truly a New Covenant, inaugurated by the death of Jesus and shared by those who place their faith in him. This is the covenant Christians remember when they celebrate the Eucharist.

Frequency of Covenant Observance

Entwined with the Lord's Supper as a covenantal meal is the frequency of its observance. How often was the new covenant remembered and celebrated? The most ancient pattern of the church was probably weekly.[40] The Jewish influence is evident even in the concept of a seven-day "week," a pattern not necessarily prevalent in the Roman reckoning of time during this period.[41] For the Jews, the week was the period from Sabbath to Sabbath, the seventh day of the week. Although the New Testament contains no unanimous prescriptive instruction on when the church should meet, the synagogue pattern was a weekly cycle. Thus, there seems to have been a conjunction of weekly meetings of the church combined with obedience to Jesus' directive, "Do this in remembrance of me" (Lk 22:19; 1 Cor 11:24-25). The commemoration of the new covenant was not limited to an annual feast day but was an ongoing activity in the church. John Calvin sums this up when he writes:

> [The Lord's Supper] was ordained to be frequently used among all Christians in order that they might frequently return in memory to Christ's Passion, by such remembrance to sustain and strengthen their faith, and urge themselves to sing thanksgiving to God and to proclaim his goodness.[42]

Preaching the Covenant through the Lord's Supper

As implied by Calvin, related to the Lord's Supper's role in remembering the atoning death of Jesus is the theological concept of proclamation through this symbolic act. As with the Lord's Supper, no true preaching of the Gospel occurs without a remembrance/rehearsal of his passion and death. This is found in Paul's enigmatic statement that by participating in the Lord's Supper, the Corinthians were *ton thanaton tou kuriou katangellete* (proclaiming the Lord's death [my translation], 1 Cor 11:26). In what way does this community observance "proclaim?" Some have seen this as a broad reference to the meeting time including verbal proclamation of the Gospel as an accompaniment to the acts of eating and drinking.[43] Yet this does not seem to fit the context. Paul is not talking about eating, drinking, and preaching. He is saying that eating/drinking in remembrance is preaching.[44]

A standard meaning of *katangellō* is recount or recite.[45] The core of the Gospel is not just words, but words about an event and person. In accordance with remembrance of the new covenant, the symbolic acts and emblems rehearse the basis of the covenant, the atoning death of Jesus. This need not be seen as simply a proclamation for outsiders. It is a recounting for covenant participants to, as Calvin said, "sustain and strengthen their faith."[46]

Covenantal Fellowship

A final theological theme related to the Lord's Supper as a Covenantal Meal is the topic of fellowship among the covenant participants. Biblical covenants are made between God and a community of people. This is true even of covenants between God and individuals (such as Abraham) because their families and descendants are included in the covenant.[47] The community impact of God's covenants is celebrated in Psalm 105:8-10 (NRSV):

> He is mindful of his covenant forever,
>> of the word that he commanded, for a thousand generations,
> the covenant that he made with Abraham,
>> his sworn promise to Isaac,
> which he confirmed to Jacob as a statute,
>> to Israel as an everlasting covenant.

The key verse in understanding the Lord's Supper as covenantal fellowship is 1 Corinthians 10:16, where the cup is called the *koinonia tou aimatos tou christou* (sharing of the blood of Christ, NRSV) and the loaf is the *koinonia tou somatos tou christou* (sharing of the body of Christ, NRSV). What does Paul intend people to understand by these references? In what way is the Lord's Supper sharing or communion (*koinonia*)?

When these two are seen as a parallel reference, Paul is drawing upon the symbolic power of the blood and body of Christ to call to mind the crucifixion, the foundational event of the covenant. Elsewhere, Paul is personally drawn to self-identification with Jesus' crucifixion.[48] The covenantal fellowship of those who have been similarly "crucified with Christ" is remembered and celebrated in the community of those who have been saved by Christ's death and who may share a similar fate if persecution awaits them. This aspect of the Lord's Supper makes it unavailable to outsiders, those with no covenant commitment. Going back to John 6:60-61, Cullmann has noted what may be a reflection of the historical reality that many outside the early Christian community were offended by the celebration of the Lord's Supper and the theological truth that one must have faith in order to properly appreciate the Lord's Supper (Jn 6:36, 47, 48).[49]

Theologically, then, the covenantal meal is both vertical and lateral in its fellowship. It recognizes the communion with the Risen Christ and the Father, the divine participants of the covenant, a communion not unknown in the history of Israel.[50] It is lateral in embracing commonality with other human covenant partners. As John Reumann has noted, "Covenant implies fellowship at a meal among those who have covenanted together and with God."[51]

This raises the question as to how the Lord's Supper is a "meal" rather than "a token consumption of a morsel of bread and a sip of wine."[52] One theory is that the early church's Lord's Supper practice arose from the context of weekly fellowship meals, somewhat disconnected to the event of the Last Supper. Therefore, some see this as the church's continuation of the tradition of inclusive fellowship meals that marked Jesus' ministry.[53] In the early church, these meals were distinct from a rite that included the "words of institution," with an accompanying emphasis upon the death/cross of Jesus.[54]

C. K. Barrett offers that Paul, pushed to find a solution to the chaotic situation in Corinth, combined the traditions of the Last Supper, a continuing Christian Passover celebration, and the weekly fellowship meal into a single entity that became the "Lord's Supper."[55] While Barrett's theory results in a tidy answer to many questions, it involves too many unprovable hypotheses to be a definitive solution. Jungmann claims that the shift away from celebrating the Lord's Supper as a part of a larger fellowship meal was the greatest change in "perhaps the whole course of the history of the Mass" and that this shift was complete and irreversible by the end of the first century.[56]

What evidence do we have for the early linking of the Lord's Supper and a fellowship meal? Several sources point to the conclusion that the early church enjoyed group meals. Klauck notes that the word *deipnon* (supper) in 1 Corinthians 11:20 was the word for the main meal of the day, eaten in late afternoon or early evening. It could refer to a festal meal or banquet.[57] Furthermore, there is evidence that the early church practiced a feast-like fellowship meal sometimes called an *agapē*.[58] This is part of the reasoning of Lietzmann, who believed that 1 Corinthians 11:26 indicates that the Corinthians were practicing something like a memorial meal (also called a "funeral feast"), an annual celebration for one who has died usually held on that person's anniversary.[59] While some of the Corinthians may have seen common features between the Lord's Supper and a funeral feast, this hypothesis ignores the Jewish presence in the early church and the continuing authority and guidance of Paul. This makes it unlikely that a practice associated with heathen religions would have found a home in the Corinthian church. Whatever the actual practices of the early churches in this regard, the *meal* characteristics of the Lord's Supper have been lost to the contemporary church.

Two Analogies of Covenant

Two analogies may help clarify some of the theological implications of the covenant for the Lord's Supper. First, many years ago a close friend of mine was separated from his beloved fiancée for the summer by many miles. The cost of long distance telephone calls was prohibitive in those days. So, the two limited their calls to once a week. But they also did something else. Often at night, at a preset time, both would go outside, look at the moon and pray for each other. They were not praying to the moon. They were connecting to and sharing the same sight despite their physical separation. On a weekly basis, the Lord's Supper is celebrated by millions of Christians who share in the cross of Christ and its benefits and remember it in a powerful communal act. Paul's words in 1 Corinthians 10:17 extend far beyond the gathering of a few dozen people in Corinth nearly two thousand years ago:

> Because there is *one bread,*
> we who are many are *one body,*
> for we all partake of the *one bread.* (NRSV, italics mine)

A second analogy comes from J. R. R. Tolkien's mythical Fellowship of the Ring, as found in his epic trilogy, *The Lord of the Rings.* As Tolkien unfolds the plot of his tale, the necessary task emerges: a perilous journey to destroy the Ring of Power and thereby save Middle Earth. Tolkien presents an array of beings from his mythical world, and they commit to this task: hobbits, an elf, a dwarf, men, and a wizard. They share little in common except their loyalty to the mission. Once they swear an oath of commitment (make a covenant), they become a "fellowship," a community of purpose. The Lord's Supper is a common act of remembrance, communion, and commitment to the covenant made possible through Jesus' sacrificial death.

The Lord's Supper as an Eschatological Meal

Feast after feast thus comes, and passes by;
Yet, passing, points to the glad feast above,
Giving sweet foretaste of the festal joy,
The Lamb's great bridal feast of bliss and love.
Horatius Bonar, 1855

Albert Schweitzer and others recovered the eschatological milieu of Jesus' ministry in the late nineteenth and early twentieth centuries.[60] Even so, not always appreciated are the eschatological aspects of the New Testament texts related to the Lord's Supper. Eschatology is necessarily theological in nature (at least biblical eschatology), making this facet of the Lord's Supper a potentially rich source for theological consideration.

Expectation of the Coming Messiah

Jeremias, after his lengthy investigation of the origins of Eucharist, is convinced that the Lord's Supper had the character of a Passover meal. For Jeremias this was not because of later theologically motivated embellishment by the early church but because this is the historical reality reflected in the Gospels. It is the "survival of an historical reminiscence."[61] According to Jeremias, an important feature of Passover was anticipation of the future redemption of Israel. In that sense, the Egyptian deliverance was but a "prototype."[62] Central to this was a tradition that the Messiah would come on Passover night. Jeremias justifies this association by citing a saying of R. Joshua b. Hananiah (c. AD 90) that reflects this belief: "On that night they were redeemed and on that night they will be redeemed."[63]

The self-understanding of first-century Judaism as an anticipatory, eschatological (even apocalyptic) community is seen in many of the writings of the time and found realization in the two great Jewish revolts in AD 66-70 and AD 132-135. The early church also understood itself as a community in waiting, an eschatological fellowship. In the New Testament this is tied to the Lord's Supper in two specific ways. First, the atmosphere of the Last Supper is eschatological, including an explicit reference to future consummation by Jesus. Luke's version records Jesus as saying, "I will not eat it until it is fulfilled in the kingdom of God" (Lk 22:16, NRSV). The reference to the future is obvious, but what does it mean to be "fulfilled in the kingdom of God?" The church's re-enactment of the Last Supper in the Lord's Supper seems inadequate as a fulfillment and does not seem to be understood this way in Acts or by Paul (who seems to have the same tradition of the Last Supper as Luke does). Added to this is the reference in Mark 14:25, where Jesus tells the disciples that he would not be drinking with them again until "I drink it new in the kingdom of God" (NRSV). Is there a connection between *fulfilled* in the kingdom of God and *new* in the kingdom of God?

The Lord's Supper as Messianic Banquet

Perhaps the answer lies in the biblical concept of a future messianic banquet, a picture found in both the Old Testament[64] and the New Testament. Luke 22:28-30 clarifies this in his statement that follows his words of institution: "You are those who have stood by me in my trials; and I confer on you, just as my Father has conferred on me, a kingdom, so that you may eat and drink at my table in my kingdom, and you will sit on thrones judging the twelve tribes of Israel" [NRSV]. Elsewhere, Jesus had presented a picture of future feasting that would include the faithful patriarchs of Israel and believers from the Gentile world at a banquet that will also feature the exclusion of many of his Jewish opponents (Mt 8:11-12, Lk 13:28-29).

This idea of sitting with Jesus at a future messianic feast involves numerous theological aspects. For example, Mark's account of the request from the sons of Zebedee to be seated on the right and left of Jesus "in your glory" (Mk 10:37; Mt 20:21, "in your kingdom"), should be understood as a banquet setting, not a throne room. Jesus leaves the determination of these positions to the Father's providence (Mk 10:40), and they are filled by two thieves at the crucifixion (Mk 15:27), ironically, tying the crucifixion to the eschatological banquet. This is even more connected in Luke 22:24, for the debate over greatness occurs at the Last Supper itself.

In John's Bread of Life discourse, participation in the Lord's Supper is linked directly to eschatological expectations when Jesus says, "Those who eat my flesh and drink my blood have eternal life, and I will raise them up on the last day" (Jn 6:54). It is a mistake to see this as a statement of magical qualities in the emblems of the Lord's Supper. As noted earlier, for John eating/drinking Jesus = believing in Jesus. The intent of this verse is to convey that believers in Jesus foretaste future reward and fulfillment when they participate in the Lord's Supper.

The idea of a messianic banquet is also reflected in the climactic "marriage supper of the Lamb" of Revelation 19:9. In this context, the Apocalypse also pictures a "great supper of God," consisting of carrion birds feasting on the corpses of the beast's vanquished army (Rev 19:17-18, 21). The image of eschatological feasting, then, is fluid in Revelation, but always embraces the idea of celebration of victory, a decisive victory for all time.

The Lord's Supper as Celebration

Christians "celebrate" the Lord's Supper, a strange expression if its theology includes only typology and covenant. Celebrating at a party could not be more distinct from mourning at a funeral, which would be the case if the Lord's Supper is only about death, forgiveness, atonement, and penitence. Would the Apostles have taught, "Jesus is dead, hallelujah!"? It is the eschatological component that justifies celebration. Christians celebrate victory over sin as a result of the cross. They celebrate victory over death as a result of the resurrection. They celebrate the coming universal reign of God as promised by Jesus. They celebrate in anticipation of his sure return.

The Lord's Supper as Eschatological Expectation
The eschatological implications of the Lord's Supper have led some scholars to see various other New Testament passages in an eschatological light. Cullmann (and others) see the *maranatha* (Come Lord!) in 1 Corinthians 16:22 as a Eucharistic prayer.[65] If the Eucharistic community act is proclaiming the Lord's death *until he comes* (1 Cor 11:26), it follows that the celebration would include an earnest prayer *that he come*. A similar analysis forms the bottom line of Jeremias's study, allowing him to write that the Lord's Supper is "an anticipatory gift of the consummation."[66]

This warrants understanding parts of Revelation beyond the messianic banquet motif as Eucharistic. Klauck theorizes that Revelation 22:6-11 may reflect invitation to the Lord's Supper and disbarment of the unworthy (22:15).[67] Whether or not this theory is valid, it is undeniable that Revelation closes on the note of eschatological anticipation and hope, and includes a Greek version of the *maranatha* (*erchou kyrie yēsou*, 22:20). Elsewhere, the anticipated fulfillment of this prayer for Jesus to come is reflected in his words in Revelation 3:20 (NLT):

> If you hear me calling and open the door,
> I will come in, and we will share a meal as friends.

This eschatological component largely defines the new covenantal community, for it is a waiting community that must fellowship without its leader (Christ) until his return.[68] Writing from the rich liturgical tradition of Roman Catholicism, Reumann states, "Eschatological hope always accompanies the celebration of the Lord's Supper."[69]

Closing Observations

> *Double-sealed and disposable, individual Remembrance(r) wafer and juice sets combine modern convenience and purity with a taste for tradition.*
> (Marketing blurb, 2005)

The Roman Catholic tradition understands the Lord's Supper and its celebration as "the summit toward which the activity of the Church is directed; at the same time it is the font from which all her power flows."[70] This study's analysis sees the Lord's Supper as a way for Christians to understand their heritage as the redeemed people of God (typological meal), their status as the fellowship of the new covenant (covenantal meal), and their future blessedness as the community awaiting the Lord's return (eschatological meal). The theological depth, breath, and richness of the Lord's Supper should cause Christians to appreciate how vital it is to Christian congregations as well as to individual believers.

Question: Celebration Today
This leads to some questions concerning how the Lord's Supper is celebrated. First, if

the Lord's Supper is a Gospel-proclaiming event, must Christians not pay more attention to how it is done? The history of the church is littered with attempts to streamline the Lord's Supper, from not offering both the bread and cup, to less frequent observances (or total neglect), and finally to the use of tiny individual cups and chips of bread that may now be purchased in a sanitary, single-serving package. Surely, all of these well-intended measures have lessened the symbolic power of the Eucharist. Whoever leads the congregation in the celebration must realize that it is a gospel-proclaiming act and speak words that fit the occasion. The cup must be filled with a red beverage to represent Jesus' blood. The loaf should be capable of being broken into individual servings in order to symbolize the unity of the redeemed body of Christ.[71]

Question: Unifying Potential of the Lord's Supper
This leads to another question. What are the implications of the Lord's Supper as a unifying factor in Christianity? James Moroney recently said, "Reuniting disparate branches of Christianity would be impossible without a common doctrine of Communion."[72] It seems unlikely that the many disparate varieties of Christianity that now exist will ever be able to solve all doctrinal issues that cause separation. Is there unity to be found in common participation in this ancient rite, celebrated in a simple way without theological encumbrances?

Geoffrey Wainwright, in *Eucharist and Eschatology*, includes a wonderful legend from the time of the persecutions of Emperor Valerian (AD 257-260). During this time of threats and frequent executions, two church leaders, Marianus and James, had this vision on the day before their deaths:

> [T]here ran up to meet us a boy, who was clearly one of the twins who had suffered martyrdom with their mother three days ago. He was wearing a garland of roses round his neck and held a green palm-branch in his right hand. "Why do you rush?" he said, "Rejoice and be glad for tomorrow you also will dine with us."[73]

Unity may yet come from embracing this New Testament picture of the Lord's Supper as it reveals the church's history as part of God's redemptive plan, its present as part of the redeemed community, and its future as Christians dine with their Redeemer.

Notes
[1]See *This Holy Mystery: A United Methodist Understanding of Holy Communion, adopted by the 2004 General Conference of the United Methodist Church*. This document may be found at www.gbod.org/worship/thisholymystery.

[2]See Robert E. Webber, *The Younger Evangelicals: Facing the Challenges of the New World* (Grand Rapids: Baker, 2002), pp. 180-82, for one example.

[3]The most extensive of these studies were the work of Hans Lietzmann, *Mass and the Lord's Supper:*

A Study in the History of the Liturgy, trans. Dorthea H. G. Reeve (Leiden: Brill, 1953), and Joachim Jeremias, *The Eucharistic Words of Jesus*, trans. Norman Perrin (Philadelphia: Fortress, 1966). See also I. Howard Marshall, *The Last Supper and the Lord's Supper* (Grand Rapids: Eerdmans, 1980).

[4]Leonard Goppelt, *Theology of the New Testament*, trans. John E. Alsup (Grand Rapids: Eerdmans, 1981), 1:214.

[5]John Reumann, "Introduction by the Editor," in Willi Marxsen, *The Lord's Supper as a Christological Problem*, trans. Lorenz Nieting (Philadelphia: Fortress, 1970), p. vi.

[6]C. K. Barrett, *Chuch, Ministry, & Sacraments in the New Testament* (Grand Rapids: Eerdmans, 1985), p. 62.

[7]Marshall, *Last Supper*, p. 15.

[8]R. H. Stein, "Last Supper," in *Dictionary of Jesus and the Gospels*, ed. Joel B. Green et al. (Downers Grove: InterVarsity, 1992), p. 444.

[9]This was *Faith and Order Paper No. 111*. It may be found online at www.wcc-coe.org/wcc/what/faith/bem1.html.

[10]Eduard Schweizer, *The Lord's Supper according to the New Testament*, trans. James M. Davis (Philadelphia: Fortress, 1967), pp. 1–3.

[11]For example the excellent handbook on hermeneutics, Grant R. Osborne, *The Hermeneutical Spiral* (Downers Grove, Ill.: InterVarsity, 1991), is silent on the issue of understanding typology for biblical interpretation..

[12]See the definition of I. Howard Marshall, "An Assessment of Recent Developments," in *It is Written: Scripture Citing Scripture: Essays in Honour of Barnabas Lindars*, ed. D. A. Carson and H. G. M. Williamson (Cambridge: Cambridge University Press, 1988), p. 16, "Typology may be defined as the study which traces parallels or correspondences between incidents recorded in the OT and their counterparts in the NT such that the latter can be seen to resemble the former in notable respects and yet to go beyond them." For discussion of current theories of typological interpretation, see W. Edward Glenny, "Typology: A Summary of the Present Evangelical Discussion," *Journal of the Evangelical Theological Society* 40 (December 1997): 627–638. What I am following here is the most basic understanding of typology, labeled by Glenny (629, n. 2), as the "literary view," which deals with the way typology functions within the Bible itself rather than as a tool for modern interpreters.

[13]Richard M. Davidson, *Typology in Scripture: A Study of the Hermeneutical ΤΥΠΟΣ Structures* (Berrien Springs: Andrews University Press, 1981), p. 191. These are 1 Cor 10:6, 1 Cor 10:11, Rom 5:14, 1 Pet 3:21, Heb 8:5, & Heb 9:24.

[14]The motif of eating and drinking is repeated in 1 Cor 10:7, but the connection to the Lord's Supper is less certain. Here the main emphasis seems to be the sacred meal associated with idol worship, which, of course, is the primary Corinthian issue causing this excursus by Paul.

[15]This has been discussed at length in many places. See, for example, C. P. M. Jones, "The Eucharist in the New Testament," in *The Study of Liturgy*, ed. Cheslyn Jones, et al. (London: SPCK, 1978), p. 152; and especially the discussion of Davidson, Typology, p. 245.

[16]Even a self-identified dynamic equivalent translation such as the American Bible Society's *Today's English Version* (Good News Bible) uses "spiritual" here.

[17]1 Cor 2:13 (2x); 2:15; 3:1; 9:11; 10:3, 4 (2x); 12:1; 14:1, 37; 15:44 (2x), 46 (2x).

[18]Rom 1:11, 7:14, 15:27; Gal 6:1; Eph 1:3, 5:19, 6:12; Col 1:9, 3:16.

[19]1 Pet 2:5 (2x).

[20]Rom 15:27, 1 Cor 3:1, 9:11.

[21]1 Cor 2:14; 15:44, 46.

[22]See Jn 3:8, where *pneuma* is used in a play on words between "wind" and "spirit."

[23]"Miraculous" is the choice of the *New Living Translation*.

[24]See Gunther Bornkamm, "Lord's Supper and the Church in Paul," in *Early Christian Experience*,

trans. Paul L. Hammer (New York: Harper & Row, 1969), p. 145.

[25]James D. G. Dunn, *Unity and Diversity in the New Testament: An Inquiry into the Character of Earliest Christianity,* 2nd ed. (Philadelphia: Trinity Press International, 1990), p. 169. In this context see Jn 6:35, 40, 47, 69.

[26]Tad W. Guzie, *Jesus and the Eucharist* (New York: Paulist, 1974), p. 61.

[27]Ignatius, *To the Ephesians* 20:2.

[28]Matt 26:28, Mk 14:24.

[29]Lk 22:20, 1 Cor 11:25.

[30]Dunn, *Unity*, p. 167. For a similar analysis, see also Willi Marxsen, *The Lord's Supper as a Christological Problem,* trans. Lorenz Nieting (Philadelphia: Fortress, 1970), p. 7.

[31]The theme of Jesus as the Passover lamb is prominent in the Gospel of John and not unknown to Paul (1 Cor 5:7), but somewhat aside from the purpose of this study.

[32]Complete reconciliation of the Synoptic accounts with that of John as to whether or not the Last Supper was an official Passover meal is difficult and unnecessary for our purposes. The Passover theme is prominent in all four Gospel accounts of the Passion Week. See Mk 14:16, Mt 26:19, Lk 22:15, and Jn 18:39, but compare Jn 19:14.

[33]There is some evidence that Ebionites, an early Jewish-Christian sect, celebrated a Christian Passover. This does not mean, however, that they did not celebrate the Lord's Supper on a more frequent, even weekly basis. See Dunn, *Unity*, p. 163, and I. Howard Marshall, "Lord's Supper," in *Dictionary of Paul and His Letters*, ed. Gerald F. Hawthorne (Downers Grove: InterVarsity, 1993), p. 574.

[34]On this point see Hans-Josef Klauck, "Lord's Supper," in *Anchor Bible Dictionary* (New York: Doubleday, 1992), 4:365. Klauck finds no evidence that the early church required a priest or ordained minister to preside over the Lord's Supper, and admits the possibility that this role may have been filled by women.

[35]See Gen 9:4. See also Ps 16:4 where the idea of drinking blood is associated with vile paganism.

[36]While blood is not mentioned specifically, the Abrahamic covenant involved splitting animals in half, undoubtedly a blood job. See Gen 15:10.

[37]See Ex 4:25, 26.

[38]Ex 24:1-8. See also Zech 9:11, Heb 9:18-20.

[39]See Ex 30:10

[40]The question as to whether or not the New Testament includes evidence for weekly celebration of the Lord's Supper is largely dependent upon Acts references to the "breaking of bread" (see Acts 2:42, 46; 20:7, 11; 27:35). If this is code language for celebration of the Lord's Supper, a case can be made for weekly (or more frequent) observance. The clearest connection between "breaking bread" and the Lord's Supper is found in 1 Corinthians 10:16. For an example of the argument in favor of weekly celebration in the New Testament, see Josef A. Jungmann, *The Early Liturgy: to the Time of Gregory the Great*, trans. Francis A. Brunner (London: Darton, Longman, & Todd, 1959), p. 29. For an example of the opinion that the "breaking of bread" refers to a regular meal and not the Lord's Supper, see Dunn, *Unity*, p. 163.

[41]The Romans traditionally did not operate on a seven-day week, but on fixed points within each month: the Kalends, the Nones, and the Ides. Romans did have a recurring market day every eight days by our reckoning, which has led some to characterize them as having an eight-day week. See S. E. Porter, "Festivals and Holy Days: Greco/Roman," in *Dictionary of New Testament Background*, ed. Craig A. Evans and Stanley E. Porter (Downers Grove: InterVarsity, 2000), p. 369. The seven-day week was eventually adopted by the Romans, but its origins came from the Jews and other eastern influences. See an article by Vincent Mallette, "The Seven-Day Week" at http://www.ac.wwu.edu/~stephan/Astronomy/7day.html.

[42]John Calvin, *Institutes of the Christian Religion*, 2 vols., ed. John T. McNeill, trans. Ford Lewis Battles (Philadelphia: Westminster, 1960), 4.17.44.

43 See Gordon D. Fee, *The First Epistle to the Corinthians*, NICNT (Grand Rapids: Eerdmans, 1987), p. 557.

44 Such quasi-non-verbal proclamation is found elsewhere in the New Testament in Acts 13:38, "through this man forgiveness of sins is proclaimed to you."

45 See Henry George Liddell and Robert Scott, *A Greek-English Lexicon*, 9th ed., rev. Henry Stuart Jones (Oxford: Clarendon Press, 1978), "καταγγέλλω ," definition #2.

46 Calvin, *Institutes*, 4:17:44.

[47]There are many examples of this in the Old Testament, keyed with language similar to "a covenant with you and your descendants." See Gen 9:9, 17:7; Num 18:19, Neh 9:8; Judg 2:1, Acts 3:25.

48 This is strongest at Gal 2:19, "I have been crucified with Christ," but see also Rom 6:6, 2 Cor 13:4, Gal 5:24.

49 Oscar Cullmann, *Early Christian Worship,* trans. A. Stewart Todd and James B. Torrance (London: SCM Press, 1953), p. 95.

50 See Exodus 24:11, where after the ceremony of the "blood of the covenant," the elders of the people and Moses ascend the mountain, see God, and eat and drink.

51 Reumann, *Supper*, p. 35.

52 Marshall, "Lord's Supper," p. 572.

53 This is the central thesis of the study by Eugene LaVerdiere, *Dining in the Kingdom of God: The Origins of the Eucharist in the Gospel of Luke* (Chicago: Liturgical Training Publications, 1994).

54 Lietzmann concluded that there were two types of Lord's Supper celebration in the early church. The fellowship meal type was called the "Jerusalem" model by Lietzmann. This was what Acts referred to as the "breaking of bread." The tradition reflected in Paul and the Gospels had an emphasis on the death/blood/cross of Jesus and the words of institution. Lietzmann called this the "Mass" model, and thought that model eventually prevailed. See a helpful summary of Lietzmann's theory in John Reumann's "Introduction" to Marxsen, Lord's Supper, p. xiv.

55 Barrett, *Church, Ministry, & Sacraments,* p. 68.

56 Jungmann, *Early Liturgy*, p. 37.

57 Klauck, "Lord's Supper," p. 362-63.

58 See Jude 12, the only unambiguous New Testament reference. See Ignatius, *To the Smyrnaeans* 13; Tertullian, *Apology* 39. The Council of Laodicea, Canon 28, outlawed the practice of holding *agape*-feasts in a church building (4th century), indicating absolute separation from the Lord's Supper.

59 Lietzmann, *Mass*, 182.

60 See Albert Schweitzer, *The Quest of the Historical Jesus: A Critical Study of the Progress from Reimarus to Wrede* (1906; Baltimore: Johns Hopkins University Press, 1998), describes this variously by saying "the world of thought in which Jesus moved was essentially eschatological" (p. 23), and as "the rock-bound eschatological world-view of Jesus" (p. 252).

61 Jeremias, *Eucharistic Words*, p. 62.

62 Ibid., p. 206.

63 Ibid. Jeremias give the reference as R. Joshua b. Hananiah, Mekilta ad Exod. 12.42. Jeremias notes that Jerome also mentions a tradition that midnight on Passover eve would be the time of the advent of the Messiah.

64 See particularly Isa 25:6, 65:13; see also 1 En 62:14, "They shall eat and rest and rise with that Son of Man forever and ever;" and 2 Bar 29:8: "And it will happen at that time that the treasury of manna will come down again from on high, and they will eat of it in those years because these are they who will have arrived at the consummation of time." Quotations from James H. Charlesworth,

ed., *The Old Testament Pseudepigrapha*, 2 vols. (Garden City: Doubleday, 1983), 2:44, 631. See also the somewhat disturbing images of an eschatological banquet celebrating war victory found in Ezek 39:17-20; see also Zech 9:15.

[65]Cullmann, *Early Christian Worship*, p. 14.

[66]Jeremias, *Eucharistic Words*, p. 261. He concludes, "As often as the death of the Lord is proclaimed at the Lord's supper, and the *maranatha* rises upwards, God is reminded of the unfulfilled climax of the work of salvation" (p. 253).

[67]Klauck, "Lord's Supper," 4:368.

[68]See Goppelt, *Theology*, 1:216.

[69]Reumann, *The Supper*, p. 26.

[70]Item #10 from the Vatican II document, "Constitution on the Sacred Liturgy," promulgated by Pope Paul VI on December 4, 1963. This may be found at www.vatican.va/archive.

[71]It has been observed that effective celebration of the Lord's Supper is very difficult in mega-churches, given their style of leaders/audience format. This begs the question as to whether the problem is on the side of the demands of the Lord's Supper or on this format itself.

[72]Monsignor James Moroney, executive director of office of liturgy for the U.S. Conference of Catholic Bishops. Quoted by Bill Broadway, "Christian Practice of Communion Becoming More Diverse," *Seattle Times* (September 25, 2004).

[73]In Geoffrey Wainwright, *Eucharist and Eschatology* (Akron: OSL Publications, 2002), p. 155.

11

THE LORD'S SUPPER AS ESCHATOLOGICAL TABLE

John Mark Hicks

The Lord's Supper is a gospel meal—"the gospel in bread and wine."[1] Consequently, its significance and dimensions are as varied as the gospel itself. It is a prism that refracts the light of the gospel in multi-faceted ways as a kaleidoscope of meaning.

The multi-dimensional nature of the Supper is quickly discerned through the common motifs that liturgies, theologians, and preachers often use. The popular idea that the Lord's Supper looks upward, outward, inward, backward, and forward reflects this perspectivalism. Or, more formally, one of the Stone-Campbell Restoration Movement's most significant sacramental theologians, William Robinson, summarizes the Supper as memorial, proclamation, covenant, communion, and feast.[2] Andrew Paris condensed its meaning to four "Cs": commemoration, confession, communion, and covenant.[3] Bryon Lambert identified ten aspects: obedience, remembrance, thanksgiving, proclamation, prophecy, covenant, altar, self-examination, communion and feasting.[4] In one of the most recent contributions from evangelical quarters, Gordon Smith organizes his presentation around the themes of remembrance, communion, forgiveness, covenant, nourishment, thanksgiving, anticipation, and presence.[5] Ecumenically, the 1982 World Council of Churches Lima document entitled *Baptism, Eucharist and Ministry* defines the meaning of the Eucharist as thanksgiving to the Father, the memorial of Christ, the invocation of the Spirit, the communion of the faithful, and the meal of the kingdom.[6]

Given its multi-dimensional nature, it is impossible to offer a comprehensive theological reflection in a brief paper such as this. Rather, I will focus on a specific dimension of the Supper that has suffered significant lack of attention in previous centuries within Western Christianity but has received increased attention in the twentieth century. But it has not yet sufficiently informed the theology nor shaped the practice of the contemporary church. I will explore the eschatological character of the Supper.

In its seventh agreement the 1957 Oberlin Faith and Order statement recognized that "there is a growing realization of the eschatological nature of the Eucharist."[7] In the almost fifty years since that recognition, several have explored the Supper's eschatological dimensions.[8] The most significant work, and perhaps most responsible for the resurgence of interest, is Wainwright's 1971 *Eucharist and Eschatology*.[9]

Drawing on this surge of discussion, this study will reflect on the eschatological nature of the Supper. First, the importance of thinking eschatologically about the Supper will be contextualized by contrasting it with discussion in the context of the Stone-Campbell tradition. Second, the Eucharistic materials in Luke-Acts will be surveyed as a way entering into the eschatological world of the New Testament. Third, suggestions will be offered regarding the significance of Eucharistic eschatology for contemporary thought and practice.

Historical Context

Wainwright's book introduced a new perspective into the history of Eucharistic thought. While previous theology and historical surveys focused on ontology (the presence of Christ), sacrifice and individualistic reception, Wainwright drew attention to the eschatological matrix of the Supper.[10] By his account, eschatological reflection, though present in the early liturgies and represented occasionally throughout the Western Church, has been largely absent.

While eschatological themes are present in the biblical and early martyrological materials, these were eclipsed by theological and institutional developments. Wainwright argues that the rise of Christianity under the Christian emperors of the Fourth Century "led to a more positive evaluation of the present age." Absorption into the political and social structures entailed "a loss of awareness" that the church was "*a witness to the coming kingdom*."[11] Accompanying this was "the increasing influence of a 'vertical' and individualized eschatology dressed in the colours of a Platonizing mysticism."[12] The combination of these two developments, among others, meant that eschatology was, on the one hand, reduced to futurist individual salvation and, on the other hand, practically lost by the identification of the Kingdom of God with the institutional church. The Eucharist was no longer a meal of the eschatological kingdom, but became an institutionalized ritual identified with the City of God upon the earth through which individuals experienced salvation and mystical—even individual—vertical relationship with God.

The loss of kingdom eschatology gave Eucharistic theology myopic vision. The church focused more on the earthly life of Jesus—especially in terms of a victim for the purposes of sacrifice and atonement—than his return. Eschatological expectation waned as the church became more comfortable with its Constantinian status.[13] Without an eschatological context, the focus of the Eucharist turned to the nature of Christ's presence and sacrifice. The Eucharist became a sacrifice; the kingdom meal became a feeding on the presence of Christ; and the table became an altar. The Eucharist became a re-presentation of the cross and almost solely focused on the death of Christ.

Western theology has generally participated in this trajectory. Even the Protestant Reformers continued the emphasis on altar and memoralism, though rejecting or reinterpreting the sacrificial imagery. Eschatology was dimly associated with the Eucharist and primarily only in relation to the promise of the future *parousia*.

There were, however, moments of eschatological light within this history. John and Charles Wesley, for example, articulate eschatological themes in their hymns and sermons.[14] Their Eucharistic hymns, though predominantly a reflection on the memorial of Christ's suffering and death, also express some eschatological themes. Their Eucharistic theology was influenced by Daniel Brevint's 1673 *The Christian Sacrament and Sacrifice*,[15] and their hymnal followed Brevint's outline. In particular, though memorializing the sufferings of the cross, they emphasized the Supper as a means of grace, a pledge of heaven, and "a sacrifice of ourselves joined to Christ."[16] Some Wesleyan hymns accentuated the communion of the saints gratefully joined together in the light of eschatological joy.[17]

On the whole, however, Western theology swam in the memoralist and presentists altar traditions of the medieval church. The Stone-Campbell Movement participated in this tradition, but with a small twist. Though memoralist, and sometimes stressing the spiritual presence of Christ in the bread and wine, the original impulse of the movement stressed the metaphor of table rather than altar. As a consequence, early traditions emphasized the role of Jesus as host at the table and the joy of table fellowship.[18]

The background to this Stone-Campbell emphasis lies in the seventeenth century when the Scottish Church began to observe "communion festivals" at tables. Participants sat at long tables as if they were sitting for a meal. They ate large portions of bread and drank wine as if at a meal. Eventually these festivals became three and four day events where hundreds and thousands communed at tables. The Cane Ridge revival in August, 1801, was designed as a communal festival.[19]

Against this background of Scottish communion festivals and the emphasis by British dissenters on the centrality and weekly character of communion (particularly Glassites, Sandemanians, and the Haldanes), Alexander Campbell focused on the "table." Campbell argued typologically that "in the house of God there is always a table of the Lord."[20] Emphasizing the weekly table, he denied all clerical distinctions and recommended joy as the primary mood of the table: "All Christians," he wrote, "are members of the house or family of God, are called and constituted a holy and a royal priesthood, and may, therefore bless God for the Lord's table, its loaf, and cup—approach it without fear and partake of it with joy as often as they please, in remembrance of the death of their Lord and Saviour."[21] Indeed, he chided Protestants in general for their joyless celebration as their experience was more like "mourners" in a "house of sorrows" than celebrants in a house of feasting. "The Lord's house," he writes, "is his banqueting place, and the Lord's day is his weekly festival."[22] The table was so central for Campbell that he wanted to substitute the table for the pulpit. His ideal "meeting-house" would have no pulpit, but "the Lord's table and the seats for the elders of the congregation" would "be at the remote end, opposite to the entrance." The gathered disciples would be placed "immediately contiguous to the Lord's table."[23]

The table-centeredness of the Stone-Campbell Movement was a distinctive of the tradition. "Gathering around the table" was common, and not just as a metaphor. Tables were more important than pulpits. When Moses Lard described his ideal church, the table extended "entirely across the house" as everyone gathered around the table and partook standing as a sign of reverence.[24] Sunday mornings were reserved for table and mutual edification, while evening services were devoted to evangelistic preaching. While table-renewal was part of the original vision, it was lost in the focus on the elements (leavened or unleavened bread, wine or grape juice), frequency of the Supper (only on Sunday and every Sunday), and the rise of a professional preaching class that shifted the focus to the pulpit. Losing the tableness of the Supper, the movement defaulted to the historic "altar" mentality. While we talked about "the Lord's table," little in our assemblies resembled a table. Instead, the atmosphere, function and practice of the Supper were decidedly "altar."

Resisting this development, James A. Harding and David Lipscomb sought to refocus the centrality of the table. They believed the exclusive use of a single preacher for the breaking of the bread service was detrimental to the spiritual health of the congregation. First Corinthians 11-14, according to Lipscomb, demonstrated that a wide number of people participated in teaching the church.[25] Harding counseled that as many "as possible should take part in the services," including "three or four" making "short talks and others reading Scripture."[26] The Spruce Street church in Nashville, for example, rarely had meetings where "fewer than four or five" edified the assembly.[27] The substitution of one preacher for mutual edification, Harding believed, was "one of the chief causes of the lack of spirituality" among the churches he visited.[28] The loss of communal participation at the table decentralized its function and the table became an altar in function and meaning.

Judging from the survey by Paul Blowers and Byron Lambert, the meaning of the Lord's Supper is understood within the Stone-Campbell Movement as either a memorialism or a spiritual presence generally characteristic of Reformed (Calvin) churches.[29] Given the Scot-Irish Presbyterian and baptistic roots of the movement, this is hardly surprising. Memorialism, however, dominated. Alexander Campbell, for example, when pressed on the exact design of the Lord's Supper insisted that it was "commemorative" as a "weekly reminder" of the forgiveness of sins. "It is not," he wrote, "an ordinance for receiving new blessings, but for commemorating those already received."[30]

The centrality of memorialism is nicely illustrated by Hiram Christopher's argument that the Lord's Supper as the "central and chief element of Christian worship" is established by the fact that the "atonement is the central and chief element of the Remedial System."[31] The worship of the church is "retrospective" as "the memory looks back to the great fact by which the soul is saved from sin."[32] Nevertheless, some, perhaps only a few, within the Stone-Campbell Movement have defended a spiritual presence of Christ. Robert Milligan, for example, writing at the same time as Christopher, insisted that the Supper is not "merely commemorative" and is "more than the mere recollection of facts. *It is intended to be the medium of furnishing and imparting spiritual nourishment.*"[33]

Absent, however, in these materials—and in most surveys of Stone-Campbell Eucharistic history and theology[34]—is a stress on the eschatological nature of the Lord's Supper. Given Paul's "till he come" statement in 1 Corinthians 11:27, it is impossible for any tradition to ignore the relationship between the Lord's Supper and the second coming. But how this relation is construed is what signals the lack of eschatological reflection.

Two recent "special issues" on the Lord's Supper in periodicals published by members of the Churches of Christ (a cappella) illustrate the point. In a 2003 issue of the *Gospel Advocate* the article "Until He Comes" only mentions the fact and hope of the second coming in brief ways while stressing solemnity, judgment and memorialism.[35] The article focused on the judgment of God against those who eat unworthily. In the 1982 *Spiritual Sword* an article entitled "Lord's Supper…Looking Forward" characterizes the Supper as a "perpetual proclamation" of the death of Christ where participants testify to their understanding "that the Lord, in fact, is coming back." This expresses a "trust in the promise" since, just as the Supper is "founded upon historical fact," it also "signifies future fact as well." Deaver summarizes the relation of past, present, and future in this way: "The keeper of the feast *presently* commemorates the past death, burial, and resurrection of Christ, as he looks forward to His *future* return."[36]

Most often the eschatological relation is taken as a temporal frame. This is something Christians do until Jesus comes. In other words, Paul provides the terminus of the Supper. Christians will remember him until he is once again present. Then, it is sometimes said, Christians will dispense partaking in the meal. Others see Paul's words as primarily stating a fact. The meal proclaims the fact of Jesus' coming. Entailed in this proclamation is a corresponding yearning or anticipation of that future reality. Christians long for the future, but the eschatology is wholly future. Still others see Paul's words as a pledge of the future. It is not only proclamation but promise. This meal is his promise that he will return. The Supper becomes a pledge of heavenly glory.

These may be properly called eschatological ideas, but they are oriented to temporality, facticity, and promise. They are decidedly futurist. They all emphasize the "not-yet-ness" of the *eschaton*; they are anthropocentric in orientation (we remember, we proclaim, we anticipate the promise). They exist alongside a memoralism and potentially a present spiritual feeding on Christ. The spiritual dynamic of the Lord's Supper remains either memory and/or nourishment. There is no eschatological dynamic in the present but only an absent Christ whose return we await through memory and spiritual sustenance. Fundamentally, this lack of eschatological "alreadiness" engenders a solemn and funerary atmosphere that is more consistent with the metaphor of altar than table.

The eschatological dimensions of the Supper have been neglected. The eschatological hope has been reduced to a promised future fact, and the supper reduced to a singular purpose. This is illustrated by this recent statement in the *Gospel Advocate*: "The chief purpose of the Lord's Supper is to emphasize only one fact of the gospel, namely, the death of Christ."[37] This memorialism even pushes thanksgiving into the background so that "eucharist" is an inappropriate designation for the Supper because it does not "express the true conception of his solemn institution."[38]

As memorialism dominated, and preaching tended to replace the table as the focus of worship, another factor contributed to a reductionistic approach to the eschatological dimensions of the Supper. The Stone-Campbell Movement never embraced the word "sacrament," William Robinson being the most notable exception. Instead, it spoke of "ordinances" in good baptistic fashion. Though the lists of ordinances sometimes varied,[39] the three central ordinances of the Stone-Campbell Movement were: baptism, Lord's Supper and Lord's Day.[40]

These are "positive institutions" in contrast to moral obligations.[41] Moral obligations have crutches. There are inducements, inclinations, and natural propensities. But a positive law is an absolute test of loyalty. The significance of the positive command is that it is unencumbered by the crutches of moral obligations and it gives a clear indication of the loyalty of the person involved. Positive law is, according to Benjamin Franklin, "the highest test of respect for divine authority" since it "tests" the condition of the "heart" as it penetrates "deep down into the inmost depths of the soul." Obedience to positive law "rises above mere morality...into the pure region of faith."[42] Disobedience to positive law reveals the "*spirit of disobedience*."[43]

As a positive ordinance, the Lord's Supper shares the nature of other positive ordinances. Tyler, for example, characterized the ordinances as (1) "divinely appointed teachers;" (2) "God's method of righteousness;" (3) "our treatment of the ordinances is esteemed as our treatment of their Author;" (4) "tests of loyalty;" (5) "special blessings" are attached to each; and (6) "obedience to ordinances should always be from the heart."[44] Each of these characterizations is framed by a legal approach to the Lord's Supper. The Lord's Supper becomes primarily an act of obedience. This is fundamentally anthropocentric and, framed by legal conceptualizations, reduces the Supper to a duty performed in memory of another. The Supper, in such a frame, becomes exactly what Campbell sought to oppose in his initial articles on the breaking of bread. The Supper becomes a time of dutiful mourning rather than joyful feasting.

Nevertheless, eschatological perspectives—even in the sense I will define below—were not wholly lacking within the Stone-Campbell tradition (and also somewhat present in Western theology). Walter Scott, for example, described the Lord's Supper as "heaven on earth" (similar to Eastern Orthodox conceptualizations).[45] Most significantly, William Robinson—who was aware of the early rumblings of eschatological thought in the twentieth century—affirmed that the "kingdom is both present and future,"[46] and therefore "we are with Him at the Lamb's great Bridal Feast" and "tread the heavenly courts."[47]

On the whole, however, the Stone-Campbell Movement, though using the language of table, was oriented in an anthropocentric direction, stressed memorialism, occasionally emphasized spiritual feeding on Christ, and reduced eschatological perspectives to the promised fact of a future reality.

Eschatology and the Lord's Supper in Luke–Acts

Braaten and Jenson note that "the twentieth century will be remembered in the history of theology for its rediscovery of the centrality of eschatology in the message of Jesus and early Christianity."[48] The reorientation of New Testament scholarship toward eschatological and apocalyptic themes began with Johannes Weiss and Albert Schweitzer.[49] C. H. Dodd moved the *eschaton* from the future into the present with his version of "realized eschatology."[50] Moltmann has been programmatic for the last quarter of the twentieth century in his affirmation that from "first to last, and not merely in the epilogue, Christianity is eschatology, is hope, forward looking and forward moving, and therefore also revolutionizing and transforming the present."[51] The New Testament is a thoroughly eschatological, if not apocalyptic, message. The practices of the early church, consequently, are likewise thoroughly eschatological.

Wainwright's book was the first comprehensive effort to interpret the Lord's Supper eschatologically. He contended that the "meal" dimension of the Supper had been obscured as "the liturgies seem to have gone to excess in disguising the fundamental phenomenological feature of the eucharist."[52] And, yet, it was the Supper's nature as a meal, as table, that embodied its eschatological realities.

Some early twentieth-century scholars recognized this point. Though much of Lietzmann's theory about the origin of the Lord's Supper as a contrast between the eschatological joy of Jerusalem meals and the memorialism of Pauline churches is now in disrepute, his emphasis on the meal character of the Supper and its continuity with the pre-resurrection meals of Jesus is a significant contribution.[53] Lohmeyer also emphasized the importance of the meal-parables and meal-acts in the ministry of Jesus as the impetus for the Eucharist.[54] More significantly, Cullmann reshaped Lietzmann's theory by emphasizing the post-resurrection meals and the Pauline extension of those meals back to the Last Supper.[55] Markus Barth, then, embraced the whole trajectory by recognizing the continuity between the pre-resurrection, post-resurrection and eccleisal meals of Jesus with his disciples.[56]

In the light of this trajectory, recent scholarship has emphasized the importance of: (1) the table in the ministry of Jesus; (2) the expression of resurrection joy in the post-resurrection meals with Jesus; and (3) the eschatological presence of Christ in ecclesial meals. In this line of thinking, the presence of Jesus is the central feature of the Lord's Supper—not as present in the bread or wine, but as host of the kingdom table. The "breaking of bread" motif in Luke-Acts grounds and illustrates this continuity.

In the Gospel of Luke the table is the primary "organizing principle" of Jesus' pedagogical method.[57] He eats with sinners and Pharisees. He models table etiquette in the Kingdom of God. In Jesus God eats with his people and by meal-acts proclaims what the Kingdom of God is like.[58] The table ministry of Jesus forms the backdrop for Luke's description of the Last Supper which, according to Wainwright, "was apparently intended to be the last of the parabolic meal-signs dispensed by the man who had come eating and drinking, and next would come with full feasting in the kingdom."[59]

In the Gospel of Luke, Jesus hosts three meals where he "breaks" bread with his disciples. Each is laced with eschatological motifs. The first is Jesus' feeding of the five thousand in Luke 9:10-17. This meal story is particularly significant for several reasons. First, it is the only meal in Luke prior to the Last Supper (Luke 22) where Jesus is the host. Second, it contains language that is explicitly tied to the Last Supper (he took the bread, blessed it, broke it and gave it to the disciples; cf. Luke 9:16 with Luke 22:19). Third, the meal has clear messianic overtones as the Messiah feeds his people and eats with them.

Just prior to this meal story, Jesus had sent "the Twelve" out to "preach the kingdom of God and to heal the sick" (Lk 9:2). Upon their return, Jesus retires with them to Bethsaida (Lk 9:11). Between these two paragraphs, Luke injects the question that shapes the rest of the narrative. Herod the tetrarch asked: "Who, then, is this I hear such things about?" (Lk 9:9, NIV). The primary question of the narrative is "who is Jesus?" The narrative answers the question in Luke 9:20 by the mouth of Peter: "The Messiah of God" (NRSV). Luke heightened the messianic character of this meal by placing it prior to the confession of Jesus as the Christ so that the hospitality, preaching, healing and feeding of his people are signs by which his messianic identity is recognized.

The meal, then, is an identity action. This is a messianic meal as the Messiah welcomes the crowd, teaches them about the kingdom of God (Lk 9:11), and provides their "food and lodging" (Lk 9:12). Jesus, as Messiah, feeds the people of God in a "remote place" (Lk 9:12), just as God did with manna in the wilderness. The table confirms Jesus' identity as God's anointed one. The meal is characterized by joy, abundance and compassion as Jesus feeds the hungry. The text has messianic banquet overtones and, therefore, is a context for interpreting the Lord's Supper.[60]

The chart below illustrates the connections between this feeding and the Last Supper. The thematic connection indicates that Luke intended his community to read Luke 9 in the light of the table in the kingdom of God. This meal is the meal of the kingdom, just as Luke 22 is the meal of the kingdom, and the ecclesial meal is the meal of the kingdom. They constitute a continuous participation in the kingdom of God. All of them anticipate the fullness of the Messianic banquet, but at the same time experience the reality of the kingdom.

Topic	Luke 9	Luke 22
Kingdom Language	Spoke about the kingdom	Fulfillment in the Kingdom
Twelve	Twelve Apostles/Baskets	Twelve Tribes/Apostles
Exodus/Wilderness	Manna in the Wilderness	Exodus Memorial
Disciples Disputing	Who's the Greatest?	Who's the Greatest?
Reclining (at table)	Table Etiquette	Table Etiquette
Liturgical Formula	Took, Blessed, Broke, Gave	Took, Blessed, Broke, Gave
Jesus as Host	Host in the Wilderness	Host at the Passover
Hospitality (Lodging)	Providing Hospitality	Accepting Hospitality
Apostolic Mission	Traveling Missionaries	Judging the Tribes
Eating a Meal	Loaves and Fishes	Passover Lamb
Service	Disciples Serve	Jesus Serves

Luke provides the longest account of the Last Supper among the Synoptics. The Last Supper, according to Luke, is a Passover meal and Luke directly links the old covenant Passover with the new covenant meal. Jesus ate this Passover in anticipation of eating with his disciples again in the kingdom of God (Lk 22:16-18). What Jesus intends to eat in the future is the fulfillment of the Passover itself. The Passover supper finds its fulfillment in the Kingdom of God where the disciples would eat and drink at Jesus' table in his kingdom (Lk 22:30).

Luke places this new covenant meal on the trajectory of redemptive history. Jesus will eat and drink with the disciples again when the kingdom comes (Lk 22:18). The fullness of the kingdom is the reign of God at the *parousia* (see the parable in Lk 19:11-27). However, Luke also believes that in the person of Jesus, who exorcises demons and raises the dead, the kingdom is already present (Lk 11:20; 17:21), and that Pentecost was the inauguration of restored Israel when Jesus ascended to the throne of David (Acts 1:6; 2:29-35 with Lk 1:30-33). The kingdom of God is already and not yet; it is present but yet future. The Passover is fulfilled in both the church and the future messianic banquet. Thus, the fulfillment in Luke 22 has a dual import. It is fulfillment in the new covenant meal of the inaugurated kingdom as well as the future Messianic or heavenly banquet.

Three days after promising he would eat and drink again with the disciples in the kingdom of God, Jesus is eating with his disciples (Lk 24:30, 42-43). Jesus' actions on that Easter first day of the week in Emmaus exactly parallel the Last Supper. At the table, Jesus "took bread, blessed and broke it, and gave it to them" (Lk 24:30), just at the Last Supper he took the bread, gave thanks, broke and gave it (Lk 22:19). Luke identifies the Emmaus meal with the Last Supper, and thus with the Eucharist.[61]

In the breaking of the bread, Jesus was "made known" (Lk 24:35). They now "recognized" him when they previously had not. Their eyes were opened at the table (Lk 24:16, 31). Cleopas and his friend saw the risen Lord and returned to Jerusalem to tell the other disciples. Then Jesus appeared to the whole group, ate with them (Lk 24:34-42) and ministered the word to them (Lk 24:44-49). The parallels between the first pericope and the second in Luke 24 are significant: the presence of Jesus, post-resurrection meal, and the ministry of the word (See also Acts 1:4; 10:41). And this experience is itself the continuation of the meals with Jesus during his ministry.[62]

The table, then, is a table of hope as it declares the presence of the kingdom through the resurrection of Jesus. The table proclaims the living Christ. The risen host is present at the table eating and drinking with his disciples. The table is about hope, joy, communion, and thanksgiving. The table on that first Easter Sunday was a table of joy and celebration (Lk 24:52).

The new community of Jesus' disciples is described in Acts 2:42 as those who "devoted themselves to the apostles' teaching and fellowship, to the breaking of bread and to prayers." Daily this new community gathered in the temple and in homes (Acts 2:46-47). They apparently gathered in the temple for prayers and teaching (Acts 3:1; 5:21 [daily]), and also gathered daily in homes to break bread.[63]

They shared food with joy and generosity. There is no substantial reason to distinguish between the breaking of bread in Acts 2:42 and Acts 2:46—they refer to a meal in the context of which the liturgical pattern was displayed [breaking bread], the Lord was remembered, and his presence experienced.[64] Whatever this "breaking bread" is ought to be interpreted against the background of Luke 9, 22 and 24 so that those texts inform our understanding of Acts 2. It seems improbable that Luke would use the same language ("breaking bread") to describe two different things within the space of five verses, especially when the Gospel of Luke informs our understanding of what it means to break bread. Consequently, "breaking bread" in Acts 2:42 and 2:46 refer to the Lord's Supper that was experienced as a daily meal in Jerusalem church.[65]

Luke intends his readers to link the "breaking of bread" with the previous events in his Gospel. Three times in his Gospel Luke gives a full description of Jesus' actions as host when he took the bread, blessed (gave thanks) it, broke it and gave it to his disciples. When Luke summarily and cryptically refers to the "breaking of bread" in Acts, he assumes the reader knows the fuller stories of his Gospel. Indeed, he assumes they understand the theological significance of "breaking bread." That significance is indicated by Luke 24:35 as the hinge text in the "breaking of bread" stories.[66] As the chart below visually represents, when the disciples of Christ broke bread they experienced the presence of the risen Christ.

The Gospel of Luke	Hinge Text	The Book of Acts
Luke 9:16 Jesus took bread, blessed, broke and gave it		Acts 2:42 the disciples continued in the breaking of bread
Luke 22:19 Jesus took bread, gave thanks, broke and gave it	Luke 24:35 Jesus was "made known to them in the breaking of the bread"	Acts 2:46 the disciples broke bread daily in their homes
Luke 24:30 Jesus took bread, blessed, broke and gave it		Acts 20:7, 11 the disciples gathered to break bread and broke it

Luke also narrates that the church continued to break bread as a community (Acts 20:7). The church gathered to break bread as its explicit purpose for assembling. The story combines several elements that illuminate the connection between breaking bread, the first day of the week and resurrection (just as in Luke 24). On this particular first day of the week when the disciples were gathered to break bread the church experienced firsthand a resurrection from the dead. The narrative links between Luke 24 and Acts 20 confirm that Luke wanted his readers to relive the resurrection of Jesus in this resurrection.[67] The resurrection of Eutychus functions as an existential reality that embodies the truth of Jesus' own presence at that table.

Topic	Luke 24	Acts 20
Gathering of Disciples	24:33	20:7
Breaking of Bread	24:30,35	20:7,11
Eating Together	24:42-43	20:11
First Day of the Week	24:1,13	20:7
Teaching the Word (logos)	24:17,19,44	20:7
Conversation (homileo)	24:14-15	20:11
A Rising from the Dead	24:5,46	20:10,12
Fear	24:37-38	20:10
The Living One (zotan)	24:5	20:12

"Breaking bread" in Luke-Acts is a meal where the Lord is present as host and the disciples sit together as a community not only in the hope of the resurrection but in the present experience of the alreadiness of the *eschaton*. Disciples share food with each other as an expression of the communion that exists among the disciples by virtue of God's redemptive act in Jesus. As they eat, they anticipate the eschatological kingdom. But they did more than anticipate. They actually experienced the presence of the risen Christ at the table. "In the reading of Scripture and at the breaking of the bread," Marshall comments, "The risen Lord will continue to be present, though unseen."[68]

"Breaking bread," then, was not a solemn funerary ritual but the new community's celebration of the presence of the risen Jesus through which God revealed the *eschaton*. The disciples ate with joy and generosity as they praised God for his redemptive work. They ate with hope as they re-experienced the victory of Jesus over death through eating together and with Jesus. Indeed, these celebratory meals were filled with joyous interaction and enthusiastic praise. Joy is pervasive in Luke's meal stories (see Acts 2:46) and is particularly appropriate to the Eucharist as well as analogous to the joy that characterized the sacrificial meals of the Old Testament (Deut 12:7, 12, 18; 14:26; 27:7).[69] It is one of the great discontinuities between the meals in Luke and the contemporary church that joy is not the most prominent way in which the contemporary Supper is experienced.

This joy is an eschatological joy. It is rooted in the presence of the living Christ at the table. As Marshall notes, "Above all, Luke's contribution is to stress that the Lord's Supper is the joyous celebration of the experience of salvation in the presence of the risen Lord."[70] In Lucan theology, it is "the Eucharist which gives the risen Christ, living and present, to the faithful. So it is that for Christians the Eucharist is the great sign of the Lord's Resurrection, the sign by which they recognize the Lord as living and present."[71]

Theological Reflection
Systematic Theology

The continuity between ministry meals (Luke 9), the Last Supper (Luke 22) and post-resurrection meals (Luke 24) is the presence of the living Christ in the breaking of the bread. "The eschatological prospect held out by Jesus at the Last Supper," Wainwright writes, "did not have to await the church's eucharist for its fulfillment, let alone remain unfulfilled until a coming of the kingdom which has even yet not occurred, but was *already fulfilled in the meals which Jesus took with His disciples immediately after his resurrection*."[72] The continuity between the Gospel of Luke and the breaking of bread in Acts is the eschatological reality of the resurrected Jesus. It is the continuation of the post-resurrection meals. "The Last Supper and those resurrection appearances," Torrance writes, "belong together in one sacramental whole. Though Jesus has withdrawn His visible presence from us, there is such an intervention by the risen Lord as the invisible reality behind each celebration of the Lord's Supper. Jesus Christ is as really present in the Eucharist as He was on that Easter day to His disciples."[73]

Yet, as Christians reflect on the continuing presence of the risen Christ at the Lord's table in the church, we are confronted with the tension that the risen Christ is also absent. Torrance calls this the "eschatological reserve" in the sense that there is "an eschatological lag waiting for the last Word or the final Act of God."[74] In our post-ascension but pre-*parousia* situation, Christians live in the tension that Jesus is both absent and present. He is absent—he no longer walks upon the earth as one of us, but sits at the right hand of God. He is present, however, sacramentally at the table. Consequently, both continuity and discontinuity occur in the post-resurrection meals. While the table mediates the presence of Christ, Jesus is not physically present in the same sense in which he was present at the post-resurrection meals. The Eucharist continues the post-resurrection meals but in a post-ascension context. Thus, the Eucharist is an anticipation of the "not yet" character of the *eschaton* but is also a participation in its "alreadiness." It is more than a pledge of what is to come; it is the present experience of the future itself, but it is not yet the fullness of face-to-face fellowship with the risen Christ.

This tension shapes the Eucharistic practice of the church. The one who bridges that tension is the Spirit of God. Pneumatology—being in the Spirit, worshipping in the Spirit—unites the church with the absent Christ so that he is truly present at the table. When Christ ascended, he poured out the Spirit upon his people. The Spirit unites heaven and earth. Moreover, this eschatological Spirit brings the future into the present. He himself is not only a down payment, an earnest or pledge of the future, but the future is now present through the Spirit. The presence of the Spirit is the presence of the *eschaton*.

When pondering the relationship between the Eucharist and eschatology, pneumatology must be front-and-center. While space to develop this point is limited, the witness of John (Jn 4:24) and Paul (Phil 3:2; Eph 5:18-19) is that the people of God worship in the Spirit. Christians worship in Spirit as people who "have immediate access to God through the Son" by the Spirit.[75] They approach the Father through the Son in the Spirit (Eph 2:18). The Spirit mediates their presence to the Father, just as the Spirit mediates the Son's presence in them. Christians are the habitation of God in the Spirit (Eph 2:22). At the table they are united sacramentally with the Father and Son through the Spirit in a communion that is given in concrete form as bread and wine at a table.

Deeper reflection on this function of the Spirit gives significance to the historic emphasis of the Eastern Orthodox tradition. They remind others that the table in the gathered church is the "sacrament of assembly."[76] The assembly, with the Eucharist at its center, involves the sacramental presence of God. The assembly is sacred—the whole assembly—because, by the Spirit, the gathered community has been lifted up into the throne room of God. There the assembly encounters the divine presence. This moves assembly, and consequently Eucharist, beyond proclamation and memory. Rather, the "newness, the uniqueness of the Christian *leitourgia* [is] in its eschatological nature as the presence here and now of the future *parousia*, as the ephiphany of that which is to come, as communion with the 'world to come'." The day of assembly, the "Lord's day," is a "symbol, i.e., the manifestation, now, of the kingdom."[77] This is no mere corporate vertical relationship, but the present experience of the future. Christians see the world with eschatological eyes in the Eucharist and authentically experience the future.

The presence of the eschatological reality in the assembly gathered around the table pulls Christians into the fullness of the kingdom of God. By the Spirit they experience the alreadiness of the kingdom as they are present in the throne room of God. The assembly is "the sacrament of the coming of the risen Lord, of our meeting and communion with him 'at his table in his kingdom.'" Through the Eucharist the church ascends and enters "into the light and joy and triumph of the kingdom" in such a way that the Eucharist is a "fully realized symbol."[78] This is the truth of the Orthodox mantra that the assembly of the church is "heaven on earth," or "standing in the temple we stand in heaven."[79] "Let us beware," Chrysostom warns, "that we do not remain on the earth."[80]

The remnants of this idea are found in Western liturgical traditions. When the church sings the *Sanctus* ("Holy, Holy, Holy"), it joins the heavenly chorus surrounding the throne of God. This is no mere distant praise. Rather, "the earthly church actually and already participates in the worship of heaven."[81]

The Wesleys also discerned this picture and spoke of it in terms of a "foretaste" of heaven. Though the imagery is "rare," according to Wainwright, "its value as an expression for the relation between the already and the not yet is undeniable."[82] In the minds of the Wesleys, this realized eschatology joined the church "in its mission of a liturgical union of praise with the whole company of heaven. The supper was understood as a vehicle that transformed the assembly of believers and gave them a present place in the 'Church Triumphant.'"[83]

The eschatological dimension of the Eucharist, therefore, is not simply a proclamation of a future fact (either the Second Advent or the kingdom of God), nor is it merely a promise or pledge of the future reality, but it is the experience of that future in the present through the Spirit who unites believers with the living Christ in the throne room of God. Jesus invites them to his table even now, and they participate in the eschatological banquet even now. They already eat at the eschatological table of the Lord; they already sit at the table with Jesus in his kingdom.

Practical Theology
Liturgical Orientation. The solemnity and apparent sadness of our current experience of the Supper in the contemporary church does not fit the Emmaus road experience. The church needs to revision the supper as an experience of resurrection joy at the

kingdom table rather than as an altar of sacrifice. As Torrance explains, "Those Easter meals gave [the disciples] their understanding of the rite in the Upper Room."[84]

Just as the Emmaus narrative moves from the non-recognition of Jesus to the recognition of Jesus at the table, so the church learns to recognize Jesus at the table. There they recognize the victory of the resurrection as they eat and drink with Jesus in hope. At the table they bring all their "Fridays" to Jesus and celebrate the victory of Christ on Sunday. The table transforms "Friday" into "Sunday." Unfortunately, the church still generally practices the supper as if it were still Friday rather than Sunday when the point of the supper is to celebrate Sunday and experience the reality that God has overcome Friday. Sunday reinterprets and renews their Fridays. As Torrance notes: "The mystery of the Resurrection is sacramentally present in the Eucharist."[85]

If the church embraces the theological idea of eschatological presence at the table as the already of a not-yet future, the Eucharistic liturgy of the church should be primarily shaped by hope, joy and spiritual communion. The Disciples' hymnal Thankful Praise is a good example of a move in this direction. For example, it emphasizes a table theology where Jesus sits as host.[86] It embodies a "meditative" or "contemplative joy."[87] But this joyous experience is a "present sharing in the eschatological banquet" rather than simply an "anamnetic thanksgiving."[88] Certainly contemplative joy is consistent with the nature of the eschatological banquet, but the joy of the eschatological banquet should not be limited to contemplation or meditation.

Missional Table.[89] If the Lord's Supper is understood as the continuation of the table ministry of Jesus in the church, it will have profound implications for the significance and practice of the table.[90] The table is a place where Jesus receives sinners and confronts the righteous; a place where Jesus extends grace to seekers but condemns the self-righteous. Jesus is willing to eat with sinners in order to invite them into the kingdom, but he points out the discontinuity between humanity's tables of social/ethnic/gender/economic/religious cultures and the table in the kingdom of God. The last (sinners, poor, and humbled) will be first in the kingdom of God, but the first (self-righteous, rich and proud) will be last and excluded from the kingdom of God (Lk 13:26-30).

The meal stories have theological and Eucharistic meaning for Luke's community. The table during Jesus' ministry should shape the table in the church because the table of Jesus is the table of the kingdom. The table of Jesus' ministry continues in the church. Jesus' table etiquette is kingdom etiquette, and the Lord's Supper is the Lord's kingdom table.

The table announces the presence of the kingdom. It announces that "today" salvation has come to the world as God communes with his people. The Jubilee motif, articulated in Luke 4:16-19, not only invests the table with great joy, but it also calls the disciples of Jesus to embrace all those who are invited to his table. The table is inclusive and extended to the poor, blind and oppressed (Lk 14:12-24). The table reaches across all socio-economic, racial and gender barriers as it unites lost humanity at one table. It embraces the "other" as Christians break bread in the presence of Jesus.[91] This inclusiveness testifies to the socio-ethical character of the table as a uniting moment in the kingdom of God.

Moreover, the table becomes a political,[92] economic,[93] and ecological[94] act within culture and against culture. It expresses the kingdom of God in all its political, economic and ecological dimensions.[95] It bears witness to how the kingdom of God in the present should transform life here and now. Christian allegiance is to the kingdom, not human political institutions. Their commitment is to the poor, not to consumerist capitalism. Their concern is for the integrity of God's creation, not self-serving exploitation of the earth. To understand that the Eucharist is the kingdom meal that embodies kingdom life, not only in the new heaven and new earth but here, is to see the Eucharist as the presence of the future that transforms the present and propels people toward the realization of the fullness of God's kingdom on the earth. The Eucharist is the meal which not only prays "Thy Kingdom Come," but also makes demands on the lives of disciples to live as if the kingdom is already present.[96]

Table Openness. One of the most significant ways in which the eschatological significance of the Supper has been employed in the last fifty years is in service to ecumenics. This partly motivates Wainwright's work, but it was pioneered by Torrance in 1952.[97] In 1993 Davies surveyed the impact of various understandings of the Supper upon ecumenics, and in 2000 Welker did the same.[98] All give significant attention to the eschatological meaning of the Supper where the primary focus is on the divine act that generates joy and gratitude in worshippers toward the expression of eschatological unity.[99]

Again, if the table ministry of Jesus is to shape our understanding and practice of the Eucharist, and if the eschatological reality is already present in the Supper, then this will move us toward emphasizing the divine invitation. Jesus invited all to the table and sat with all. If the table embodies the gospel and bears witness to the gospel, then it should reflect the universal intent of the gospel. Just as our preaching invites all to faith, so the table invites all to eat. The table, just as the ministry of the Word, offers grace and testifies that Jesus died for all. The table is a place where sinners can not only hear but experience the gracious message of the gospel through eating with the community of faith. The community of faith today, just as Israel in the past, receives aliens at its table.[100]

This should resonate with the Stone-Campbell tradition, especially in regard to ecumenics. Our historic beginnings involved significant conflicts regarding the table. Thomas Campbell was censured and ultimately defrocked for sharing communion with Presbyterians outside the Seceeder tradition in Western Pennsylvania. Alexander Campbell refused to take communion at the approval of a token-giving clergy. In the last 150 years the slogan "we neither invite, nor debar" has characterized our practice but this was mostly rooted in an individualistic understanding of "self-examination" rather than a call for unity.[101] Unity assumes an invitation to the table where all are welcome, unlimited by institutional lines. An eschatological vision turns the discussion away from institutional concerns toward the fullness of the kingdom of God.

Conclusion

Through the Lord's Supper disciples experience the eschatological joy of the risen Christ as he hosts our communal meal. The Lord's Supper is an eschatological meal of the partially realized kingdom of God.

The church should not, of course, abandon memorialism (we remember Jesus) or a sense of mystical presence through the bread and wine (Calvin's emphasis). But these perspectives must be brought under the horizon of the *eschaton*.[102] As Dix reminds us, "The whole conception of anamnesis is in itself eschatological….What the church 'remembers' in the eucharist is partly beyond history—the ascension, the sitting at the right hand of the Father and the second coming."[103]

The horizon of the Christian faith is eschatological. In the Eucharist we "remember the future"[104] because the eschatological human, Jesus the Messiah, is present at the Eucharist as an earnest of the future. In the Eucharist we experience the presence of Christ-not so much in the bread and wine, but at the table.

The eschatological horizon reminds us that the root metaphor of the Eucharist is neither tomb nor altar, but table.[105]

Notes

[1]Alexander Campbell, "Ancient Gospel. No. II. Immersion," *Christian Baptist* 5 (4 February 1828), p. 414 [D. S. Burnett edition; St. Louis: Christian Publishing Co., 1889], available at http://www.mun.ca/rels/restmov/texts/acampbell/tcb/TCB507.HTM#Essay6.

[2]William Robinson, *Essays on Christian Unity* (London: James Clark & Co., 1924), pp. 275-278, available at http://www.mun.ca/rels/restmov/texts/wrobinson/eocu/EOCU10H.HTM.

[3]Andrew Paris, *What the Bible Says about the Lord's Supper* (Joplin, Mo.: College Press, 1986), pp. 151-243.

[4]Byron Lambert, "Have We Understood the Lord's Supper?" in *The Lord's Supper: Historical Writings on Its Meaning to the Body of Christ*, ed. Charles R. Gresham and Tom Lawson (Joplin, Mo.: College Press, 1993), pp. 208-210.

[5]Gordon T. Smith, *A Holy Meal: The Lord's Supper in the Life of the Church* (Grand Rapids: Baker, 2005). Leonard J. Vander Zee, *Christ, Baptism and the Lord's Supper: Recovering the Sacraments for Evangelical Worship* (Downers Grove, Ill.: 2004), pp. 187-219, discusses meaning under the headings: presence of Christ, mediation of the Holy Spirit, Supper and sacrifice, remembrance, and meal of hope.

[6]Available at http://www.wcc-coe.org/wcc/what/faith/bem4.html.

[7]*The Nature of the Unity We Seek; Official Report of the North American Conference on Faith and Order*, ed. Paul S. Minear (St. Louis: Bethany, 1958), p. 203.

[8]Some representative examples are Scott McCormick, Jr., *The Lord's Supper: A Biblical Interpretation* (Philadelphia: Westminster, 1966), pp. 88-108; Paul E. Deterding, "Eschatological and Eucharistic Motifs in Luke 12:35-40," *Concordia Journal* 5 (May 1979): 85-94; Patrick Regan, "Pneumatological and Eschatological Aspects of Liturgical Celebration," *Worship* 51(1977): 332-350; William Hill, "The Eucharist as Eschatological Presence," *Communio* 4 (Winter, 1977): 306-320; John H. McKenna, "The Eucharist, The Resurrection and the Future," *Anglican Theological Review* 60 (1978): 144-165; Horton Davies, *Bread of Life and Cup of Joy: Newer Ecumenical Perspectives on the Eucharist* (Grand Rapids: Eerdmans, 1993), pp. 80-116; Arthur A. Just, *The Ongoing Feast: Table Fellowship and Eschatology at Emmaus* (Collegeville, Min.: Liturgical, 1993); Debra Dean Murphy, "Bread, Wine, and the 'Pledge of Heaven': A (Wesleyan) Feminist Perspective on Eucharist and Eschatology," *Quarterly Review* 14 (Winter 1994-1995): 401-412; Peter Leithart, "The Way Things Really Ought to Be: Eucharist, Eschatology, and Culture," *Westminster Theological Journal* 59 (Fall 1997): 159-176; Robert G. Clouse, "Eschatology and the Lord's Supper: Hope for the Triumph of God's Reign," in *The Lord's Supper: Believers Church Perspectives*, ed. Dale R. Stoffer (Scottdale, Pa.: Herald P, 1997), 129-139; Jason Fout, "Beginnings and Ends: Eucharist and Eschatology," *Quodlibet Online Journal of Christian Theology and Philosophy* 2.4 (Fall 2000), available at http://www.quodlibet.net/fout-eucharist.shtml; Rebecca Kuiken, "Hopeful Feasting: Eucharist and Eschatology," in *Hope for Your Future: Theological Voices from the Pastorate*, ed. William H. Lazareth (Grand Rapids: Eerdmans, 2002), pp. 192-198; Martha L. Moore-Keish, "Eucharist: Eschatology," in *A More Profound Alleluia: Theology and Worship in Harmony* (Grand Rapids: Eerdmans, 2005), pp.109-132.

[9]Geoffrey Wainwright, *Eucharist and Eschatology* (London: Epworth, 1971)

[10]Wainwright, *Eucharist*, pp. 1-2. He organizes his discussion under three themes: antepast of heaven, marantha, and firstfruits of the Kingdom.

[11]Wainwright, *Eucharist*, p. 125.

[12]Ibid.

[13]See the discussion of William R. Crockett, *Eucharist: Symbol of Transformation* (New York: Pueblo, 1989), pp. 256-258.

[14]Steven T. Hoskins, "Eucharist and Eschatology in the Writings of the Wesleys," *Wesleyan Theological Journal* 29 (1994): 64-80, available at http://wesley.nnu.edu/wesleyan_theology/theo-jrnl/26-30/29-04.htm. See also Murphy, "Bread, Wine, and the 'Pledge of Heaven'," 406-8.

[15]Daniel Brevint, *The Christian Sacrament and Sacrifice by way of Discourse, Meditation, & Prayer upon the Nature, Parts and Blessings of the Holy Communion* (Oxford: At the Theater in Oxford, 1673).

[16]J. Robert Nelson, "Methodist Eucharistic Practice: From Constant Communion to Benign Neglect to Sacramental Recovery," *Journal of Ecumenical Studies* 13 (Spring 1976): 280-281. See also Kathryn Nichols, "The Theology of Christ's Sacrifice and Presence in Charles Wesley's Hymns on the Lord's Supper," *Hymn* 39 (October 1988): 19-29 and "Charles Wesley's Eucharistic Hymns: Their Relationship to the Book of Common Prayer," *Hymn* 39 (October 1988): 13-21.

[17]For example, see J. E. Rattenbury, *The Eucharistic Hymns of John and Charles Wesley* (London: Epworth, 1948), #96; #102.

[18]Paul A. Crow, Jr., "The Lord's Supper in Ecumenical Dialogue," *Theology Today* 22 (April 1965): 45-6, available at http://theologytoday.ptsem.edu/apr1965/v22-1-article3.htm.

[19]Leigh Eric Schmidt, *Holy Fairs: Scottish Communion and American Revivals in the Early Modern Period* (Princeton: Princeton University, 1989).

[20]Alexander Campbell, "Breaking the Loaf," in *The Christian System* (1839; reprint ed., Nashville: Gospel Advocate, 1970), p. 265.

[21]Campbell, "Breaking the Loaf," p. 269.

[22]Alexander Campbell, "A Restoration of the Ancient Order of Things, No. IV. On the Breaking

of Bread, No. 1," *Christian Baptist* 3 (1 August 1825): 175.

[23]Campbell, "Meeting-Houses," *Millennial Harbinger* 5 (January 1834): 8.

[24]Moses Lard, "My Church," *Lard's Quarterly* 1 (1864): 150-151.

[25]David Lipscomb, *Queries and Answers,* ed. J.W. Shepherd, 5th ed. (Nashville: Gospel Advocate, 1963), p. 267.

[26]James A. Harding, "An Interesting Letter from C. E. J.," *The Way* 5 (9 July 1903): 707.

[27]James A. Harding, "The Pastor—A Letter from Brother J. E. Dunn and a Reply by the Editor," *The Way* 2 (June 1900): 84.

[28]Harding, "An Interesting Letter," p. 707.

[29]Paul M. Blowers and Byron C. Lambert, "Lord's Supper, The," in *The Encyclopedia of the Stone-Campbell Movement,* ed. Douglas A. Foster, et. al. (Grand Rapids: Eerdmans, 2004), pp. 493-495. See also K. C. Richardson, "The Lord's Supper as a Sacrament in the History of the Stone-Campbell Movement" (M.Div., thesis, Emmanuel School of Religion, 1996); James O. Duke, "The Disciples and the Lord's Supper: A Historical Perspective," *Encounter* 50 (Winter 1989): 1-28; and Richard L. Harrison, Jr., "Early Disciples Sacramental Theology: Catholic, Reformed and Free," *Mid-Stream* 24 (July 1985): 255-292.

[30]Alexander Campbell, "What is the Real Design of the Lord's Supper?" *Millennial Harbinger* 17 (September 1846): 396.

[31]Hiram Christopher, *The Remedial System; or, Man and His Redeemer in Two Parts* (Lexington, Ky.: Transylvania Printing and Publishing Co., 1876), p. 348.

[32]Ibid., p. 341.

[33]Robert Milligan, *The Scheme of Redemption* (1868; reprint ed.,Nashville: Gospel Advocate, 1977), 429-30. See also Robert Richardson, *Communings in the Sanctuary* (1872; reprint ed., Abilene, Tex.: Leafwood Publishers, 2000) and R. H. Boll, *Truth and Grace* (Cincinnati: F. L. Rowe, 1917), p. 272: "The import of the Lord's Supper is not exhausted in the word 'memorial'...It has a further power...the Lord's Supper is not simply a reminder of the Lord's death, but a real participation in the body and blood of Christ."

[34]It is absent, for example, in Blowers and Lambert's survey ("Lord's Supper") in *The Encyclopedia of the Stone-Campbell Movement* except in the person of William Robinson.

[35]David Brag, "Until He Comes," *Gospel Advocate* 145 (6 June 2003): 21-22. Other articles (pp. 12-21) included "The Lord's Supper and the Lord's Day" by Cecil May, Jr., "A Memorial to the Lord's Death" by Dale Jenkins, "Discerning the Lord's Body" by Howard Justis, and "The Christian's Holy Meal" by Kevin Cauley. The overarching theme stressed memorialism and solemnity. The issue is apparently a response to my *Come to the Table: Revisioning the Lord's Supper* (Abilene, Tex.: Leafwood Publishers, 2002), without naming it.

[36]Mac Deaver, "Lord's Supper...Looking Forward," *Spiritual Sword* 13 (July 1982): 12.

[37]J. M. Powell, "The Purpose of the Lord's Supper," *Gospel Advocate* 123 (5 February 1981): 78.

[38]J. W. McGarvey, "Dedicatory Sermon, Campbell Street Church of Christ, Louisville, Ky. (1877)," available at http://www.mun.ca/rels/restmov/texts/jwmcgarvey/DEDSERM.HTM.

[39]Milligan, *Scheme*, p. 361-441, lists seven: preaching the word, prayer, praise, fasting, baptism, Lord's Day, and the Lord's Supper.

[40]Alexander Campbell, *Christian Baptism: With Its Antecedents and Consequents* (Bethany, VA: Campbell, 1851), p. 17: "The Christian ordinances—baptism, the Lord's day, and the Lord's supper—as taught and observed by the Apostles." Cf. Calvin L. Potter, "Thinking Our Way Into the Future with Truth Behind Our Backs," *Mid-Stream* 25 (July 1987): 307.

[41]Alexander, Campbell, "Essays on Man in his Primitive State, and under the Patriarchal, Jewish, and Christian Dispensations.—No. XVI. Christian Age—No. II.," *Christian Baptist* 7.12 (5 July 1830): 656; Campbell, *Christian Baptism*, p. 246.

[42]Benjamin Franklin, "Positive Divine Law," in *Gospel Preacher: A Book of Twenty-One Sermons* (Cincinnati: G.W. Rice, 1877), 2.193, available at http://www.mun.ca/rels/restmov/texts/bfranklin/tgp2/TGP209.HTM.

[43]Franklin, "Positive," p. 194. See John Mark Hicks, "The Gracious Separatist: Moral and Positive Law in the Theology of James A. Harding," *Restoration Quarterly* 42.3 (2000): 129-147, available at http://johnmarkhicks.faithsite.com/content.asp?CID=17867.

[44]J. Z. Tyler, "The Ordinances of the Lord," in *New Testament Christianity*, ed. Z. T. Sweeney (Columbus, IN: New Testament Christianity Book Fund, 1926), pp. 113-124. This article is immediately followed by Franklin's "Positive Divine Law," pp. 125-165, cited above. Both are available at http://www.mun.ca/rels/restmov/texts/zsweeney/ntc2/NTC200.HTM.

[45]Letter cited by William Baxter, *The Life of Elder Walter Scott* (Cincinnati: Bosworth, Chase & Hall, 1874), p. 410, available at http://www.mun.ca/rels/restmov/texts/wbaxter/lews/LEWS26.HTM.

[46]William Robinson, *Completing the Reformation: The Doctrine of the Priesthood of All Believers* (Lexington, KY: College of the Bible, 1955), p. 59.

[47]William Robinson, "The Administration of the Lord's Supper," in *The Lord's Supper: Historical Writings on Its Meaning to the Body of Christ*, ed. Charles R. Gresham and Tom Lawson (Joplin, Mo.: College Press, 1993), p. 89-90.

[48]C. E. Braaten and R. W. Jenson, *The Last Things: Biblical and Theological Perspectives on Eschatology* (Grand Rapids: Eerdmans, 2002), p. vii.

[49]Johannes Weiss, *Jesus' Proclamation of the Kingdom of God* (1892, German; Philadelphia: Fortress, 1971) and Albert Schweitzer, *The Quest of the Historical Jesus* (London: Adam & Charles. Black, 1911).

[50]C. H. Dodd, *The Parables of the Kingdom* (London: Nisbet, 1935).

[51]J. Moltmann, *Theology of Hope: On the Grounds and Implications of a Christian Eschatology* (New York: Harper & Row, 1967), p. 16.

[52]Wainwright, *Eucharist*, p. 18.

[53]Hans Lietzmann, *Mass and the Lord's Supper: A Study in the History of Liturgy* (1926, German; trans. D. H. G. Reeve; Leiden: E. J. Brill, 1979).

[54]J. Lohmeyer, "Das Abendmahl in der Urgemeinde," *Journal of Biblical Literature* 56 (1937): 217-252.

[55]Oscar Cullmann, "The Meaning of the Lord's Supper in Primitive Christianity," pp. 5-23, in *Essays on the Lord's Supper*, trans. J. G. Davies (Richmond, Va.: John Knox Press, 1958 [French original, 1936]).

[56]Markus Barth, *Abendmahl: Passamahl, Bundesmahl und Messiasmahl* (Zollikon-Zurich: Evangelischer Verlag, 1945). See Markus Barth, *Rediscovering the Lord's Supper: Communion with Israel, with Christ, and Among Guests* (Atlanta: John Knox, 1988).

[57]John Koenig, *The Feast of the World's Redemption: Eucharistic Origins and Christian Mission* (Harrisbug, PA: Trinity Press International, 2000), p. 181.

[58]See Eugene LaVerdiere, *Dining in the Kingdom of God: The Origins of the Eucharist in the Gospel of Luke* (Chicago: Liturgy Training Publications, 1998).

[59]Wainwright, *Eucharist*, p. 35.

[60]Albert Schweitzer, *The Mysticism of St. Paul the Apostle* (London: A. & C. Black, 1931), p. 44, proposed an eschatological understanding of the Lord's Supper in relation to this feeding..

[61]Augustine, *Letter* 149: "And no one should doubt that his being recognized in the breaking of bread is the sacrament, which brings us together in recognizing him." Cited by Arthur A. Just, Jr., ed., *Luke*, ACCS, NT III (Downers Grove: InterVarsity, 2003), p. 382. See Just, *Ongoing Feast*, for an extended defense of this identification.

[62]Jon A. Weatherly, "Eating and Drinking in the Kingdom of God: The Emmaus Episode and the Meal Motif in Luke-Acts," in *Christ's Victorious Church*, ed. Tom Friskney and Jon A. Weatherly (Eugene, Ore.: Wipf and Stock, 2001), pp. 18-33.

[63]See Eugene LaVerdiere, *The Breaking of Bread: The Development of the Eucharist According to Acts* (Chicago: Liturgy Training Publications, 1998).

[64]Cf. William A. Dowd, "Exegetical Notes: Breaking Bread (Acts 2:46)," *Catholic Biblical Quarterly* 1.4 (October 1939): 358-362, for an extended defense of this understanding.

[65]Many support this understanding of Acts 2:42 and 2:46. For example, Brad Blue, "The Influence of Jewish Worship on Luke's Presentation of the Early Church," in *Witness to the Gospel: The Theology of Acts*, ed. I. Howard Marshall and David Peterson (Grand Rapids: Eerdmans, 1998), p. 489, and C. K. Barrett, *A Critical and Exegetical Commentary on the Acts of the Apostles,* ICC (Edinburgh: T&T Clark, 1994, 1998), 1:164-165.

[66]R. J. Dillon, *From Eyewitnesses to Ministers of the Word: Tradition and Composition in Luke 24*, Analecta Biblica, 82 (Rome: Biblical Institute, 1978), p. 105, regards Lk 24:35 as the "connecting link" between the ministry of Jesus and the Eucharistic meals in Acts.

[67]Luke Timothy Johnson, *The Acts of the Apostles*, Sacra Pagina (Collegeville, Minn.: Liturgical Press, 1992), p. 358: "Is it by accident that the story takes place on the first day of the week (Lk 24:1), or that it occurs in an 'upper room' (Lk 22:12; Acts 1:13), or that the disciples are gathered to "break bread" (Luke 24:30-35)? All of these are clear verbal pointers back to the resurrection of Jesus and the experience of his risen presence by the first disciples."

[68]I. Howard Marshall, *The Gospel of Luke*, NIGTC (Grand Rapids: Eerdmans, 1978), p. 900.

[69]See Philippe Henri Menoud, "The Acts of the Apostles and the Eucharist," in *Jesus Christ and the Faith,* 1953, French; trans. E. M. Paul (Pittsburgh: Pickwick, 1978), pp. 84-106; see Barth, Rediscovering, p. 74.

[70]I. Howard Marshall, *The Last Supper and the Lord's Supper* (Grand Rapids: Eerdmans, 1980), p. 133.

[71]Jacques Dupont, "The Meal at Emmaus," in *The Eucharist in the New Testament: A Symposium,* ed. J. Delorme, trans. E. M. Stewart (Baltimore: Helicon, 1965), p. 121.

[72]Wainwright, *Eucharist*, p. 38.

[73]T. F. Torrance, "Eschatology and Eucharist," *Intercommunion*, ed. Donald Baillie and John Marsh (N.Y.: Harper & Brothers, 1952), p. 334

[74]T. F. Torrance, *Royal Priesthood,* 2nd ed (Edinburgh: T & T Clar, 1993), p. 45. I am indebted to Vander Zee, *Christ*, p. 216, for this reference and the substance of this paragraph.

[75]J. E. L. Oulton, *Holy Communion and Holy Spirit: A Study in Doctrinal Relationship* (London: S.P.C.K., 1954), p. 129

[76]Alexander Schmemann, *The Eucharist: Sacrament of the Kingdom*, trans. Paul Kachur (Crestwood, N.Y.: St. Vladimir's, 1987), pp. 27-48.

[77]Ibid., p. 43.

[78]Ibid., pp. 43-44.

[79]Ibid., p. 45.

[80]As quoted by Schmemann, *Eucharist*, p. 169. See also Pope John Paul II, "Eucharist: Pledge of Future Glory" (General Audience, October 25, 2000), available at http://www.cin.org/pope/eucharist-glory.html.

[81]Wainwright, *Eucharist*, p. 117.

[82]Ibid., p. 152. See also Rattenbury, *Eucharistic Hymns*, pp. 61-78.

[83]Hoskins, "Eucharist and Eschatology."

[84]Torrance, "Eschatology and Eucharist," pp. 333-334.

[85]Ibid., p. 338.

[86]Keith Watkins, ed., *Thankful Praise: A Resource for Christian Worship* (St. Louis: CBP Press, 1987), nos. 55 (p. 73), 178 (p. 140), and 179 (p. 140). See also Keith Watkins, *Celebrate with Thanksgiving* (St. Louis: Chalice, 1991).

[87]Keith Watkins, *The Feast of Joy: The Lord's Supper in Free Churches* (St. Louis: Bethany, 1977), pp. 19-20.

[88]Gerard Francis Moore, "The Eucharistic Theology of the Prayers for Communion Service of the Lord's Supper of the Christian Church (Disciples of Christ): 1953-1987," (Thesis, Licentiate of Theology, Catholic University of America, 1989), p. 125.

[89]See Koenig, *The Feast of the World's Redemption*, pp. 215-259.

[90]Hicks, *Come to the Table*, pp. 51-66.

[91]Jim Forest, "In the Breaking of Bread: Recognizing the Face of Jesus," *Sojourners* 14.4 (1985): 34-36; See Murphy, "Bread, Wine, and 'the Pledge of Heaven,'" pp. 402-404.

[92]William T. Cavanaugh, *Torture and Eucharist: Theology, Politics, and the Body of Christ* (Malden, Mass: Blackwell, 1996).

[93]See Joseph A. Grassi, *Broken Bread and Broken Bodies: The Lord's Supper and World Hunger,* rev. ed. (Maryknoll, N.Y.: Orbis, 2004).

[94]See Leithart, "The Way Things Ought to Be."

[95]William Robinson, *Completing the Reformation*, p. 51, writes: "No one can partake of the Christian sacraments without realizing the terrific impact this ought to have on his life in economic and political realities, in fashioning the events of our time nearer to the pattern of 'God's time' which will be fulfilled in the 'last time.' We cannot escape the responsibility laid upon us if we are truly 'partakers of Christ.'"

[96]William Robinson, *Completing the Reformation*, p. 60, writes: "Men and women should see in the church, in its fellowship life, in those who commune with the body and blood of Christ, the spearhead of the kingdom. It is our Lord's express purpose that the will of God should be done on earth as it is in heaven, and it cannot be so done until it is done in us. What this is to mean in the sacrifice of our own selfish interests, in the economic, social, and political life of our time may be left to the imagination of each reader, as he comes face to face with the reality of our Lord's sacrificial life and death in the service of Holy Communion. If he does not find here that judgment upon his own conscience and that strength and grace to enable reformation, he will find them nowhere else."

[97]Torrance, "Eschatology and Eucharist," pp. 303-350.

[98]Davies, *Bread of Life and Cup of Joy*; and Michael Welker, *What Happens in Holy Communion?* (Grand Rapids: Eerdmans, 2000).

[99]See also Paul A. Crow, Jr., "The Lord's Supper in Ecumenical Dialogue," *Theology Today* 22 (April 1965): 39-58, available at http://theologytoday.ptsem.edu/apr1965/v22-1-article3.htm.

[100]Here is where the "breaking of bread" on the ship in Acts 27 contributes to a missional and open understanding of the Eucharist. For a defense of this reading, see Barrett, *Acts*, 2:1208-1210.

[101]Blowers and Lambert, "Lord's Supper," pp. 492-493.

[102]Dupont, "The Meal at Emmaus," p. 121: "We are familiar with the idea that the Eucharist is the memorial of the Saviour's Passion, and so it is. But it would be to restrict it significance if we saw in it only the death of Jesus without seeing his Resurrection at the same time. For the early Christians the death and Resurrection formed only one mystery, which was likewise inseparable from its third factor: the *parousia.*

[103]Gregory Dix, *The Shape of the Liturgy* (London: Dacre, 1945), p. 264.

[104]Kuiken, "Hopeful Feasting," p. 197.

[105]See Leithart, "The Way Things Ought to Be," pp. 166, 172-173. See Paul H. Jones, *Christ's Eucharistic Presence: A History of the Doctrine* (New York: Peter Lang, 1994), p. 45. This is the major thesis of Hicks, *Come to the Table: Revisioning the Lord's Supper.*

12

RESPONSE

I. Howard Marshall

T hese three presentations paint an interesting and attractive picture of the significance of the Lord's Supper in the Stone-Campbell Restoration Movement. My response will demonstrate implicitly that every major element in Stone-Campbell understanding is shared and indeed should be shared by evangelical Christians in other denominations.

Response to Lynn McMillon
The paper on the Scottish Restorationists is an intriguing piece of Scottish church history reaching right up to the present day with its description of a service in an Edinburgh congregation in 1985. Most of the points mentioned in the paper would be generally accepted by all Christians holding to an independent form of church polity. Certainly John Glas himself was something of a scriptural literalist, demonstrated by his insistence that the Lord's Supper, as he rightly called it, should be celebrated in the *evening*, thereby canonizing what may have been an adventitious circumstance in Corinth into an ecclesiastical rule.

His insistence that the primary function of the Lord's Supper is the recollection of the Lord in his body and blood given for us rightly puts first things first. Moreover, the denial that the Lord's Supper repeats his sacrifice merits continual repetition over against the ongoing tendency to sacerdotalism in many churches. I also affirm most strongly the recognition that the presence of an ordained minister is not required.

I also appreciated the implicit suggestion that the number of people present should not be excessive; something valuable gets lost when the company is so large that the process of passing round the bread and the cup is wearily prolonged and the atmosphere of a meal with fellow-members of the body of Christ disappears; at the same time some occasions may require this loss in the interests of other factors.

So I fully agree with the practical comments at the end of Krause's paper (note 71) about the size of congregations and buildings. On the one hand, recently I looked around a congregation of 2,500 seated on two levels in the enormous Nairobi Baptist Chapel at an ordinary worship service. While I felt I could have fellowship and sense unity with the brothers and sisters seated adjacently in the second front row downstairs, this was not possible with those seated in the back row of the gallery. On the other hand, I have been acutely conscious of spiritual unity in the large tent meeting of the Keswick Convention, with the banner proclaiming "All One in Christ Jesus" dominating the proceedings and the distribution of the bread and cup taking place in a quiet, dignified fashion.

The emphasis on Jesus' earthly poverty in the Glasite movement is unusual but appropriate. The call to wash one another's feet takes up a gesture of humble service that was eloquent in the first century but may require adaptation to be meaningful in ours.

Another interesting feature is the stress on discipline, which may stand in tension with the fact that in a famous Scottish tradition it is emphasized that the Supper is precisely for sinners.[1] In my own (Wesleyan) tradition it is for all who sincerely desire to be saved from their sins through faith in the Lord Jesus Christ. The saddest feature presented in the paper, however, is that its author was not permitted to partake in the Edinburgh meeting, which of course was a Sandemanian assembly and not a Stone-Campbell one. As soon as an assembly or denomination refuses the Lord's Supper to other Christians who love the Lord, then something drastically has gone wrong with their self-understanding as part of the body of Christ. The other papers in our symposium make it abundantly clear that this would emphatically not be the attitude of congregations in the Stone-Campbell tradition. Thank God for Christian progress towards recognition of our common participation in salvation no matter what our denomination.

Response to Mark Krause

The following points struck chords of agreement:

First, the reference to all the Israelites eating the same food as one another and drinking the same cup as one another is significant; if we carry over this typology, as I am sure that we are meant to do, then it follows that the tradition of "communion in one kind" that used to be practiced in the Roman Catholic Church went clearly against the New Testament understanding and practice in the Lord's Supper.

Second, emphasis on the unity of the participants seems correct: the common loaf and cup implies that all who participate are equally God's guests and recipients of his provision, and this secures the same thought as the one baptism. For me this was brought home vividly when Chris Wigglesworth introduced the Divinity community in Aberdeen to the practice of each person passing the elements to the next, each of us saying to our neighbour "The body of Jesus was broken for you" and "the blood of Jesus was shed for you." This may not be a New Testament practice, but it seems to me to be very much in harmony with it, and it creates a situation of fellowship in which I cannot treat my brother or sister in Christ as an enemy nor can I despise them. "A common oath of commitment" joins together the persons who have a common loyalty and love.

Third, if we carry over the typology of the spiritual food, then we are saying that those who participate in the Lord's Supper participate in the Holy Spirit or in Christ, not necessarily understood as residing in the elements but spiritually real to the participants.

Fourth, the paper emphasizes that the meal is hosted by the risen Lord, unseen and unheard.

Interestingly, fifth, the stress is on action rather than elements. This is open to misunderstanding in the Roman Catholic tradition where it appears that on occasion the action of the priest in consecrating the elements and celebrating the Mass has been regarded as more important than the participation of the people in taking, eating and drinking.

The substance of the paper is concerned with the character of the Lord's Supper as a covenant meal. Here there are some points that deserve mention for further discussion. I pick up on the five points listed for questioning the Passover character of the church's meal:

(1) While no mention of a lamb occurs at the Lord's Supper, the question does arise whether a lamb was included at the Last Supper. Luke 22:15 may well imply it.[2] Its absence would have been noteworthy. But it is unlikely that this aspect of the Last Supper was carried over into the Lord's Supper, even if the church meal could have included meat. The vital argument from silence is that Jesus used the bread and cup as the symbols: why did he not use the lamb, which would have been very effective in view of the symbolism of Jesus as the Lamb of God that we find in the New Testament and specifically in 1 Corinthians 5:7? One possible, very pragmatic reason is the comparative rarity of meat in the meals of ordinary people and the shift from an annual festival meal to a weekly ordinary meal could have dictated the nature of the food available.

(2) Was the Lord's Supper a sacrificial meal? Recently this interpretation has been proposed by C. J. Collins who argues that the Lord's Supper should be understood as a peace offering leading to communion with God.[3] However, Aalen makes a much better case for seeing the Lord's Supper as the meal after the sacrifice.[4] Certainly, the absence of explicit mention of a lamb would point away from this sacrificial interpretation of the meal. But the memory of the Savior's death could have been influential.

(3) How is the weekly celebration to be explained? This is generally linked to the symbolism of the first day of the week as the day of resurrection; in effect, Easter became a weekly event, and this may have been decisive. Also, the other meals of the disciples with Jesus were probably relevant. Even though the Last Supper was not a *haburah* meal, this Jewish practice could have provided part of the context in which the development of the Lord's Supper among the disciples of Jesus was natural. The question of the relationship between the Lord's Supper and fellowship meals with Jesus is left unresolved in the paper. But once the meal is seen as being hosted by the risen Lord, and once the Christian celebration shifts from the Sabbath to the first day of the week, the conditions are created for a celebration of the risen presence of the Lord whose risen presence was revealed when he shared the bread at Emmaus.

(4) The New Testament gives no evidence of a specified presider/celebrant. As I have already indicated, it is, therefore, precarious to insist that the president must be "ordained," whatever that means. Nevertheless, as the church developed as a spiritual household, the "householder" may have been the obvious person to do so. But it is not laid down in so many words.

(5) Drinking blood has no role in the Passover. However, it has no role at all in Judaism. So this point does not specially distinguish the Lord's Supper from the Passover in particular.

My point, then, is that the differences from the Passover meal should not be exaggerated. If the Lord's Supper retained some paschal associations, the linking of it to the covenant may perhaps be strengthened. I almost wondered whether preaching "the covenant" and having "covenantal" fellowship were perhaps read into the material, and it was not clear to me whether the themes that are developed in relation to the covenant were entirely dependent on the presence of the covenant motif. Perhaps we should be asking what specifically is missing from our understanding of the meal if the covenantal aspect is missing. May it be particularly the element of commitment on the part of both sides, God pledging himself to be our faithful God and we pledging ourselves to be his faithful people? The participation in the meal is thus a concrete expression of this mutual commitment, a meaningful symbol that helps to convey what it symbolizes.

Response to John Mark Hicks

In commenting on this third paper I return to a point that recurs in all the papers, namely the character of the Lord's Supper as a meal, which is why I prefer the scriptural title "the Lord's Supper" for it. So here I welcome the emphasis on the identification of the significant piece of furniture as a table. Nevertheless, the phrase "stressed the metaphor of table rather than altar" might be misinterpreted by some to think that both appellations are acceptable (although one is better than the other). Let me say it plainer: the metaphor of altar has no place whatever in the Lord's Supper. We gather round a table in the appropriate posture for a meal, which in our culture is sitting. The practices of kneeling and even designating the piece of furniture as an altar, as in some fellowships, both suggest a profound misunderstanding of the situation. As Hebrews emphasizes, Jesus died once for all and entered the presence of God to make his offering once for all (Heb 7:27; 9:12, 25-28; 10:10), and this is not what the Lord's Supper symbolizes.

It is supper, communion, and memorial, but not sacrifice. It is true that from a very early date the post-apostolic church did introduce the language of offering and sacrifice.[5] But we are governed by Scripture and not by the early church. The question that might arise is whether the early church's understanding guides us as to how Scripture should be understood, particularly when the interpretation is fairly widespread. For myself I prefer the practical evidence of the Protestant church's practice in Scotland, where this truth of the Lord's Supper as meal is firmly enshrined in our history.

However, Hicks's main point is to rehabilitate two essential factors: the spiritual presence of Christ and the eschatological hope at the meal. I thoroughly support this aim, and I am grateful to the author for citing things that I have written that support his case. Nevertheless, a word of gentle warning may be needed. Emphasis on other functions of the Lord's Supper can threaten to eclipse the fundamental purpose of the meal to proclaim the Lord's death, a proclamation that includes expounding its role in reconciling God and sinners. It is one thing to be reductionist, but it is another to recognise primacy, and the proclamation of the cross is to my mind primary: as Luther said, *crux sola nostra theologia.*

This, however, is a point that needs to be made more when I am confronting liberal Christians for whom the atoning sacrifice of Jesus and the justification of the individual sinner by faith in his blood are not the central element in Christianity and, consequently, the Lord's Supper becomes a fellowship meal rather than a memorial of the cross. In present company I surely do not need to beat that particular drum, and I insist that I am not criticizing the presentation at this point, but merely pointing to a dangerous tendency elsewhere in the church.

In this connection, let me stress the importance of the opening up of Scripture as part of the heart-warming experience. Some tend to identify this only with the breaking of the bread, and so elevate the actual partaking of the elements as the means of communion with the Lord. It is not so in the New Testament, where it was *as the Lord opened up the Scriptures* that the disciples felt their hearts strangely warmed, indeed burning within them (Lk 24:32). Opening up the Scriptures and preaching and teaching the Word occupy a far greater place in the New Testament than celebration of meals. We must not disjoin the Word from the sacrament of the Lord's Supper as if the latter were somehow the apex of revelation and communion.

Nevertheless, it is right to emphasize that this is an eschatological meal, in the sense that it is a real foretaste on earth of what we shall enjoy in all its fullness in the age to come. "Until he comes" (1 Cor 11:26) sets the limit and promises the fulfillment.

So, having been blessed by sharing in your heritage, I share mine by bringing to you one of the glories of Primitive Methodism that my church to its infinite shame has cast aside for a mess of ecumenical pottage. Sadly absent from our present liturgical aids is the culmination of the Supper in the singing of the immortal lines of Charles Wesley:

> Love's redeeming work is done;
>   Fought the fight, the battle won:
> Vain the stone, the watch, the seal;
>   Christ hath burst the gates of hell:
> Hallelujah!
>
> Soar we now where Christ hath led,
>   Following our exalted Head:
> Made like him, like him we rise;
>   Ours the cross, the grave, the skies:
> Hallelujah![6]

Notes

[1] I am thinking of the invitation of the saintly Scottish professor John Duncan (known as "Rabbi" Duncan, 1796-1870) to a woman whose feelings of unworthiness made her shrink back from participation in the Lord's Supper: "Tak' it; it's for sinners."

[2] C. K. Barrett, "Luke XXII.15: To Eat the Passover," *Journal of Theological Studies*, ns 9 (1958): 305-307. However, the broader question of whether the Last Supper was a Passover meal in the strict sense remains the subject of controversy.

[3] C. John Collins, "The Eucharist as Christian Sacrifice: How Patristic Authors Can Help Us Read the Bible," *Westminster Theological Journal* 66 (2004): 1-23.

[4] S. Aalen, "Das Abendmahl als Opfermahl im Neuen Testament," *Novum Testamentum* 6 (1963): 128-152.

[5] Did 14:1; 1 Clem 40-44; Ign., Phld. 4; Justin, Dial. 41:3; 117:1; Irenaeus, Haer. 4:17:5 (interpreting Mal 1:10-11). See J. N. D. Kelly, *Early Christian Doctrines* (London: A. & C. Black, 1958), pp. 196-97.

[6] These words from the hymn "Christ the Lord is risen today," traditionally sung at the Lord's Supper in Primitive Methodist congregations, were included in the alternative order of service for the Lord's Supper in *The Book of Offices* (London: Methodist Publishing House, 1936), p. 39, of the United Methodist Church. The hymn is perhaps not as well-known outside Methodism as the somewhat similar "Jesus Christ is Risen Today" (a translation from the mediaeval Latin in *Lyra Davidica*, 1708), but it is infinitely superior. The final verse (not included in the order of service but continuing the theme to its climax) runs:

> King of glory, soul of bliss,
>   Everlasting life is this,
> Thee to know, thy power to prove,
>   Thus to sing, and thus to love.
> Hallelujah.

Part 4

UNDERSTANDING ESCHATOLOGY
THROUGH DIALOGUE
WITH PRETERISM

13

MILLENNIALISM IN THE
EARLY STONE-CAMPBELL MOVEMENT

Richard J. Cherok

From the very beginning of Europe's colonization of North America, the "New World" began to be linked to the millennial hopes and expectations of its settlers. In a manner unlike Europe, however, where millennialism usually resided "on the fringes of society," millennialism in America, Richard Kyle explains, became "more central to the religious experience."[1] By the antebellum period of the nineteenth century, apocalypticism not only held a position of primacy in American Christian thought, but it reached beyond the realm of religion to influence society more profoundly than at any other period in American history. "America in the early nineteenth century," Ernest Sandeen correctly asserts, "was drunk on the millennium." From nearly every quadrant of American thought in the era prior to the Civil War, Sandeen continues, the inhabitants of the newly formed republic were "preoccupied with the millennium."[2]

The enchantment of the millennium so captivated the American mind during this period that its terminology and ideology were imbedded in the rhetoric of both Christians and non-Christians alike. Charles Grandison Finney, the most renowned evangelical revivalist of the era, repeatedly announced the approach of the millennium and even told an audience in Rochester, New York that "the Millennium might be brought about in three months" if the church could be united in its evangelistic effort.[3] Similarly, Robert Owen, a noted deist and opponent of Christianity, used language that resonated with millennial imagery as he spoke to the participants in his anti-religious social experiment at New Harmony, Indiana.[4] The "principles" of his social experiment, Owen claimed, "shall lead us to the commencement of measures, which may not improperly be termed the beginning of the MILLENNIUM." With the millennium's arrival, he added, "We shall know what vice and virtue really are: how to avoid the one and secure the other; and how, in [the] future, to bring up our children ignorant of crime."[5]

The most popular schools of eschatological thought in nineteenth-century America were the historic form of premillennialism and postmillennialism. The Puritan divines of the seventeenth century first carried historic premillennialism to the shores of New England, from where it eventually spread to the rest of the country.[6] The characteristic trait of premillennialism is a belief that society will grow progressively worse until Christ returns to bring the social decline to a cataclysmic end by the establishment of his millennial reign upon the earth. Postmillennialism—sometimes referred to as progressive millennialism—displays itself as an optimistic view in which the spread of the gospel will bring about positive social changes that will climax in a utopian millennial period of Christian predominance. Following this thousand-year period of millennial harmony and bliss, Christ will return to earth and bring the created world to its conclusion. Postmillennialism's first American advocate was Jonathan Edwards, who saw the excitement of the Great Awakening as the opening chapter of the millennial era. The optimism spawned by the American Revolution and the progress of American society in the years after the revolution only served to intensify the postmillennial illusions of optimism that became so popular among nineteenth century proponents of reform within the United States.[7]

In light of this heightened period of eschatological awareness, it is absurd to assume that millennialism did not make an impression upon the thoughts, actions, and writings of the early leaders of the Stone-Campbell Restoration Movement. Nevertheless, a historiographical examination of the survey studies of the movement, especially the earlier works, gives the unlikely impression that the millennial fervor of antebellum America had a negligible impact upon the movement's initial patrons. By comparing the comments about millennialism contained in the movement's histories with the actual apocalyptic views of the movement's founding figures it will become readily apparent that Stone-Campbell historians for the most part have failed to pay millennialism the respect it deserves as an influence on the growth and development of this movement. The purpose of this study will be to compare the historiographical reporting of millennialism with the actual millennial views of the movement's early leaders. An effort will also be made to explain the obvious variance between the history and historiography of millennialism within the movement.

Setting a Precedent for Millennial Neglect

With respect to the four primary leaders of the Movement at its outset—Barton W. Stone, Thomas Campbell, Alexander Campbell, and Walter Scott—all were motivated by deep-rooted apocalyptic beliefs. Yet, the earliest histories of the movement have very little to say about the influence of millennialism on their thought. The first effort to write a comprehensive history of the movement came when Benjamin B. Tyler (1840-1922), a well-known minister among the Disciples of Christ, wrote *A History of the Disciples of Christ* as a part of *The American Church History Series*.[8] Tyler's 1894 study was included as volume twelve of the multi-volume series edited by the renowned historians Philip Schaff, Henry Codman Potter, and Samuel Macauley Jackson.[9] Though written during the lifetime of many who knew the founders of the movement, and only fifty years after the earliest death among the founding forefathers of the movement, Tyler failed even to hint that the millennial beliefs of the early Disciple leadership may have influenced their thought and actions.

James H. Garrison (1842-1931), a leading figure among Disciples and the influential editor of *The Christian-Evangelist*, compiled a series of essays into a 1901 history of the restorationists of the century that had just passed.[10] In addition to his edited work of 1901, Garrison produced two brief historical overviews of the Disciples, one in 1888—some six years earlier than Tyler's comprehensive history—and another in 1904.[11] He also wrote a 1909 history entitled *The Story of a Century*, to honor the centennial celebration of the Stone-Campbell Movement.[12] As a result of his importance to both the recording of Disciple history through the pages of his periodical and his undertakings to produce Disciple historical works, Garrison may aptly be recognized as the father of Stone-Campbell Movement historiography. Nevertheless, the issue of millennialism and its influence on early leadership of the Disciples is nowhere to be found among his chronicles of the movement.

The first historical study of the Disciples written by a professional historian came from the pen of Errett Gates (1870-1951), a historian with the Disciples Divinity House at the University of Chicago. Like the earlier works of Garrison and Tyler, however, Gates' book, The Disciples of Christ, refrains from touching upon the role that apocalyptic thought played in the early growth and development of the movement.[13] As the earliest historians of the movement's origin and expansion, Garrison, Tyler, and Gates set a precedent for overlooking millennialism that numerous historians of the Stone-Campbell Movement have modeled in their published historical surveys.[14]

The Introduction of Millennialism to Stone-Campbell Historiography

Not until 1909, when William Thomas Moore (1832-1926) published his massive 830 page volume, *A Comprehensive History of the Disciples of Christ*, did millennialism gain recognition as having influenced the early Disciple Movement. Unfortunately, Moore viewed millennialism as a problem rather than a contribution to the Stone-Campbell Movement. Following a brief discussion of Campbell's contentions with the Mormons, Moore noted that "troubles never come singly" and went on to explain how many of the "Reformers" became "greatly excited with respect to the Millennium." "Their success in preaching the 'ancient Gospel' and the restoration of New Testament Christianity was so great that they became deeply impressed with the idea that the Millennial period was near at hand."[15] At fault for this over-zealousness, Moore further explained, was Walter Scott. Not only was Scott consumed with millennial fever, but in Moore's words, "He imparted his own enthusiasm to many who were associated with him, and the result was that the churches everywhere were more or less affected by this Millennial anticipation." This growing apocalyptic interest, he further contended, "was not conducive to the best development of the plea which the Disciples were making."[16] As a result, Campbell "saw that something must be done to check the abnormal [millennial] excitement which had already become widespread."[17] So, even though he agreed with many of Scott's claims, Campbell responded to his fervent millennialism with an anonymous series of articles that were written for the Millennial Harbinger of 1834. "In the course of a few years the [millennial] excitement subsided," according to Moore, "at least so far that it was no longer a danger to the propagation of the Ancient Gospel."[18]

That Campbell named his journal the Millennial Harbinger, Moore asserted, is evidence that he also had eschatological concerns. Nevertheless, Moore pointed out, Campbell "held tentatively" to his millennial views and was "always level-headed" in his handling of these beliefs. Moreover, he posited, it was not clear whether Campbell "took any particular side in the controversy between Pre-Millennialists and Post-Millennialists."[19] In essence, Moore suggested that the millennial beliefs of Campbell and Scott were simply by-products of the Restoration plea's early success, rather than the previously embedded theological convictions that they believed were coming to fruition through the successful propagation of the Restoration plea.

In addition to his belief that millennial interest was merely an outgrowth of the movement's prosperity, Moore offered three additional interpretations of the apocalyptic beliefs of Campbell, Scott, and essentially all of the other first-generation leaders. First, he insisted, the issue of millennial excitement was problematic for the continued advancement of the Disciples. Second, he suggested that the eschatological views of the early leaders were neither identifiable nor of any substantive value to their overall thought.[20] Finally, he maintained, the millennial issue was only a brief concern for the movement's leaders and had a notable influence on them for only a brief period of time.

Moore's first idea, that the issue of millennial excitement was problematic to the early leadership of the movement, gained little support from subsequent historians.[21] His second and third contentions, however, that the millennial views of the early leaders were neither discernable nor valuable and had only a limited impression on the movement, garnered considerable support from later historians. Following in the ideological footsteps of Moore, many historians have advanced his interpretation of the budding movement's apocalyptic beliefs by downplaying the significance of millennialism in both the movement and the initial leadership of the Disciples. These historians provide only a brief mention of the millennial ethos of the early movement's most influential figures—focusing primarily on Alexander Campbell—and they fail to define the views of the early leaders with any distinctiveness and certainty.[22]

The Millennial Views of Alexander Campbell and Walter Scott

An overview of the eschatological views of Campbell and Scott, in contrast to the claims of Moore and many later historians, show that they held to very distinct millennial beliefs that profoundly colored the Stone-Campbell Movement. Driven by a postmillennial understanding of Christ's Second Coming, Campbell viewed the advancement of primitive Christianity as the inaugural step in the institution of the millennium.[23] "I believe that there will be…a Millenium," he informed Robert Owen, "a long period of general or universal peace, happiness, and political and religious prosperity."[24] This utopian period, he told his readers, will be enjoyed as a result of the restoration of ancient Christianity. "Just in so far as the ancient order of things, or the religion of the New Testament, is restored," he insisted, "just so far has the Millennium commenced, and so far have its blessings been enjoyed."[25]

As a debater, preacher, educator, and religious leader, Campbell saw himself as a reformer of Christianity. Just as other postmillennialists sought to reform their society—and thus hasten the coming of the millennium—by such activities as eliminating alcoholic consumption, ending slavery, and putting Bibles and tracts into the hands of all Americans, Campbell believed his restoration of the Bible's "ancient order of things" was a social reform that would expedite the approach of the millennium. For this reason he dubbed his monthly journal the *Millennial Harbinger*. This magazine, he wrote in the first installment, "shall have for its object the developement [sic], and introduction of that political and religious order of society called THE MILLENNIUM, which will be the consummation of that ultimate amelioration of society proposed in the Christian Scriptures."[26] To Campbell, the only thing necessary for the introduction of the millennium, which he referred to as "the last and most beneficial change in society," is "to let the gospel, in its own plainness, simplicity and force, speak to men."[27] When divested "of all the appendages of human philosophy…and of all the traditions and dogmas of men," he was convinced, "it will pass from heart to heart, from house to house, from city to city, until it bless the whole earth."[28] Campbell maintained his postmillennialism throughout the remainder of his life, though its optimism waned with the coming of the Civil War "and his hope turned more to what lies beyond 'the present material universe.'"[29]

In contrast to Campbell's expressed postmillennial conviction was Walter Scott's early acceptance of historic premillennialism. As early as 1826, Scott had produced a pair of essays on the millennium that were published in the Christian Baptist. Scott's prediction of a sudden apocalyptic change that would occur during the era in which he lived was an unmistakable identification of his premillennial belief. In the first of his two articles, Scott wrote:

The time is certainly arrived, when the great political establishments, the powers and principalities of the world, which have created and fostered those warlike feelings, and mercantile and rival interests, so hostile to the spirit of the gospel, and which have led men so far away from nature, must speedily be dissolved; and when the economy of God, which shall be more in unison with the religion of his Son and with nature, shall suddenly make its appearance.[30]

Upon accepting the Mahoning Baptist Association's 1827 invitation to serve as their evangelist in the Western Reserve, Scott abandoned plans to publish a periodical entitled "The Millennial Herald," but he did not forsake his fervent premillennialism. To his hearers in the Western Reserve, Scott announced:

The Christian of the nineteenth century has been permitted to witness the accomplishment of wonderful events. Providence has stationed him on a sublime eminence, from which he can behold the fulfillment of illustrious prophecies, and look backward upon nearly the whole train of events leading to the Millennium.[31]

To Scott, the proclamation of the ancient gospel was the inaugural step in a sequence of events that would precede the cataclysmic arrival of the millennium. The spread of the ancient gospel, he believed, would convert the lost, bring an end to sectarianism, unite the churches, and transform society. All of this, he was convinced, would be preliminary to the Lord's institution of his millennial reign upon the earth. Through the pages of his magazine, *The Evangelist*, Scott expressed his anticipation of the Lord's return with a flurry of premillennial speculations that were published in the mid-1830s and early 1840s.[32] By 1842, Scott appears to have been fairly committed to the eschatological schemes of William Miller (1782-1849), a New England farmer who predicted the inauguration of the millennium in 1843 and 1844. Though intrigued by Miller's apocalyptic reckonings, Scott "never succumbed to the fatal date-setting millennial disease, nor did he ever completely endorse the Miller calculation."[33] Nevertheless, when Miller's appointed times for the Second Advent proved to be a disappointment, Scott grew disillusioned with premillennialism and gradually adopted the postmillennial view that he would espouse for the remainder of his life.[34]

Recent Historiographic Acknowledgements of Stone-Campbell Millennialism

That millennialism had a profound influence on Scott, Campbell, and their ideals for the Stone-Campbell Restoration Movement is beyond question. Yet the majority of the movement's survey histories fail to recognize this contribution within the lives of the early leaders and the rapid growth and development of the movement. Only the historical studies of David Edwin Harrell, Jr., Leroy Garrett, Henry E. Webb, and Richard T. Hughes identify millennialism as having significantly influenced the early movement and its leadership.

Garrett's *The Stone-Campbell Movement* completely overlooks the eschatology of Walter Scott but points to the moniker of the *Millennial Harbinger* as an expression of

Alexander Campbell's "conviction that he was a catalyst…for a coming millennium."[35] These sentiments are echoed in Webb's *In Search of Christian Unity*, when the author warns that "the significance of the name of [Campbell's] journal should not be over-looked." Despite his admonition, however, Webb neglects to identify Campbell as a postmillennialist in his all-too-brief overview of the movement's millennialism. Furthermore, Webb only mentions Scott's millennialism for the purpose of suggesting that he did not use the doctrine of the Lord's return as a scare tactic in his evangelistic efforts.[36]

Perhaps the most probing investigation of millennialism's effect on the movement is found in Harrell's *Quest for a Christian America, 1800-1865*. Harrell notes that "not one first-generation leader of the church ignored the apocalyptical portions of the Scriptures and some of them were almost totally preoccupied with discussing prophetic passages." He goes on to provide an extensive analysis of apocalypticism within the thought and lives of Alexander Campbell and Walter Scott. Like every historian before him, however, Harrell fails to investigate the millennial ideas of Thomas Campbell and Barton W. Stone.[37]

Only Hughes' history of the Churches of Christ, *Reviving the Ancient Faith,* contains an exposé of the millennial ideas of Stone (though it neglects Thomas Campbell). In addition to his brief comments about the millennialism of Scott and Alexander Campbell, Hughes reports that Stone adhered to premillennialism from at least the early 1830s throughout the remainder of his life. Much of Hughes' book, however, deals with the manner by which an emerging group of leaders within the movement relied on Stone's "apocalyptic worldview" to set themselves apart as the Churches of Christ (a cappella). This "apocalyptic worldview," Hughes further explains, is not an eschatological theory, but an outlook on life that leads its proponents to live as though "the final rule of the kingdom of God were present in the here and now."[38] As such, Hughes offers only a minimal overview of Stone's premillennial beliefs and their impressions upon him and the movement.

The Eschatological Views of Barton Stone and Thomas Campbell

Though the movement's historians seem to have relegated to uncertainty the millennial perspectives of Stone and Thomas Campbell, it may be accurately claimed that both were highly influenced by their millennial views. Both Harrell and Hughes agree that Stone was indeed a devout premillennialist, yet they only touch upon his eschatological beliefs in their histories.[39]

Stone corroborates their judgements in a correspondence he had with an 1834 reader of his *Christian Messenger.* "The second coming of Christ," Stone wrote, "is at the commencement of his millennial reign on earth-here on earth he will reign till the 1000 years be finished—nor will he cease to reign on earth till he has raised from death the wicked, and judged them according to their works."[40] To Stone, Newell Williams explains, "The union of Christians was the hinge on which the millennium turned."[41] Only with the achievement of Christian unity, Stone believed, would the millennial reign of Christ be consummated. Yet, because of the efforts that he and his fellow workers had put forth on behalf of Christian unity, Stone was convinced that the millennium was imminently at hand.

Though Thomas Campbell's millennial view is less apparent because of the paucity of information about it, two sources provide insight into his apocalyptic belief. In an 1839 essay entitled "Christian Union," the senior Campbell stated that he was "looking for a Millennium of universal peace and prosperity, in which peace shall universally triumph." In addition, he wrote, it was his "grand concern and present duty… to adopt the proper means for accomplishing this truly blissful and desirable object."[42] The postmillennial optimism that exudes from Thomas Campbell's 1839 article can also be found, according to Hans Rollman, in his *Declaration and Address of the Christian Association of Washington*.

Few documents even come close to paralleling the efficacy of the *Declaration and Address* for defining and elucidating the core ideals of the Stone-Campbell Movement. Nevertheless, this foundational document has only recently been considered for its millennial ideology and expression.[43] The *Declaration and Address*, Rollman maintains, was Thomas Campbell's "eschatological action plan" for instituting the millennium in our world. "By restoring to the church its original unity and purity," Rollman argues, "He hoped to create the irenic conditions for effective evangelization, which were to eventually prosper into a millennial Zion, when Jews would convert and the fullness of the Gentiles was to be completed."[44]

The Rise of a New Millennial View: Amillennialism

Ironically, the premillennial and postmillennial traditions that the movement's earliest leaders so avidly embraced began to dissipate in the thought of second- and third-generation restorationists. The debacle of the Millerite predictions discredited premillennialism in the thought of many people (as it did with Walter Scott), while the bloodshed and brutality of the Civil War eroded the optimistic hope for universal progress that characterized postmillennialism. From the ashes of these disillusionments with pre- and postmillennialism, however, arose an interest within the Stone-Campbell Movement in the Augustinian view of a "realized millennium." Though nowhere to be found in the thought of their Restoration forefathers, the Augustinian or amillennial view of eschatology dismisses the literal interpretation of the thousand-year millennium in Revelation 20. The true reign of Christ, amillennialists insist, is not in an earthly kingdom, but in the lives of his followers. As such, they interpret the millennium as a symbolic representation of the Christian age that began at Christ's death and will end with his return.

The shifting sands of millennial belief that followed the Civil War reached across all lines of Protestantism in the United States. The disenchantment with historic premillennialism and postmillennialism caused a growing class of liberal Protestants to pursue a social gospel and political progressivism. Conservative Christians, on the other hand, tended to adopt the recently developed dispensational form of premillennialism.[45] The conservative heirs to the Stone-Campbell Movement, however, were unwilling to accept dispensationalism because of the theological value they placed on the church. Having struggled for so many years to emphasize the need to restore the church to its apostolic purity, the Disciples could not, en masse, accept the dispensational belief that the church's very existence is nothing more than God's response to Israel's rejection of Jesus as the Messiah.[46] As a result, dispensationalism has had only a limited influence within the movement, though it has been far more widely embraced among other conservative evangelical groups.

The transition from antebellum pre- and postmillennialism to the wide acceptance of amillennialism that seemed to permeate the Stone-Campbell Movement's twentieth-century leaders was both slow and uncertain. Several second-generation leaders retained historic premillennial ideas, including Moses Lard, David Lipscomb, James A. Harding, and T. W. Brents. At the same time, men like Tolbert Fanning, J. W. McGarvey, Robert Milligan, and E. G. Sewell continued to advocate postmillennialism.[47] Yet, by the start of the twentieth century it appeared that amillennialism was gaining a large hearing within the movement. In a 1901 article for the *Christian Standard*, Edgar H. Olmstead wrote that it was

> doubtful whether the dogma of a millennium would have received any currency worth mentioning except for the bold attempt to interpret literally the highly apocalyptic passage in Rev. XX. 1-10, which, in common with many other pictorial representations of spiritual realities, was probably never intended for exact or literal fulfillment.[48]

Olmstead's obvious amillennial leanings became the predominant eschatological belief of the movement throughout the remainder of the twentieth century.

Why the Historical Neglect?

One question yet remains to be answered: Why have the historical surveys of the Stone-Campbell Restoration Movement not reflected the highly influential eschatological beliefs of its early leaders? The answer to this question may present itself in the movement's substitution of a figurative for a literal interpretation of the millennium and the resultant effect it had on the movement.

As second- and third-generation Disciples became more heavily influenced by amillennialism, they lost all hope for the arrival of an earthly millennial period. Without the millennium as an objective, Disciple leaders turned their attention to other goals that they could claim as the ultimate pursuits of the movement. As a result, the restoration of the ancient church and the unity of Christ's followers, which were initially recognized as instruments to be used for the implementation of the millennium, displaced the millennium as the culminating aim of the movement. Thus, the pursuit of the millennium by the earliest Disciple leaders became a quest for restoration and unity among second- and third-generation Disciples. So completely did these new pursuits take hold within the Stone-Campbell Movement that its historians have repeatedly overlooked the movement's original millennial influences and endorsed the concepts of restoration and unity as the central concerns of the early Disciple Movement.

Notes

[1]Richard Kyle, *The Last Days are Here Again: A History of the End Times* (Grand Rapids: Baker, 1998), p.77.

[2]Ernest R. Sandeen, *The Roots of Fundamentalism: British and American Millenarianism, 1800-1930* (Chicago and London: University of Chicago Press, 1970), pp. 42-43.

[3]Quoted in Paul E. Johnson, *A Shopkeeper's Millennium: Society and Revivals in Rochester, New York, 1815-1837* (New York: Hill and Wang, 1978), p. 109. Finney is more often quoted as saying, "If the Church will do all her duty, the millennium may come in this country in three years." See Charles G. Finney, *Lectures on Revivals of Religion*, ed. William G. McLoughlin (1835; Cambridge: Belknap Press of Harvard University Press, 1960), p. 306.

[4]See Richard J. Cherok, "A Comparison of Millennial Rhetoric: Alexander Campbell's Christian Millennialism and Robert Owen's Secular Millennialism," *Journal of Millennial Studies* 2 (Winter 2000): www.bu.edu/mille/publications/winter2000/winter2000.html.

[5]Robert Owen, "New-Harmony Sunday Meeting for Instruction in the New System," *New Harmony Gazette* 1 (12 July 1826): 334.

[6]Kyle, *Last Days are Here Again*, p. 78.

[7]Sandeen, *Roots of Fundamentalism*, p. 43.

[8]Benjamin B. Tyler, *A History of the Disciples of Christ*, vol. 12, *American Church History Series* (New York: Christian Literature Company, 1894).

[9]Philip S. Schaff, Henry Codman Potter, and Samuel Macauley Jackson, eds., *American Church History Series*, 13 vols. (New York: Christian Literature Company, 1893-1897).

[10]J. H. Garrison, ed., *The Reformation of the Nineteenth Century: A Series of Historical Sketches Dealing with the Rise and Progress of the Religious Movement Inaugurated by Thomas and Alexander Campbell, from its Origin to the Close of the Nineteenth Century* (St. Louis: Christian Publishing, 1901).

[11]J. H. Garrison, *Our Movement; Its Origin and Aims: A Paper read Before the Baptist Ministerial Association of Boston, Mass.* (St. Louis: Christian Publishing, 1888); and J. H. Garrison, *A Nineteenth Century Movement* (St. Louis: Christian Publishing, 1904). Garrison produced this brief history to read at an 1897 unity conference between Disciples and Congregationalists. He later published it as a thirty-three page pamphlet.

[12]J. H. Garrison, *The Story of a Century: A Brief Historical Sketch and Exposition of the Religious Movement Inaugurated by Thomas and Alexander Campbell* (St. Louis: Christian Publishing, 1909).

[13] Errett Gates, *The Disciples of Christ* (New York: Baker and Taylor, 1905).

[14] See M. M. Davis, *The Restoration Movement of the Nineteenth Century* (Cincinnati: Standard, 1913); M. M. Davis, *How the Disciples Began and Grew* (Cincinnati: Standard, 1915); Alonzo W. Fortune, *Origin and Development of the Disciples* (St. Louis: Bethany, 1924); Walter Wilson Jennings, *A Short History of the Disciples of Christ* (St. Louis: Bethany, 1929); P. H. Welshimer, *Concerning the Disciples: A Brief*

Resume of the Movement to Restore the New Testament (Cincinnati: Standard, 1935); Harold W. Ford, *A History of the Restoration Plea* (Joplin, Mo.: College Press, 1952); Winfred E. Garrison, *Whence and Whither the Disciples of Christ* (St. Louis: Christian Board of Publication, 1959); Oliver Read Whitley, *Trumpet Call of Reformation* (St. Louis: Bethany, 1959); James DeForest Murch, *Christians Only: A History of the Restoration Movement* (Cincinnati: Standard, 1962); Enos E. Dowling, *The Restoration Movement* (Cincinnati: Standard, 1964); Richard M. Tristano, *The Origins of the Restoration Movement: An Intellectual History* (Atlanta: Glenmary Research Center, 1988); Morris Womack, *Thirteen Lessons on Restoration History* (Joplin, Mo.: College Press, 1988); and James B. North, *Union in Truth: An Interpretive History of the Restoration Movement* (Cincinnati: Standard, 1994).

[15]William Thomas Moore, *A Comprehensive History of the Disciples of Christ* (New York: Fleming H. Revell, 1909), p. 303.

[16]Ibid.

[17]Ibid., p. 304.

[18]Ibid.

[19]Ibid., pp. 304-305.

[20]While it is certainly true that most antebellum evangelicals used millennial rhetoric that sometimes blurred the distinctions between the cataclysmic pessimism of premillennialism and the progressive optimism of postmillennialism, it is generally true that a single millennial belief could be discerned within their thought. See David Edwin Harrell, Jr., "Walter Scott and the Nineteenth-Century Evangelical Spirit," *Walter Scott: A Nineteenth-Century Evangelical*, ed. Mark G. Toulouse (St. Louis: Chalice, 1999), p. 28.

[21]Only a few histories of the Stone-Campbell Movement have concurred with Moore's interpretation of the millennium as a problem among early Disciple leaders. See Walter Wilson Jennings, *The Origin and Early History of the Disciples of Christ* (Cincinnati: Standard, 1919), pp. 306-307; and Louis Cochran and Bess White Cochran, *Captives of the Word* (1969; reprint ed., Joplin, Mo.: College Press, 1987), pp. 69-70.

[22]Winfred E. Garrison, *Religion Follows the Frontier: A History of the Disciples of Christ* (New York: Harper & Brothers, 1931), p. 147; Winfred E. Garrison, *An American Religious Movement: A Brief History of the Disciples of Christ* (St. Louis: Bethany, 1945), p. 91; Homer Hailey, *Attitudes and Consequences in the Restoration Movement* (Los Angeles: Citizen Print Shop, 1945), p. 92; W. E. Garrison and A. T. DeGroot, *The Disciples of Christ: A History* (St. Louis: Christian Board of Publication, 1948), pp. 206-207; Earl Irvin West, *The Search for the Ancient Order* (Nashville: Gospel Advocate, 1949) 1:71-72; Bill J. Humble, *The Story of the Restoration* (Pensacola: Firm Foundation, 1969), p. 35; Lester G. McAllister and William E. Tucker, *Journey in Faith: A History of the Christian Church (Disciples of Christ)* (St. Louis: Bethany, 1975), pp. 145-146; and Max Ward Randall, *The Great Awakenings and the Restoration Movement* (Joplin, Mo.: College Press, 1983), p. 269.

[23]For additional research into Campbell's millennial ideology, see Robert Frederick West, *Alexander Campbell and Natural Religion* (New Haven: Yale University Press, 1948); Richard T. Hughes, "From Primitive Church to Civil Religion: The Millennial Odyssey of Alexander Campbell," *Journal of the American Academy of Religion* 44 (March 1976): 87-103; Hiram J. Lester, "Alexander Campbell's Millennial Program," *Discipliana* 48 (Fall 1988): 35-39; Tim Crowley, "A Chronological Delineation of Alexander Campbell's Eschatological Theory from 1823-1851," *Discipliana* 54 (Winter 1994): 99-107; Mark G. Toulouse, "Campbell and Postmillennialism: The Kingdoms of God," *Discipliana* 60 (Fall 2000): 78-96; Kevin James Gilbert, "The Stone-Campbell Millennium: A Historical Theological Perspective," *Restoration Quarterly* 43 (2001): 33-50; and Craig M. Watts, "Millennial America and the Vision of Peace in the Thought of Alexander Campbell," *Discipliana* 62 (Spring 2002): 25-31.

[24]Alexander Campbell and Robert Owen, *The Evidences of Christianity: A Debate Between Robert*

Owen and Alexander Campbell (1829; reprint ed., St. Louis: Christian Publishing Company, 1906), p. 595.

[25]Alexander Campbell, "A Restoration of the Ancient Order of Things—No. I," *Christian Baptist* (February 1825): 126.

26 Alexander Campbell, "Prospectus," *Millennial Harbinger* (January 1830): 1.

27 Alexander Campbell, "An Oration in Honor of the Fourth of July," *Popular Lectures and Addresses* (1863; reprint ed., Hollywood, Calif.: Old Paths Book Club, n.d.), p. 68.

28 Ibid.

29 Leroy Garrett, *The Stone-Campbell Movement: The Story of the American Restoration Movement* (1981; revised ed., Joplin, Mo.: College Press, 1994), p. 16.

30 Walter Scott, "On the Millennium—No. I," *Christian Baptist* (July 1826): 250-251.

31 A. S. Hayden, *Early History of the Disciples in the Western Reserve, Ohio: With Biographical Sketches of the Principal Agents in Their Religious Movement* (Cincinnati: Chase and Hall, 1875), p. 171.

32 William A. Gerrard III, *Walter Scott: American Frontier Evangelist* (Joplin, Mo.: College Press, 1992), pp. 181-182.

[33]Harrell, "Walter Scott and the Nineteenth-Century Evangelical Spirit," p. 29. Miller received a great amount of attention when he announced that 1843, and later 1844, would be the year of the Lord's return. He derived these dates from his calculations of Biblical prophecy and chronology. For additional information see Ronald L. Numbers and Jonathan M. Butler, eds., *The Disappointed: Millerism and Millenarianism in the Nineteenth Century* (Knoxville: University of Tennessee Press, 1993).

[34]Gerrard, Walter Scott, p. 183. Scott presented an exhaustive explanation of his postmillennialism in his book, *The Messiahship, or Great Demonstration* (Cincinnati: H. S. Bosworth, 1859).

[35]Garrett, *The Stone-Campbell Movement*, 16. See also pp. 53-54 and pp. 438-439.

[36]Henry E. Webb, *In Search of Christian Unity: A History of the Restoration Movement* (1990; revised ed., Abilene, TX: ACU Press, 2003), pp. 149-151.

[37]David Edwin Harrell, Jr., *Quest for a Christian America, 1800-1865: A Social History of the Disciples of Christ* (1966; reprint ed., Tuscaloosa: University of Alabama Press, 2003), pp. 39-48. By simply identifying Stone as a premillennialist, Harrell moves beyond previous historians in his treatment of Stone's eschatological views.

[38]Richard T. Hughes, *Reviving the Ancient Faith: The Story of Churches of Christ in America* (Grand Rapids: Eerdmans, 1996), pp. 92, 109-110.

[39]There is little evidence of Stone's millennial views prior to 1827, when he began publishing his *Christian Messenger,* and soon clarified his premillennial views. For additional information on Stone's millennial ideology, see C. Leonard Allen, "'The Stone the Builders Rejected': Barton W. Stone in the Memory of Churches of Christ," *Cane Ridge in Context: Perspectives on Barton W. Stone and the Revival,* ed. Anthony L. Dunnavant (Nashville: Disciples of Christ Historical Society, 1992), pp. 43-61; D. Newell Williams, *Barton Stone: A Spiritual Biography* (St. Louis: Chalice, 2000), pp. 223-229; Kevin James Gilbert, "The Stone-Campbell Millennium: A Historical Theological Perspective," *Restoration Quarterly* 43 (2001): 33-50; D. Newell Williams, "From Trusting Congress to Renouncing Human Governments: The Millennial Odyssey of Barton W. Stone," *Discipliana* 61 (Fall 2001): 67-81; David Edwin Harrell, Jr., "The Legacy of Barton W. Stone's Millennialism in the Churches of Christ," *Discipliana* 61 (Fall 2001): 82-91; and James B. North, "The Legacy of Stone's Millennialism in the Christian Churches," *Discipliana* (Fall 2001): 92-96.

[40] Barton W. Stone, "Barton W. Stone to Elder William Caldwell," *Christian Messenger* 8 (May 1834): 148.

[41] Williams, *Barton Stone*, p. 224.

[42]Thomas Campbell, "Christian Union," *Millennial Harbinger* (April 1839): 155.

[43]See Hans Rollman, "The Eschatology of the Declaration and Address," *The Quest for Christian*

Unity, Peace, and Purity in Thomas Campbell's Declaration and Address: Text Studies, eds. Thomas H. Olbricht and Hans Rollman (Lanham, Md.: Scarecrow, 2000), pp. 341-363.

[44]Ibid., pp. 352, 357.

[45]Damian Thompson, *The End of Time: Faith and Fear in the Shadow of the Millennium* (Hanover and London: University Press of New England, 1996), p. 101. See also George Marsden, *Fundamentalism and American Culture: The Shaping of Twentieth-Century Evangelicalism, 1870-1925* (New York: Oxford University Press, 1980), pp. 43-71.

[46]Gilbert, "The Stone-Campbell Millennium," p. 43.

[47]Ibid., pp. 41-42.

[48]Edgar H. Olmstead, "Millennial Theories and Faiths," *Christian Standard* 37 (27 July 1901): 944.

14

A CRITIQUE OF CONTEMPORARY PRETERISM IN THE STONE–CAMPBELL MOVEMENT AND EVANGELICALISM

Edward P. Myers

No one would debate the current popular interest in eschatology, as illustrated by the immense popularity of the *Left Behind* novels.[1] Also, the Middle East Crisis, transmitted hourly via television and the Internet, has caught the attention of many Bible students who see sure signs civilization is at the beginning of the End.

In 1970, Hal Lindsey popularized premillennial eschatology when he published *The Late Great Planet Earth*.[2] From coast to coast and around the world, Bible-believing people began to express an interest in a study of end times. The impact of Lindsey's writing was felt everywhere.

The next year, 1971, Max King printed his book, *The Spirit of Prophecy*. It went virtually unnoticed by the religious world, but it initiated an unsettling atmosphere in Churches of Christ (a cappella) that continues today. This influence is also being felt among evangelicals. This book introduced a new, enticing form of preterism.

In studies of eschatology, the term preterism usually refers to the belief that all the eschatological prophecies of the New Testament were fulfilled in the first century. This new, current preterism, however, is probably best identified as hyper-preterism, believing that all prophecies from both Old and New Testaments were fulfilled in the first century by the destruction of Jerusalem in AD 70.[3] King explains:

> We mean the fulfillment of every aspect of God's purpose relative to the complete restoration of man through Christ. This takes in all promises, prophecies, types, patterns, figures and shadows in Old Testament Scripture with respect to 'things to come' in terms

of the New and everlasting Covenant. From this perspective, we hold that every facet of eschatology in New Testament Scripture fulfilled the prophesied end of the Old Testament dispensation. Concerning His eternal purpose, God, through Christ, has spoken and acted. There is nothing more to be written and nothing more to be fulfilled. God's work through Christ is finished. It is full, complete and everlasting.[4]

Edward C. Stevens, president and founder of the International Preterist Association, begun in the mid-1990s, has greatly extended the influence of King, especially within evangelical circles. Stevens was also Director of the Northeast Ohio Bible College in Ashtabula, Ohio, a school specifically to train men for ministry from a preterist eschatological position.[5] Stevens's most influential book is *What Happened in A.D. 70?*[6]

In 2004, Keith A. Mathison edited a book that challenges the ideas of King and Stevens and shows the growing impact of their ideas among evangelicals.[7] The preterist claim to have the backing of leading evangelicals most recently received a boost with the endorsement by R. C. Sproul. The fact is, however, that R. C. Sproul did not completely endorse preterism. He would correctly be called a partial-preterist, but he does not fit within the same category with King and Stevens. In fact, his son, R.C. Sproul, Jr., wrote the foreword to Mathison's volume. Part of this foreword is printed on the back cover and reads, "Eschatologies have consequences. That is why I am so delighted that my friend Keith Mathieson has put together this outstanding book....What follows is meticulous, scholarly, and devastating to...hyper-preterism....My prayer is that those who have been ensnared by this error will, in reading the book, come under conviction, and so be set free." The IPA website contains a massive amount of material that is definitely not people-friendly.[8]

Though most would list five to seven key points in King and Stevens's hyper-preterism, Mathison lists seventeen:

1. The kingdom has arrived.
2. The kingdom is spiritual.
3. The kingdom must be entered and dwelt in through spiritual means.
4. All things written about Christ in the Old Testament have been fulfilled (Luke 21:22).
5. The Great Commission has been fulfilled (Matt. 28:18-20).
6. All things have been made new (Rev. 21:5).
7. The scheme of redemption has been consummated.
8. The old heavens and earth have passed away, and the new heavens and earth are here (Matt. 5:17-20)
9. The time of reformation has occurred (Heb. 9:10).
10. Christ has returned.
11. The "perfect" has come (1 Cor. 13:10; Eph. 4:13).
12. The Bridegroom has returned.
13. The first covenant became obsolete and disappeared (Heb. 8:13).
14. The mystery is finished (Rom. 16:25-26; 1 Cor. 2:6-8; Eph. 3:4-10; Rev. 10:17).
15. Death and hades have been thrown into the lake of fire (Rev. 20:13-14).

16. All things have been "restored" (Acts 3:21).
17. Armageddon has passed.[9]

A point-by-point response to these seventeen positions would be a book-length undertaking. However, most of the points of preterism, even in this new form, can be found in the history of the church.

Critiquing Preterism
The Claim that What He Teaches is New

In the foreword to King's book, *The Spirit of Prophecy*, C. D. Beagle, King's father-in-law, declares the book to offer a "new vision of scriptures," and brags that it is "the most enlightening book ever written about Bible prophecy and its fulfillment."[10] However, Beagle also states that what they taught did not involve "anything that has not been preached since the beginning of the REFORMATION"[11] (capitalization original). King says he

> believes that this great purpose and power of God's word was lost in the dark ages, and our need today is to return, to re-establish spiritual Israel, and maintain her in the strength and power of God's word. Away with the bitter enemy of literalistic concepts that are treading her underfoot by looking for a future literal fulfillment of what has already happened, and there, belongs to God's Israel now.[12]

While King claims the "great purpose and power of God's word was lost in the dark ages," he never tells us the what, who, when, or how of this loss. We are not told how many centuries before the Dark Ages it was lost nor by whom. This teaching they claim is "new" is not as new as they would have one think. A close look at the history of the church, as done by Terry Varner, shows this is not the case.[13]

Stevens tries to make a similar point related to the creeds of the church. According to Stevens, "The early saints made so many blunders in so many areas, because of their shallow understanding, pagan background, and political motives." He continues by saying, "The Creeds are not mistaken just because they reflect too little of the Biblical position and too much human opinion. They are wrong because they reflect the NT's transitional futurist perspective which is no longer applicable to our fulfilled perspective in the Kingdom today after 70 A.D."[14] Kenneth L. Gentry, pastor of Fairview Presbyterian Church and a research professor in Systematic Theology at Christ Church, Lynchburg, Virginia, observes that this claim has serious implications for the perspicuity of Scripture: "This viewpoint not only has implications for the later creeds, but for the instructional abilities of the apostles: no one in church history knew the major issues of which they spoke—until very recently! Are the Scriptures that impenetrable on an issue of that significance?"[15] Gentry then lists a number of writings from the church fathers showing that they had "absolutely no inkling of an A.D. 70 resurrection or a past second Advent."[16]

This claim, as valuable as King may believe it to be, is not the most critical issue of his theology. More important in the critique of preterism is King's basic key to understanding eschatological prophetic passages—what he calls "the spiritualizing hermeneutic."

The Spiritualizing of All Prophecy
King writes:

> Does end-time prophecy have primarily "literal" (material) or a "spiritual" application, and if both kinds of applications are involved, how can one consistently distinguish between the two? Until this issue of "methods of interpretation" is settled, there can be no hope of a true and consistent interpretation and application of prophecy. . . It is the belief of the author that the spiritual method of interpretation is firmly established in the Bible, and that it is the basic and primary method of interpretation involved in end-time prophecy.[17]

With these words King sets up his hermeneutical principle. Every prophecy is treated figuratively, never literally. In taking this position, King sets on its head a basic way of interpreting Scripture and, in the end, confuses our usual understanding of the use of words. Two examples of this are Ephesians 6:10-20 and 1 Corinthians 15.[18]

Stafford North says, "The 70 A.D. view is wrong because it makes figurative events the Bible intends literally."[19] King argues that the natural, weak, corruptible body that Paul refers to as dying and being buried is the "fleshly or carnal system of Judaism" and that the primary application of the resurrection is the death of Judaism and the rise of Christianity.[20] There is no resurrection of the body; it is only a figurative resurrection of Christianity (or, as he says elsewhere) the AD 70 event is the coming of the kingdom with power.[21] Any resurrection passage receives the same treatment in his spiritualizing hermeneutic.

This spiritualizing of terms is found in the interpretation of eschatology texts. The word "world" refers to the "Jewish Age." The word "body" refers to "Judaism" or at times "christianity" (according to the context in which it is found). "This world" refers to the Old Covenant, Judaism, or the Jewish system. "The world to come" is the Christian system or the eternal covenant. The "day of the Lord" or "that day" refer to AD 70 and the fall of Jerusalem.[22]

Since King creates his own dictionary by employing words differently from everyone else, it makes evaluating his work a challenge.

The Second Coming with the Destruction of Jerusalem
King explains the Second Coming with reference to the destruction of Jerusalem: "This was the end of the world, the destruction of the temple, and the coming of Christ (Matt 24:1-3). This was when heaven and earth passed away (Matt 24:35; Rev 20:11). This was when the greater and more perfect tabernacle was entered by all the

redeemed."[23] "There is no time period between the fall of Jerusalem and the second coming of Christ. They are synchronous events time-wise."[24] "There is no scriptural basis for extending the second coming of Christ beyond the fall of Jerusalem."[25] "The destruction of Jerusalem did not leave unfulfilled one single prophecy, promise, or blessing."[26] And Stevens writes, "What we traditionally call 'the second coming' of Christ happened in that generation when Jerusalem was destroyed!"[27]

In addition, King believes the Apostle John lived to see Jesus' second coming. Commenting on John 21:19-23, he writes: "Jesus meant to live the impression that John would tarry till he came, otherwise he would not have said it, but he did not say what they concluded from his statement namely that John would not die....Surely John lived to see Christ's coming, not only in vision, but in actuality."[28]

In the McGuiggan-King debate,[29] the second proposition was: "The Scriptures clearly teach that the second coming of Christ is yet future." King denied this proposition.

King believes that the second coming of Christ at Jerusalem was a time when he was visible. He writes, "He was seen (Mt 24:30). It was a visible coming, as predicted, and furthermore, we are told what was seen, even 'the man Jesus Christ."[30] But King does not mean that Christ was seen physically; rather, "it is figurative language of Christ's revelation, especially the effect it would have on the Jewish Commonwealth."[31]

While the certainty or fact of the second coming is clearly taught in Scripture, the time is not. From the days of the first century until today many have been curious about the time of the Lord's return. But the Bible makes it clear that no one knows the exact time when Jesus will return. God, the Father, knows the time but he is the only one who does. Jesus said that neither he, nor the angels, knew the time of his return (Mt 24:36-44). If Jesus, in the days of his flesh, did not know the exact time, and if the angels had been denied that knowledge, and if no one up to Jesus' time had been given that knowledge, then it is certainly clear that God meant for the exact time to be unknown. Anyone, therefore, who tries to set a time for the return of our Lord is being presumptuous—even if they set that time as fulfilled in the first century.

King's doctrine that the second coming of Christ occurred at the destruction of Jerusalem is hermeneutically unfounded and theologically misguided. King says that this AD 70 event ushered in the beginning of the new heaven and the new earth. The new heavens and earth stand in contrast to the Jewish world (and not the material creation).[32] The old heavens and old earth was the carnal Jewish world.[33]

If we live today in the new heaven and the new earth, then the world in which we live will continue without end. When asked about the end of the present world, King says the answer to this question is in the mind of God and has not been revealed to us. Of course, he has to say that. If all the passages that normally are taken to refer to the future establishment of a new heaven and a new earth have already been fulfilled, then God must have nothing to say about the future of this world.

The General Resurrection

No preterist teaching fills people with more emotion than the doctrine of the general resurrection of the dead. More than any other preterist teaching, this is the one that causes people to back-peddle away from it. Preterists do not deny the resurrection; what they deny is a literal, bodily resurrection of humanity.

Max King writes that he "sincerely believes that the general resurrection belongs to the same time and event as given to the coming of Christ, the judgment, end of the world, and receiving of the eternal kingdom. It completes, not hinders, God's plan of redemption."[34] He says, "I deny John 5:28 is a literal grave out here in the cemetery somewhere. That's what I deny about John 5:28."[35]

> Judaism was the metaphorical grave of the spiritual dead out of which this resurrection took place, just as ancient Babylon was the grave of national Israel. The fall of Judaism was the defeat of the 'ministration of death' and the opening of the graves. Those who had previously heard and obeyed Christ were found worthy of eternal life in the new heaven and earth. The disobedient were raised to eternal hell or separation from God (2 Thess 1:7-9).[36]

In other words, the texts generally understood to tell us of a general resurrection do not teach that at all. John 5:28-29 is discussing the death of the Jewish economy and the resurrection of Christianity. It is at this time that Christians experience a spiritual resurrection. Those who obeyed the gospel on Pentecost were not spiritually raised until AD 70. Paul affirms that Christians were "raised together with Christ" but this did not occur, according to King, until Jerusalem was destroyed.

The Final Judgment

Max King believes the second coming of Christ and the final judgment are inextricably tied together. As he addresses the subject, he says he wants "to deal primarily with the judgment of the last days."[37] Notice also the following:

Judgment was inseparably related to the second coming of Christ and his kingdom.[38]

> Again, emphasis needs to be given to the fact that 'the great judgment day' of the Bible does not fulfill all need or manner of judgment. There was judgment enacted before that day, and certainly God's judgment of the world, the nations, and his people continues in active power today. Because the judgment day of prophecy is applied to the fulfillment of prophecy, does not mean that every form or power of judgment in all subsequent time is being denied. The author does believe, however, that the judgment that resulted in the establishment of the eternal kingdom at the coming of Christ transpired in the end of that world (Matt. 24:14), being necessary to complete the redemption begun at the cross. A future judgment day, coming of Christ, or establishment of a kingdom is no more needed than a future cross.[39]

Notice that King acknowledges that this "does not mean that every form or power of judgment is being denied." Does this also apply to a future judgment? Not as far as

King is concerned; he says a future judgment day is no more necessary than a future cross. In the McGuiggan-King debate, King denied the following proposition: "The New Testament teaches there is yet to be a day in which all the dead will be raised to life. And that they with the people yet alive n that day will be judged relative to where they shall spend eternity."[40]

It is also significant to understand how this doctrine relates to the centrality of the cross. It is at this point that evangelicals should posit a fierce objection.

Replaces the Cross with the Destruction of Jerusalem
Preterism makes AD 70 and the destruction of Jerusalem the primary focus of the will of God and replaces the cross as the central point in the history of the scheme of redemption. Paul says the gospel, which is of "first importance," is the death, burial and resurrection of Jesus Christ (1 Cor 15:1-4). The idea of Max King and others that the kingdom of Christ came at the cross but the kingdom of God did not come with power until the destruction of Jerusalem is unfounded in Scripture.

King and other hyper-preterists do not agree. In their thinking the cross plays an important part in the *eschaton*, defined as the period beginning with the cross and ending in AD 70. The cross plays a role; but the main point of reference is the destruction of Jerusalem and the ending of the Jewish economy, not the role of Jesus on the cross. Surely this has major implications for soteriology.

Conclusion
Why is the hyper-preterist view of biblical eschatology making gains in Christian circles? Why is such an extreme reading of Scripture finding receptive ears, not only in Stone-Campbell churches, both Churches of Christ (a cappella) and Christian Churches (independent), but also among all sorts of evangelical churches?

There are two possible reasons. First, preterism is a reaction to the growth of "rapture theology" that was popularized first by Hal Lindsey in *The Late Great Planet Earth* and then most recently in the *Left Behind* novels by Tim LaHaye and Jerry Jenkins. Lindsey's book was published in 1970, just one year before King's book *The Spirit of Prophecy*. King is an equal and opposite of Lindsey: one is guilty of extreme literalizing, the other of extreme spiritualizing; one places all prophecy in the future, the other in the past.

Second, preterists believe they have the answer to liberal theology, and this has an appeal to conservative believers.

However, a tremendous loss occurs to Christianity in the over-spiritualizing of all eschatological passages to speak only to the church 2,000 years ago.

Notes

[1]Tim LaHaye and Jerry Jenkins, *Left Behind: A Novel of Earth's Last Days* (Wheaton, Ill.: Tyndale, 1995).

[2]Hal Lindsey, *The Late Great Planet Earth* (Grand Rapids: Zondervan, 1970).

[3]"Preterism" seems too generic to identify all those who hold to what is called the AD 70 Theory. The term "hyper-preterism" has its own drawbacks.

[4]Max R. King, *The Cross and the Parousia of Christ* (Warren, Oh.: Parkman Road Church of Christ, 1987), p. 669.

[5]This Bible college was started specifically to address realized eschatology. It is difficult to date exactly when Stevens served in this position. The school opened its doors on January 3, 1977, and the last bulletin for the school was published in the winter 1979-1980. A brief survey and analysis is presented in Terry Varner, *Studies in Eschatology*, vol.1 (Marietta, Oh.: Therefore Stand Publications, 1981), pp. 9-12.

[6]Ed Stevens, *What Happened in A.D. 70?* (Ashtabula, Oh.: N.E.O.B.I., 1981; reprint ed., Bradford, Penn.: Kingdom Publications), p.19.

[7]Keith A. Mathison, ed., *When Shall These Things Be?* (Phillipburg, N.J.: P & R Publishing, 2004).

[8]Kenneth L. Gentry, "The Historical Problem with Hyper-Preterism," in *When Shall These Things Be?* ed. Keith A. Mathison (Phillipsburg, N.J.: P & R Publishing, 2004), p. 4, writes, "Hyper-preterism is a small but active, militant, and growing theological movement. Its enthusiastic adherents loudly demand that those who disagree with them stop their full-time labors and deal with all their questions—or die the death of a thousand emails." However, Todd Dennis, "An Introduction to Preterism," writes, "This view of eschatological fulfillment is gaining a strong foothold in every niche of Christianity, and its revolutionary world view may very will [sic] usher in a great reformation rivaling that of the 16th Century for size and scope. Gladly the 'Preterist Movement' has seen a gathering of fine people from nearly every doctrinal background, as opposed to the denominational splintering that was associated with the Reformation period." http://www.preteristarchive.com/Preterism/dennis-todd)

[9]Edward E. Stevens, "Doctrinal Implications of Preterist Eschatology," at www.preterist.org as cited by Mathison, *When Shall*, pp. xiii-xiv.

[10]Max King, *The Spirit of Prophecy* (Warren, Oh.: Parkman Road Church of Christ, 1971), p. v.

[11]D. B. Beagle, *Christ in Prophecy, Preparation, and Establishment of the Glorious Kingdom*, as cited in Varner, *Eschatology*, p. 33.

[12]King, *The Spirit of Prophecy*, p. 353.

[13]Varner, *Eschatology*, pp. 78-97, shows from external evidence that what King says is not new. In debates and writings over the last one hundred years there have been people who have taken similar positions. One of Varner's best responses is in demonstrating that the writings of the Apostolic Fathers (AD 110-165) contain abundant testimony that they did not accept the doctrine of AD 70 being the end of all things. The implication is that if the early church fathers understood the Second Coming of Christ to be in the future, how did they miss the fact that it had already occurred in AD 70? He says the study of the Church Fathers is the "missing link in Kingism."

[14]Ed Stevens,. http://www.preterist.org/articlesold/what_if_the_creeds_are_wrong.htm. p. 13

[15]Kenneth L. Gentry, Jr., "A Brief Theological Analysis of Hyper-Preterism," at www.reformed. org./eschaton/gentry_preterism.html., pp 1-2.

[16]Ibid.

[17]King, *Spirit of Prophecy,* pp. 1-2.

[18]Charles J. Aebi, "An Expose of the A.D. 70 Doctrine," in *The Future of the Church*, ed. William Woodson (Henderson, Tenn.: Freed-Hardeman College, 1978), p. 13.

[19]Stafford North, "Did Jesus Return in 70 A.D.?" (Unpublished paper), p. 2.

[20]King, *Spirit of Prophecy*, pp. 199–204.

[21]King, *The Cross*, p. 32 (pp. 425, 662 comment on Col 1:13).

[22]Charles Aebi and others refer to this as "redefining words" for their own use. What they are saying in "redefining words" is the same thing as using the "spiritual interpretation" of eschatology texts.

[23]King, *Spirit of Prophecy*, p. 68.

[24]Ibid., p. 81.

[25]Ibid., p. 105.

[26]Ibid., p. 105.

[27]Edward C. Stevens, *What Happened in A.D. 70?* (Bradford, Penn.: Kingdom Publications, 1997), p. 2.

[28]King, *Spirit of Prophecy*, p. 111.

[29]Jim McGuiggan and Max King, *The McGuiggan-King Debate* (Warren, Oh.: Parkman Road Church of Christ, 1975).

[30]Ibid., p. 89

[31]King, *Spirit of Prophecy*, p. 269.

[32]Ibid., p. 37.

[33]Ibid., p. 57.

[34]Ibid., p. 212.

[35]Max R. King, *The Nichols-King Debate* (Warren, Oh.: Parkman Road Church of Christ, 1973), p. 97.

[36]King, *Spirit of Prophecy*, p. 220.

[37]Ibid., p. 155.

[38]Ibid.

[39]Ibid., p. 180.

[40]*McGuiggan-King Debate*, p. 206.

15

RESPONSE

Grant Osborne

F ew movements in our times have experienced every major eschatological position. It was very interesting to discover that this has indeed been the case in the Stone-Campbell Restoration Movement. My task is to sum up the issues and interact with these aspects of the movement. I will be considering four primary positions: postmillennialism, the preterist movement, amillennialism, and premillennialism. The latter two are by far the most viable, so I will discuss them together.

The Postmillennial Position

Postmillennialism was prominent and most viable at the beginning of the Stone-Campbell movement; that makes sense historically. This eschatological belief flourished in times of revival (Jonathan Edwards and the Great Awakening). So the early part of the nineteenth century, with its revivalism and the explosion of the missionary movement, was a natural time for postmillennialism to develop. In fact, America was seen as the God-sent means of fulfilling this "millennium." This school of thought believes that before Christ returns we will see the triumph of the gospel worldwide and an era of peace ushered in. They base this on the Great Commission (Mt 28:19, "disciple all nations"), the promise in the Olivet Discourse (Mt 24:14, the gospel "preached in the whole world...and then the end will come"), and the kingdom parables (the growth of the kingdom in Mt 13:31-33).

Historically, this system flourished in the first half of the nineteenth century and then at the turn to the twentieth century, but in both cases the optimism disappeared due first to the Civil War and second to World War I. Hopes of an era of peace centered on the success of the gospel seemed unlikely in this world. Biblical evidence for this position is insufficient, especially given constant reminder of the absolute depravity of humankind. Each time people believe the "millennium" may have started, history proves it wrong. Moreover, the biblical promises yield only the truth that the mission of the church will continue until Christ returns, not that there will be a triumph and period of peace before the end. Mark 13:7-8 states the opposite: wars and disasters will continue until the End.

The Preterist Position

Preterism has become quite popular of late. It holds that the prophecies and Revelation refer not to future events but to the present ("preterist") situation at the time when Revelation was written. Those who hold this position believe it was penned in AD 68 in the middle of the destruction of Israel by the Romans (AD 66-70) in order to explain why God was so judging the nation for rejecting his Messiah.

Preterist teaching includes two schools of thought. The moderate type exemplified by the reconstructionists[1] restricts this mainly to Revelation. The more extensive type sees all the prophecies of the New Testament, even those regarding the Second Coming of Christ, as all fulfilled in AD 70. Unfortunately, it is this wider type that has become influential of late in some parts of the Stone-Campbell Restoration Movement. Primarily, this is due to the influence of the writings of Max King[2] and Edward Stephens.[3] Their more hyper view has given rise led to a new label, "transmillennialism," because it transcends the issue of a millennium. They believe that all the prophecies are allegorical/spiritual rather than literal. So the return of Christ refers to his establishment of the church with himself as Head; the bodily resurrection is the establishment of the "body of Christ," the church; and the "Day of the Lord" is the "end of the world," or the end of Judaism, in AD 70. At that time the old "heaven and earth" passed away (the Jewish system), and the "new heaven and new earth" (the church) appeared. Final judgment then is not a future event but was completed at the judgment of the Jewish people in AD 66-70.

What are we to say about this recent movement? This growing position is seriously flawed, even dangerous. If the Second Coming of Christ and the resurrection of the dead are cardinal doctrines at the core of the Christian faith—and everyone (including Paul in 1 Corinthians 15) says they are—then radical preterism is a heresy.

Let's take the biblical evidence one section at a time. First, the teachings of Jesus: The Olivet Discourse (Mark 13 = Matthew 24-25 = Luke 17, 21) is much debated, to be sure. Some, like R. T. France and N. T. Wright,[4] would also take the whole passage to refer allegorically to the destruction of Jerusalem. None of them, though, would extend this to Paul or the rest of the New Testament!). Others see the destruction of Jerusalem only pertaining to Mark 13:5-23, with 13:24-27 speaking of the future *parousia*, like David Wenham and D. A. Carson.[5] Still others, such as Darrell Bock, Craig Blomberg, and myself,[6] see the whole discourse as apocalyptic language referring to the destruction of Jerusalem as proleptic of the events of the future *eschaton*. None would interpret Jesus' teaching on his future *parousia* (Matt 16:27; Luke 17:30; John 14:2-3; Acts 1:11) as referring only to the events of AD 70.

The great number of future prophecies from Paul or other NT writers (1 Thess 4:13-5:11; 2 Thess 1-12; 1 Cor 15:51-52; Phil 3:20; Tit 2:12-13; Heb 9:28; Jas 5:8, 1 Pet 4:7) were not interpreted by the church fathers as having already been fulfilled, nor can they be taken in this way and be true to the meaning of Scripture. The event will take place when earthly history is finished and eternity inaugurated. That event has not happened yet.

Finally, a preterist understanding of Revelation is more viable. However, it is still not the more likely understanding. First, a preterist perspective requires Revelation to be written in AD 68. This view is defended by some, but the historical circumstances behind the seven letters and the imagery of the book favor the view that it was written late in the reign of the emperor Domitian about AD 95.[7]

Second, for preterist interpreters, the Beast is Rome, the kings from the east (16:12, 17:12-14) are Roman generals, Armageddon is the siege of Jerusalem, and the "great tribulation" (7:14) is the present suffering of Christians at the hands of the Jews. The locust plague of 9:1-11 refers to the five months of terror at the hands of the Roman tribune Gessius Florus from May to September, AD 66; the 200 million demonic horsemen of 9:12-21 are the Roman army invading Palestine. The "court of the Gentiles" trampled in 11:2 is unbelieving Israel, and "the kingdom of this world" that has become "the kingdom of our Lord" (11:17) is the establishment of Christianity as a result of the fall of Jerusalem.

All this is possible, but is it likely? The atmosphere of Revelation is global and cannot be so easily applied to Palestine and the fall of Jerusalem. Throughout the book the action effects "every tribe, people, language, and nation" (5:9; 7:9; 10:11; 13:7; 17:15) and "all the inhabitants of the earth" (3:10; 6:10; 8:13; 11:10; 13:8, 14; 17:8). That only the people of Israel are in view is never even hinted. The locusts fall on "all who do not have the seal of God" in 9:4, and the demonic horsemen kill one-third of humankind in 9:18 (note also 6:8, where "a fourth of the earth" are killed). How can such clear language be read as limited to Israel alone?

The trampling of the court of the Gentiles in 11:2 is almost certainly the persecution of the saints (a major theme in Revelation), not the punishment of the Jewish people. Also, nowhere in the New Testament does the fall of Jerusalem inaugurate the church age. The debate is whether the church is initiated at Pentecost or at Jesus' choice of the twelve (my preference), but no one other than a preterist would have it starting in AD 70.

In conclusion the preterist view on Revelation is possible but unlikely. However, to extend the preterist view to all the promises of the New Testament quite frankly appears heretical. If we are now living in the perfect "new heaven and new earth" and this world is all there is (with no hope of a future resurrection), we must echo Paul's statement "our preaching is useless and so is your faith" (1 Cor 15:14)!

The Amillennial and Premillennial Positions
Amillennialism and Premillennialism are the most tenable eschatological positions. They will be discussed together to allow comparison.

The amillennial position is the dominant belief in churches of the Stone-Campbell Movement currently. So, detailed description of this position is not needed. The movement's embracing of amillenialism originally developed as a reaction against the overly literal interpretation of the millennium in the first three centuries of the church. Augustine cemented the predominance of the amillennial perspective until the nineteenth century. This view believes that Revelation 20 should be understood symbolically as the triumph of God's mission during the church age. It is the final of a series of cycles in the book describing the people of God between the advents.

Premillennialism, on the other hand, takes Revelation 20:1-10 as a literal prophecy of a future reign of Christ on earth, though many would take the "thousand" as a symbol of a lengthy reign rather than a literal thousand years. Not everyone is aware that premillennialism includes four subgroups: By far the best-known type of premillennialism to those in the Stone-Campbell Movement, and most groups today, is the prophecy movement of Hal Lindsay, Jack Van Impe and Tim LaHaye.

However, this form of premillennialism is least likely to be correct. It employs a weak hermeneutic based on the fact that Israel is now an independent nation. It assumes all the prophecies and symbols were meant to be fulfilled in our own day. So the eagle is the United States and the bear is Russia. The number "666" (Rev 13:18) must refer to something current, like Ronald Wilson Reagan (three names, each with six letters), the bars of the credit card, or some embedded system in Microsoft.

This kind of coding is impossible. God hardly inspired a series of symbols that were incomprehensible in their own day and meant only for our day. Rather, every symbol in the Book of Revelation was understood in John's day and drawn from the stock of apocalyptic symbols stemming from the OT and intertestamental period as well as the situation in the first century. The key to 666 is either: 1) gematria, an ancient technique drawn from the fact that all ancient numbers were letters of the alphabet (a = 1, b = 2 etc.); so every word or name had a numerical value when the letters were added up, and 666 meant something like "Nero Caesar" (in Hebrew); or 2) a three-fold stress on the incompleteness/sinfulness of humankind, with 777 as absolute completeness and 888 (the gematria of "Jesus") equaling perfection. A combination of the two may be the best answer; the main thing is that the attempt to find a name today that adds up to 666 is very wrong-headed.

The other three are more viable. The second, dispensationalism (connected to the first but without the hermeneutic) believes there will be a seven-year tribulation period (Dan 9:24-27) and that the "rapture" (return of Christ for the church) will occur at the beginning of the period (1 Thess 4:13-18; Rev 3:10). The third, the mid-tribulation position, agrees but places the rapture in the middle of the period (Matt 24:22; Rev 11:11-12). The fourth, the post-tribulation position places the return of Christ at the end of the tribulation period (Matt 24:29; 2 Thess 2:1-3).

The fourth will be the focus of the rest of the discussion. It is often called "historic premillennialism" because it was the dominant view for the first three centuries of the church age. This position agrees with amillenianalism in several areas. For instance, they agree that Christ will only return once, whereas the second and third positions above also believe Christ will return a second time to destroy the enemies of God (Rev 19:11-21). They also agree that the so-called Old Testament prophecies of a millennial reign (Ps 72:8-14; Isa 11:2-11; Zech 14:6-21) are probably looking forward to the immediate future of Israel, the church age, or eternity. Their view of Revelation 20:1-10 is the main difference, with amillennialism holding it is symbolic of the church age and premillennialism that it is a literal future reign of Christ on earth.

Each section of the passage will be examined in an effort to compare these two options. The first is 20:1-3 in which an angel descends from heaven, "seizes the dragon" by the scruff of his neck, "binds" his hands and feet in chains (the meaning in the first century) and throws him into the abyss (his prison for the next thousand years), sealing/locking it behind him. The amillennial interpretation is that Satan is bound in this age (Mk 3:27; Jn 12:31; Col 2:15) and therefore unable to stop the gospel from going forth. Yet the imagery seems very strong, so the premillennialist sees it as a final period in which Satan can no longer "deceive the nations" (the very thing he does in this age).

The second section 20:4-6 involves the reign of the saints, with the key term being ez_san, the saints "coming to life" at this time. This is understood either as a coming to spiritual life following conversion (Augustine), the heavenly exaltation of the saints in the intermediate state (most amillennialists today), or to the physical resurrection of the saints at the parousia (most premillennialists). The term is used of a physical "coming to life" (Mt 9:18; Jn 11:25; Rom 14:9) and of Jesus' resurrection (Rev 1:18, 2:8; 13:14—the beast). Most importantly, the very next verse (Rev 20:5) uses *ezesan* of the unsaved dead "coming to life" at the end of this period, certainly the resurrection to judgment in terms of Daniel 12:2, Matthew 25:46, and John 5:29. Therefore, while it could be the second (the first in unlikely in the context), the third seems to make more sense in this context.

The final section is 20:7-10, in which Satan is released at the end of the period and gathers the nations to destroy the saints. Here the amillennial position may have the stronger argument, for the wording, "gather them for battle" in 20:8b is the exact phrase used in 16:14 for Armageddon. So the two wars of 19:17-21 and 20:8-9 may be the same battle. Premillennialists say the differences between the two (surrounding the Holy City, destroyed by fire from heaven) outweigh the similarities and favor 20:8-9 being a different battle.

Both views are almost equally viable, each with strengths and weaknesses. The premillennial position seems most persuasive to me, while most of those in the Stone-Campbell Movement are persuaded by the amillennial interpretation. Let iron sharpen iron while we continue to study the evidence, each challenging other with mutual respect.

Conclusion

Eschatology will always remain an uncertain field of study. God has deliberately not made clear in his Word exactly how he plans to end this world and introduce the next. The only cardinal, certain truth is the fact of Christ's future coming. Issues like the exact timing of Christ's return and the events by which the Day of the Lord will take place must await God's own will and revelation. As Jesus said, "No one knows about that day or hour, not even the angels in heaven, nor the Son, but only the Father" (Mt 24:36; Mk 13:32). We must realize that we know no more about the Second Coming than the Jews did about the first. God has revealed everything in symbols, and we can only do our best in interpreting the data in Scripture. He will reveal all in due time. Until then we must be humble and avoid turning eschatology into a new holy war between factions.

Notes

[1] David C. Chilton, *The Days of Vengeance: An Exposition of the Book of Revelation* (Fort Worth: Dominion, 1987).

[2] Max R. King, *The Cross and the Parousia of Christ: The Two Dimensions of One Age-Changing Eschaton* (Warren, Oh.: Parkman Road Church of Christ, 1987).

[3] Edward Stephens, *What Happened in A.D. 70?* (Ashtabula, Ohio: N.E.O.B.I., 1981; reprint ed., Bradford, Penn.: Kingdom Publications).

[4] R. T. France, *Matthew*, TNTC (Grand Rapids: Eerdmans, 1985); N. T. Wright, *Jesus and the Victory of God* (Minneapolis: Fortress, 1996).

[5] David Wenham, *The Rediscovery of Jesus' Eschatological Discourse,* Gospel Perspectives 4 (Sheffield: JSOT Press, 1984); D. A. Carson, "Matthew," ed. Frank E. Gaebelein, *The Expositor's Bible Commentary* (Grand Rapids: Zondervan, 1984), pp. 1-599.

[6] Darrell Bock, *Luke*, IVP New Testament Commentary (Downers Grove, Ill.: InterVarsity, 1994); Craig Blomberg, *Matthew*, New American Commentary (Nashville: Broadman, 1992); Grant R. Osborne, *Matthew* (Grand Rapids: Zondervan, forthcoming).

[7] Colin J. Hemer, *The Letters to the Seven Churches of Asia in Their Local Setting* (Grand Rapids: Eerdmans, 2001); David Aune, *Revelation*, 3 vols., WBC 52 (Dallas: Word, 1997-1998); G. K. Beale, *The Book of Revelation: A Commentary on the Greek Text*, NIGTC (Grand Rapids: Eerdmans, 1999); Simon J. Kistemaker, *Exposition of the Book of Revelation,* New Testament Commentary 20 (Grand Rapids: Baker Academic, 2001); Robert H. Mounce, *The Book of Revelation*, NICNT 17 (Grand Rapids: Eerdmans, 1977); Grant R. Osborne, *Revelation,* Baker Exegetical Commentary on the New Testament (Grand Rapids: Baker, 2002).

Part 5

Understanding the Bible Through Contemplating the Role of the Old Testament as Christian Scripture

16

THE OLD TESTAMENT IN
THE EARLY STONE-CAMPBELL MOVEMENT

Gary Hall

T he Stone-Campbell Restoration Movement has had a love-hate relationship with the Old Testament. Many do not see it as having any authority or relevance for the church. On the one hand, it is a part of the Bible and the Bible is the inspired word of God. So the Old Testament must remain in the canon. On the other hand, many find much in the Old Testament that is useful and helpful but do not know quite how to interpret it. This essay will review the early founders' perspectives and teachings on the Old Testament-from Alexander Campbell to David Lipscomb. The survey will cover some of the major figures in the nineteenth century. An analysis of their writings will provide insights into our current situation. Space prohibits addressing some of the short-coming that will surface. However, a few suggestions will be offered by way of critique.

Thomas Campbell

The earliest explicit reference to the Old Testament in published works of the leaders of the Stone-Campbell Restoration Movement is in Thomas Campbell's "Declaration and Address" written in 1809. The fourth proposition (of 13) states:

> That although the scriptures of the Old and New Testament are inseparably connected, making together but one perfect and entire revelation of the Divine will, for the edification and salvation of the church; and therefore in that respect cannot be separated; yet as to what directly and properly belongs to their immediate object, the New Testament is as perfect a constitution for the worship, discipline and government of the New Testament church, and as perfect a rule for the particular duties of its members; as the Old Testament was for the worship, discipline and government of the Old Testament church, and the particular duties of its members.[1]

In an appendix in which Campbell explained and interpreted his views, he reiter-
ates that the New Testament is the proper and immediate rule for the church. Yet the
Old Testament was of equal authority and the very same in its moral requirements. But
our Lord taught his people in the New Testament what they should observe and do.
"Thus we come to the one rule, taking the Old Testament as explained and perfected
by the new, and the new as illustrated and enforced by the old; assuming the latter as
the proper and immediate directory for the christian church."[2]

Thomas Campbell published very little that would allow us to see how he would
interpret and apply the Old Testament to the Christian life. However unintentional
he sowed the seeds for future attitudes toward the Old Testament with this and
similar statements.[3]

Alexander Campbell

Understanding Alexander Campbell's hermeneutical approach to the Old Testament
requires an understanding of the approach to the Old Testament then in vogue in
Protestant America, especially among the Presbyterians and Baptists on the American
frontier. The Old Testament law was commonly divided into three parts: the moral, the
civil, and the ceremonial law. The Mosaic or old covenant was considered to be the
same as the new covenant but only the moral part of the old law was binding on
Christians. Furthermore, many American Protestants upheld John Calvin's view of the
law, including its three main functions: 1) bringing knowledge of sin; 2) restraining sinners; 3) arousing one to obedience and better knowledge of God's will.

Calvin further taught that whoever wished to do away with the law misunderstood
it, for Moses commanded it to be obeyed. Jesus abrogated it for the believer only in
that he came to remedy transgressions of it so that it no longer condemns us.[4] Calvin's
teaching was embodied in the *Philadelphia Confession of Faith* adopted by the Redstone
Association. The Brush Run church attended by the Campbells was part of this association, though it had never subscribed to the confession. The *Philadelphia Confession* was
a Baptist revision of the *Westminster Confession* of 1677.[5] The evangelistic preaching of
the day included long dissertations on the law in order to convict the hearers of their
sin and bring them to the point of repentance.

Into this setting Alexander Campbell's "Sermon on the Law" dropped like a bomb
shell, provoking charges of heresy against him. Campbell testified that without these
circumstances he probably would not have advocated the "present reformation."[6] At
every point Campbell refuted the traditional view on the value and use of the law.

The main part of the sermon consisted of four points (covering 12 published
pages). Campbell first established the meaning of the word "law," noting it had at least
two major meanings: the Old Testament in general and the Mosaic law. He rejected the
three-fold division as unbiblical and the designation of the Ten Commandments as
"moral law" as a misnomer. They were not all moral laws, nor did they cover all of

morality. Secondly, he pointed out what the law could not accomplish, and thirdly, explained why this was so: it could not bring righteousness or life because of human weakness. Finally, he pointed out that God had remedied the law's defects by sending his Son who brought an end to the law, revealed the full demerit of sin and condemned it, and accomplished what the law could not: righteousness.

The conclusion to the sermon covered fourteen printed pages and consisted of five points: (1) the law and the gospel, the old covenant and the new, essentially were different; (2) those in Christ were no longer condemned, and therefore Christians were not under the law even as a rule of life; (3) preaching the law to prepare a person for the gospel was not necessary; (4) all arguments from the Old Testament to support infant baptism, tithe, holy days, etc. were repugnant; (5) Jesus must be venerated in the highest degree, not Moses. The third point was expounded at some length with copious quotes from the New Testament.

The most common reaction to the sermon was that Campbell had rejected the Old Testament as authority for the church.[7] Charges of heresy on this point were later dropped. His hermeneutic in this sermon has become the hallmark of Old Testament interpretation for the Stone-Campbell Restoration Movement down to the present day. The sharp distinction between the old and new covenants is the mainstay of that hermeneutic.[8]

Campbell refined his views in further publications and debates. The most significant formulations were his understanding of the several different covenants and three dispensations. In the 1820 debate with John Walker, Campbell exhibited his strong concern for the historical context of the Bible. He considered it crucial to understand under which covenant administration and during what dispensation a particular event or word occurred. In the debate Campbell enumerated eight covenants in the Bible[9]: with Adam, Noah, two with Abraham (the first a promise of a great nation which was established with circumcision in Genesis 17, and the second the promise of blessing of all the nations through him which was not fulfilled until the coming of Christ[10]), at Sinai, with Aaron (priesthood), with David, and the new covenant.

For Campbell the new covenant was the most important and superseded all others. The covenant with Abraham in Genesis 12 was the most important in the Old Testament. It preceded the covenant of circumcision and was completely fulfilled by Christ. Thus, Campbell could argue against Walker and the entire Reformed tradition that Christian baptism did not replace circumcision. There was no direct connection because the Abrahamic covenant that Christ fulfilled was prior to circumcision and did not include it. This formulation also led to his diminishment of the Mosaic covenant as secondary and temporary, and in effect only until Christ. Campbell was using Paul as his guide here.

Campbell also developed the concept of three dispensations: the patriarchal, the Mosaic, and the Christian.[11] Each age had its own priesthood and nothing from one age carried over into the next. By analogy with the growth of living things, Campbell characterized the three ages as stages to spiritual maturity: infancy, childhood, and adulthood stage, or as the starlight, moonlight, and sunlight ages. Campbell repeatedly admonished that when studying the Bible one had to determine which age the text belonged to.

This became his second rule of Bible interpretation:

> In examining the contents of any book, as respects precepts, promises, exhortations, etc., observe *who it is that speaks, and under what dispensation he officiates.* Is he a Patriarch, a Jew, or a Christian? *Consider also the persons addressed: their prejudices, characters, and religious relations.* Are they Jews or Christians—believers or unbelievers—approved or disapproved? This rule is essential to the proper application of every command, promise, threatening, admonition or exhortation, in Old Testament and New.[12]

This rule is repeated throughout his writings and debates. The Christian dispensation began in Acts 2 so that the Gospels and Jesus' life on earth were part of the Mosaic dispensation. The Jewish dispensation ended on the cross.[13] Campbell's views on the covenants and dispensations contradicted the Reformed view, which taught that the old and new covenants (the Mosaic and Christian) were basically one covenant with two administrations.[14] Campbell asked that if the Jewish and Christian covenants were one covenant of grace, why not include the covenant with Abraham and have three dispensations of the one covenant?

Campbell's' perspective led to a sharp dichotomy between the Old Testament and New Testament. However, he was not a Marcionite. Campbell promoted an essential relationship between the two under the concept of typology, taking the book of Hebrews as his guide. The Old Testament was full of types and shadows of the new covenant. All of Israel's religious institutions and her history were types. Leviticus 16 was an important chapter in this regard.

The study of the tabernacle is of utmost importance. No one, according to Campbell, can thoroughly understand Christianity who has not mastered its topography. Every element of it is a type, for Moses had the perfect pattern of everything and was told to make everything according to the pattern.[15]

Also all illustrious persons were prophetic and typical of the life of the Messiah, from Adam to Jonah. But most important was the language of the old that explains the language of the new. Campbell insisted that the Old Testament and New Testament were united, for no one can understand the language of the new kingdom without understanding the language of the old. Nor can one understand either the old or new covenant by itself.[16] The old was full of the doctrine of the new, and all who want to understand the Christian institution must approach it through Moses and make Paul their commentator.[17]

Fulfilled prophecy was also an important part of Campbell's use of the Old Testament. It was an important proof of the Bible's inspiration.[18] Campbell, in his debate with the skeptic Robert Owen, used fulfilled prophecy as one of his many proofs of the truthfulness of Christianity. He listed five categories of fulfillment: (1) the fates of the ancient cities and empires; (2) the symbolic import of Jewish institutions; (3) the double references that point to the Messiah and his kingdom; (4) the direct and literal predictions of the Messiah and his kingdom; (5) the literal and symbolic prophecies in the New Testament reaching down to our own times.[19]

These principles laid out by Alexander Campbell have had wide influence in the Stone-Campbell Movement. The leaders who followed remained faithful to his hermeneutic and one sees similar principles repeated often.

Campbell's insistence on putting biblical texts in their appropriate historical context was a crucial hermeneutical principle. His dispensational scheme helped readers see the Bible in its interrelatedness while paying attention to the historical context. This concept, coupled with his understanding of the sharp break between the old (Mosaic) covenant and the new (Christian) covenant, provided a salvation-historical approach to the Bible. It was intended as a corrective to the weaknesses in the view taken by his contemporaries who saw little difference between the two testaments.

However, Campbell's formulations arouse several concerns. (1) The sharp break between the covenants could be easily interpreted as a sharp break between the two testaments. The old covenant could easily come to be associated with the Old Testament, the law with the Hebrew Bible. Then the whole Old Testament would be seen as irrelevant for the Christian. This did happen as we know. Though Campbell's point was that it was the old law that was abolished in Christ, that fine point was not observed. Also, that the law need not be preached to lead to Christ could be understood to mean that the Old Testament did not need to be preached at all. That the law was not viable for justification led to the conclusion that it was not useful at all. But if the law is God's revealed will for his covenant people this cannot be true. God's will reveals his character so certainly that there is great teaching value in the law for the Christian in matters of morality and holiness to name just two areas.

(2) Campbell's understanding that the Jewish dispensation continued up to Acts 2 meant that, as he said, John the Baptist and Jesus died under the old law. This seemed to suggest that the Gospels were mostly Jewish and of little importance for the Christian. In fact Paul was Campbell's favorite New Testament author. Later authors like Walter Scott almost skipped the Gospels. Yet the Gospels were written for the church and were certainly intended to be an important part of instructions for Christians. As just one example, the Sermon on the Mount is hardly irrelevant for Christians.

(3) Is the dispensational scheme misleading? It is helpful for reminding the student of the proper historical context for interpreting texts, but are there not important continuities between the eras? The nature of God, human beings, sin, holiness, grace, morals and a host of other items are very similar.

(4) Campbell's perspective on covenants seems to conflict with his view of dispensations. Is there really a two-fold covenant given to Abraham with two distinct fulfillments? If so then the Patriarchal period would in some sense continue until the coming of Christ. But the Bible does not explicitly suggest there were two Abrahamic covenants. Could the Mosaic covenant be a continuation of the covenant with Abraham and on the way to complete fulfillment in Christ? Jesus himself said he fulfilled the law and the prophets.

(5) The use of constitution language by Thomas Campbell, Rice Haggard, and later Isaac Errett was understandable given the excitement generated by the new national constitution of 1781. But that language also added to seeing a sharp break between the testaments. Furthermore, conceptualizing the covenant as a constitution made it a legal arrangement between God and his people, downplaying or ignoring the relational side and eliminating grace as the motivating principle. The Old Testament law defined the conditions of the covenant but it was not the covenant. The covenant was made prior to the law and involved a voluntary commitment by both parties and a relationship that could be expressed by several metaphors including that of father-son and marriage. Constitution language does not convey these important concepts.

(6) Advocating typology as the major way to relate the two testaments provided a limited model for use of the Old Testament in the church. Recognizing in addition a promise-fulfillment scheme still did not provide enough models to handle the complexity of the relationship. Large sections of the Old Testament did not fit either model and one could deduce that they could be ignored, which they subsequently were by Walter Scott and Robert Milligan.

Campbell regularly studied and lectured from the Old Testament. He advocated serious study of it and a deep familiarity with it as essential for the Christian. Yet he unconsciously provided a hermeneutic that led in a different direction than he might have intended.[20]

Walter Scott

Scott was a close associate of Alexander Campbell and popularized the reformation in the Western Reserve. He is credited by Boring with writing the first systematic theology of the Stone-Campbell Movement.[21] This was *The Gospel Restored*.[22] He accepted both the Old and New Testament as part of the unified Bible. He united them with a salvation-historical approach like Campbell. He began his exposition by starting with the Fall in Genesis with its introduction of sin. This first section of the book occupied pages 9-128! The second section moves immediately to discussion of the Messiahship of Jesus. This had two parts, the Messiahship of Jesus and the human response. The last part occupied over 300 pages in which he detailed his famous five steps to salvation.

Therefore, of the Old Testament only Genesis 2-3 is discussed. Other references to the Old Testament come in various sections that deal with the Old Testament prophecies of the Messiah found in the law, prophets and psalms (Luke 24), Moses and John the Baptist stand at the two ends of the law. John is the end of the law when the kingdom of God began to be preached. The great object of the Old Testament prophecies was the redemption of humankind. Thus, the Old Testament prophecies and the Gospels are linked together, the New Testament depending on the Old Testament for prophecy and the Old depending on the New for fact. The difference was that the Old Testament's purpose was to show that the Messiah was to come and the New Testament's purpose was to show that he had come.[23]

The Pentateuch contains prophecies mainly of Jesus' descent and ancestry. The Psalms speak of his descent from David and picture events from his birth to his resurrection. The prophets limit the descent of the Messiah to a virgin of the house of David and point to numerous events in his birth, life, ministry and death. Scott devoted considerable space to the book of Daniel because he saw that it portrayed the role of Christ in history. Therefore, Scott's chief hermeneutic for the Old Testament is christological. Its importance is that it points to the coming of Christ. A further comparison between the new covenant and the old was by analogy. The first was physical and defiled with sin; the latter was spiritual and pregnant with life and joy. The analogy was typified by the contrast between Adam and Christ.[24]

Though Scott held to the unity of the Bible his major theological work ignored most of the Old Testament. Despite his conviction that one needed to understand the Old Testament in order to understand the New, this gap in his writing would not have gone unnoticed. His convictions did not translate in a practical way into his theological formulation.

Barton W. Stone

Stone came from a similar Presbyterian background as Alexander Campbell. His views were forged in dialogue with and against some of their Calvinistic views.

Stone had an intimate knowledge of both the Old and New Testament and quoted often from them. In his early work he seemed to make little distinction between them, but as he developed his thought he came to recognize a difference. Though he had little formal education he knew and used Hebrew and Greek in his expositions and lectures. He appealed often to the importance of context for interpretation and to the whole teaching of Scripture.

One of his early investigations was the biblical doctrine of atonement.[25] He disagreed with the Calvinistic position of a covenant of works, as well as with limited election and atonement. In defining the doctrine he began with the Old Testament to try to understand the relationship between God and Israel. The law addressed only fleshly matters not spiritual and applied to the political relationship between God and Israel. The system of sacrifice in the Old Testament informs the New Testament teaching in the form of typology. Leviticus 16 is best understood as a type of Christ and his sacrifice. The law was taken out of the way by Christ's blood, nailed to the cross and abolished.[26] This does not include the moral law but only the ceremonial laws, which were types and shadows of Christ. Jesus abolished the political curse of the moral law–death–not the moral law itself.

The basis of the old law or covenant was God's grace and love. Jesus through the gospel made it possible for both Jew and Gentile to receive the blessing of Abraham through faith. But the old law was removed. The death of Christ abolished the old and brought in the new.[27] So Christians were not under the old law. Everything good in it was brought forward into the new covenant, so there was no need to go back beyond the new.

How then did Jesus fulfill the law (Matt 5:17)? The testimony of the law and prophets will continue until the end of time for through the law, Psalms and prophets, Jesus' life, death, burial, and resurrection were typified and predicted. When these took place the types and prophecies were fulfilled. Yet the law remained unfulfilled in two particulars: Christ as the antitype of the high priest has gone into heaven (the antitype of the Holy of Holies), but he has yet to return; also as the antitype of the scapegoat he will not accomplish the final abolishment of sin until the end, so disease, sickness and death still remain.

Stone recognized, as did Campbell, the sharp distinction between the old and new covenant and the significance of the death of Christ for the old law/covenant. The concept of constitution was important for Stone as for Campbell. Stone used the example of the state of Kentucky, which had rewritten its constitution. The good things in the old constitution were brought forward into the new one. The state citizen was only bound by the new constitution.

Isaac Errett

In his position as founder and long-time editor of the *Christian Standard*, Errett had a strong influence on the movement, indeed he was considered by some to be the most influential disciple of his time.[28] He was not an educated man, but with an excellent mind and through hard work he gained a reputation as a good Bible expositor. His position on the Old Testament can be gleaned from his published works, *First Principles, Our Position,* and *Evenings With the Bible*.[29] In *Our Position* he states:

> While agreeing as to the divine inspiration of the Old and New Testaments, we differ on the question of their equal binding authority on Christians. In our view, the Old Testament was of authority with Jews, the New Testament is now of authority with Christians. We accept the Old Testament as true, and as essential to a proper understanding of the New, and as containing many valuable lessons in righteousness and holiness which are of equal preciousness under all dispensations; but as a book of authority to teach us what we are to do, the New Testament alone, as embodying the teachings of Christ and his apostles, is our standard.[30]

Errett made the same points about the authority of the Old Testament in other places. Its lack of authority for Christians was especially true for him when it involved knowing what to do for salvation. In this regard the old covenant had been done away with, and only the new covenant provided the instruction from God. As the old will, it now had no effect for Christians who were under the new will or covenant. The authority of the Old Testament was in its witness to Christ, not in its authority as law for us. It was also essential for people in understanding God's plan of redemption. It shows that that plan was a progressive development. Sinful human nature required a gradual unfolding of this plan, and the Old Testament shows how that developed. The Jewish nation served the purpose of educating the people through their experience and through the teaching of the need for salvation, so that in the fullness of time Jesus came and the gospel was preached.[31]

Errett followed Campbell in understanding that the Bible witnesses to three dispensations: the Patriarchial, the Jewish, and the Christian. The Jewish age continued up to Acts 2.

He also taught that the connection between the testaments was to be understood in terms of typology. The Old Testament is antitype for the New Testament and all is clear in the Old Testament only when it is viewed through the New Testament. The Old Testament is basically a system of types, figures and symbols. The Old Testament had six uses: (1) it contains "a historic development of the purpose of God to redeem a sinful race"; (2) it presents a record of God's purpose through the ages to prepare the race for the coming of the Redeemer; (3) it reveals the "will of God, as addressed to the patriarchs and Jews-not his will in reference to us"; (4) it contains "the types and prophecies of the coming salvation" and is therefore "a great storehouse of evidence for the divinity of the New Testament"; (5) it provides moral principles that are "immutable and eternal" and precious lessons in "truth, righteousness and piety...which are of equal application to persons under all dispensations" (Rom 15:4); and (6) its development of human character, both positive and negative, is the most genuine in any literature, but it is not a book of authority to teach us what to do.[32]

Errett's *Evenings With the Bible* reveals how he treated the Old Testament on a practical level. He intended his essays to awaken a new interest in the Old Testament to prepare the way for better understanding of the New Testament. He searched for lessons and the truth that could be appropriated by the Christian for spiritual growth.[33] The first two volumes progressed through the Old Testament from Genesis to Esther, with a last lesson on Job. Each lesson is a devotional approach, attempting to draw out moral observations and instructions that could serve for family devotions. When applicable the New Testament is used to explicate the Old Testament text. Typology is not used; rather, straight-forward application is made. Conspicuous in their absence from these volumes are Psalms and any prophets, texts that would provide the basis for typology. Errett concentrates on people, though he does notice a few events, like Exodus 5-15.

He completely skips over the law in Exodus, Leviticus and Deuteronomy. He considers Balaam in Numbers 23-25, comes back to Nadab and Abihu in Leviticus 10, then goes directly to Joshua 24.[34]

Errett was aware of the new arena of critical studies of the Old Testament making its way from Germany to the United States. But his work was aimed at the "popular mind" and he did not intend to deal with this "new school" that brought "doubt on the inspiration of the Old Testament."[35]

Errett made clear that the worth of the Old Testament for the Christian was limited to moral lessons, which in his writings came mostly from persons and events. This kind of interpretation can lead to what John Bright called a "dreary moralism" which prompts the question of how the Old Testament would differ in its moral lessons from other literature.

Errett's failure to utilize the law, Psalms, and prophets in his exposition should cause concern. Though not removed from Alexander Campbell in years, he was some distance from him in understanding the importance of the Old Testament for the Christian. We do not find the deep study or strong emphasis on its importance outside of moral lessons.

Robert Milligan

Milligan was a contemporary of Errett's and became a prominent educator, finishing his career at the College of the Bible in Lexington. Milligan wrote one of the most influential books in the movement, *The Scheme of Redemption*,[36] the closest to a systematic theology written by anyone in the movement.[37] His earlier work, *Reason and Revelation*, also provides insight into his views.[38]

The Scheme of Redemption is organized into three books, each with several parts and/or chapters. Milligan's goal was to show that the organizing principle of the Bible is God' plan to redeem the human race. Book I begins with Creation and the Fall (pp. 17-62) to set the scene for the need for redemption. Book II attempts to show the progress of development in the scheme of redemption (pp. 63-284). The section moves from Adam to the death of Christ. Book III is the major section (pp. 285-577) and covers the foundation of the church and its ministry, ordinances, and organization. One recognizes Alexander Campbell's three dispensations, with the Mosaic dispensation continuing from Moses up to Acts 2.

Milligan's focus on the Old Testament is surprisingly minimal. From Creation to the death of Joshua covers 176 pages, with the death of Joshua to the coming of John the Baptist covering just 11 pages. The history and prophets were apparently of little interest. His chief principle for interpreting the Old Testament was typology. Thus, his main interest in the Pentateuch, after covering the fall, was to show how parts of the law and sacrifices provided types for the New Testament. Theological type is described as "a shadow of things to come."[39] There were legal, historical, and prophetic types.

They were designed to give a pictorial outline of *The Scheme of Redemption* and to serve as proof and demonstration of the divine origin of the antitype.[40] Milligan goes so far as to assert that "the Jews were all their lives engaged in setting up types and printing documents that they themselves could neither read nor understand."[41] In other words, ancient Israel could not understand its own Scriptures.

Much of the information included in the discussion of material from the Pentateuch seems irrelevant to the modern reader. It is heavy on description, especially on the tabernacle. The law was designed to provide the Jews with civil government, to convict of sin, to prevent idolatry, and to provide the religious nomenclature for the Scheme of Redemption.[42] The Law itself had been abolished but the principles behind the Decalogue were immutable and of perpetual obligation. These were moral principles that came from the nature of God.[43]

In *Reason and Revelation,* Milligan appeals to fulfilled prophecy as proof of the divine origin of the Bible.[44] The prophecies he referred to were those in Daniel 7, 8, 9 and 10-12. He gave precise dates and events for their fulfillment. He used the quotes in the New Testament to prove the scope of the Old Testament canon. Types and prophecy are also proof of the unity of the Bible.[45]

The fact that Milligan ignored such a large part of the Old Testament in his major work speaks for itself. Its value and validity for the Christian was minimal. His suggestion that Israel could not understand its own scripture seems the height of Christian arrogance. At the least it suggests that God was deceiving his people.

J. W. McGarvey

McGarvey was the premier Bible interpreter of the second half of the nineteenth century. He had great influence because of three roles: as professor of Bible and president of the College of the Bible in Lexington, as writer of a column in the *Christian Standard*, and as author of commentaries on the New testament, especially the Gospels and the book of Acts.

Although McGarvey wrote several volumes he did not compose a work on hermeneutics. His *Guide to Bible Study*[46] was not a guide in the expected sense but contained summaries of the major divisions of the Bible and brief summaries of each book with reference to historical contexts. In the introduction Herbert L. Willett laid out ten rules for Bible study, but they did not deal with hermeneutical issues either, but rather practical issues such as Bible chronology and which Bible translation to use. McGarvey's concern was to find practical lessons in the books. Deuteronomy 1-4 was a guide to preachers for it drew practical lessons from Israel's history and based some exhortations on them. The lives of the great Old Testament people taught some great lessons. He did find many passages throughout Isaiah that looked forward to the Messiah. He also recognized that the Psalms were under a different dispensation.[47]

In one of his lectures on the study of Scripture, McGarvey advocated the historical study of the text, by which he meant not the historical context of passages, but the placing of texts in their proper historical chronology in the Bible. This approach allowed one to see the "progress of revelation and the consequent gradual elevation of mankind."[48] This ignoring of context is paradoxical in light of the fact that he made a great effort to travel to the Bible lands in order to understand the cultural and geographical context of the Bible. The detailed book he wrote of his travels was required of his students in the College of the Bible.[49]

McGarvey's approach to the Old Testament can be ferreted out of his New Testament commentaries to some extent. When considering passages that contain quotes from the Old Testament in his *Fourfold Gospel*, he exhibits a variety of understanding. In commenting on the use of Isaiah 7:14 in Matthew 1:22-23, he lists four ways prophecies can be fulfilled: (1) when a thing clearly predicted comes to pass; (2) when the substance of the type becomes reality; (3) when elevated language describing an event is used of an ensuing event more suited to the language; and (4) when parabolic or figurative language may be applied to a subsequent event.

The third way applies to the use of Isaiah in Matthew 1. Isaiah 7:14 had an immediate application, but it also prefigured the birth of Jesus. The use of Hosea 11:1 in Matthew 2:15 was typological. McGarvey used the metaphor of the shell and kernel of a nut. Israel was the outer shell and Jesus was the kernel. Matthew's use of Jeremiah 31:15 in 2:18 was the adoption of some words of the prophet to the current situation. The Jeremiah text was not a prediction.[50]

McGarvey's commentary on Acts demonstrates little interest in addressing how the quotes and references to the Old Testament should be understood. He never reflects on the appropriateness of the Old Testament texts chosen or the hermeneutics involved in Stephen's sermon in Acts 7. He has only brief comments on other passages. Most comments simply state that the event fulfilled the Old Testament passage being referenced. In Acts 15 he notes that James' quote of Amos 9 is from the Septuagint but makes no comment on its difference from the Hebrew text.[51]

McGarvey's numerous articles on biblical criticism in *Christian Standard* center mostly on the Old Testament. His main concern is to respond to the negative criticism being leveled at the Old Testament in Germany and England and mediate it to the common person. He had read all of the leading critics, including Colenso on the Old Testament,[52] so was speaking from first hand knowledge. He was uniformly critical of the critics.[53]

McGarvey's teaching demonstrates that the earlier concern of the movement's first generation of thinkers for serious Bible study through the original languages had declined. He was designated Professor of English Bible at the College of the Bible and never required Hebrew or Greek of his students. Four-year Bible students only studied from the English Bible. Only McGarvey's own *The Land of the Bible* and a few other books outside of the Bible were assigned to students.

McGarvey opposed the introduction of the organ into church worship and by his arguments gives us insight into his understanding of the minimal authority of the Old Testament for Christians. As part of the old covenant it no longer could be used to ascertain the demands of God. Instrumental music—in the same category as sacrifices and incense in the Old Testament and therefore only part of Jewish worship—was not included in the Christian system. Additionally, he held that what is not expressly authorized by the New Testament writers and apostles—instrumental music among these—is forbidden.[54]

McGarvey represents a hardening position and further move away from the early leader's desire for a deep knowledge of both Old and New Testament. His practice of teaching only from the English Bible seems to suggest little interest in deeper study of the text. Yet his trip to the Middle East and resulting book exhibits a strong concern for the historical and cultural setting of the Bible. He also read widely but did not seem to demand that his students do so. McGarvey seemed to conceive of the whole Old Testament as a legal document that was abolished in Christ. Thus, his resistance to instrumental music discounted anything it said, even in the Psalms, because it was a part of the old covenant. The concept of covenant as constitution was rigidly applied to the whole Old Testament.

David Lipscomb

Lipscomb was one of the most influential men in Churches of Christ (a cappella), a fact attested by the fact that Lipscomb University bears his name. Like Isaac Errett his influence came from his position as an editor of an important periodical, in his case, the Gospel Advocate. He had little formal education but possessed a good intellect and could write clearly and well. He was a pacifist during the Civil War and an advocate of eliminating racial barriers. As a result he suffered personal loss and opposition but persevered.

His views on the Old Testament were very similar to Alexander Campbell's regarding dispensations, covenants, the end of the Law, and typology as the means to relate the testaments.[55] There were three dispensations, Patriarchal, Mosaic, and Christian,[56] and two covenants grounded in the promise to Abraham, the Mosaic or old covenant and the new covenant.[57] The Mosaic covenant was added because of sin and ended by the death of Christ, but the Christian should study it because it contained many things for our admonition. It was a schoolmaster to train Jews to receive Christ. It was temporary until Christ and only Jesus ever fully obeyed it and fulfilled it.[58] Jesus nailed it to the cross and introduced a better and higher covenant.

Therefore, the law regulating the Sabbath was not binding nor was the law on tithe.[59] However, all that was good for man from the old was adopted into the new. Even though the Sabbath was not for the Christian the principle of rest is. A day of rest should be secured. The laws under the old covenant are of value to see how to interpret the laws of the new covenant. Lipscomb also used constitutional language by comparing the old and new covenants to an old and new state constitution. Principles from the old covenant were transferred into the new, meaning that the principle behind the law on the son who cursed the parents is carried over in the principle of how children are to relate to their parents, though the punishment is not the same.

The Old Testament is full of types of Christ and the church. Aaron, Moses, and David are all types of Christ. The priests and kings typify Christians. The Jewish assembly was a type of the church.[60] Abel's lamb was a type of Christ and every lamb since. Everything that happened under Moses was typical of what took place under the perfect dispensation. The Old Testament is also full of lessons to be learned from the nation of Israel and from individuals within it.

Nevertheless, Lipscomb held strongly to the unity of the Bible. It is in perfect harmony, indissolubly linked, with each testament dependent on the other for completeness. They are connected by one spirit and purpose.[61] Yet the Old Testament is not complete and was preparatory for the New Testament. Prophecy was a major way the testaments were connected. Jesus Christ came as a fulfillment of them.[62] In an extended discussion of the nature of God, the Holy Spirit, and the Kingdom of God, Lipscomb depends heavily on the Old Testament.[63]

Lipscomb shared with Alexander Campbell both the strengths and weaknesses of a similar approach to the Old Testament. The stress on typology tended to lead to suggesting large portions of the Old Testament were unusable. Yet when formulating a theology he found much in the Old Testament that was important, especially in understanding God (of course he had little choice). However, he shared McGarvey's position on instrumental music and the Old Testament, which meant the latter had little authority for the Christian. In practice Lipscomb had difficulty being consistent with what he said about the unity of the Bible.

Conclusion

The traditional teaching on the Old Testament that has developed in the Stone-Campbell Restoration Movement was solidified early and changed little in the nineteenth century after Alexander Campbell. It was characterized by dividing history up into three dispensations: Abraham, Mosaic, and Christian. It promoted a hermeneutic that first of all sought the setting of a passage in the proper dispensation. Under this historical scheme different covenants were recognized. A distinguishing characteristic was the recognition of a complete break between the Old (Mosaic) covenant and the New (Christian) covenant. This was grounded in several New Testament passages in the teaching of Jesus and Paul. The covenant concept was strongly influenced by constitution language.

The major interpretative principle applied to the Old Testament was a prophecy and fulfillment scheme, which pointed to Christ or the Kingdom. Typology was also a method used to make sense of the Old Testament and understand its place as crucial background to the New Testament. At a practical level the early leaders, when preaching, teaching or writing, made copious use of the Old Testament. However, in some areas a sharp distinction was maintained. This was especially notable toward the end of the era in the debate over the introduction of an organ into church worship.[64]

Unfortunately, the sharp distinction that was drawn between the covenants influenced how the Old Testament was viewed. Whether intentional or not, the position taken by the early leaders of the movement sowed the seeds of a deliberate ignoring or explicit denigration of the Old Testament that seems to have characterized the movement in the twentieth century.

The Christian churches continue to exhibit a practical Marcionism. The views of the early leaders of the Stone-Campbell Movement have had the unintended consequence of creating a negative view of the Old Testament. Coupled with such slogans as "New Testament Christianity" or the "New Testament church," widespread neglect of the Old Testament among the churches is not surprising. Decades ago G. E. Wright warned the church against a "Christomonism" based on its neglect of the Old Testament. Contemporary expressions of the Stone-Campbell Movement must heed that warning and give serious thought to the place of the Old Testament in the life of the church.[65]

Notes

[1] James deForest Murch, *Christians Only* (Cincinnati: Standard, 1962), p. 45.

[2] Ibid., p, 50.

[3] A similar attitude was stated by Rice Haggard in his proposal for Christian unity, "Address to the Different Religious Societies" in 1804: "Let us have one form of discipline, and government, and let this be the New Testament. The Old Testament is necessary as a guide to our faith: for by it we are led to those things we find accomplished in the new, and which we are to believe. But for the constitution of a Christian church; its conduct when constituted; the reception of its members and upon what principles; the manner of expelling and for what, we have sufficient guide in the New Testament, independent of every other Book, in the world." See Everett Ferguson, "Alexander Campbell's Sermon on the Law: A Historical and Theological Examination," *Restoration Quarterly* 29 (1987): 79.

[4] John Calvin, *Institutes of the Christian Religion*, Book II, Section VII, 7-12, ed. John T. McNeill; trans. Ford Lewis Battles (Philadelphia: Westminster, 1960), 1:355-361.

[5] The *Philadelphia Confession* stated in chapter XIX that the moral law in the Ten Commandments was the same law written on the heart of man after the fall. God also gave to Israel ceremonial laws that were effective until Christ and judicial laws that expired with the nation. The moral law was forever binding. Christ did not dissolve it but strengthened it. True believers were not under the Law to be justified but it could be used as a rule of life, informing them of the will of God and in that sense it directed and bound them. For a convenient full stating of these articles see Everett Ferguson, "Alexander Campbell's Sermon," pp. 76-77.

[6] Alexander Campbell, "Sermon on the Law," *Millennial Harbinger* (1846): 493. The sermon was

delivered at the annual meeting of the Redstone Association on September 1, 1816. Campbell was not originally invited to speak at the meeting but someone cancelled. With only two hours notice Campbell delivered the sermon without notes. But its organization and depth reflect the fact that he had been studying and thinking about the issue for some time. In a letter to his father four years earlier he had expressed similar thoughts (see Ferguson, "Alexander Campbell's Sermon," p. 79, for the quote). The sermon was published in a little tract at the time but it had little circulation. Thirty years later (1846) it was published in the *Millennial Harbinger* because of many requests. It still reflected Campbell's sentiments.

[7]See some of the remarks collected in Elmer Prout, "Alexander Campbell and the Old Testament," *Restoration Quarterly* 6, 3 (1962): 131-34. Campbell's response was that the charges were malicious and unfounded and as far from his sentiments "as the east is distant from the west," as quoted in Robert Richardson, *Memoirs of Alexander Campbell* (Philadelphia: Lippencott, 1868-1870): 2:28.

[8]See Wayne Strickland, ed., *Five Views on Law and Gospel* (Grand Rapids: Zondervan, 1996). Four of the five views disagree with Campbell and would find ready acceptance among his opponents.

[9]Alexander Campbell, *Debate on Christian Baptism: between John Walker and Alexander Campbell* (Pittsburgh: Eichbaum and Johnston (1822; reprint ed., Rosemead, CA: Old Paths Book Club, n.d.), pp. 153-174.

[10]Alexander Campbell, *Christianity Restored* (1835; reprint ed., Rosemead, CA: Old Paths Book Club, 1959), p. 136.

[11]These thoughts were developed in a series of articles in *The Christian Baptist*, 6-7 (1828-1829). The full title of the 16 essays was: "Essays on Man in his Primitive State and Under the Patriarchal, Jewish and Christian Dispensations." Though I have not yet found direct evidence, it seems to me that Campbell got his idea about the three dispensations from the English scholar T.H. Horne who published his massive *Introduction to the Critical Study and Knowledge of the Holy Scripture* (London: n.p., 1818). It became a major textbook in England. Campbell quotes approvingly from Horne in *Christian Baptism* (p. 58) and elsewhere.

[12]Campbell, *Christianity Restored*, p. 97. Italics are in the original.

[13]Campbell, "Essays on Man," *Christian Baptist* 7 (1929): 78-79.

[14]Calvin, *Institutes*, Book II, section X, (McNeill, Battles) 1:421-429

[15]Alexander Campbell, *Familiar Lectures on the Pentateuch* (St. Louis: Christian Publishing Co., 1867), pp. 189-191. Reading this volume is a frustrating experience for one searching for examples of Campbell's interpretation of Old Testament texts based on his hermeneutical principles. The book is a collection of verbatim reports of his early morning lectures to the students of Bethany College. Each day a text was read and Campbell commented on it. Very seldom do the comments bear any relationship to the text. Only in the early chapters of Genesis does he offer appropriate comments to help understand the text. After that the comments range far and wide, apparently covering items Campbell thought in important for his young charges to know. Comments based on the actual text are rare.

[16]For example in the Rice debate he insisted that no one could fully understand the Christian institution of baptism "without a thorough knowledge of the five books of Moses, as well as of the five historical books of the New Testament." See Alexander Campbell, *Campbell-Rice Debate* (Lexington: A.T. Skillman and Son, 1844), p. 161.

[17]As Campbell, *Familiar Lectures*, p. 313, says, "The Law and the Gospel stand together—a monument of eternal truth."

[18]*Christian Baptism* (Bethany, VA: by author, 1852), pp. 42-43.

[19]*The Evidences of Christianity* (1829; reprint ed., Nashville: McQuiddy Printing, 1946), pp. 352-380.

[20]Compare Eugene Boring, *Disciples and the Bible* (St. Louis: Chalice, 1997), pp. 70-72.

[21]Boring, *Disciples*, p. 44.

[22]Walter Scott, *The Gospel Restored* (Cincinnati: Donogh, 1836)

[23]Scott, *Gospel Restored*, pp. 165, 168.

[24]Though not germane to this discussion, it is interesting that Scott's emphasis on the importance of the book of Acts had a profound influence on the movement. Campbell and Stone preferred Paul's epistles, but because of the influence of Scott's plan of salvation and its grounding in the book of Acts, that book became central in the movement's canon.

[25]See D. Newell Williams, "The Power of Christ's Sacrifice: Baron W. Stone's Doctrine of Atonement," *Discipliana* 54 (1994): 20-31; Barton W. Stone, *Atonement: The Substance of Two Letters Written to a Friend* (Lexington, Ky.: Joseph Carless, 1805); James M. Mathes, ed., *Works of Elder B.W. Stone* (Cincinnati: Moore, Wilstach, Keys and Co., 1859), pp. 85-141.

[26]Mathes, *Works*, pp. 112-113.

[27]Ibid., pp. 287-88.

[28]Boring, *Disciples*, p. 117.

[29]*First Principles* (Cincinnati: Standard, 1869); *Our Position* (Louisville: Broadhurst, 1872); *Evenings With the Bible,* 3 vols. (Cincinnati: Standard, 1884, 1887, 1889).

[30]Errett, *Our Position*, pp. 8-9. Italics in the original.

[31]Errett, *First Principles,* pp. 3-9. See also Isaac Errett, "The Law of Progressive Development" in *The Living Pulpit of the Christian Church*, ed. W.T. Moore (Cincinnati: R.W. Carroll, 1868), pp. 472ff, available at http://www.mun.ca/rels/restmov/texts/wmoore/tlp/TLP23.HTM.

[32]Errett, *First Principles,* pp. 12-14.

[33]Errett, *Evenings With the Bible,* 1:5-6.

[34]In light of the current fad in Evangelical Christianity with Bruce Wilkerson and David Kopp, *The Prayer of Jabez* (Multnomah, 2000), it is fascinating that Errett, *Evenings*, 1:232-237, follows his lesson on Joshua 24 with one on the prayer of Jabez! Half of his application is to widowed mothers who persevere. His interpretation was that the sorrow of the occasion was the perhaps the death of the father, or poverty of the family.

[35]Errett, *Evenings*, 2:6.

[36]Robert Milligan, *The Scheme of Redemption* (St. Louis: Christian Board of Publication, 1868) and reprinted many times by several publishers up into the 1970s. It was still in use in some colleges in the 1970s and 80s.

[37]Boring, *Disciples*, p. 142.

[38]Robert Milligan, *Reason and Revelation* (Cincinnati: R.W. Carroll and Co., 1867), revised and published often.

[39]Milligan, *Scheme*, p. 68.

[40]Ibid., p. 71.

[41]Ibid.

[42]Ibid., pp. 83-85.

[43]Ibid., p. 114.

[44]Milligan, *Reason and Revelation,* pp. 63-153.

[45]Ibid, pp. 27-30

[46]J. W. McGarvey, *Guide to Bible Study* (Cleveland: Bethany C.E. Company, n.d. ; reprint ed., Old Paths ed., 1950).

[47]He considered the Song of Solomon's inclusion in the Old Testament to be a mistake. He could not see how it fit into the design of the whole Old Testament and found little edification or practical value in it. See McGarvey, *Guide*, p, 46.

[48]J. W. McGarvey, "Preacher's Methods," *Missouri Christian Lectures, July, 1883*, available at

http://www.mun.ca/rels/restmov/texts/jwmcgarvey/etc/PRECHMTHD.HTM, p.3.

[49]J. W. McGarvey, *The Land of the Bible* (Cincinnati: Standard, 1880).

[50]J.W. McGarvey and Philip Y. Pendleton, *The Fourfold Gospel* (Cincinnati: Standard, 1914).

[51]J. W. McGarvey, *New Commentary on the Acts of the Apostles* (Cincinnati: Standard, 1892).

[52]An impressive achievement if he read all of Colenso, a British bishop in South Africa, who published 3,500 pages between 1862 and 1879.

[53]Many of McGarvey's essays were collected and published as *Short Essays on Biblical Criticism* (Cincinnati: Standard, 1910).

[54]J. W. McGarvey, "Instrumental Music in Churches," *Millennial Harbinger* (1864): 510-14 and "Instrumental Music" (1865): 186-88. See also J. W. McGarvey, *What Shall We Do About the Organ* (Nashville: McQuiddy Printing, 1903), available at http://www.bible.acu.edu/crs/doc/mcal.htm. In the latter publication he developed the argument that from the beginning there were two groups at worship in the Jewish temple on the Lord's day, Jewish Christians who followed the Jewish worship practices and other Christians who followed the apostles and which did not include sacrifice nor music. This purely hypothetical and highly unlikely situation was proof that all Jewish things were unsuitable for Christian worship.

[55]Most of Lipscomb's views can be conveniently found in *Queries and Answers*, ed. J.W. Shepherd (1866-1867; reprint, 5th ed.; Nashville: Gospel Advocate, 1963)

[56]Lipscomb, *Queries*, pp. 82-83.

[57]Ibid., pp. 108-113.

[58]Ibid., p. 258.

[59]Ibid., pp. 370-372 and 420.

[60]Ibid., pp. 19, 84.

[61]David Lipsomb, *Salvation From Sin*, ed. J.W. Shepherd (Nashville: Gospel Advocate, 1913), pp. 5, 10-11, 18.

[62]Ibid., pp. 17, 55-64.

[63]Ibid., pp. 26-51, 76-108, 129-134.

[64]Unfortunately, a significant anti-Catholic sentiment shows up in other discussions also.

[65]Understanding the relationship between the testaments is a complex issue that has been addressed often in recent years. Some helpful suggestions can be found in David Baker, *Two Testaments, One Bible*, rev. ed. (Downers Grove: InterVarsity, 1991) and Sidney Greidanus, *Preaching Christ From the Old Testament* (Grand Rapids: Eerdmans, 1999). I have briefly addressed the issue in Gary Hall, *Deuteronomy*, College Press NIV Commentary (Joplin, Mo.: College Press, 2000), pp. 128-131.

17

A CRITIQUE OF THE PLACE OF THE OLD TESTAMENT IN THE CHURCHES OF CHRIST (A CAPPELLA)[1]

Terry Briley

How does someone who grew up in a fairly traditional Church of Christ in Tennessee end up at a Jewish school (Hebrew Union College), preparing to teach Old Testament at Lipscomb University? If that question even seems valid to anyone with a Church of Christ background, it affirms the relevance of the topic at hand. I would like to think the notion of studying and teaching Old Testament would not seem as impractical as pursuing a Ph.D. in medieval bathing habits, but I fear that among many of our brethren such is not the case.

I should also confess at the outset that my conclusions in this paper about the present situation in Churches of Christ are not based on extensive studies with statistical validity. I speak, not as an authority on the history of the Stone-Campbell Restoration Movement, but as one who has breathed its atmosphere his entire life and yet also deeply loves the Old Testament. I am drawing largely upon observations from 39 years as a member of Churches of Christ, 32 years of ministry, and 20 years of teaching at Lipscomb University. These experiences are limited not only chronologically but also geographically, since I have lived only in Nashville, Tennessee, and the northern Kentucky/Cincinnati, Ohio, area. I have consulted, however, with colleagues at Harding University, Harding Graduate School, Abilene Christian University, and Pepperdine University. The findings on this subject are remarkably similar, regardless of the school or region of the country.

Where We Are

In my opinion, we have a long way to go in Churches of Christ to incorporate the Old Testament in a sound and meaningful way. As I attempt to describe, substantiate, and later explain that situation in a generalized fashion, a few equally general qualifications are in order. First, people in Churches of Christ sincerely love God and his Word. They hold strongly to the inspiration and authority of Scripture. Any neglect or abuse of the Old Testament is rooted in something other than intentional disrespect. Although certain historical circumstances make the issue of the Old Testament's relevance more pronounced in Churches of Christ, the difference is only one of degree from the Baptists, Methodists, and others.[2] In addition, the picture this study will present has individual and congregational exceptions. Finally, the appreciation for the Old Testament in Churches of Christ appears to be growing.

The picture of American biblical literacy does not seem to have changed substantially from the findings of the Gallup Organization over a decade ago: "Americans revere the Bible—but, by and large, they don't read it. And because they don't read it, they have become a nation of biblical illiterates."[3] My years of teaching incoming freshmen at Lipscomb, many of whom have grown up in Churches of Christ and even attended Christian schools, indicate that the situation in these churches is not remarkably better than Gallup's overall findings.

Biblical literacy tests administered to freshmen at Lipscomb show their factual knowledge of the Bible tends to be best in the narrative of the Old Testament up to the division of the kingdom and in the Gospels and Acts. Conversations with colleagues at sister institutions indicate that these conclusions are not the result of regional factors, but reflect the general state of the young people coming to Churches of Christ college programs from our churches. Even where their factual knowledge of the Old Testament is good, students are rarely able to relate these details to the larger picture of the biblical message.

In a required course I teach for Bible majors and minors on Old Testament Exegesis and Hermeneutics, I spend a significant amount of time defending the relevance of the various genres of the Old Testament (especially Law). Students have clearly learned, either directly or indirectly (by neglect), that this portion of Scripture does not constitute a priority. I manifested similar shortcomings in understanding and appreciating the Old Testament as an undergraduate thirty years ago, and I quickly learned in my subsequent ministry the detrimental effects of these shortcomings.

I occasionally have the opportunity to hear one of our students make use of an Old Testament text in a devotional setting. One example will illustrate the pain such an experience can bring. A young man once spoke in chapel on Jeremiah 38 and the incident where Zedekiah allowed Jeremiah to be cast into a muddy cistern. When Ebed-Melech intervened to have Jeremiah drawn out of the cistern, he threw down some old rags and worn-out clothes to pad the ropes. The point the student drew from the text was that if these old rags could be used to serve God's purpose, so can the least of us. Such allegorizing of the Old Testament, unfortunately, is common.

Since most of these students are the product of our churches, I must assume that this is where they have learned to ignore the Old Testament and/or to view it as a source for stories "that will preach" (even if at the expense of their true intent). A number of my graduate students who are involved in ministry have told me of elderships that have discouraged or even forbidden them from preaching from Old Testament texts.

Where I find hope for initiating a healthier view of the Old Testament is in the academic arena. As co-editor of the College Press Old Testament commentary series, I have been encouraged that there were more than enough well-qualified Old Testament scholars to handle the task. While I do not have precise numbers, more individuals with doctorates in Old Testament teach at Churches of Christ colleges and universities than at any previous time.[4] Academic credentials, of course, are not an end in themselves. What is most encouraging is the sense I get from conversations with my colleagues and reading their works that they have a passion for improving their students' understanding and appreciation of the Old Testament. They are, after all, participating in the training of the next generation of leaders in the church.

The academic community can also serve the church through the written word. Articles in church-related journals, Bible School literature, commentaries, and other books provide an opportunity to demonstrate the benefits and proper place of the Old Testament for Christians. It will be interesting to see, however, if the College Press Old Testament Commentary series, for example, will be read as widely as the New Testament series.

In summary, then, Churches of Christ continue to feel the legacy of some unfortunate internal tendencies to minimize the Old Testament as well as to demonstrate the general biblical illiteracy that has characterized American society over the past half century. Optimism over signs of improvement in the situation must be tempered by a continued lack of a clear vision for the role of the Old Testament. The need pointed out by Tony Ash over twenty years ago still applies:

> No one seems to have been able to bring the Old Testament before the brotherhood as a matter of deep and abiding interest in any way that has had staying power. Hence, we need a rationale to demonstrate why and how we must be concerned with the Old Testament.[5]

How We Got Here

The remainder of this study will analyze the view of the Old Testament in Churches of Christ from J. W. McGarvey to the present. Before considering that period, a brief comment must be made regarding Alexander Campbell's "Sermon on the Law" and his continued influence on the way the Old Testament has been viewed, whether or not later generations are aware of this influence. If the subsequent generations had understood

Campbell's strong distinction between the Mosaic and Christian covenants within the context of his overall thought, however, the Old Testament might not have been neglected to the extent it has. Everett Ferguson refers to Campbell's daily lectures on the Pentateuch to his students at Bethany College, for example, in light of his belief that the Old Testament "contains eternally valid principles about God and man."[6]

It appears that the tendency within Churches of Christ in the post-McGarvey era, however, was to emphasize the distinction between the testaments to a radical degree. This trend led to the implicit (and sometimes explicit) conclusion that the Old Testament is an irrelevant relic of the past. An example of this attitude appears in a sermon delivered by N. B. Hardeman in a significant series of gospel meetings held at the Ryman Auditorium in Nashville, Tennessee, in the 1920s. At the time the Ryman was the largest auditorium in the state of Tennessee, seating 6,000-8,000 people, and some estimated that 2,000-3,000 people had to be turned away.[7] In a two-part sermon entitled "Rightly Dividing the Word of Truth," Hardeman used the following language to distinguish the covenants:

> Let it be remembered, brethren, that you and I, as Gentiles, descendants of Japheth, were never subjected to the law of Moses. It was never applicable unto us. Its promises were never ours, neither its threats nor punishments. Strange, it is not, therefore—passingly so—that, notwithstanding two thousand years have passed since it was taken out of the way and nailed to the cross, there perhaps are people to-night, never included in it, that are blinded, deceived, and deluded by the thought that they are amenable to it?…Thus on the pages of God's word it is clearly declared that the law is blotted out, wiped away, stricken from existence, become dead, that we might serve in newness of spirit and not in the oldness of the letter.[8]

What is striking about this quotation is the extremity of the language used to refer to the removal of the law. What conclusion would his audience likely draw from this language regarding the Old Testament in general? One of Hardeman's former students, however, told me that they studied the Old Testament extensively in Hardeman's "Scheme of Redemption" class. One would not expect that to be the case in light of the words quoted above. Herein lies an important clue regarding the historic tendency to devalue the Old Testament. Ferguson notes the same principle at work in the subsequent reading of Campbell's "Sermon on the Law": "The strictures on the law arose in a polemical context….It is a common occurrence in Christian history to extract a position from a polemical context and absolutize it. That seems to have occurred in Restoration churches in regard to the Old Testament."[9]

Other areas of significant debate that have occupied Churches of Christ have promoted a tendency to overstate the distinction between the covenants. In issues of worship, for example, the matter of instrumental music comes to mind. In response to appeals to the Old Testament in favor of instrumental music, Guy N. Woods affirmed that "Every argument which its supporters make, in an appeal to Old Testament usage, opens the floodgates for the introduction of the entire Jewish ritual, including infant sprinkling, and the burning of incense and the other shadows of the law (Heb. 10:1-4)."[10]

Opposition to premillennialism has also led to a diminishing of the relevance of the Old Testament. Foy E. Wallace, Jr., was probably the most prominent debater of this issue in the mid-twentieth century. In an attack on Seventh Day Adventism and its millennial views, Wallace wrote the following:

> When the law, the decalogue, the old covenant was abolished, annulled, abrogated and taken out of the way, it was not so done in part but in whole. The whole thing went—decalogue and all. But God gave us a new constitution and we are governed by what it says. We do or 'don't do' a thing not because it was or was not in the Old Testament. We do or don't do things because they are or are not in the New Testament. It so happens that every moral principle, every law founded on moral conduct, is repeated in the new constitution. Such things were not right because they were in the law. They were in the law because they were right-because they are moral within themselves. We do not refrain from doing such things now because the Ten Commandments prohibited them, but because, being right or wrong in themselves, the New Testament incorporates them. That has to do with the basic principles of moral conduct, universal moral principles. They were not moral because they were in the law. They were in the law because they were moral. For the same reason they were put into the New Testament code.[11]

It should be pointed out that the quotations above from both Hardeman and Wallace reflect a common misreading of Colossians 2:14 in regard to what was "canceled" and "nailed to the cross" at Christ's death. These words are frequently applied to the Old Testament in its entirety, or at least to the Law of Moses. Most interpreters, however, understand the *cheirographon* which was nailed to the cross to be the debt of sin ("certificate of debt," NASB).[12]

These debates have led to an overstatement of the contrast between the covenants because the New Testament passages frequently used to support this distinction are themselves polemical. Whether it is Paul's battles with Judaizing teachers or the contentions of the author of Hebrews, the primary goal in such texts is not to present a balanced view of the Old Testament but to address the abuses and dangers at hand, dangers which arose in many cases from a misreading of the Old Testament. Despite this fact, a careful reading of the New Testament should make clear that its authors highly valued and made use of the Old Testament, and consequently that one cannot understand the New Testament well without a firm grounding in the Old Testament.

A debate-driven reading of the Old Testament has resulted in a second-hand knowledge of a major section of the Bible. A view of the Old Testament as the repository of obsolete beliefs and practices leads to the conclusion that one should focus on the New Testament alone. Thus, knowledge of the Old Testament has come to be derived largely from what the New Testament says about it, frequently in a polemical context, resulting in a stunted and increasingly negative view of the Old Testament. Is it possible to break out of this cycle?

Where We Should Be Going

Perhaps it is best to address ways to break out of the negative cycle regarding the Old Testament at a personal level. I did not grow up with especially negative views toward the Old Testament, but neither was I led to greatly value or understand it. How then did I break out of the cycle and end up as a professor of Old Testament?

The answer to the question begins with two names: Jack Lewis and John Willis. These two men, in my opinion, have been the most influential figures in promoting the serious study of the Old Testament in Churches of Christ over the past half-century. After earning a Ph.D. in New Testament at Harvard University, Lewis went on to receive a second doctorate from Hebrew Union College in Old Testament, subsequently teaching at Harding Graduate School since its inception. John Willis, longtime professor at Abilene Christian University, completed his Ph.D. in Old Testament at Vanderbilt University. Both men have set a marvelous example of teaching, scholarly activity, and dedication to the church. They have aided in the training of hundreds of ministers and influenced many of their students to pursue academic training in the Old Testament to the highest level. The academic genealogy of practically every teacher of Old Testament in Churches of Christ educational institutions can be traced to one of these two men, or both.

I am part of the third generation of students influenced by Lewis and Willis. I never studied directly under either one, but the bulk of my training in Hebrew and Old Testament at Lipscomb was with Rodney Cloud, who was educated by both Lewis and Willis.[13] My own enlightening experience under Cloud regarding the immense potential of the Old Testament to speak to Christians has motivated me to pass on this experience to others.

The current generation of Old Testament scholars has also had access to a tremendous resource in the wealth of evangelical Old Testament scholarship. J. W. McGarvey joined other biblical conservatives early in the previous century in the defense of Scripture against the destructive effects of higher criticism. By the second half of the twentieth century, however, a number of highly trained evangelical scholars were able to take the positive elements within critical approaches (such as redaction and form criticism) and apply them in insightful ways to improve the understanding of Scripture. The literary artistry within the Bible has been increasingly appreciated as a result.

Groundbreaking works such as John Bright's, *The Authority of the Old Testament*, first published in 1967, challenged Christians to reconsider the prevailing neglect of the Old Testament.[14] An explosion of evangelical works on hermeneutics has provided insight into the interpretation of the Old Testament. Progress has also been made in quality commentary series which incorporate the Old Testament such as the Tyndale commentaries (InterVarsity), the New International Commentary (Eerdmans), and the Word Biblical Commentary (Nelson), and individual volumes on Old Testament books. Many helpful works on Old Testament theology, critical issues, backgrounds, ethics, and other subjects have emerged.

One of the greatest opportunities for growth in appreciation for the Old Testament in Churches of Christ, therefore, resides with those of us who are the heirs of Lewis, Willis, and anyone else inside or outside Churches of Christ who has equipped us to teach the Old Testament to ministers and other young people at our colleges and universities. We must strive to introduce or maintain appropriate courses within our curricula. We must show our students how to interpret the Old Testament, how to relate it to the New Testament, and how to think theologically about the content of the Old Testament. Only then will they be equipped to apply the Old Testament most effectively to their lives and their ministry within the church.

Those of us trained in the Old Testament also need to respond to Tony Ash's lament, quoted earlier. His challenge calls us to publish works directed to the church that demonstrate the relevance of the Old Testament. The College Press commentary series is a step in that direction, but we also need works that grapple directly with the underlying issues of our attitude toward the Old Testament. Leonard Allen's challenge to Churches of Christ in *The Cruciform Church*,[15] for example, contains a chapter entitled "The Strange World of the Bible." He speaks of the need for "enlarging our canon," a call in part to reaffirm the value of the Old Testament. He also addresses the importance of recognizing the literary forms of the Bible. A possible model for some of us to share our experiences is Philip Yancey's, *The Bible Jesus Read*, in which he describes his struggle to overcome negative preconceptions of the Old Testament and the insights he was able to gain as a result.[16]

In addition to training ministers and writing for the church, we need to be ministers in the church as well. My experience in preaching, including fifteen years at my present congregation, has confirmed for me that the Old Testament is a vital resource for helping Christians understand God and their relationship with him. Admittedly, some worshippers are uncertain about strange sermons from unfamiliar books like Deuteronomy and Ecclesiastes at first, but the rewards of successfully overcoming that uncertainty make the effort worthwhile.

One of the requirements for dealing with reservations Christians have about the value of the Old Testament is to address the fundamental issue of the relationship between the testaments. This issue returns us to Alexander Campbell's "Sermon on the Law." Campbell addressed a legitimate concern: the failure to make an adequate distinction between the covenants. Subsequent generations, however, took that concern too far and committed the opposite error: the failure to appreciate the massive areas of continuity between the covenants. Jesus' emphasis in Matthew 5:17 on *fulfilling* the Old Testament rather than *abolishing* it calls us to appreciate and learn from this continuity. As one work on biblical interpretation concludes:

> Matthew 5:17, therefore, suggests the following hermeneutical principle for applying the OT in the NT age: All of the OT applies to Christians, but none of it applies apart from its fulfillment in Christ. Thus, we reject both the opposing views often found, respectively,

in classic covenant theology (all the OT applies except what the NT repeals) and in classic dispensationalism (none of the OT applies except what the NT repeats).[17]

This perspective, combined with a sound hermeneutical approach, frees Christians to see the vital elements of the Old Testament message that underlie and illuminate the New Testament.

Learning from the Old Testament

Let me close by briefly suggesting four areas in which the church could profit from a proper hearing of the Old Testament.

Covenant

Campbell's constitutional view of covenant tends to obscure the richly relational nature of covenant revealed in the Old Testament. Rick Marrs has addressed the value of the Old Testament teaching on covenant in *Leaven*, a periodical published by Pepperdine University.

> Community models and programs often reflect more the wisdom of the age than the genius of scripture. In this context, the Old Testament concept of covenant remains largely unknown and untried. I would suggest that the covenant (and its attendant terms—steadfast love, justice, righteousness, knowledge of God, et al.) have significant potential for the creation of vibrant and meaningful communities of faith.[18]

The false dichotomy that labels the former covenant as one of law and the new covenant one of grace collapses when one examines the Old Testament more closely. God is gracious in calling and redeeming Israel before giving the law. When law is seen within the relational nature of covenant, it no longer looks like the basis of a relationship with God, but gracious guidance from a loving Father that maximizes the blessing of the relationship and warns of dangers that threaten the relationship. The same is true of the instruction given in the New Testament to those who are in relationship with God through the gracious work of Christ. Old Testament passages, such as Deuteronomy 1-11; 29-30 and Psalms 1, 19, and 119, reveal the positive view of the law which wise Old Testaments saints possessed and from which wise New Testament saints could benefit.

The theme of God's grace in the covenant relationship permeates the narrative of the Old Testament as well. Unfortunately, the perspective of many adults in Churches of Christ has been formed by accounts such as the judgment of Nadab and Abihu and Uzzah, warning stories viewed by many preachers as highly relevant to Christians. When such incidents are viewed as typical, God comes across as harsh and vindictive. Viewed within the context of the whole Old Testament, however, these exceptional situations are overshadowed by the tremendous patience and loyalty God shows to Israel.

Holiness

Another theme that ties the testaments together is God's holiness and his call for a holy covenant community in which he can dwell and manifest his redemptive purpose to the world.[19] As irrelevant and uninteresting as most Christians find Israel's purity laws, those regulations symbolize the pervasive problem of sin and the need for every area of life to be submitted to God. They point out how essential the presence of God is for the profitable existence of God's people and how sin jeopardizes that presence. The centrality of these concepts in the Old Testament reinforces and clarifies the same situation in the New Testament in passages such as 1 Corinthians 3:16-17; 6:19-20; 2 Corinthians 6:14-7:1.

The very notion of community, with its emphasis on corporate solidarity, is foreign and even offensive to many Christians in an individualistic society. Yet the concept appears frequently in the New Testament, most notably in Paul's use of the body analogy.[20] Many of Israel's laws and national experiences reinforce the fact that our individual relationship with God does not override the necessity of forging a meaningful community through which God can most effectively accomplish his purpose. Failure in this area seriously endangers God's presence with his people.

Worship

The Old Testament also has much to say to the Christian about worship. This issue is a sensitive one because the debate about the applicability of the Old Testament has been most heated in Churches of Christ over whether instruments may or may not be used in Christian worship.[21] The greatest contribution of the Old Testament, however, relates not to the acts of worship but rather the spirit of worship. A common, unfair caricature of Old Testament worship is that it consisted of superficial outward acts. The Psalms (Psalm 50) and the prophets (Isaiah 1) debunk such a notion. The New Testament has relatively little to say about the relationship of one's view of God or the quality of one's life to the acceptability of worship before God. The Old Testament, however, has an abundance of insights for Christians on this vital matter.

Christology

The Old Testament is vital to the Christian's understanding of the Savior. He is revealed against the backdrop of such concepts as kingship, priesthood, sanctuary, and sacrifice. To a large extent, the New Testament writers assume their readers are well-grounded in the meaning of these concepts. Those who do not have this background are subject to a limited, if not distorted, understanding of the one to whom they commit their lives.

Conclusion

The final two sections of this study, therefore, represent one proposal as to the means and result of giving the Old Testament a greater place of prominence in the life and teaching of the church. If those of us who are privileged to train ministers will instill in them the knowledge, understanding, and appreciation of the Old Testament, and if we will write and speak to the church directly and effectively, the power of God's full revelation can be unleashed. The potential of such a situation would be to give the church a stronger foundation for understanding the nature of God and his Anointed, the meaning of the call to be a holy community, the overarching story of God's gracious work of redemption, and the type of worship which pleases God and draws us closer to him.

Notes

[1]For the rest of this article, references to "Church of Christ" or "Churches of Christ" will apply to a cappella congregations and the parenthetical note will not appear.

[2]The relationship of the testaments has been a thorny issue since the beginning of the church. Cf. David L. Baker, *Two Testaments, One Bible: A Study of the Theological Relationship Between the Old and New Testaments*, rev. ed. (Downers Grove, Ill.: InterVarsity, 1991).

[3]George Gallup, Jr. and Jim Castelli, *The People's Religion: American Faith in the 90s* (New York: Macmillan, 1989), p. 60.

[4]Mention should also be made of individuals such as Paul Watson and Harold Shank, who are highly trained academically in Old Testament but primarily serve the church rather than the academy.

[5]Tony Ash, "Old Testament Scholarship and the Restoration Movement," *Restoration Quarterly* 25:4 (1982): 221.

[6]Everett Ferguson, "Alexander Campbell's 'Sermon on the Law': A Historical and Theological Examination," *Restoration Quarterly* 29 (1987): 84.

[7]N.B. Hardeman, *Hardeman's Tabernacle Sermons*, vol. 1 (Henderson, Tenn.: Freed-Hardeman University, 1990), p. 11.

[8]Ibid., p. 38.

[9]Ferguson, "Sermon," p. 84.

[10]Guy N. Woods, *Questions and Answers: Open Forum, Freed-Hardeman College Lectures* (Henderson, Tenn.: Freed-Hardeman College, 1976), p. 29.

[11]Foy E. Wallace, Jr., *God's Prophetic Word* (Lufkin, Tex.: Roy E.. Cogdill, 1946), pp. 261-262.

[12]The similar text in Ephesians 2:15 is a bit more difficult, but appears to focus on detailed aspects of the law which were designed to keep Jews separate from Gentiles.

[13]I also studied Old Testament at Lipscomb under Clyde Miller, who attended Hebrew Union College. My primary Greek and New Testament teacher, Harvey Floyd, was highly supportive of the study of Hebrew and Old Testament.

[14]John Bright, *The Authority of the Old Testament* (Nashville: Abingdon, 1971).

[15]C. Leonard Allen, *The Cruciform Church: Becoming a Cross-Shaped People in a Secular World* (Abilene, Tex.: ACU Press, 1990).

[16]Phillip Yancey, *The Bible Jesus Read* (Grand Rapids: Zondervan, 2002).

[17]William W. Klein, Craig L. Blomberg, and Robert L. Hubbard, *Introduction to Biblical Interpretation* (Dallas: Word, 1993), p. 280.

[18]Rick Marrs, "The Role of the Old Testament in Training Students for Christian Ministry," *Leaven* 9.2 (2001): 67.

[19]See 1 Pet 1:15-16 and Lev 11:44-45; 1 Pet 2:9 and Ex 19:6.

[20]See 1 Cor 12:12; Eph 4:11-16.

[21]The issue of instrumental music in Christian worship is closely tied to Campbell's distinction between the covenants. Instruments were clearly used in the Old Testament, but they are not explicitly mentioned in regard to New Testament worship. The debate over this issue in the Stone-Campbell Movement has been multifaceted, but one major point of disagreement relates to whether the New Testament's "silence" is permissive or restrictive.

18

THE OLD TESTAMENT IN THE STONE-CAMPBELL MOVEMENT TODAY: PROPOSALS FOR CHANGE

Paul J. Kissling

W hile reaction against abuse of the Old Testament in Calvinistic Protestantism and Catholicism by the early pioneers of the Stone-Campbell Restoration Movement was understandable, inevitable and necessary, the retention of their over-reaction in what Alexander Campbell called "this continuing reformation" is a cause for concern in all current streams of the movement, Churches of Christ (a cappella), Christian Churches (independent), and Disciples of Christ. This is all the more the case when it is recognized that many of the other principles of New Testament Christianity have far wider acceptance today than they have had at any time since the early church. If the reformation continues, if Stone-Campbell restoration is, in fact, a movement, then reconsideration of the traditions of that movement must be ongoing and in process. This chapter identifies some difficulties in the tradition and suggests some conceptual tools that might further reconsideration of the traditional understanding of the Old Testament—both as text and as covenant—among the churches and people who would trace their spiritual roots to Campbell's continuing reformation

What Is the Tradition?

Before difficulties within the tradition can be identified, the tradition must be defined, no matter how vaguely or tentatively that definition be made. While no cookie-cutter pattern can be used to trace the understanding of the place of the Old Testament in the Stone-Campbell Movement, from the *Declaration and Address* through the "Sermon on the Law" to present-day use of the Old Testament, certain themes and concepts advocated in the earliest period continue to be widely influential.

First, while the Stone-Campbell Restoration explicitly disavows Marcionism, it has typically asserted that there is a radical discontinuity between the Old and New Covenants and between the authority of the Old and New Testament texts.[1]

Second, while the movement has been inconsistent in applying this hermeneutical position (one thinks of sermons on tithing and the Lord's Day being based on the Sabbath for example), there has been widespread agreement that both in terms of canonical emphasis and covenant we are New Testament people. The early reformers used the language of constitutions to distinguish between the guiding authority for the Jewish church, the Old Testament, and for the Christian Church, the New Testament.

Third, while the Old Testament is essential in that it confirms the accuracy of the New through fulfilled prophecy and in typological anticipations of the new covenant,[2] its direct relevance to the Christian Church has generally been rejected. While the Old Testament is full of lessons for life, the Old Testament does not apply directly to the church.[3]

Fourth, even within the New Testament itself we have tended to focus on Acts of the Apostles, beginning with chapter 2 and the Epistles (particularly Hebrews) as a sort of canon-within-the-canon. Anything recorded as occurring prior to the day of Pentecost is to be understood as standing under the old covenant and as such is not directly relevant to the church. Thus, history rather than text has been the basis for this inner canon. The event of Pentecost is the turning point. No matter that the Gospels are written to the church, they speak of the time under the previous dispensation. Conversion accounts in the Gospels, for example, are not directly relevant since they fall under the previous dispensation.

Fifth, it has been commonly understood that the basis for salvation in the old covenant is completely different from the basis for salvation as revealed in Acts and the Epistles. The Old Testament as a result functions as a rather long prolegomenon for the New Testament. Most of it, therefore, can be safely disregarded.

Sixth, the movement has traditionally used a threefold dispensational paradigm for understanding the flow of salvation history with the Abrahamic, Mosaic and Christian dispensations being set up within a particular understanding of progressive revelation— thus starlight, moonlight, sunlight.[4]

Other commonalities relate to the understanding of the Old Testament in Stone-Campbell churches, but all such churches do not subscribe uniformly even to those mentioned above. However, the above are a fair representation of the Stone-Campbell Movement's distinctive approach to the Old Testament.

Problems with the Tradition

To begin with, the tradition responds to legitimate concerns in an exaggerated way. Some level of discontinuity between the old and new covenants does exist. However, to portray that discontinuity in such radical terms is inappropriate. No fair-minded reading of Hebrews 8 and Galatians 3:17-20, for example, leads to the conclusion that the Abrahamic covenant is radically discontinuous with the new covenant. The Old Testament itself plainly recognizes that in some sense the Mosaic covenant is outmoded and in need of replacement (Jer 31:31-34). But the Mosaic covenant is not coterminous with the Old Testament nor is the era prior to the time of Jesus defined by the Mosaic covenant. In fact, within the text of the Old Testament the Abrahamic covenant has chronological and theological priority over the Mosaic covenant.[5]

The covenant forged between Yahweh and Israel and mediated by Moses is viewed as a nationalization and specification of the promises to Abraham. While it has the potential to be the means God uses to accomplish his universal plan, that potential is only to be realized if the nation honors its promise to obey God's voice and keep his covenant (Ex 19:5-8). It is the fulfillment, partial fulfillment or non-fulfillment of the promises to Abraham, which drives the narrative of the Primary History,[6] not the fulfillment or non-fulfillment of the covenant mediated by Moses.

The Abrahamic promises seem on the verge of finding fulfillment early in the reign of Solomon, only to see the nation rather quickly (in both textual and historical terms) fall into persistent and increasingly serious covenant unfaithfulness. That unfaithfulness ultimately results in the breaking of the covenant, and in dispersion and exile. But God's purpose for the descendants of Abraham is not frustrated even by the radical unfaithfulness of Israel. A new covenant is promised to replace the broken Mosaic covenant.

To portray the Abrahamic covenant as star light, compared to the moonlight of the Mosaic covenant, and to see both as radically deficient compared to the sunlight of the new covenant does not do justice to the canonical narrative within the Old Testament itself or to the New Testament's understanding of the Old Testament.

Furthermore, although the Abrahamic covenant has priority over the Mosaic covenant within the Old Testament, the discontinuities between the two are easily overstated. The Mosaic covenant, like the Abrahamic, is based on God's prior action in grace.[7] Both require a human response to that grace of faith and obedience. Both are universalistic in aim. Both are based on a decision by God to narrow the focus of his work with humankind to a specific group of people. The covenant document which begins the Mosaic covenant begins its ten "words" or "matters" with a word of God's grace, "I am the LORD your God who brought you out of the land of Egypt, out of the house of slavery."[8] Human response is a response to grace. All of these characteristics that the Abrahamic and Mosaic covenants share are also shared with the new covenant. The polemics of Paul in contexts where Judaizers[9] base a legalistic approach to religion on Old Testament texts, among other things, must not cloud recognition of the prevailing continuities between the Abrahamic, Mosaic, and new covenants.

Another example of the tendency to deal with legitimate concerns in an exaggerated way is the fashion in which the ideologies of the Old Testament and New

Testament texts are contrasted. While this is not unique to the Stone-Campbell Movement, it is a problem in this tradition. The Old Testament's God is alleged to be a God of War while the New Testament's God is a God of Love.[10] The supposedly vengeful God of the Old Testament, however, cannot hold a candle to the God of the book of Revelation, for example. The stories of Achan and Ananias and Sapphira do not seem to be radically different in their ideologies.

At certain turning points in the story of God working out his purpose, a rather unusually strict form of divine discipline surfaces, perhaps as a warning to the people of God, the canonical audience. This strictness is not seen in more "normal circumstances." One thinks of the flood, which according to the explicit statements of Genesis does not succeed in driving out the human tendency for evil that brought on the flood initially (Gen 6:5 and 8:21). Since the flood does not succeed in driving evil from the human heart, it functions then, canonically, as a sort of warning to humankind at a key turning point. This is true in both Old and New Testaments.

The anger of a Holy God at human sin is just as much a part of his portrayal in the New Testament as the incomprehensible love of that God is a part of his portrayal in the Old Testament. The classic text Christians sometimes stumble over, the punishing of the children for the sins of the fathers to the third and fourth generations,[11] in context is designed to contrast the limited scope of God's righteous judgment compared to the unlimited extent of his faithful love.

In addition to the tendency to exaggerate differences between the Old and New Testaments and the covenants described therein, the Stone-Campbell Movement struggles with hermeneutical consistency in a variety of ways. For example, the pattern of consistent practices in the early New Testament Church is advocated as a way of determining what the church in all times and circumstances should do. But when it comes to the defining and use of Scripture, this principle is quickly set aside. The New Testament Church demonstrates consistent use of the Old Testament as Scripture,[12] not the New Testament. Yet, the pattern of consistent practice in current churches of the Stone-Campbell tradition de-emphasizes the Old Testament (as Terry Briley's chapter in this volume documents). Ironically, this condition conflicts with the practice of the early church, which is supposed to provide the pattern for restoring church practice.[13]

Hermeneutical inconsistency also appears in the basic assertion in the Stone-Campbell Movement that the Old Testament applies to Israel and the New Testament applies to the church. But, does any of the Bible (Old or New Testament) actually apply to the contemporary church directly? The failure to recognize the historical distance of the New Testament documents leads to an exaggeration of the differences in the hermeneutical challenges of applying the Old and New Testaments to the contemporary church. While it is true that the New Testament, generally speaking, was written to Christians while the Old Testament was not, it was not written to *us*. The principle of applying promises and doctrines to those to whom they were given (whether to

Israel or to the church) is sound, but somehow the Stone-Campbell tradition has forgotten at times that North American Christians are not the Corinthians.

A specific example of this form of hermeneutical inconsistency is the failure to take seriously the New Testament use of the Old Testament as a guide for interpreting and appropriating the Old Testament in the church. For example, when Paul[14] addresses the issue of material provisions for Christian workers, he contrasts his own human authority with the divine authority of the Law, quoting Deuteronomy 25:4, "You shall not muzzle an ox while it is treading out the grain." He continues, "Is it for oxen that God is concerned? Or does he not speak entirely for our sake? It was indeed written for our sake." Well, yes, God is concerned about oxen.[15] But Paul here argues that there is a more fundamental principle underlying that Law and its continuing appropriation in the church. For Paul, at least some issues in how the church should be run and organized are based on principles drawn from Old Testament Scripture, which are viewed in the Stone-Campbell Movement as irrelevant for matters in the church.

Another hermeneutical inconsistency in the Stone-Campbell Movement is the (un)conscious canon-within-the-canon that is advocated. Rightly concerned that the Protestant Reformation had stopped the process of reformation in part because of its imposition of Luther's canon-within-the-canon centered on his interpretation of Romans, the Stone-Campbell Movement responded by creating an alternative canon-within-the-canon centered on Acts, the epistles and, according to Boring, especially the general epistles.[16] In addition to the subjectivity of such decisions about canons within the canon, one does not successfully reject Protestant or Roman Catholic inner-canons by replacing their inner-canons with another. In regards to the Old Testa-ment, over three-fourths of Scripture is excluded by this means.

In addition, the use of events recorded in canonical texts as the basis for distinguishing an inner-canon is perplexing. While the event of Pentecost certainly does inaugurate the age of the Spirit in a new way, all of the New Testament texts are *written* after Pentecost. In fact, the Old Testament Scriptures are appropriated after Pentecost as Scripture for the church. Why should events referred to outside of the text be the basis for determining the applicability of the Old Testament when the New Testament documents written after those events still use the Old Testament as Scripture for the church?

A final area of concern is the "dispensationalist" approach to reading Scripture that underlies the Stone-Campbell Movement and flows from hermeneutical inconsistencies within it. Each covenantal dispensation, according to Campbell, has its own system of salvation and particularly its own signs of that salvation. Each covenant dispensation has its own constitution, king, members, entrance requirements, and laws.[17] While each successive dispensation brings over elements from the previous constitution, the outdated constitution[18] has no authority in the new dispensation. It is again ironic, despite rejecting dispensationalism in eschatology (in particular, the notion of a rebuilt temple with a re-institution of Temple sacrifices), the movement does not see the plank in its own eye in regard to the three dispensations. Once again the movement runs up against what the New Testament itself actually says. Paul argues vehemently in Romans 4:1–12 that Abraham was saved by the same means Christians are saved, by faith and not by circumcision or other observances of the Law understood within a system of works righteousness.

What Is Salvageable from the Tradition?

While the above critique is fairly wide-ranging, elements of the Stone-Campbell thought about the Old Testament are helpful and worth retaining. Recognition of the historical distance and the distinction in covenants between the people of God prior to the time of Christ and those after the time of Christ is helpful. A key text emphasized in the movement is Jeremiah 31:31–34 and its use in Hebrews. The new covenant is different from the Mosaic Covenant, and the tradition has rightly emphasized this.[19]

One ought not to read the Old Testament as though it were addressed directly to Christians. One ought not argue for candidates for baptism on the basis that prior to time of Jesus God's people entered the covenant at birth or at eight days after birth. The Old Testament legal materials do not apply directly to Christians, including the Ten "Commandments."[20] The Ten Commandments are given in a specific historical context and their content is related to that context.[21]

Recognition of the artificiality of distinguishing between moral, civil, and ceremonial law (popular during the time of the early reformers and still today) is a related insight that continues to be helpful. Campbell's point in the "Sermon on the Law" that the Ten Commandments are not all moral law and not all moral law is found in them is well taken.[22] The so-called golden rule, "Love your neighbor as yourself," illustrates the arbitrariness of these distinctions. In Leviticus 19:19, immediately following the golden rule, the audience is prohibited from cross-breeding animals, intermixing seeds, and wearing clothing made of mixed fibers. Why should verse 19:18b be moral and 19:19 not be? The Law is not arranged in these categories. By bringing those categories to the text, authority is transferred to the interpreter's preconceived schema. Finally, the notion of progressive revelation that underlies the starlight, moonlight, sunlight schema can retain its usefulness if it is separated from the schema and it is carefully qualified.[23]

Some Recommendations for the Future

As a way forward, a clearer recognition of and greater emphasis on the single plan of God throughout Scripture should be advocated. That plan takes the form of a canonical story. First revealed in the creation mandate in Genesis 1:26-28, the plan is frustrated by human sin. The ensuing chapters of Genesis demonstrate that even the universal purging judgment of the flood will not restore the relationship lost through human sin. Babel confirms that the strategy must change. That change in strategy occurs with the calling of and promises to Abram.[24]

This set of promises forms the theological spinal cord of the rest of the Bible. Because of the persistence of human rebellion the LORD's strategy is focused on one faithful man and his descendants.25 That promise begins to see its fulfillment in the development of the nation while in Egypt, its deliverance in the Exodus, and its establishment in the land of promise in the Conquest. But the covenant the nation enters at Sinai is conditional and tenuous, even though the underlying promise is not.

Before the plaster has dried on the copies of the covenant documents, the covenant is broken and the LORD is ready to make alternative arrangements as to whom he will work through. The promise itself, however, is still intact.26 The persistent disobedience of Israel and its leaders leads to the undoing or breaking of the covenant by both Yahweh and Israel.27 It is not fully restored in the post-exilic period.28 The promise of a new covenant finds initial fulfillment in the elect man, the New Israel, Jesus the Messiah. The ultimate fulfillment of that plan awaits the eschatological future promised by him.

The Sinai covenant within the canonical story is only one potential means of fulfilling the plan of God. The promise to Abraham is not so conditional, although even here the means of fulfillment is not confined to our rather limited imaginations.29 This approach avoids the hermeneutical confusion of applying promises and commands made to Israel directly to Christians while recognizing that the Bible has one story line. Within that story line the Mosaic covenant is ultimately a cul-de-sac. The Abrahamic covenant is not.

Fuller appreciation for the single plan of God would enable the movement to recognize a common basis for salvation throughout Scripture. Although that salvation is marked in differing ways in differing times and circumstances, salvation is based on grace and responded to by faith(fullness) throughout Scripture. That response, is not, however, the ultimate basis of salvation.

This reading of the canonical story is informed by a greater emphasis on the notion of conditionality in prophecy, covenants and promises and the use of process metaphors in the understanding of how God works out his plan in the text. While I would not advocate that our movement accept the so-called "open view of God" as a standard theological operating procedure, I would suggest that the Mosaic covenant is conditional and is portrayed as an experiment—an experiment that ultimately fails. While the language may well be anthropomorphic, the story of the Old Testament reads like an account of God using a series of strategies in his relationship with humankind.

The story begins with a covenant based on a single prohibition and is radically dependent on human obedience. That strategy (Plan A) fails due to lack of faith and obedience. The next strategy is life east of Eden where humanity calls on the name of the LORD. Escalating sin and violence however prove that merely removing humanity from the garden will not resolve the problem of human estrangement. It only leads to universal judgment. Plan B also fails.

Plan C is founded on the purging of humanity's sin and the retention of a faithful remnant. The story of the fall of Noah in Genesis 9:18-29 and the rebellion against the new creation mandate at Babel makes clear, however, that merely starting over will not further God's purpose. Plan D is to narrow the focus from humanity as a whole to one faithful family. While the national concretization of this promise also ultimately fails, the promise to Abram does result in one faithful descendant of Abraham, Jesus the Messiah the son of Abraham, the son of David. The plan only works, however, when God takes on human flesh and the fulfillment of the promise is dependant on him. He inaugurates a covenant in which the presence of the Spirit is an ongoing and continual experience and as a result human response is aided and in some senses produced by the work of the Spirit.

Promises made to Israel are understood conditionally in this view. The so-called spiritualization of those promises in the New Testament is not, I would argue, an indication of an allegorical hermeneutic. Instead the promises are reinterpreted for the church because the conditions for their literal fulfillment were not met by the nationally defined Israel. The recognition of the conditionality of those promises helps to make sense of how the New Testament actually interprets the Old.

In regard to a new hermeneutic of Law, the Stone-Campbell Movement would benefit from a more nuanced understanding and positive evaluation of the Torah as a gracious gift that sustains the life of God's people. Torah usually is better rendered "instruction" or "guidance for life."[30] It is not intended within the text of the Old Testament itself as the means of salvation.[31] While history proves that it has the potential to be distorted into some form of legalism, it is unfair to the Old Testament to suggest that such legalism is inherent within it. The Torah is guidance given to God's people about building a community that lives out its gratitude for God's gracious work in the way that its members treat one another.

While the church is not Israel, and, in that sense, is not under the Law, the New Testament consistently looks to the Old Testament for guidance in Christian living. An example is Paul's instructions to children in Ephesians 6:1-3. Obedience is enjoined on Christian children because it is right and because it is based in Scripture. The commandment to "honor your father and mother" in its original Old Testament context is a command probably given to adult[32] children to guide their treatment of their aged parents. Paul makes an application of that commandment to children who are still in the home.

He regards the promise attached to the commandment as applying not just to adult Israelites and their life in the promised land but to Christians in all stages of life in all places. The Old Testament Scriptures, including the Torah, have much to teach the church, even though those laws were not directly addressed to the church. In Paul's mind, underlying principles transcend the particular circumstances of their original propagation. This faithful search for such principles is the needed antidote to the wholesale rejection of the Torah's relevance in the Stone-Campbell Movement.

A more positive evaluation of the usefulness of the Torah for the church would be fostered if there was a more widespread appreciation of the situational nature of the law within the Old Testament. The law is often viewed as the unbending and rigid standard of right and wrong. This fails to account for the fact that the Old Testament text itself gives two versions of the Ten Words and two or more versions of many individual laws. The differing versions have typically been explained in source critical terms or in some artificial harmonization. But textually speaking, these varying laws have a narrative context. The laws of Deuteronomy are given after the Exodus generation has failed. The canonical text portrays Moses as changing the laws in slight ways in light of the pattern of rebellion so obvious in the previous generation.

The Torah must be propagated anew for a new generation. The differences between the laws in Exodus and Leviticus and Deuteronomy cannot be swept away as merely the rhetorical stance of each book. Moses, in faithfully proclaiming to the Israelites "all that the LORD commanded him concerning them" (Deut 1:3), changes the law.[33] While the differences are not major, this does suggest that the Torah is to some extent situational while always being founded on underlying principles. It is the underlying principles and not the situationally specific concretizations which speak through the ages. The Stone-Campbell Movement's hermeneutic in general and its understanding of the Old Testament in particular would be advanced by widespread appreciation of this concept.

The concept of natural law is a related issue. The book of Genesis seems to operate with a concept of natural law. Prior to the revelation at Sinai, at various times, the characters in Genesis seem aware of laws that are not made concrete until later in Exodus through Deuteronomy. Noah knows the difference between clean and unclean animals. Abram and Jacob know about tithing. The Cain and Abel story presumes an understanding on the part of the participants of basic principles of sacrifice. Isaac is promised that his descendants will participate in the universal promises made to Abraham "because' he "kept [God's] requirements, commands, decrees and laws" (Gen 26:5). The Sabbath laws are anticipated by God's pattern of work and rest in creation. Underlying the particular concrete laws given to Israel in the legal sections of the Pentateuch are principles built into the very nature of the created universe and these principles are part of the relationship between God and humanity from the earliest times. This encourages the interpreter to look for the unchanging principles behind the legal materials of the Old Testament without being bound to the particular historical manifestations of those principles in the Law.

Let me conclude with some suggestions about reading theory. The concept of progressive revelation Alexander Campbell acknowledged is still helpful if it is not exaggerated into a criticism of the earlier portions of the Old Testament. Doctrines such as the Trinity, Satan, and the eternal state are only revealed gradually in history and in the canon. The movement would be ill advised to abandon this insight. But how does one retain historical interpretation, acknowledge progressive revelation, and yet see the Bible holistically, with Old and New Testament theology combining to form a biblical theology.

A helpful metaphor to encourage this asks the biblical interpreter to distinguish between forward and backward reading of the Bible and to give forward reading only temporal priority. In other words, interpreters should read the Bible forward first—from Genesis through Revelation—as though they are first-time readers.[34] They should then read it backwards in light of the whole.[35] The procedure of reading forward first helps to prevent losing layers of meaning within the Old Testament text itself, misunderstanding of what the New Testament is actually doing with the Old Testament, and the adoption of a sort of "Gnostic" hermeneutic in which the Bible is read in complete separation from human authorship. Reading backwards helps to insure that our interpretation is Christian, adds new levels of meaning to the Old Testament in light of God's fuller revelation, and prevents potential mis-readings of the Old Testament that would be clarified from fuller scriptural revelation.

Conclusion

While some of the comments in this study may seem like a wholesale rejection of an important part of the traditional hermeneutic of the Stone-Campbell Restoration Movement, this is not what is intended. The tradition teaches people to be careful in applying the Old Testament to the church without careful forethought. It warns against simplistic transference of texts to completely inappropriate circumstances. It calls people to be self-critical in interpretive theory. It reminds people that historical and theological context must guide interpretation. The ongoing self-critical evaluation of the interpretive tradition of the movement is one of the practices that keeps it moving and the reformation continuing.

My desire is that that these reflections may contribute to that process and make us less inclined to see our own tradition as the norm by which we judge all others.

The Ten Commandments - Right and Responsibilities[36]

God Given Rights (that had been denied them in Egypt)	Responsibilities
Freedom to worship	Worship the LORD (Yahweh) Alone
	Worship without idolatry
	Worship without abusing the name which redeemed them
To work and rest freely	Preserve Sabbath rest for man and beast
Freedom from oppression in family life	Preserve parental authority
	Preserve sexual integrity in marriage
Freedom from terror & violence	Do not kill
Their own land & property	Do not steal
	Do not covet
Freedom from injustice	Protect neighbor from false witnesses

Notes

[1]M. Eugene Boring, *Disciples and the Bible. A History of Disciples Biblical Interpretation in North America* (St. Louis: Chalice, 1997), p. 282, referring to Robert Earl Woodrow, "The Nature of Biblical Authority and the Restoration Movement" (M.A. thesis, Abilene Christian University, 1983), p. ii, can say: "A clear hermeneutic had been developed and accepted by the majority of the Churches of Christ, so that a masters thesis surveying this period could simply list its major emphases as its assumed point of departure. Generally speaking, the main tenets of this hermeneutic have been (a) The Scripture is the sole source of religious knowledge; (b) the Old Testament has been superseded by the New; (c) the New Testament is a constitution for the church; (d) the New Testament is a "pattern" or "Blueprint" for the church, sanctioning (and binding) forms and practices mentioned in the canon, and prohibiting those elements not recorded; and (e) New Testament authorization is ascertained through a logical system of commands, approved examples, and necessary inferences."

[2]Boring, *Disciples*, p. 145: "Milligan does succeed in incorporating the Old Testament as an essential part of the Christian Bible. In doing this, typology is his main hermeneutical method."

[3]Boring, *Disciples*, p. 132, quoting Isaac Errett, *Our Position* (Cincinnati: Standard, 1900), p. 8, says, "While agreeing as to the divine inspiration of the Old and New Testaments, we differ on the question of their equal binding authority on Christians. In our view, the Old Testament was of authority with Jews, the New Testament is now of authority with Christians. We accept the Old Testament as true, and as essential to a proper understanding of the New, and as containing many valuable lessons in righteousness and holiness which are of equal preciousness under all dispensations; but as a book of authority to tell us what we are to do, the New Testament alone, as embodying the teaching of Christ and his apostles is our standard."

[4]Robert Milligan, *The Scheme of Redemption*, pp. iii-ix, is divided in the following manner: Book One : God, Creation, Fall; Book Two: the Scheme of Redemption in Process of Development; Book three: the Scheme of Redemption Developed in and through the Church of Christ. Boring, *Disciples*, p. 142, "The book thus institutionalizes Alexander Campbell's own division of the canon."

[5]The Abrahamic covenant itself is a nationalization and specification of the creation mandate in Gen 1:26-28. Notice how Ex 1:7 records the multiplication of Israel in Egypt in terms which are an obvious echo of the promise of a great nation in Gen 12:2 and the creation mandate in Gen 1:26-28.

[6]The classic statement of this view for the Pentateuch is D. J. A. Clines, *The Theme of the Pentateuch*, JSOTS, no. 10 (Sheffield: JSOT Press, 1978).

[7]Ex 19:4 prior to the offer of the covenant at Sinai.

[8]All translations throughout are the author's.

[9]I am reminded of E. P. Sanders work suggesting that a legalistic understanding of the religion of the Old Testament is not typical of Judaism in the first century C.E.

[10]Boring, *Disciples*, p. 65, referring to Royal Humbert, *A Compend of Alexander Campbell's Theology with Commentary in the Form of Critical and Historical Notes* (St. Louis: Bethany Press, 1961), p. 49, says: "Thus, in his debate with Robert Owen, Campbell was able to meet the objection that the biblical God was a God of war and vengeance by acknowledging that the Old Testament did not have a complete picture of God, and that Christians can affirm 'the whole Bible' without being bound to defend all that the Bible says about God." If Boring is correct this goes back to Alexander Campbell. In any case it is a common criticism of the Old Testament, even if this is not distinctive to the Stone-Campbell Movement.

[11]Ex 20:5-6. Notice how the order is reversed in Ex 34:6-7.

[12]Albert C. Sundberg, *The Old Testament of the Early Church*, Harvard Theological Studies 20 (Cambridge, Mass.: Harvard University Press, 1964), pp. 134-138, argues that the New Testament church recognized a wider Jewish canon by merely listing the allusions to the Apocrypha from the list in Nestle-Aland. This misses the point, since nowhere in the New Testament are books in the Apocrypha quoted as Scripture.

[13]Gary Hall, in a private communication, helpfully points out that the early church after the apostolic era faced a similar dilemma in light of Marcion.

[14]1 Cor 9:8-10.

[15]See Ex 20:8; Jon 4:11

[16]For the argument that Alexander Campbell's canon-within-the-canon was focused more on Hebrews than on Acts, see Boring, *Disciples*, pp. 69-79.

[17]Boring, *Disciples*, p. 251

[18]For the Bible as Constitution see Boring, *Disciples*, pp. 25, 52, 282,

[19]I would like to thank Gary Hall for reminding me of this.

[20]The rationale for the Sabbath command in Ex 20:9-11 gives me pause. By founding the Sabbath command in God's creative activity, one approaches the notion of natural law. See Rom 14:5-7.

[21]The giving of the ten "commandments" is another. Often the word "commandments" is viewed as negative and restrictive, but, actually the Hebrew Bible never uses the Hebrew word for commandment. Instead they are actually ten "words" or "covenant matters" and in the original context they are covenant obligations based upon Israel's own experience of God graciously bringing them out of slavery in Egypt. The ten "words" in effect tell Israel never to do to each other what has been done to them by their Egyptian oppressors. They are given freedom from their oppressors by the work of God. That God calls them to not abuse those freedoms ("rights") but to recognize the responsibilities that go along with those freedoms. They are not stern and oppressive restrictions on human freedom but the logical living out in daily life the implications of their redemption from Egypt. See the chart appended to this chapter.

[22]Alexander Campbell, "Sermon on the Law," *Millennial Harbinger* (1846): 498.

[23]Campbell's position on progressive revelation, if Boring has understood him correctly, is another issue. See footnote 10 above and Boring, *Disciples*, pp. 63-65

[24]The theme of the name shem and how one achieves a great name links the Babel through the genealogy of shem to the promise to Abram. The builders of Babel wanted to make a name for themselves and not fill the earth as directed by God after the flood. In judgment they are scattered anyway, but God switches strategy by focusing his work on one man who in faith and obedience accepts the divine gift of a great name.

[25]For the possibility that originally the promise was offered to Abram's father, Terah see Paul J. Kissling, *A Sketch of Old Testament Theology* (Lansing, Mich.: GLCC, 1999), p. 22.

[26]Ex 32:7-14. Notice how the LORD offers to make Moses into a great nation in 32:14.

[27]Jer 11:10, 14:21; Ez 16:59; 44:7. See Tyler F. Williams, "Parar," in Willem A. VanGemeren, ed., *New International Dictionary of the Old Testament Theology and Exegesis* (Grand Rapids: Zondervan, 1997), 3:697, saying, "Noteworthy, however, is that in both Jeremiah and Ezekiel the possibility of Yahweh's breaking the covenant is inextricably linked to the idea of a new covenant."

[28]Zech 11:10-14.

[29]Mt 3:9 "Do not presume to say to yourselves, 'We have Abraham as our ancestor'; for I tell you, God is able from these stones to raise up children to Abraham."

[30]See Ps 119 or Ps 19:7-13.

[31]C. Leonard Allen, *The Cruciform Church* (Abilene, Tex.: Abilene Christian University, 1990), pp. 62-64.

[32]All of the ten words seem to be addressed to the adult members of the community. This seems to be no exception.

[33]Another example of changing the Law, is Josh 8:2 where the rules for the plunder at Ai are changed from the stricter rules disobeyed by Achan at Jericho. See Paul Kissling, *Reliable Characters in the Primary History*, JSOTS, no. 22 (Sheffield: Sheffield Academic Press, 1996), pp. 90-93 .

[34]For first-time reading, see Laurence Turner, *Announcements of Plot in Genesis,* JSOTS, no. 96 (Sheffield: JSOT Press, 1990), p. 17.

[35]See Paul Kissling, "Old Testament Interpretation in Preaching: Reading Forwards Before Reading Backwards," in *Preaching through Tears: Essays in Honor of Wayne E. Shaw*, ed. John C. Webb and Joseph C. Grana II (Lincoln, Ill.: Lincoln Christian College, 2000), pp. 63-77.

[36]Paul J. Kissling, *Old Testament Theology*, p. 33.

19

RESPONSE

M. Daniel Carroll R. (Rodas)

It is a privilege to respond to these essays by scholars who are contributing to an important "in-house" debate about the authority and place of the Old Testament within the history of the Stone-Campbell Restoration Movement and churches associated with it. To enter into and respond to these serious—even personal—reflections is to tread on sacred ground. I am honored by the invitation.

The Old Testament and the Stone-Campbell Movement

Apparently, the negative appraisal of the Old Testament within the Stone-Campbell movement in large measure can be traced to Thomas Campbell's *Declaration and Address* of 1809 and Alexander Campbell's "Sermon on the Law" in 1816. These pronouncements by the movement's early voices made a sharp dichotomy between Law and Gospel and affirmed the absolute priority of the New Testament in matters of faith and practice. The Old Testament was understood to be the charter of God's ancient people, whereas the New Testament presents the constitution for the new people of God.[1] This perspective yielded a devaluation of the Hebrew Bible that has persisted since that time. The essays by Hall and Briley survey the views of prominent leaders that echo these sentiments from those early days until the mid-twentieth century.[2]

From this point of view, wherein lies the authority and value of the Old Testament? The interpretive key is christological: What are of continuing importance (in addition to isolated moral and spiritual lessons) are those things that point to Jesus. Allegory and typology demonstrate the enduring significance of sacrifices, institutions, events, and persons of the Old Testament, since these find their ultimate fulfillment in him. The history of salvation begun in the early chapters of Genesis leads to Christ's first coming and the launching of the Church in Acts 2 and ultimately to his return in glory. This history is divided into three dispensations (the Abrahamic, the Mosaic, and the Christian), and believers should establish guidelines for their daily living and corporate worship only according to what is revealed in the last.[3]

Although the three contributors can appreciate the legitimate insights that have been gleamed from the pages of Scripture over the years, they are of one voice in critiquing what they feel are the extremes and blind spots of this treatment of the Old Testament. The movement confesses that the entire Bible is the inspired Word of God, but in actuality the Hebrew Bible is relegated to a very secondary role, producing what Gary Hall calls a "practical Marcionism."[4] To counter this mishandling of the text, Briley lists several themes that provide continuity across the testaments: the covenant relationship, the divine demand for holiness, the role of the heart in worship, and the foundations for a full-orbed Christology. With the same goal in mind, Kissling argues for a single purpose of God throughout the Bible, divine grace as the common grounds for salvation, and a more nuanced appreciation of the conditionality of the Old Testament promises, covenants, and Law. As a fundamental hermeneutical principle, continues Kissling, the Old Testament first should be interpreted in its own right and from within its own context in order to avoid imposing inappropriate Christian ideas ("reading forwards before reading backwards").

Especially praiseworthy is that these scholars and others of like conviction are not on a crusade to simply point out weaknesses in their tradition's use of the Old Testament. Out of a deep commitment to the movement's history and churches, they contribute to the forum that is the *Stone Campbell Journal* and are involved in producing the College Press NIV Commentary series. Here, in other words, are not mere clanging symbols or cynical critics, but instead serious scholars offering weighty initiatives designed to remedy longstanding shortcomings, all with the goal of playing a constructive part in maturing the study and application of the Bible.[5]

The Challenge of Appropriating the Old Testament

How can one who stands outside of the Stone-Campbell Restoration Movement assess its use of the Old Testament? What strikes me as I read these essays is the sense that "there is nothing new under the sun." The Old Testament has always posed a challenge. That is, this issue of how to understand it as Christians is one that all traditions have wrestled with since Pentecost.

As a practicing Jew and rabbi, Jesus naturally and consistently utilized the Old Testament to teach his disciples and the crowds. After the resurrection he again returned to it to explain his life and work. What had occurred could not be comprehended apart from the Scripture (Lk 24:25-27, 32). The other apostles and Paul continued to cite the

Old Testament in their preaching and writing. At the same time, however, the New Testament makes it abundantly clear that many of the clashes in those local churches revolved precisely around its proper interpretation and appropriation. In those early years the apostolic leadership in Jerusalem had to adjudicate the significance of Gentiles being introduced into the fold for Old Testament theology (the identity of the people of God and the fulfillment of the promises), rituals (circumcision, sacrifices, and the feasts), dietary laws, and ethics. This confusion and friction are evident in several New Testament epistles (Rom 4:9-11; Gal 2:11-5:15; Eph 2:11-22; Heb 1-10; See also Acts 15:1-35).

Interest in questions surrounding the Old Testament has continued unabated for two millennia. The helpful surveys by John Bright, A. H. J. Gunneweg, and David Baker demonstrate that it has not been confined to ecclesiastical and popular discourse.[6] Within Old Testament studies viewpoints cover a broad range. At one end are those who dismiss or underestimate the value of the Old Testament. The negative reaction against the Hebrew Bible (and everything Jewish) within Old Testament scholarship reached its horrific excess in Nazi Germany.[7] This extreme is an exception. Christian theological and/or practical dismissal of the Old Testament has been held with sincere conviction and almost always without any malice toward Jews. Its supposed flaws are perceived through a lens that emphasizes distinction between Law and Gospel distinction lens.

Others claim the Old Testament portrays an external religion of dead rituals instead of the life-giving faith of the New. Some are skeptical of all Christian efforts to embrace the Old Testament, because its world is too unlike our own. This difference can be theological[8] or an indicator of an inadequate worldview for contemporary moral concerns.[9] This latter perspective is especially prevalent within much feminist scholarship (both Christian and Jewish), where appraisals of the value of the Old Testament range from a guarded appreciation of its worth for faith and life to outright rejection.[10]

Old Testament scholars who have a more positive evaluation of the potentiality of the Old Testament for Christians vary greatly in their proposals. A significant illustration of this conviction from the first half of the twentieth century is Gerhard von Rad.[11] He opted for a typological connection between the testaments, but his was a typology distinct from the conventional. He discerned a pattern of redemptive acts in the history of Israel, which were celebrated in the cult and "actualized" (his term) in new contexts by subsequent generations of God's people. The Old Testament contained dynamic that continually pointed forward to fresh redemptive actions by God; the New Testament reinterpreted and reemployed those same traditions in order to explain the saving event wrought in Christ.

Brevard Childs has taken a different tack. Over the last three decades he has championed what is called canonical criticism. The Old Testament, he says, should be recognized for what it is and always has been: an integral part of the Christian scripture.[12] Whatever the possible redaction history behind the received form of a text and its probable meaning within ancient Israel, it was appropriated by the New Testament authors and by the church and read with another set of convictions. Childs often juxtaposes these various layers of understanding and attempts to demonstrate how Old Testament texts found their place within Christian belief.

More recent Old Testament theologies continue to engage the issues pertaining to how Christians are to read the Old Testament as Scripture. Bernard Anderson, for example, gives a Christian confession at the beginning of his work, but he never clearly articulates a method of how to move from the Old to the New.[13] Walter Brueggemann is hesitant to say that the Old Testament itself anticipated Jesus as Messiah (though the New Testament authors looked back to their sacred text and found him there), but he openly declares the importance of the Hebrew Bible for shaping a vision of realty and mission in the world.[14] Goldingay prefaces the first volume of his narratival approach to Old Testament theology with an extended discussion on what it might mean to read it in light of the New Testament revelation; his is a concern to help the Christian church heed the entirety of Scripture.[15] In the field of social ethics, Christopher Wright suggests a paradigmatic approach that ripples from the Old Testament into the New,[16] while others look to the text to mold Christian character.[17] Liberation theologians also have appealed to the Old Testament for its imperatives of justice and care for the poor in order to find inspiration for social change.[18]

Conclusion

Two lessons should be learned. First, Christians will always grapple with how best to interpret and utilize the Old Testament for faith and practice. After two thousand years no end to that fundamental quest seems likely. Second, the multiplicity of proposed solutions, whether longstanding (like allegory, typology, the history of salvation) or more contemporary (such as feminist, canonical, and liberationist approaches), underscore that no single way to handle the Old Testament should exclude other means. Hebrews 1:1 rings true: "In the past God spoke to our forefathers through the prophets at many times and in various ways." The Hebrew Bible is a diverse source of genres written over a long time, and its rich fund of truth is limitless. No one interpretive scheme is comprehensive enough to expound totally its depths without remainder; every slant on the text is inescapably partial. Goldingay correctly appreciates that many models for understanding for Scripture within the Old Testament are possible, and each one offers its own contribution to explicate ways by which the Old and New Testaments are related to one another and to help see how we are to live before God in the world.[19]

In sum, the concerns within the Stone-Campbell Movement regarding the proper interpretation and application of the Old Testament are another chapter in an historic and global debate among Christians of all stripes. The conversation around the

Stone-Campbell Movement's table, in other words, is part of an ongoing family discussion. May those who participate in this foray into new and important territory for that tradition be encouraged by this family context-they are part of something bigger-and in their faithfulness to the Scripture seek in turn to enrich that broader discourse for the sake of God's people and for his glory.

Notes

[1]Hall contends that the constitutional interpretation of the Old Testament can be traced, at least in part, to the political context at the beginning of the nineteenth century. The U.S. Constitution had been ratified in 1781.

[2]For a more comprehensive review, see M. Eugene Boring, *Disciples and the Bible: A History of Disciples Interpretation in North America* (St. Louis, Mo.: Chalice, 1997).

[3]One of the major topics of contention along these lines within the Stone-Campbell Restoration Movement is the propriety of using instrumental music in church services.

[4]Marcion was a second-century heretic (died AD 160), who rejected the Old Testament altogether. His ideas, which many connect to the dualism of Gnosticism, were refuted vigorously by Justin Martyr, Irenaeus, Tertiullian, and Origen.

[5]From another quarter another recent attempt to reorient thinking and overcome common, simplistic mishandlings of the text with regard to the Old Testament is Peter Enn, *Inspiration and Incarnation: Evangelicals and the Problem of the Old Testament* (Grand Rapids: Baker, 2005).

[6]John Bright, *The Authority of the Old Testament* (Grand Rapids: Baker, 1967), pp. 58-109; A. H. J. Gunneweg, *Understanding the Old Testament* (trans. J. Bowden; OTL; Philadelphia: Westminster, 1978), pp. 34-176; David L. Baker, *Two Testaments, One Bible: A Study of the Theological Relationship between the Old & New Testaments* (rev. ed.; Downers Grove, Ill.: InterVarsity, 1991).

[7]See Robert P. Ericksen, *Theologians under Hitler: Gerhard Kittel, Paul Althaus and Emanuel Hirsch* (New Haven, Conn.: Yale University Press, 1985); Cornelia Weber, *Altes Testament und völkische Frage: Der biblische Volksbegriff in der alttestamentlichen Wissenschaft der nationalsozialisteschen Zeit, dargestellt am Beispiel von Johannes Hempel* (FAT, 28; Tübingen: Mohr Siebeck, 2000); Richard Steigmann-Gall, *The Holy Reich: Nazi Conceptions of Christianity, 1919-1945* (Cambridge: Cambridge University Press, 2003). This antipathy in Germany actually began decades before during the nineteenth century and culminated in (and actually contributed to laying the foundations for) the anti-Semiticism of the Nazi regime.

[8]Erhard S. Gerstenberger, *Theologies in the Old Testament* (trans. J. Bowden; Minneapolis: Fortress, 2002), pp. 5-18, 283-306, accentuates how different ancient religious views are from those of modern, pluralistic European societies. He also disallows that there is any single theological stream within the Old Testament to connect neatly to the New.

[9]Cyril S. Rodd, *Glimpses of a Strange Land: Studies in Old Testament Ethics* (Old Testament Studies; Edinburgh: T. & T. Clark, 2001); Carol Dempsey, *Hope amid the Ruins: The Ethics of the Hebrew Prophets* (St. Louis, Mo.: Chalice, 2000).

[10]Without attempting to categorize the following individuals as to where they are located on the spectrum, one could mention as examples Carol Meyers, Phyllis Bird, Carol Dempsey, Lilian Klein, Gale Yee, Yvonne Sherwood, Cheryl Exum, Athalya Brenner, Alice Laffey, Renita Weems, and Alice Bach.

[11]Gerhard von Rad, "Typological Interpretation of the Old Testament" in C. Westermann, ed,

Essays on Old Testament Interpretation (Richmond, Va.: John Knox, 1963), pp. 174-92; idem, *Old Testament Theology, vol. 2: The Theology of Israel's Prophetic Traditions,* trans. D.M.G. Stalker (New York, N.Y.: Harper & Row, 1965).

[12]Brevard S. Childs, *Introduction to the Old Testament as Scripture* (Philadelphia: Fortress, 1979); *Old Testament Theology in a Canonical Context* (Philadelphia: Fortress, 1985); *Biblical Theology of the Old and New Testaments: Theological Reflection on the Christian Bible* (Minneapolis: Fortress, 1993).

[13]See Bernard W. Anderson, *Contours of Old Testament Theology* (Minneapolis: Fortress, 1999), pp. 1-15.

[14]Walter Brueggemann, *Theology of the Old Testament: Testimony, Dispute, Advocacy* (Minneapolis: Fortress, 1997), pp. 729-35; *Prophetic Imagination* (rev. ed.; Minneapolis: Fortress, 2001)

[15]John Goldingay, *Old Testament Theology, vol. 1: Israel's Gospel* (Downers Grove, Ill.: InterVarsity, 2003), pp. 15-41.

[16]Christopher J. H. Wright, *Old Testament Ethics for the People of God* (Downers Grove, IL: InterVarsity, 2004).

[17]See William P. Brown, *Character in Crisis: A Fresh Approach to the Wisdom Literature of the Old Testament* (Grand Rapids: Eerdmans, 1996); Gordon J. Wenham, *Story as Torah: Reading the Old Testament Ethically* (Old Testament Studies; Edinburgh: T. & T. Clark, 2000).

[18]For a survey of Latin American liberationist Old Testament studies see M. Daniel Carroll R., "Liberation Theology: Latin America," in *The Oxford Illustrated History of the Bible,* ed. J. Rogerson (Oxford: Oxford University Press, 2001), pp. 316-29.

[19]John Goldingay, *Models for Interpretation of Scripture* (Grand Rapids: Eerdmans, 1995). His basic categories are narrative, legal material, the prophetic, and "experienced revelation" (which would include wisdom, poetry, and apocalyptic).

APPENDIX TO CHAPTER 5

"John's Gospel in the Early Restoration Movement" by Carisse Mickey Berryhill

Chapter citation frequency, by year, 1800-1852,
in Campbell mss & selected documents from Campbells, Stone, and Scott

Thomas Campbell = t   Alexander Campbell = a   Barton Stone = b   Walter Scott = w

John chapter	Citations (by year, 1800–1852)	Total	Percent
21	a	1	
20	bbb a bbb ww ta bbbbbb a a taa wwww	27	8.5%
19	aa	2	0.6%
18	ttt aaaa a	8	
17	t bbb t t a a aa bbbbb t a bbb a a w ttt 9a ab t www wwwwww	45	14.2%
16	t a ta wvv aa a ww	11	
15	bb t a b a t	7	
14	aa bbbb t aa	9	
13	b t	2	
12	bbb a ta	6	
11	b a bb o	4	
10	b bb aaa	6	
9	b a	2	
8	t bbb aa a aaaaaaa w	15	
7	b aa a w	5	
6	t ttt bbbb aa bbb a bbbb w aaaaaa t w	30	9.4%
5	t bb aaaaa a bbbbbb ta bbbb a a a	26	8.2%
4	t ttt bb a a a	0	
3	t 10b aaa aaa bbb aaa aaa bbbbb a aa aaa aaa abb t 12a t w	59	18.6%
2	a a	2	
1	tttt bbbbbb tttt bbbbbbb tttt bb a 20a t ww	51	16.0%
Totals		**318**	

Years: 1800 1801 1802 1803 1804 1805 1806 1807 1808 1809 1810 1811 1812 1813 1814 1815 1816 1817 1818 1819 1820 1821 1822 1823 1824 1825 1826 1827 1828 1829 1830 1831 1832 1833 1834 1835 1836 1837 1838 1839 1840 1841 1842 1843 1844 1845 1846 1847 1848 1849 1850 1851 1852

Contributors

William R. Baker, professor of New Testament, Cincinnati Bible Seminary-Graduate Division of Cincinnati Christian University, received his Ph.D. from University of Aberdeen, with previous degrees from Trinity Evangelical Divinity School and Lincoln Christian College. He has published *1 Corinthians* (Tyndale, forthcoming), *Preaching James* (Chalice, 2004), *2 Corinthians* (College Press, 1999), *Sticks and Stones* (InterVarsity, 1996) and edited *Evangelicalism and the Stone-Campbell Movement* (InterVarsity, 2002). He is a board member of the Stone-Campbell Study Group for Evangelical Theological Society and General Editor, *Stone-Campbell Journal.*

Randall Balmer, professor of American Religious History, Barnard College, Columbia University, received his Ph.D. from Princeton University, with previous degrees from Trinity Evangelical Divinity School and Trinity College. His most recent publication is *Thy Kingdom Come: How the Religious Right Distorts the Faith and Threatens America* (Basic Books, 2006), having previously authored many well-received books, including *Encyclopedia of Evangelicalism* (Westminster John Knox, 2002) and *Mine Eyes Have Seen the Glory* (Oxford University Press, 1989).

Carisse Mickey Berryhill, special services librarian, Brown Library, Abilene Christian University, received her Ph.D. from Florida State University, with previous degrees from Harding University and subsequent degrees from University of North Texas and Harding University. She contributed "From Dreaded Guest to Welcoming Host: Hospitality and Paul in Acts," in *Restoring the First-century Church in the Twenty-first Century,* ed. Warren Lewis and Hans Rollman (Wipf and Stock, 2005) and "Common Sense Philosophy" in *Encyclopedia of the Stone-Campbell Movement,* ed. Douglas Foster et al. (Eerdmans, 2004) and edited *Earl Irvin West, Searcher for the Ancient Order* (Gospel Advocate, 2004).

Terry Briley, dean of the College of Bible and Ministry and professor of Old Testament, Lipscomb Unviversity, received his Ph.D. from Hebrew Union College, with previous degrees from Hebrew Union and Lipscomb University. He has published *Isaiah,* 2 vols. (College Press, 2000, 2004) and serves as coeditor of the College Press NIV Commentary series.

Gary M. Burge, professor of New Testament, Wheaton College & Graduate School, received his Ph.D. from University of Aberdeen. He has published *Whose Land? Whose Promise?* (Pilgrim, 2003); *John* (Zondervan, 2000), *Letters of John* (Zondervan, 1996), and *The Anointed Community: The Holy Spirit in Johannine Tradition* (Eerdmans, 1987).

M. Daniel Carroll R. (Rodas), Earl S. Kalland Chair of Old Testament, Denver Seminary, received his Ph.D. from University of Sheffield. He is co-editor of *Character Ethics and the Old Testament: Appropriating Scripture for Moral Life* (Westminster John Knox, 2006) and editor of John Rogerson, *Theory and Practice in Old Testament Ethtics,* JSOTSup 405 (T & T Clark/Continuum, 2004).

Richard J. Cherok, associate professor of church history, Cincinnati Christian University, received his Ph.D. from Kent State University, with previous degrees from The University of Akron and Kentucky Christian University. He has published numerous essays and reviews in scholarly journals and contributed articles to the *Encyclopedia of the Stone-Campbell Movement,* ed. Douglas Foster et. al.; Eerdmans, 2004) and the *Encyclopedia of Fundamentalism.* He is an editor for *Stone-Campbell Journal.*

Jack Cottrell, professor of theology, Cincinnati Bible Seminary-Graduate Division of Cincinnati Christian University, received his Ph.D. from Princeton Theological Seminary and previous degrees from Westminster Theological Seminary, University of Cincinnati, and Cincinnati Bible College and Seminary. He has published *The Faith Once for All: Bible Doctrine for Today* (College Press, 2002), *Romans,* 2 vols. (College Press, 1996, 1998) and served as coeditor of the College Press NIV Commentary Series on the New Testament.

Gary Hall, professor of Old Testament, Lincoln Christian Seminary, received his Ph.D. from from Union Theological Seminary in Virginia, with previous degees from Gordon-Conwell Theological Seminary, Lincoln Christian Seminary, and Milligan College. He has co-authored *Introduction to the Old Testament* (College Press, 2005) and published *Deuteronomy* (College Press, 2000), "Violence in the Name of the Lord: Israel's Holy Wars," in *Issues of Life and Death,* ed. Larry Chouinard, David Fiensy, and George Pickens (College Press, 2004). He is a consulting editor for *Stone-Campbell Journal.*

John Mark Hicks, professor of theology, Lipscomb University and adjunct professor of Christian Doctrine, Harding University Graduate School of Religion, received his Ph.D. from Westminster Theological Seminary, with previous degrees from Western Kentucky University and Freed-Hardeman University. He has published *Kingdom Come: Embracing the Spiritual Legacy of David Lipscomb and James A. Harding* (Leafwood Press, 2006) with Bobby Valentine, *Down in the River to Pray: Revisioning Baptism as God's Transforming Work* (Leafwood Press, 2004), with Greg Taylor, *Come to the Table: Revisioning the Lord's Supper* (Leafwood, 2002), *1 and 2 Chronicles* (College Press, 2001), *Anchors for the Soul: Trusting God in the Storms of Life* (College Press, 2001). He is an editor for *Stone-Campbell Journal.*

Brian D. Johnson, associate professor of New Testament, Lincoln Christian College, is a Ph.D. candidate, University of Aberdeen, with previous degrees from Cincinnati Bible Seminary and Cincinnati Bible College. He has published "'Salvation is from the Jews': Judaism in the Gospel of John," in *New Currents through John: Global Perspectives,* ed. Tom Thatcher and Francisco Lozada, Jr. (SBL Publications, 2006), and "The Temple in the Gospel of John," in *Christ's Victorious Church: Essays on Biblical Ecclesiology and Eschatology in Honor of Tom Friskney,* ed., Jon Weatherly (WIPF and Stock, 2001).

Paul J. Kissling, professor of Old Testament and biblical languages and director of research, TCMI Institute, received his Ph. D. from University of Sheffield, with previous degrees from Trinity Evangelical Divinity School, Lincoln Christian Seminary, and Great Lakes Christian College. He has published *Genesis,* vol. 1 (College Press, 2004), *Reliable Characters in the Primary History,* JSOT Supplements 224 (Sheffield Academic, 1996) and *A Sketch of Old Testament Theology* (GLCC, 1999) and serves as coeditor of the College Press NIV Commentary Series on the Old Testament. He is an editor for *Stone-Campbell Journal.*

Mark S. Krause, Dean of the College, professor of Bible and theology, Puget Sound Christian College, received his Ph.D. from Trinity Evangelical Divinity School, with previous degrees from Puget Sound Christian College and Emmanuel School of Religion. He has published "Ethics in a Postmodern World," in *Christian Ethics* (Parma Press, 2003) and co-authored *John* (College Press, 1998). He is a consulting editor for *Stone-Campbell Journal.*

Robert C. Kurka, professor of Bible and theology, Lincoln Christian College and Seminary, is in residence for a Ph.D. from Trinity Evangelical Divinity School and has received a D.Min. from Trinity Evangelical Divinity School, with previous degrees from Lincoln Christian Seminary and Minnesota Bible College. He has published "The Role of the Holy Spirit in

Conversion" in *Evangelicalism & the Stone-Campbell Movement,* ed. William R. Baker (InterVarsity, 2002), and "The Unity of Scripture: The Theology of Promise," in *Taking Every Thought Captive,* ed. Richard Knopp and John Castelein (College Press, 1997). He is a board member of the Stone-Campbell Study Group for the Evangelical Theological Society.

Lynn A. McMillon, distinguished professor of Bible and dean of the College of Biblical Studies, Oklahoma Christian University, received his Ph. D. from Baylor University, with previous degrees from Harding Graduate School of Religion and Oklahoma Christian University. He has published "John Glas," "Robert Sandeman," "Greville Ewing," "Haldanes," in *Stone-Campbell Encyclopedia* (Eerdmans, 2004), "The Restoration of Baptism by Eighteenth and Nineteenth Century Restorers in Britain," in *Baptism and the Remission of Sins* (College Press, 1990), and *Restoration Roots* (Gospel Teachers, 1983). He is president and editor of *The Christian Chronicle.*

I. Howard Marshall, honorary research professor of New Testament, University of Aberdeen. His many publications include *New Testament Theology* (InterVarsity, 2004), plus commentaries on *Luke* (Eerdmans, 1978), *Acts* (InterVarsity, 1980), *Pastoral Epistles* (T. & T. Clark, 1999), *1 Peter* (InterVarsity, 1991), *Epistles of John* (Eerdmans, 1978), and a monograph on the Lords' Supper entitled *The Last Supper and the Lord's Supper* (Eerdmans, 1980).

Edward P. Myers, professor of Bible and doctrine, Harding University, received his Ph.D. from Drew University, with previous degrees from Southern Christian University, Cincinnati Bible Seminary, Harding Graduate School of Religion, and Lubbock Christian University. He has published *After These Things I Saw: A Commentary on the Book of Revelation* (College Press, 1997) and *Letters from the Lord of Heaven: Studies in Revelation 1-2* (Howard, 1993). He is a board member of the Stone-Campbell Study Group for the Evangelical Theological Society.

Grant Osborne, professor of New Testament, Trinity Evangelical Divinity School, received his Ph.D. from University of Aberdeen. His publications include *John* (Tyndale, forthdcoming), *Romans* (InterVarsity, 2004), *Revelation* (Baker, 2002), *3 Crucial Questions about God* (Baker, 1995), and *The Hermeneutical Spiral* (InterVarsity, 1991), and he serves as editor for the IVP New Testament Commentary.

Paul Pollard, professor of Greek and New Testament, Harding University, received his Ph.D. from Baylor University, with previous degrees from Harding Graduate School of Religion, Lipscomb University and postgraduate study at Oxford University, Andover Newton and Pepperdine University. He has contributed "Colossians" for a one-volume commentary (ACU Press, forthcoming). He is a board member of the Stone-Campbell Study Group for the Evangelical Theological Society and an editor of *Stone-Campbell Journal.*

John Sanders, visiting professor of theology, Hendrix College, received his Th.D. from University of South Africa. He edited *Violence and Atonement: Is the God of the Cross Violent* (Abindgon, 2006), and has published among other volumes *Does God Have a Future? A Debate on Divine Providence* (Baker, 2003) and *The God Who Risks: A Theology of Providence* (InterVarsity, 1998).

Duane Warden, professor of Bible and associate dean, Harding University, received his Ph.D. from Duke University, with previous degrees from Harding Graduate School of Religion and Harding University, and postgraduate study at Columbia University, and the American School of Classical Studies (Athens, Greece). He is the author of *1 and 2 Peter and Jude* (Resource Publications, forthcoming).